# ZONDO
# AT YOUR
# FINGERTIPS

First published by Jacana Media Pty (Ltd) in 2023

10 Orange Street
Sunnyside
Auckland Park 2092
South Africa
+2711 628 3200
www.jacana.co.za

ISBN 978-1-4314-3326-1

Cover design by publicide
Editing by Russell Martin
Proofreading by Lara Jacob
Set in Sabon LT Std 10.5/14pt
Printed by ABC Press, Cape Town
Job no. 004031

See a complete list of Jacana titles at www.jacana.co.za

# ZONDO
# AT YOUR
# FINGERTIPS

Paul Holden

*In memory of Richard Mark Holden, 1952–2021*

# Contents

# Acknowledgements

THE PUBLICATION OF any book, not least this one, is the work of many hands.

I'd like to thank the team at Jacana, especially Maggie Davey and Bridget Impey, who were extremely patient in waiting for something book-like from me after our first meetings a number of years ago. The production team at Jacana was, as ever, helpful as can be. My thanks go to Russell Martin, Lara Jacob, Megan Mance, Shay Heydenrych and all the others.

I had the immense privilege to give evidence before the Zondo Commission. In preparing this evidence, I was helped by an absolutely crack team of investigators and advocates at the commission, who deserve my endless thanks. So my thanks to Advocate Matthew Chaskalson, Advocate Mabongi Masilo, Advocate Sibusiso Tshikovi, Advocate Sanmarie Pieterson and Advocate Ko Pather.

My colleagues at Shadow World Investigations, Andrew Feinstein and Rhona Michie, have been a great source of support and assistance, and extremely understanding about why I've not attended a team meeting for so long.

My friends and colleagues at Open Secrets were amazing collaborators in putting together numerous submissions to the commission, and acted as an important sounding board for our work.

I am very grateful for Liat Davis's invaluable assistance, delivered at breakneck speed, in tackling the Bosasa chapter.

I was able to stay sane while writing this book at rapid speed because of the endless joy that Jessica and Zoe bring into my life, and because of the love and support of my extended family. My thanks and love to all of them.

During the nightmare of Covid-19, and as I was preparing to give my evidence before the commission, my father passed away unexpectedly and much too young. I dedicate this book to him and the love of his life, William.

# Introduction

THE JUDICIAL COMMISSION of Inquiry into Allegations of State Capture, Corruption and Fraud in the Public Sector was an epic endeavour, as is saying its full name. As a result, most South Africans simply refer to it as the Zondo Commission, after the preternaturally calm Judge Raymond Zondo, who presided over the commission as its chairperson.

The Zondo Commission held over 400 days of hearings, taking the testimony of over 300 witnesses over the course of four years. The transcript of all this evidence runs to 75,099 pages. Altogether 1,438 people and companies were implicated in testimony and more than 3,099 notices were sent out to individuals and companies to inform them they would be named. The commission issued 3,171 summonses between 2018 and 2021. A total of 1,731,106 pages of documentary evidence were submitted in support of the hearings; as the commission had to produce multiple copies of the evidence bundles, it eventually printed out 8,655,530 pages for public hearing purposes, no doubt heartening Johannesburg's various distributors of printer ink.

All of the evidence, reports, hearings and other material, gathered in digital format, comes to a petabyte of data – 1,000 terabytes or 1,000,000 gigabytes. That is an insane amount of data. If you laid out a petabyte of 1 gigabyte flash drives end to end, it would stretch to over 8 kilometres (about 8,400 metres, to be exact). And, of course, the consolidated findings and recommendations of the commission, set out in 19 volumes, run to over 4,750 pages.

All this evidence is impressive; it is also extremely daunting. Indeed, only a handful of professionals and maniacs are going to read every report of the Zondo Commission, let alone dive into the underlying materials.

But this is something of a tragedy. The commission itself is globally unique. There has been no comparable attempt, anywhere in the world, to dig so deeply and so thoroughly into state corruption over such a long period. The findings of the Zondo Commission, too, are profound. It is simply not possible to understand the last decade of South African history without coming to grips with the extensive evidence of state capture unearthed by the commission. Nor, arguably, will it be possible to understand where the country is heading in the wake of the commission, not least because the commission's recommendations on issues like the legislature and anti-corruption enforcement – if implemented – will reconfigure key aspects of our democratic state. I firmly believe that when future historians consider South Africa in the 21st century, the Zondo Commission will loom large in their telling. Simply put, while it is not above legitimate criticism, the Zondo Commission was the real deal.

I'm so certain about this because my thirties have been bookended by two quite distinct commissions of inquiry: the Zondo Commission and the Seriti Commission. I attempted to give evidence to the Seriti Commission, established to investigate and making findings on the notorious Arms Deal. Along with my colleague Andrew Feinstein, I submitted thousands of pages of evidence.

But the Seriti Commission was such a shameful whitewash that we eventually refused to participate, together with our colleague Hennie van Vuuren. In the entire time I engaged with the Seriti Commission, it refused to give me a *single page* of the evidence I asked for in order to prepare for my testimony before the commission. In 2019, the High Court agreed with our view of the commission, setting aside Seriti's report on the basis that his commission had failed to conduct a meaningful investigation. Recently, we filed a complaint with the Judicial Service Commission to discipline Seriti and his co-chair, Judge Hendrick Musi, for their total failure to do their jobs.

My engagement with the Zondo Commission couldn't have been more different. I ended up presenting over 15,000 pages of evidence and reports to the commission, attempting to help the commission trace the money stolen by the Gupta family and their allies. I testified over a number of days about this evidence, first in December 2020 and then again in June and July 2021. Unlike the Seriti Commission, the Zondo Commission allowed me to see thousands of pages of evidence to back up my findings, while I worked collaboratively with an extraordinary team of dedicated, competent and professional investigators at the commission to trace the Gupta money through labyrinthine networks.

The work I performed with the Zondo Commission was – to my pleasant surprise – summarised and affirmed in a volume of its own.

## What this book is – and isn't

This book is meant to avert the potential tragedy that Zondo's report may remain largely unread and partially understood, by presenting its content in a much briefer form. This, however, has some caveats: there are things this book does, and things this book explicitly doesn't do.

Let's start with what this book doesn't do: it does not attempt to summarise the entirety of the evidence before the commission, which would frankly be impossible to achieve with any sort of brevity. The book is also not a summary of the phenomenon of state capture in all its forms, or a historical blow-by-blow retelling of over a decade of wrongdoing. That, again, is a much bigger endeavour.

As for what it does do: this book primarily summarises and condenses the commission's final reports, its findings and its conclusions. In doing so, it teases out the key facts and findings and, where necessary, clarifies any thorny legalese.

But it would be remiss of me to jump feet first into the commission's reports without providing any context. It would also be an oversight, I think, not to highlight some broad issues that I feel were not dealt with sufficiently at the commission, or with which I take particular issue. And, finally, I have taken some liberties with the chapter that deals with money flows section of the commission's report, which is based on my evidence before the commission.

This book does three further things. First, in the next chapter, I give a very brief set of contextual explanations about things you'll need to know to make sense of the commission's reports. This includes, for example, an explanation of just what state capture is

– or at least what the commission thinks it is. It also sets out to explain an idea that runs through the commission's reports, namely, that the Gupta family ran an organised crime network as defined by South Africa's prevailing law, which the commission calls the 'Gupta enterprise'. And, with apologies in advance, I explain the network of legislation and laws that govern procurement in South Africa, as well as the legal framework that creates various criminal offences such as corruption, racketeering and money laundering.

Second, although I keep myself to covering only those things the commission broadly affirmed, I have decided to try to enliven the commission's report where it relates to my evidence on money flows. To make my evidence more intelligible, this chapter will include, among other things, visualisations of money flows that formed part of my evidence before the commission, but that were not included in the final reports.

Third, and finally, I address some of my bigger criticisms of the Zondo Commission's report. These are not to be read as undermining the work of the commission as a whole, which is in many respects properly remarkable; they simply serve to highlight the areas where more truth-telling is needed, and which companies and people should face further scrutiny.

## How to read this book
This book is intended to be easy to read, and, in that vein, we have published a website that provides reading guides and assistance you can use alongside this text. This includes a 'master' timeline of state capture as covered by the commission, a chapter-by-chapter timeline, and an extended list of characters with relevant biographical detail. The website can be viewed at www.zondoatyourfingertips.info.

I have also provided, at the end of each chapter, a section containing all the commission's recommendations about the topics covered in that volume.

## The commission's voice vs my voice
As I've already pointed out, the primary aim of this book is to present the commission's findings in a brief and accessible way, and, except where I specifically mention it, I do not try to correct the commission

about things I think they've got wrong.

Practically, this raises some stylistic issues. It would be extremely tedious for both the reader and this poor writer if every sentence started with 'The commission found that', or 'The commission notes that', or 'The commission quizzically opines with pointed sarcasm that' (you'll be surprised how often that last phrase is apt). To avoid this, I have had to adopt the voice of the commission as my own for much of the book. Thus, when I write, for example, 'Anoj Singh held a safety deposit box at Knox Vault', what I intend to convey is that 'The commission found that Anoj Singh held a safety deposit box at Knox Vault'.

But this means I need to clear up a point of potential confusion: where I set out matters contained in the reports, I do not personally validate or confirm the findings of the commission. So, in the above example, I am not personally telling the reader of this fact as if I know it to be true based on everything I have seen (although I have no reason to doubt it): I am rather relaying the gist of the commission's version.

I point this out because there may, indeed, be errors of fact in the commission's reports that I am not aware of or not competent to readily appreciate. My repetition of the commission's version is therefore not necessarily an endorsement of the commission's findings or version of events. In summary: if the commission got stuff wrong, take it up with them – and please refrain from shooting this messenger.

## Referencing

There is also the matter of referencing. Most of this book is based on the commission's final reports. So, if I had to reference every fact or assertion emanating from the commission, the footnotes would simply be a long list of paragraph numbers. This is both extremely tedious and would probably add a good thirty or forty pages to a book that I have tried – believe me – to keep to a reasonable length.

What I've decided to do, instead, is give a broader set of references. So, where I address a particular topic or theme – you'll know this by the heading – I will provide the range of paragraphs in which the material appears. I have included, at the end of this book, a table setting out the headings and the relevant source references.

This, I think, is an elegant solution that saves my own sanity and a good few trees while, simultaneously, giving you, dear reader, enough information to go rooting through the commission's reports should you want to delve deeper into its work.

## The structure of this book

The commission delivered its 19 volumes of findings contained in 6 'parts', which were released approximately a month apart. The sequence of the volumes and parts does not follow any particular internal logic or order, presumably because the commission released the reports as they were completed by the various teams that worked on them.

Part 1 of the commission's final report, for example, is made up of three volumes, the final of which is a set of reflections on South Africa's procurement framework based on *all* the evidence of the commission. In an ideal world, where the commission had a longer time frame to deliver and had everything ready to publish at once, one would have expected this overarching set of findings to appear at the end of the commission's final report.

As this suggests, it would be somewhat strange to simply summarise the commission's reports precisely in the order they were published: we would be jumping between topics and themes somewhat haphazardly, referring at times to events not yet described or, as you reached the end of the book, harking back to events in the early commission volumes that might have slipped your mind. To avoid this, I have exercised some editorial judgement in how I present the volumes, of which two things are noteworthy.

First, I have kept with the commission's volume structure, because the commission generally devoted each volume to a specific theme or area of inquiry, like the capture of Transnet or an account of the infamous Waterkloof landing. While the volumes often cross-refer, it would ultimately be more confusing, and show less fidelity to the commission's own findings, if the individual volumes were emptied and their contents ordered in ways the commission did not see fit to do.

Second, and in order to impose some sort of logical or thematic order on the commission's scattergun approach to publishing, I have grouped together volumes according to a broader theme or issue, or a particular type or site of state capture. In total, I have identified eight broad themes in the commission's findings, into which I have slotted specific reports.

In the interests of transparency, and to make it easier for the reader to locate specific volumes in the commission's final report, I set out in the accompanying table the broad themes I've identified, the volumes I include in each theme, and the part and volume number used by the commission, should you want to go find the original source material.

| Commission's original part and volume number | Subject |
| --- | --- |
| **Part 1: The capture of state ministries or institutions** | |
| Part 4, volume 1 | Treasury |
| Part 1, volume 3 | South African Revenue Service |
| Part 5, volume 1 | State Security Agency |
| **Part 2: State capture at state-owned enterprises** | |
| Part 2, volume 1 | Transnet |
| Part 4, volumes 3 & 4 | Eskom |
| Part 1, volume 1 | SAA |
| Part 2, volume 2 | Denel |
| Part 1, volume 2 | *New Age* |
| Part 5, volume 2 | SABC |
| Part 4, volume 1 | Alexkor |
| Part 5, volume 2 | PRASA |
| **Part 3: Bosasa** | |
| Part 3, volumes 1 to 4 | Bosasa |
| **Part 4: State capture in the Free State** | |
| Part 6, volume 1 | Estina/Vrede dairy scandal |

| Commission's original part and volume number | Subject |
|---|---|
| Part 4, volume 2 | Free State asbestos scandal |
| | Free State housing debacle |
| **Part 5: Particular events** | |
| Part 5, volume 2 | The Waterkloof landing |
| Part 6, volume 1 | Investigations into the closure of Gupta accounts |
| **Part 6: Bits and pieces** | |
| Part 6, volume 3 | Duduzane Zuma |
| Part 6, volume 3 | Vytjie Mentor |
| Part 6, vVolume 3 | Guptas' knowledge of the appointment of Fikile Mbalula |
| Part 4, volume 1 | EOH and the City of Johannesburg |
| **Part 7: The President, the ANC and Parliament** | |
| Part 6, volume 2 | President Cyril Ramaphosa |
| | The ANC |
| | The failure of parliamentary oversight |
| **Part 8: The money** | |
| Part 6, volume 3 | The cost of state capture, the amounts earned by the Gupta enterprise from state capture, and the laundering networks used by the Guptas |

| Commission's original part and volume number | Subject |
| --- | --- |
| Part 9: The commission's structural reflections and observations | |
| Part 1, volume 4 | Corruption in state procurement and the commission's ten recommendations to tackle it |
| Part 10: A critique | |

## Some things you need to know

Truly getting to grips with the Zondo Commission's final report requires some background knowledge, which the commission sometimes assumes the average reader might already have. Below, I set out some key facts about the commission, explain some key concepts used throughout its work, explain just exactly who the Guptas are, and then give a whirlwind tour of the three key laws you need to understand in reading the commission's findings.

## How did the commission come about and what was its job?

The South African public first started becoming aware of the Gupta family in the early years of Jacob Zuma's presidency. Early reports hinted at the potential influence wielded by the Guptas over the state and, in particular, the close friendship they shared with President Jacob Zuma.

By 2013, they had become a household name. A plane-load of wedding guests landed at the Waterkloof Air Force base in April 2013. Waterkloof is a military installation that was only supposed to be used by high-level dignitaries, government ministers and presidents. The media furore about a group of wedding guests landing at a national security key point was only made more intense because of the nature of the wedding they were attending: the union of Aakash Jahajgarhia and Vega Gupta, the latter the daughter of Achla Gupta, sister of the three Gupta brothers Ajay, Atul and Rajesh. The sumptuous and luxurious wedding was held at Sun

City and attended by a raft of senior government officials. Photos of the event were carried in national newspapers, confirming both the Guptas' extraordinary lack of taste and their previously under-the-radar wealth and influence.

Over the next two years, further scandals involving the Guptas came to light, largely through investigations undertaken by the crack investigative journalism team, amaBhungane. Questions began to be asked about how the Guptas, owners of an IT business, had become involved in a dodgy dairy farm in the Free State, while stories began breaking about the Guptas earning pots of cash from government contracts elsewhere in the state.

Then came the Weekend Special: in December 2015, Finance Minister Nhlanhla Nene was fired and replaced by a hitherto unknown MP, Des van Rooyen. Van Rooyen famously arrived at the Ministry of Finance with two advisors, both of whom had links to a group of individuals and companies orbiting the Gupta family operation. After the rand crashed over that weekend, Van Rooyen was removed and replaced by Pravin Gordhan.

But the incident had set off the country's fire alarms and they weren't going to be switched off so soon, not least because the Deputy Minister for Finance, Mcebisi Jonas, would soon publicly tell of how he had been offered the post of finance minister during a meeting with Ajay Gupta at the Guptas' luxury compound in Saxonwold. The idea that a family of businessmen was making crucial Cabinet appointments seemed astounding.

Four months later, the Guptas were again embroiled in highly contentious public scandals when they seemed to get extraordinarily special treatment from Eskom and the Department of Mineral Resources (DMR) in order to help them buy Optimum coal mine. The mine was a key supplier of coal to Eskom.

Precisely as that deal was going through, South Africa's commercial banks decided to close down all the accounts controlled by Gupta companies. The banks claimed that providing the Guptas with banking facilities invited serious reputational damage and possible involvement in criminal wrongdoing. With little attempt to hide the clear favour in which the Guptas were held by Zuma and his Cabinet, an Inter-Ministerial Panel was appointed to investigate the closure of the accounts. The commission would later hear evidence that many of the banks considered this investigation to be little more than an act of intimidation.

Amidst this fury of scandal, in March and April 2016, three complaints were lodged with Advocate Thuli Madonsela, the Public Protector: one by Father S Mayebe on behalf of the Dominican order of Catholic priests, another by Mmusi Maimane, the leader of the opposition Democratic Alliance, and the third by an unknown individual. Madonsela had been appointed to the position of Public Protector by Jacob Zuma in 2009 for a non-renewable seven-year term. Unlike those appointed to the position before and after her, Madonsela took her job seriously. She had, for example, already written a stinging report about 'security' upgrades to Jacob Zuma's residence, finding that he should repay over R200m that had been spent by the state on pimping his pad.

Madonsela investigated a wide range of allegations related to the influence of the Gupta family and published her final report, *State of Capture*, on 14 October 2016. While her findings about Gupta influence were dynamite, the 'remedial action' that she published was even more combustible: Jacob Zuma had to appoint a commission of inquiry into the Gupta family and their influence over his administration. And because he was a potentially implicated party, Zuma could not choose his preferred judge (as he had done with the lamentable Seriti Commission into the Arms Deal, which failed to once mention his role in the transaction despite his being a co-accused in a criminal case *about* the Arms Deal). Instead, the judge had to be chosen by Chief Justice Mogoeng Mogoeng, another Zuma appointee, who ended up being far less forgiving of Zuma than was widely expected.

Zuma naturally challenged the remedial action, which delayed any implementation of Madonsela's recommendation. The High Court eventually handed down judgment in December 2017. As a result, on 9 January 2018, Jacob Zuma, who would be forced to resign just over a month later, appointed the Judicial Commission of Inquiry into Allegations of State Capture, Corruption and Fraud in the Public Sector. Chief Justice Mogoeng identified Judge Raymond Zondo, then the Deputy Chief Justice, as his candidate to head the commission. Thus the Zondo Commission was born.

Laughably, considering how long the commission would

eventually sit and the extraordinary volume of evidence it gathered, the commission was initially granted six months to do its work. It ultimately sought and received eight extensions, and delivered its final report on 22 June 2022, four and a half years after it had been appointed.

The commission was given nine terms of reference. They ranged from the very specific to the very general – which is the reason why the commission was able to spread its investigative net so wide. In the interest of completeness – and I promise this will be one of the few times I include such a daunting block of quoted text – the terms of reference ran as follows:

1.1 whether, and to what extent and by whom attempts were made through any form of inducement or for any gain of whatsoever nature to influence members of the National Executive (including Deputy Ministers), office bearers and/or functionaries employed by or office bearers of any state institution or organ of state or directors of the boards of SOEs. In particular, the commission must investigate the veracity of allegations that former Deputy Minister of Finance Mr Mcebisi Jonas and Ms Mentor were offered Cabinet positions by the Gupta family;

1.2. whether the President had any role in the alleged offers of Cabinet positions to Mr Mcebisi Jonas and Ms Mentor by the Gupta family as alleged;

1.3. whether the appointment of any member of the National Executive, functionary and/or office bearer was disclosed to the Gupta family or any other unauthorised person before such appointments were formally made and/ or announced, and if so, whether the President or any member of the National Executive is responsible for such conduct;

1.4. whether the President or any member of the present or previous members of his National Executive (including Deputy Ministers) or public official or employee of any state-owned entities (SOEs) breached or violated the Constitution or any relevant ethical code or legislation by facilitating the unlawful awarding of tenders by

SOEs or any organ of state to benefit the Gupta family or any other family, individual or corporate entity doing business with government or any organ of state;

1.5. the nature and extent of corruption, if any, in the awarding of contracts, tenders to companies, business entities or organizations by public entities listed under Schedule 2 of the Public Finance Management Act No. 1 of 1999 as amended.

1.6. whether there were any irregularities, undue enrichment, corruption and undue influence in the awarding of contracts, mining licences, government advertising in the *New Age* Newspaper and any other governmental services in the business dealings of the Gupta family with government departments and SOEs;

1.7. whether any member of the National Executive, including Deputy Ministers, unlawfully or corruptly or improperly intervened in the matter of the closing of banking facilities for Gupta owned companies;

1.8. whether any advisers in the Ministry of Finance were appointed without proper procedures. In particular, and as alleged in the complaint to the Public Protector, whether two senior advisers who were appointed by Minister Des van Rooyen to the National Treasury were so appointed without following proper procedures;

1.9. the nature and extent of corruption, if any, in the awarding of contracts and tenders to companies, business entities or organizations by Government Departments, agencies and entities. In particular, whether any member of the National Executive (including the President), public official, or functionary of any organ of state influenced the awarding of tenders to benefit themselves, their families or entities in which they held a personal interest.

One note of clarification: in point 1.5 of the terms of reference, they stipulate a list of public entities included under schedule 2 of the Public Finance Management Act (PFMA). The PFMA is discussed below, but suffice it to note here that this schedule listed 21 different state-owned entities and their subsidiaries. These are:

1.   Traffic and Navigation Services Company
2.   Airports Company
3.   Alexkor Limited
4.   Armaments Corporation of South Africa
5.   Broadband Infrastructure Company (Pty) Ltd
6.   CEF Pty (Ltd)
7.   Denel
8.   Development Bank of Southern Africa
9.   Eskom
10.  Independent Development Trust
11.  Industrial Development Corporation of South Africa Limited
12.  Land and Agricultural Bank of South Africa
13.  SA Broadcasting Corporation Limited
14.  SA Forestry Company Limited
15.  SA Nuclear Energy Corporation
16.  SA Post Office Limited
17.  South African Airways Limited
18.  South African Express (Pty) Limited
19.  Telkom SA Limited
20.  Trans-Caledon Tunnel Authority
21.  Transnet Limited

# What is a commission of inquiry and how is it different from a court?

When reading the commission's report (and this summary), it is very important to bear in mind precisely what a commission of inquiry is, and how this compares with a court. To cut to the quick, there are four essential differences.

First, a commission of inquiry is set up to investigate a matter of public interest. Its job is to use its powers, including the power to seize documents and subpoena witnesses, to establish the truth of a situation. In general terms, they are appointed when the public does not know the truth of a matter so that an investigation can be made to find out what happened.

A commission has a wide range of discretion to decide how it might go about finding out the truth of a matter. It can, for example, appoint experts to provide specific reports, or call witnesses, conduct its own investigations behind closed doors, subpoena bank statements and company records, and even use legal mechanisms to get access to information abroad. But, fundamentally, what is supposed to drive a commission is the attempt to get as much relevant evidence as possible, ask probing questions of this evidence, and then make findings of facts based on this evidence.

A court of law is very different. In a court case, the judge sits and decides between the versions put forward by two sides. The facts that judges can refer to in making their decision (besides quoting other cases) are the facts that are put before them by the litigants. In addition, a judge only hears the testimony of witnesses chosen by the two opposing sides. So while a judge in a commission of inquiry is supposed to be actively seeking evidence to make up his or her mind (and can call whatever witnesses they want or look for information within their powers), a judge in a court of law is limited to considering only the evidence that either side introduces into the court record.

Second, court proceedings are adversarial: they are a contest between two opposing sides – a fight, if you will. In a court, two sides put their versions before a judge, who must make a ruling based on which side puts forward the most compelling evidence when read against the law. Each 'side' of the litigation is responsible for testing, probing and disproving the evidence of the other side through, for example, cross-examination. The judge then decides the case on this basis.

A commission is not adversarial. It is primarily involved in finding out the facts for itself. The judge, or the evidence leaders used by the commission, are the people who decide which witnesses to call and are also responsible for questioning those witnesses to figure out the truth. Implicated parties can, of course, apply to cross-examine any witness called by a commission. Yet it is ultimately up to the commission to decide on the witness list, and then sufficiently probe that evidence to find the truth. Most importantly, commissions are supposed to be neutral: they are not prosecutors. They must treat each witness fairly, and, while they can robustly test the evidence, they do not approach the investigation with a charge sheet of wrongdoing that they try to prove through examination.

Third, and this is the second most important thing to bear in mind, commissions of inquiry are not bound by the same rules of evidence as a court of law. Courts are bound by very strict rules of evidence;

they cannot admit hearsay evidence (what a witness says another person said), for example, or rely on newspaper articles as evidence. Commissions of inquiry can and do adopt a more flexible and wide-ranging approach, because their job is to satisfy themselves as to the facts of a matter, and sometimes this can actually best be achieved by testing hearsay evidence, or considering media reports, or using other types of evidence normally discounted by a court of law.

Finally, and most importantly, a commission of inquiry's findings are not binding. A commission's final report is, without being too dismissive, a very proper-sounding research report. So when a commission of inquiry recommends to the President that he must brush his teeth twice a day and floss after every meal, the President can decide to ignore this recommendation, instead embracing plaque as a constant companion. But when a court of law makes a decision, it *must* be followed. There are no ifs and buts. If a judge tells the President to adopt the correct oral hygiene routine, the President must do so, regardless of how much we all hate flossing.

This last point is very important to bear in mind, because many people may be confused as to why the Zondo Commission has found numerous people guilty of wrongdoing, yet they remain at liberty. This is because the commission is not a court of law; and, in fact, a court of law might find differently from the commission, and it will be the court's decision that is final and binding.

So, to summarise, commissions of inquiry are unique instruments because they:

i.   are supposed to actively investigate matters to make their own determination about the facts as they present themselves;

ii.  can call their own witnesses, or subpoena documents, or use a wide range of other investigative methods, to establish the truth of a matter;

iii. are not adversarial, and are responsible for testing the evidence of all witnesses before them;

iv.  can rely on a much wider range of evidence than a court of law, and can use much more flexible rules of evidence to determine the truth; and

v.   produce findings and recommendations that, while compelling, are not legally binding.

## What is state capture?

In its penultimate volume, the commission spent a good eighty pages pondering the nature and definition of state capture, recording the inputs and opinions of a wide range of witnesses before it, such as academics. After considering all this, the commission then set out what it saw as its own understanding of state capture.

Somewhat unexpectedly, the commission does not define state capture in abstract terms, or give a wide definition that can be used to determine whether state capture has occurred in other contexts. Instead, the commission grounds its understanding of state capture in the facts of the investigation it conducted and, in particular, in the terms of reference that guided its investigation.

As a first step, the commission explored the implications of its wide terms of reference, and then distilled the essential nature of the investigation it had to perform. At its broadest, the commission summarised the terms of reference as being 'predominately concerned with the practices of executive members of the state, and the nature of their relationships with private individuals, and specifically the Gupta Enterprise'.

Drawing on the concrete evidence it considered, the commission then described the South African experience of state capture, calling it, quite interestingly, a 'project'. The notable implication of this is that the 'project' was not a series of quickly organised and opportunistically parasitic endeavours conceived on the fly. Instead, it was a considered and motivated scheme that sought not only to seize and wield influence for financial gain, but fundamentally to transform the political environment to embed this project for good. Perhaps state capture was therefore only the first step, and, if left uninterrupted, the end result would have been radical state transformation (of the anti-democratic and unconstitutional, rather than economic, kind).

In a powerful and compelling paragraph, the commission distilled the 'project' of state capture in South Africa as follows:

> state capture in the South African context evolved as a project
> by which a relatively small group of actors, together with their
> network of collaborators inside and outside the state, conspired
> systematically (criminally and in defiance of the Constitution)

to redirect resources from the state to their own gain. This was facilitated by a deliberate effort to weaken or exploit state institutions and public entities, but also including law enforcement institutions and intelligence services. As just intimated, to a large extent this occurred through strategic appointments and dismissals at public entities and a reorganisation of the procurement process. The process involved undermining of oversight mechanisms, and the manipulation of the public narrative in favour of those who sought to capture the state. Moreover, the subversion of the democratic process which the process of state capture entailed was not simply about extracting resources but was further geared towards securing future power and consequently shaping and gaining control of the political order (or significant parts of that order) in a manner that was necessarily opaque and intrinsically unconstitutional.

The commission fleshed out this definition by providing a sort of checklist of the notable features of state capture. It identified these features present in the South African example of state capture:

i. The allocation and distribution of state power and resources, directed not for the public good but for private and corrupt advantage;

ii. A network of persons outside and inside government acting illegally and unethically in furtherance of state capture;

iii. Improper influence over appointments and removals;

iv. The manipulation of the rules and procedures of decision-making in government in order to facilitate corrupt advantage;

v. A deliberate effort to undermine or render ineffectual oversight bodies and to exploit regulatory weaknesses so as to avoid accountability for wrongdoing;

vi. A deliberate effort to subvert and weaken law enforcement and intelligence services at the commanding levels so as to shield and sustain illicit activities, avoid accountability and to disempower opponents;

vii. Support and acquiescence by powerful actors in the political sphere, including members of the ruling party;

viii. The assistance of professional service providers in the private sphere, such as advisors, auditors, legal and accounting firms, in masking the corrupt nature of the project and protecting and even supporting illicit gains;

ix. The use of disinformation and propaganda to manipulate the public discourse, in order to divert attention away from their wrongdoing and discredit opponents.

The checklist is worth considering because it provides some sense of the interlocking developments and schemes that came together to produce a 'project' that was more sinister – and more programmatic – than a series of hit-and-run con jobs. It could also, in future years, act as a sort of early warning system, identifying those things that, if they emerge in concert again, point the way to another crisis of capture.

## Who are the Guptas and what is the Gupta enterprise?

In general terms, when people refer to 'the Guptas', they are referring to the three Gupta brothers: Atul, Ajay and Rajesh (also called Tony). These three brothers arrived in South Africa in the wake of South Africa's first democratic election and set about establishing an IT empire called Sahara. Sahara largely acted as an importer and reseller of computer equipment. As time progressed, Sahara grew its client base and, importantly, started receiving a wide range of government contracts.

The Guptas were drawn into the ambit of senior ANC decision-makers under the Mbeki presidency. In 2000, Mbeki's administration created an entity called Brand South Africa, a marketing vehicle designed to promote South Africa abroad. In 2006, Ajay Gupta was appointed to the board of Brand South Africa. In a statement later put out by the Thabo Mbeki Foundation, it confirmed that Ajay had been recommended to the board by Essop Pahad, 'who rightly or wrongly thought that [Ajay Gupta] had the skills, knowledge and capacity to facilitate the work of the Council'.[1] Pahad was, at the time, Thabo Mbeki's bruising enforcer who served as Mbeki's Minister in the Presidency. Ajay Gupta served on the board of Brand SA until 2016.

According to evidence heard by the commission, the Guptas

---

1   https://amabhungane.org/stories/guptaleaks-how-ajay-gupta-was-trusted-with-crafting-sas-global-image/.

became close to Jacob Zuma during his period in the wilderness; the four years between 2005 and 2009, after he had been fired as Deputy President in the wake of the conviction of his financial advisor, Schabir Shaik, his own indictment on charges of fraud and corruption, and his triumphal accession to the Presidency of the country. Zuma, in his truncated appearance before the commission, confirmed that the Guptas were his friends. Other witnesses before the commission, including the three erstwhile heads of South Africa's intelligence services, testified that Zuma had told them that part of his loyalty to the Guptas derived from the fact that they had agreed to employ his son Duduzane during the wilderness years when others would not touch the family with a barge pole.

The commission first refers to the operations of the Gupta brothers as 'the Gupta enterprise' (also written as 'the Gupta Enterprise') in the first volume of its second part, which focused on the capture of Transnet, although it somewhat abstrusely describes the enterprise that captured Transnet only at the very end of its report.

The term 'the Gupta enterprise' is derived from a piece of legislation (more about which below) called the Prevention of Organised Crime Act (POCA), which was first passed into law in 1998. POCA criminalises a range of nasty behaviours like money laundering and criminal gang activity, among which is the act of racketeering. In layman's terms, racketeering takes place when a group of people and entities all operate together as a sort of criminal business. The criminal business exists to commit crimes for its own gain, and to commit those crimes on an ongoing and systematic basis (there are more specific requirements than this in the law, which I'll describe in more detail later). POCA refers to this type of business as a 'racketeering enterprise'.

Section 1 of POCA helpfully defines a racketeering enterprise to include 'any individual partnership, corporation, association or other juristic person or legal entity, and any union or group of individuals associated in fact, although not a juristic or legal entity'. A racketeering enterprise thus exists *de facto* rather than *de jure*.

In non-legalese, an 'enterprise' is not some sort of formal legal entity. There is no company called 'Get All Your Gupta Loot Here (Pty) Ltd', even if that would be an amazing company name to register as a prank. The 'enterprise' is something that exists in fact: it is a recognisable group of people and companies that may not be related in formal terms, such as through shared company directorships, but through the way they interact with one another, forming an association of wrongdoers who work in concert to commit crimes.

Of course, not all crimes are equal, and not all crimes are considered to be part of racketeering activity. If the Guptas were a group of furiously organised jaywalkers who littered occasionally, they would not be a racketeering organisation, regardless of what Mrs Grundy might say.

In order to be considered part of a 'pattern of racketeering activity', the enterprise must commit crimes that are listed in schedule 1 of POCA. There is quite an incredible list of crimes in Schedule 1. I won't name them all, but they run the gamut from the greatest hits of the criminal class like murder, rape, kidnapping, arson and assault, to more specialist endeavours like money laundering, exchange control violations or, indeed, any offence for which the punishment may be a period of imprisonment for one year without the option of a fine.

There is, in addition, one final requirement for racketeering to exist: at least two crimes must be committed by the racketeering enterprise, and they must be committed within ten years of each other. So, if the Guptas had paid a single bribe, they would be guilty of the offence of corruption. But if the Guptas paid the bribe, then used money laundering techniques to disguise their ill-gotten gain, all the people involved would be considered party to a 'pattern of racketeering activity' performed by a 'racketeering enterprise'.

Frustratingly, the commission does not actually describe all the people and entities that fall within the Gupta enterprise, although it does at times make findings that specific individuals could be considered parties to racketeering activity. But, inferentially from its descriptions and findings, one can determine that the commission believed the participants in the Gupta enterprise to include, at the very least:

i.   The Gupta brothers and their relatives, including wives and descendants;

ii.  All of the companies registered in South Africa and abroad that were controlled by the Guptas both in law (i.e. they were shareholders or directors) and in fact (i.e. where they may not have been on any of the paperwork, but the company was run at their direction);

iii. Employees of Gupta-controlled companies who were involved in criminal behaviour;

iv. Senior Gupta lieutenants, including, most notably, Salim Essa and Kuben Moodley;

v. Outside companies and their directors that were not necessarily directed by the Guptas but were associates or co-conspirators in a consistent pattern of illicit activity – companies like Albatime, Regiments and Trillian, and their directors like Eric Wood.

The commission would also make a number of recommendations, based on the evidence before it, that particular individuals should be investigated for racketeering offences to benefit the Gupta enterprise. These individuals included public officials like Brian Molefe, Anoj Singh and Matshela Koko.

## What were the GuptaLeaks?

The term 'GuptaLeaks' refers to the disclosure of a large amount of internal Gupta enterprise emails and work content. However, colloquially, GuptaLeaks has come to mean both the existence of the leak and the extensive media reporting on it. The material was leaked to investigative journalists sometime in either 2015 or 2016. The existence and scale of the leak was announced on 1 June 2017 by amaBhungane and the *Daily Maverick*; shortly thereafter, a deluge of stories provided shocking details about the extent of the Guptas' capture of the country and their audacious corruption schemes.

The most notable dataset within the GuptaLeaks consists of the email inboxes for Ashu Chawla for a whole range of years ending in 2016. Chawla, as we shall see, was a key lieutenant of the Guptas; he acted as a sort of chief operations officer for the Gupta enterprise. His emails show him involved at all levels of the enterprise; he is, at some times, organising visas for friends and families and booking limos for the Gupta brothers while, simultaneously, presiding over grand corruption schemes and the laundering of vast sums of money.

His emails provide a granular insight into how the Gupta enterprise went about its business from day to day. They also provided access to emails sent or forwarded to Chawla by the infamous 'Business Man' email address which, as we will see, the commission found was run by Salim Essa and used to orchestrate the activities of captured public officials and criminal co-conspirators. His emails were also invaluable in tracing how the Guptas gathered and laundered their ill-gotten gains abroad, as he was frequently copied into correspondence containing internal accounting ledgers and other banking documents.

Another key dataset within the GuptaLeaks consists of calendar entries and records for Ashu Chawla and, importantly, for some of the Gupta brothers themselves. These calendar entries have been vital in stitching together which actors – including senior politicians – the Guptas were inviting for 'chats' at their Saxonwold compound.

## The laws you need to know to understand the commission's report

In practice, the primary business of state capture in South Africa was the distortion and corruption of government procurement. This was facilitated and enabled by captured public officials at the highest levels of South African government structures and, in particular, the country's state-owned enterprises (SOEs). This sort of behaviour is criminalised by a series of laws, which are useful to understand upfront before even confronting the nitty-gritty of the commission's findings. Here, I focus on three particular pieces of legislation (not including the Constitution).

The primary law of South Africa – the 'apex law' – is the Constitution. All government action must abide by the prescripts of the Constitution, and all laws in South Africa must either fall within the parameters set by the Constitution or give effect to some constitutional requirement.

Section 217(1) of the Constitution establishes the principles that should guide the way the government goes about buying goods and services. It states that 'when an organ of state in the national, provincial or local sphere of government, or any other institution identified in national legislation, contracts for goods or services, it must do so in accordance with a system which is fair, equitable, transparent, competitive and cost-effective'. This requirement is given effect through a major piece of legislation that was passed in 1999, called the Public Finance Management Act (PFMA). It is this law that the commission ends up referring to the most. The PFMA, in broad terms, sets out the legal framework through which all government procurement must be conducted in a fair and efficient way.

The PFMA creates two very important legal entities, and imposes duties on them. The first entity is known as an 'accounting officer'. The accounting officer is the person within a government department that is responsible for creating and instituting a fair procurement system and, most importantly, ensuring that all procurements follow the rules. Generally speaking, the accounting officer is usually the head of a government department, although the National Treasury can, in extraordinary circumstances, appoint somebody else to this role.

The second entity is an 'accounting authority'. Section 49 of the PFMA requires that every public entity have an accounting authority. In practical terms, the accounting authority is almost always the board of that entity. Thus the board of directors of Transnet is considered the 'accounting authority' under the PFMA. In the rare cases where a board does not exist, it is the CEO or other person 'in charge' of the entity that serves in this role.

Accounting authorities have fiduciary duties. A fiduciary is, simply, somebody who manages funds on behalf of someone else; the duties they have to perform are, in broad terms, to manage those funds fairly. According to section 50, fiduciary duties include:

- exercising the 'utmost care' to protect the assets of a public entity;
- acting honestly and with integrity and in the interests of the public entity;
- preventing financial prejudice to the state;
- reporting every decision or fact before the accounting authority to relevant oversight authorities such as Parliament; and
- refraining from using this position for personal gain or the improper benefit of another person.

Section 51 establishes a further set of 'general responsibilities' for these accounting authorities, which mirror many of the responsibilities of accounting officers. There is quite a range of responsibilities, but some of the most important and relevant for the commission's work are the responsibility to:

- ensure a fair procurement system is in place;

- take steps to prevent irregular, fruitless and wasteful expenditure;
- safeguard assets of the company and manage how the entity collects and spends money;
- take disciplinary action against any employee who violates the PFMA or 'makes or permits' irregular, fruitless or wasteful expenditure; and
- ensure that the public entity is compliant with all and any other legislation.

So, in broad terms, the PFMA requires accounting officers (usually heads of departments) and accounting authorities (usually the board of directors) to stop public money being spent in any way that is unfair, untoward, fruitless and wasteful, and enjoins that accounting authorities exercise their duties with honesty and integrity and in the interests of the public.

Crucially, the PFMA creates what are known as 'statutory crimes' or 'statutory offences'. In layman's terms, this means that if a person violates the PFMA, they are guilty of a crime. If any accounting officer or accounting authority violates the requirements I've just outlined, they can be prosecuted and, if convicted, either fined or imprisoned for up to five years. This is serious stuff: when the commission thus finds that people like Brian Molefe or Anoj Singh may have violated the PFMA, what the commission is saying is that they have committed an actual crime and must go to jail.

The second key piece of legislation is the Prevention and Combating of Corrupt Activities Act (PRECCA), which was passed in 2004. Unlike the PFMA, PRECCA is pretty straightforward: it criminalises the acts of corruption and bribery. Somewhat uniquely in international law, PRECCA also creates a legal duty on any person who 'holds a position of authority' to report any corruption they may become aware of. If this is not done, that person is guilty of a criminal offence for which they can be fined or sentenced to three years' imprisonment by a magistrate's court or ten years by a decision of the High Court.

The third piece of legislation, which has already been mentioned, is the Prevention of Organised Crime Act (POCA), which was passed in 1998. POCA creates a range of statutory offences. For our purposes, two are most important. I have already described the first in some detail above: the creation of the offence of racketeering.

What I didn't mention, and what always surprises me when I reread it, was the penalties for being involved in racketeering, or otherwise receiving money or assets from a racketeering enterprise. Under POCA, any person found guilty of this offence can be fined up to R1000 million (i.e. one billion rand) or sentenced to life imprisonment.

The second notable crime is that of money laundering. This is defined widely under POCA. In a nutshell, it states that a person is guilty of money laundering if they tick two boxes:

- they engage in any transaction or activity involving funds that they know, or 'ought reasonably to have known', were the proceeds of a criminal activity; and
- their involvement in this transaction or act has or 'is likely to have' the effect of concealing or disguising their criminal origin, or helps a person who has committed an offence to avoid prosecution.

Like PRECCA, POCA also creates a legal obligation on any person who carries on a business or is involved in a business to report any suspicion they may have that they have been involved in a transaction involving funds from a criminal source, where they reasonably ought to have known this to be the case. Any person convicted of the offence of money laundering can be fined up to R100 million or sent to jail for 30 years; any person who fails to report their suspicions of wrongdoing is liable to a fine (whose upper value is not stipulated) and a prison sentence of 15 years.

Together, the PFMA, PRECCA and POCA create a fearsome legal framework that requires that state money is spent fairly, punishes those that fail to ensure this is the case, and fairly nails any person who benefits from corruption or handles any of the illicit loot that this may generate.

# PART ONE

# The Capture of State Ministries or Institutions

*The commission's broad terms of reference empowered it to investigate capture at many levels of government. This included examining whether state capture, or other forms of wrongdoing, took place within key state institutions. To this end, the commission investigated and produced three reports that form part of this theme, investigating allegations of state capture at the National Treasury, the South African Revenue Service and the State Security Agency.*

# The attempted capture of the National Treasury

THE COMMISSION, IN THE very first paragraph of its report on the 'attempted capture of the national treasury', clarifies that the focus of the investigation was, primarily, whether President Jacob Zuma, Minister Joemat-Pettersson and Dudu Myeni (then chairperson of the board of SAA) used pressure and influence to get Treasury to approve certain transactions. These transactions were either 'not in the interests of the country' or, if not objectionable in principle, were problematic because of the terms and conditions foisted on the Treasury.

The pressure placed on the Treasury took place under two different finance ministers. The first was Pravin Gordhan, who held the post between May 2009 and May 2014, and again from 13 December 2015 until 31 March 2017. The second was Nhlanhla Nene, appointed in May 2014 and fired in dramatic and controversial circumstances by Zuma on 9 December 2015. This pressure took multiple forms and included the dramatic dismissal of the finance minister on two separate occasions.

The pressure placed on the Treasury revolved around five transactions or deals that Zuma and others sought to pursue. Not all of these deals are dealt with in detail below, but for completeness they included:

i.   the infamous 'nuclear deal' to pursue a huge nuclear power project;

ii.   the Airbus leasing transaction at SAA which was pursued with particular vigour by Dudu Myeni;

iii.  the creation of a Khartoum route to be serviced by SAA;

iv.   the purchase of Engen by PetroSA; and

v.    the creation of Denel Asia.

## The context: Evidence of Lungisa Fuzile

The commission begins its Treasury report by quoting, at length, from a statement furnished to it by Lungisa Fuzile. Fuzile started working at the National Treasury in 1998 as a deputy director in the Department of Finance. He rose through the ranks and was appointed the director general of the Treasury in 2011. In this position, Fuzile was one of the most senior civil servants in the entire country. He resigned in early 2017 when he became aware of plans to fire Pravin Gordhan.

Fuzile's statement traverses a range of issues, including his experiences around the nuclear deal and other transactions, which Treasury resisted because of their potentially disastrous economic consequences. Fuzile used these experiences to draw three broad conclusions about the Treasury at the time:

i.    The Ministry of Finance and the Treasury acted as a 'stumbling block' to the corruption or erosion of due process and policy-making;

ii.   The Ministry of Finance and Treasury played a role in stopping or delaying numerous 'bad decisions' that would have had 'dire' fiscal consequences for the country;

iii.  In certain cases, government decisions were manipulated to achieve certain predetermined outcomes; if they had been implemented, 'the country would most likely have been bankrupt at some point in the future'.

Fuzile's evidence is particularly notable for the picture it paints of Zuma's hostility to Treasury. According to Fuzile, he started hearing rumours in the second half of 2015 that Zuma had become unhappy with the budget process and the budget as a whole. Treasury, Zuma was said to believe, had become an obstacle to the National Development Plan (NDP).

Fuzile was told as much when he met with Khulekani Mathe

in November 2015. Mathe, who worked at the National Planning Commission (NPC), told Fuzile that, unbeknown to Treasury, Zuma had been having engagements with the NPC. During these meetings, Zuma was said to have expressed 'grave dissatisfaction' with Treasury and its failure to aid the NDP. Mathe further told Fuzile that Zuma had directed the NPC to start gathering evidence to show that Treasury was thwarting the President's ambitions. Zuma, Mathe claimed, had said of the Treasury that he would 'shake the tree; if it falls, so be it'.

## Jonas meets the Guptas

After using Fuzile to paint a picture of the extraordinary pressure piled on Treasury by Zuma and others, the commission moved on to one of the most controversial moments in the history of state capture: the Guptas' attempt to bribe Mcebisi Jonas in person. Jonas had been appointed the Deputy Minister of Finance on 26 May 2014, the same day that Nene was appointed the minister. Jonas would serve in this position until March 2017, when he was dismissed alongside Pravin Gordhan.

Jonas's infamous meeting with the Guptas was facilitated by two people: Fana Hlongwane and Duduzane Zuma. Hlongwane made his fortune by receiving tens of millions of rand in 'commissions' from BAE Systems in relation to the sordid 1999 Arms Deal. According to Jonas, and seemingly despite Hlongwane's questionable pedigree, the two were friends. Hlongwane, meanwhile, was also a friend of Duduzane Zuma; Duduzane considered Hlongwane one of his 'uncles' from exile.

Duduzane Zuma and Jonas spoke to each other for the first time on 17 October 2015. Zuma had reached out to Jonas to invite him to the 'South African of the Year' ceremony held by ANN7, the Guptas' TV station, but Jonas declined. This led to a series of ping-pong texts and calls leading up to 23 October 2015, when he received another call from Duduzane. Jonas told Duduzane that he had a meeting in Rosebank, Johannesburg, and they could meet thereafter. The two then met at the Hyatt in Rosebank, one of the city's swankier locations.

Jonas recalled that Duduzane was nervous and conveyed little of substance – only that Jacob Zuma was a fan of Jonas. During the meeting, Duduzane was called by Hlongwane. Shortly thereafter, Duduzane complained that the Hyatt was too crowded and that he would prefer to speak in a more private location. Jonas would later testify that, while he agreed to the proposition, he thought it would involve a trip to a nearby office or other facility. Duduzane tried to argue before the commission that, in fact, Jonas already knew where Duduzane wanted to take him: the Gupta compound. On this, and on every disputed fact about what happened on 23 October 2015, the commission believed Jonas's evidence was more credible.

Jonas was escorted to a car in the parking lot and, together with Duduzane, was driven the short distance from Rosebank to the Gupta compound in neighbouring Saxonwold. They were soon joined by Hlongwane, with whom they had a nondescript chat. Eventually, Rajesh (Tony) Gupta walked into the room.[2] Jonas would recall a lengthy chat, while Hlongwane and Duduzane later claimed that Tony Gupta merely 'peeped' into the room to ask Duduzane a question. The commission would find that Jonas's version of this meeting was most likely accurate.

Jonas testified that Tony Gupta started the conversation by saying that the Guptas had been gathering intelligence on Jonas, his friends and advisors; that the Guptas had the means to gather all sorts of information on anybody they wanted. All of this, it appears, was to serve as a prelude to the threat Tony Gupta then delivered: if Jonas told anyone about the meeting, the Guptas would ruin his career.

Jonas eventually intervened to ask Tony Gupta to get to the point. Tony told Jonas that Zuma was a fan of his, but not of Nene. Indeed, Zuma was poised to fire Nene shortly, Tony claimed, because Nene failed to cooperate with the Guptas. Tony then told Jonas that 'we are in control of everything', including the National Intelligence Agency and the National Prosecuting Authority, and that 'the old man [Jacob Zuma] will do anything we tell him to do'. Zuma, Tony told Jonas, wanted to appoint Jonas as Minister of Finance.

No doubt to the surprise of Tony Gupta, Jonas was unreceptive: he didn't want to take up the position. Tony insisted that he must accept the role, but to sweeten the deal, he told Jonas that it would

2    In a statement Jonas gave in affidavits filed at the High Court, he initially claimed it was Ajay Gupta. He later told the commission it was likely Rajesh. The commission's investigations led it to believe it was most likely Rajesh.

make him a very wealthy man, and said he could pay Jonas R600m if he accepted the post and worked with the Guptas. To prove his point, Tony then pointed at Duduzane and bragged that the Guptas had made him a billionaire and bought him a house in Dubai. When Duduzane testified before the commission, Tony Gupta's boast was put to him. Zuma, the commission drily noted, 'did not dispute the correctness of the statement that the Guptas had made him a billionaire by October 2015'.

Despite Jonas's refusal of the offer, Tony Gupta began to set out a vision of what he wanted to achieve. The Guptas, he said, were already earning about R6bn from government entities every year, and they wanted to increase this to R8bn a year. But, the Gupta brother ruefully noted, this was being prevented by National Treasury. If Jonas were to take the position, therefore, he would need to 'clean up Treasury' by firing some of the most senior civil servants: Director general Fuzile, his long-time deputy Andrew Donaldson, Ismail Momoniat, and chief procurement officer Kenneth Brown.

Jonas began to leave. Tony Gupta motioned to Hlongwane and Duduzane to remain where they were, and approached Jonas on his own. He escorted him to a bar area near the front door, where he repeated the R600m offer, and offered to help him stash the money in Dubai. He then sought to prove his bona fides by giving him R600,000 in cash on the spot, and asked if Jonas had a bag he could use. Jonas believed that Tony Gupta was about to show him the cash, so he made a swift exit.

Jonas contacted both Pravin Gordhan and Nhlanhla Nene, although he only disclosed the full details of the various bribe offers to Nene (when Jonas met Gordhan, they were siting with Gordhan's wife, so he did not go into detail). Nene would corroborate Jonas's version, and confirm that Jonas was extremely disturbed and agitated by the encounter.

## Nene's resistance to state capture and his eventual dismissal

As Jonas's evidence made clear, by the end of October 2015 Nene's days were numbered. He had already had a number of run-ins with Zuma and Zuma's close confidante, Dudu Myeni, about a range of questionable transactions. One of the most contentious was the infamous 'nuclear deal', which would have involved the purchase of a nuclear power facility sufficient to produce 9.6 gigawatts (GW) of power by 2030. The idea was first included in an Integrated Resource Plan approved in 2011. But when Treasury reviewed the plan, it was immediately obvious it was not feasible. The purchase would be the single largest procurement in South African history and one of the largest ever public investments in the world. The implications for South Africa's debt and fiscal stability would be profound.

Nevertheless, Zuma's Cabinet pushed hard for the deal. In September 2014, Minister of Energy Tina Joemat-Pettersson announced that South Africa had already signed an 'intergovernmental framework' with Russia to lay the foundation for the procurement. On 10 June 2015, she presented a further five bilateral agreements signed with other nuclear powers as the prelude to a formal acquisition process. On the same day, Cabinet decided that the Minister of Energy, in consultation with the Minister of Finance, should present a memorandum setting out the fiscal and financial implications of the deal. This was to be done as a matter of urgency.

A month later, on 8 and 9 July 2015, Zuma attended a BRICS summit hosted by Russia. The memorandum had not yet been completed. Zuma criticised Nene for failing to produce it, as the President had been keen to present something to Russia's President Vladimir Putin. Perhaps seeking something else helpful, Joemat-Pettersson gave Nene a draft letter addressed to the Russian government. She asked him to sign the letter so it could be presented; Nene refused because he believed it created an implied commitment to contract with Russia. Nene continued to refuse even after Joemat-Pettersson presented him with a revised and edited version. Nene later recalled that she fretted about how she could explain this to Zuma.

Nene testified that, as a result of refusing to sign the letter, he came to be seen as one of the primary obstacles to the nuclear deal. A number of Cabinet members accused him of insubordination, and some were openly hostile. Nene would later hear from Jonas that the latter had been called to a meeting by Jacob Zuma after the summit in Russia, and that Zuma had expressed his dissatisfaction with Nene's refusal to play ball.

Running parallel with developments and pressures around the nuclear deal were similar pressures emanating from SAA. One of these related to a bizarre proposal from SAA to begin operating a route to Khartoum, which was floated not long after the brutal dictator of Sudan, Omar al-Bashir, visited South Africa. Dudu Myeni, then chairperson of the SAA board, wrote to Nene in June 2015, asking for his response to a 'business case' that had been submitted on the route. A review of the plan showed that SAA would lose money on it for at least two years, something the airline could ill afford. Nene refused to support the proposal.

Two months later, in August 2015, SAA approached Treasury to ask for a R5bn guarantee. A guarantee is basically a standing offer to lend money to an entity if needed; it is not actually a loan, but a promise to deliver a loan if need be. Nene had previously approved a guarantee of about R7bn in December 2014, without which SAA would have run out of cash by January 2015.

This time, however, Nene refused because a specialist finance committee called the Fiscal and Liability Committee had recommended against it. The committee feared that there was the very real possibility that SAA's dire financial position could lead to the guarantee being 'called in', in which case the South African government would have to find billions of rand to lend to the airline.

By way of response, Nene wrote to Myeni in September 2015, saying that certain outstanding matters would have to be resolved quickly if there was any chance of the guarantee being issued. Among the requirements was that SAA finalise a particularly bizarre and contentious deal involving the purchase of Airbus aircraft. I describe this deal in much more detail in the section on SAA, but suffice it to note here that, at the time, SAA had negotiated a highly favourable deal to lease aircraft from Airbus to modernise its fleet. SAA had previously been on the hook to buy the aircraft on onerous terms. The lease agreement would have dug SAA out of a significant hole. The deal was sufficiently advantageous that it was approved by National Treasury as a clear way to improve SAA's financial position.

Soon after Treasury's approval, Myeni threw a spanner in the works. She proposed a whole new deal, whereby SAA would buy the aircraft, sell them to a local intermediary, and then lease the aircraft back from the intermediary. Nene responded by asking for a new business case and new information, which was belatedly handed over. When Treasury reviewed the plan, it realised it would make SAA's already parlous financial position even worse.

By November 2015, Nene had become disturbed by Myeni's running of SAA, not least because of an exodus of senior management, who cited a breakdown in trust with the board led by Myeni. In a meeting on 3 November 2015 with an ANC study group, Nene said that 'either Ms Myeni leaves or I leave'. Nene's comment was reported to Myeni and, sometime later in November 2015, he was summoned to a meeting with Myeni and Zuma at Zuma's official residence. Nene would later testify that he believed the meeting had mostly been called so that Myeni could complain about Nene. Nene, for his part, doubled down in the meeting and reiterated his opinion that Myeni should step down from the board.

On 2 December 2015, not long after this apparently 'awkward' meeting, Nene made his final decision on the Airbus leasing deal: it would not be approved. Nene publicly announced the decision the following day.

Matters began to come to a head on the nuclear deal scarcely a week later. On 8 December 2015, a Cabinet meeting was called, which was to be attended by all those members whose portfolios touched on the nuclear deal. Zuma was to chair the meeting, which was arranged to begin at 3 pm, although Treasury was subsequently told it would take place an hour later. This seemingly innocuous change in schedule was, in fact, all-important. According to Nene and Fuzile, in the rescheduled hour Zuma had held a preliminary meeting with other Cabinet members overseeing the nuclear deal, including State Security Minister David Mahlobo, Minister of International Relations Maite Nkoana-Mashabane, Minister of Public Enterprises Lynne Brown and Tina Joemat-Pettersson. Nene's exclusion from the meeting was striking.

The substance of the meeting was to seek approval from the subcommittee to finally confirm the issuing of tenders for the nuclear deal. The centrepiece of the meeting was the presentation of a proposed nuclear programme by the Ministry of Energy. The presentation recommended the purchase of 9.6 GW of nuclear power. To Nene's and Fuzile's consternation, this was described as the joint recommendation of the Treasury and the Department of Energy. But this was clearly not true, as Treasury had already, in September 2015, made it clear that South Africa at that time could only afford to procure just over 2 GW of energy.

Nene and Fuzile were asked to respond to the proposal. Fuzile pointed out that this was definitely not Treasury's recommendation and ran through the reasons why. It was at this point that Zuma launched into a stinging criticism of Treasury. He began by attacking Treasury's refusal to support a hare-brained scheme for PetroSA to purchase Engen, which had apparently been a project that Zuma was keen to pursue, but which had run aground during Pravin Gordhan's time as Minister of Finance. Zuma then lamented Nene's failure to 'find the money' to fund projects the President wanted to pursue.

Despite Treasury's stated reservations, the Cabinet subcommittee approved the proposal. A full sitting of Cabinet would approve it the following day, mandating the government to begin issuing requests for proposals. The nuclear deal was on its way.

The Cabinet meeting ended at approximately 5.30 pm. On his way home, Nene received a call from Zuma's office asking him to attend a meeting at the Union Buildings. Nene turned round. In a meeting that lasted no more than two or three minutes, but would end up costing the country vast sums of money, Zuma fired Nene. Nene stood up, shook Zuma's hand, and left. On his way home, he texted Fuzile: 'the axe has fallen'.

Nene's unexpected firing, and his replacement by the little-known Des van Rooyen, would send South Africa's markets into free-fall. The rand depreciated from R13.40 to R15.40 against the US dollar overnight. A later National Treasury study calculated that the firing of Nene would cost 1.1% of GDP by the end of 2017, lead to the loss of 148,000 jobs, and reduce the value of Johannesburg Stock Exchange shares by R378bn.

Zuma, in his conversation with Nene and in his subsequent public announcements, explained that he had decided to remove Nene so that the latter could take up a role with the newly formed BRICS Bank. The commission found this was clearly nonsense, and posited the real reason: 'The reason given by President Zuma for Mr Nene's dismissal must be rejected. The reasons why President Zuma dismissed Minister Nene is that he was not co-operating or working with the Guptas and he was resisting President Zuma's and Dudu Myeni's attempts to get National Treasury to approve transactions or projects or measures that were not in the interests of the country.'

## The Weekend Special and the hand of the Gupta enterprise

The shock of Nene's dismissal on 9 December 2015 was compounded by the announcement of his successor: a relative non-entity called Des van Rooyen.

In an initial statement before the commission, Van Rooyen would deny any connection to the Guptas. Instead, he insisted that Zuma had started taking an independent interest in him in mid-November 2015, when Zuma summoned him to a meeting to discuss his qualifications. On 30 November 2015, Zuma asked him for his CV, and on 6 December Zuma called him to request a meeting sometime between 7 and 10 December 2015; on the 9th, Zuma offered him the job, which he accepted.

The only problem with Van Rooyen's version was a plethora of contradictory evidence. Thuli Madonsela's *State of Capture* report confirmed that Van Rooyen could be placed in the Saxonwold area – the home of the Guptas – on at least seven occasions prior to his appointment, including the day he was appointed. When Van Rooyen testified before the commission, he admitted that he had, in fact, met with the Guptas, on 9 December as well, and that he had first met Tony Gupta at Luthuli House, the ANC headquarters, in October 2015.

Van Rooyen, however, was adamant: at no stage did he ever discuss his appointment as Finance Minister with Tony Gupta, and he was not appointed at the behest of the Guptas. The commission was scathing in its dismissal of this idea: 'The probabilities are overwhelming that Mr Tony Gupta spoke to Mr Van Rooyen about his possible appointment as Minister of Finance. President Zuma may have met with Mr Van Rooyen and looked at his CV but there can be no doubt that Mr Van Rooyen was either suggested to President Zuma by the Guptas or that his appointment as Minister of Finance had the blessing and approval of the Guptas.'

Van Rooyen's real relationship with the Guptas was revealed by his choice of special advisors, whom he appointed soon after he accepted the role of minister. The first advisor was Mohamed Bobat, who was appointed on 10 December 2015, the day after Van Rooyen's appointment. The second was Ian Whitley, who was appointed as Van Rooyen's chief of staff.

At the time of his appointment, Bobat held a senior position at the advisory company Regiments, which was headed by Eric Wood. I describe the pernicious role of Regiments in later chapters, but, in brief, Eric Wood was extremely close to Salim Essa, a key Gupta lieutenant, and his companies would earn vast sums from dodgy contracts with Transnet and Eskom. Van Rooyen later claimed he had no idea Bobat was at Regiments when he appointed him, which suggests that he had not even bothered to ask Bobat for his CV. Bobat, in the few days that he served in this role, would use his position to send a confidential National Treasury presentation to Eric Wood and Salim Essa.

According to Van Rooyen's version, he met his chief of staff, Whitley, for the first time on 11 December 2015 during a business meeting at Melrose Arch: the same day he was appointed minister. Van Rooyen claimed he was introduced to Whitley by Malcolm Mabaso, who was, at the time, part of the support staff of Minister Mosebenzi Zwane (Zwane, as I'll show in much more detail later, was a major Gupta ally and associate). Following a brief meeting, Van Rooyen claimed, he was sufficiently impressed to appoint Whitley as his chief of staff on the spot.

The commission rejected these versions out of hand, seeing instead the controlling influence of the Guptas: 'it is Mr Tony Gupta or one of the Gupta brothers who must have arranged for him to appoint Mr Bobat. So, Mr Van Rooyen knew that he got the appointment as Minister of Finance through the Guptas and that he got Mr Bobat and Mr Whitley through the Guptas. They were all Gupta people.'

## The reappointment of Gordhan – and the race to his dismissal

The collapse of South Africa's markets forced Zuma's hand, as did an intervention by the ANC Top 6 leaders, who met with Zuma and recommended action on Van Rooyen. On 13 December 2015, Gordhan was summoned to a meeting with the President and asked to accept the position of Minister of Finance. Gordhan agreed but noted that he was determined to deal with three key things: the mismanagement of SAA under Myeni, the nuclear deal, and the performance of Tom Moyane at SARS. Gordhan was announced as the new Finance Minister on Monday, 14 December 2015. Van

Rooyen's ignominious four-day tenure had come to an end.

Gordhan's second tenure as Minister of Finance was marked by continued friction between Zuma as well as those close to him and the Treasury, and by an extraordinary attempt to concoct criminal charges against the minister. Famously, on 17 February 2016, General Berning Ntlemeza, the Hawks head, whom Gordhan accused of being an agent of state capture, delivered a letter to Treasury. The letter included 27 questions posed to Gordhan that were related to bogus claims that Gordhan had been party to the creation of a so-called rogue unit within SARS. The 27 questions were subsequently leaked to the press soon after Gordhan had completed his budget statement for the year.

The pressure continued to mount throughout 2017. Gordhan noted two separate flashpoints. The first was when Minister of Social Development Bathabile Dlamini wrote a lengthy letter to Zuma, which demanded that Zuma intervene because the National Treasury had raised objections to her problematic plans for paying out social grants.

The second revolved around amendments to the Financial Intelligence Centre Act (FICA). The Act codified, among other things, how banks had to report suspicious transactions to the Financial Intelligence Centre. The amendments to FICA included introducing greater levels of scrutiny over politically exposed persons (PEPS). PEPs are people who either serve as government officials or are linked to politicians or senior government officials and may present a corruption risk. The amendments also required banks to record the true beneficial owners of bank accounts. Gordhan claimed that there were attempts to undermine this process, including a mooted plan to move the Financial Intelligence Centre to a different part of the Cabinet security cluster. Zuma, for his part, refused to sign the amendments until litigation was brought to force him to do so.

On 11 October 2016, the political temperature increased even further. The National Director of Public Prosecutions, Shaun Abrahams, announced that charges were being pursued against Gordhan related to his role in approving the early retirement of the former Deputy SARS Commissioner Ivan Pillay. Media reports soon confirmed that Abrahams had met with Zuma and other Cabinet ministers the day before. The announcement led to another pummelling of financial markets. On 31 October, following weeks of intense civil society pushback, Abrahams announced he was withdrawing the charges. He claimed there was now evidence that Gordhan and his two co-accused had no intention to act unlawfully.

But, in the highly charged interregnum between Abrahams's two announcements, Gordhan took a somewhat audacious step. As I'll discuss in more detail later, in April 2016 numerous banks shut down the Guptas' bank accounts because of potential reputational risk and criminal exposure. Zuma's Cabinet responded aggressively, and appointed an Inter-Ministerial Task Force to investigate. Gordhan was purportedly on the task force but effectively refused to participate. Instead, on 14 October, Gordhan brought a High Court application that sought a declaration that the Minister of Finance had no powers to intervene in the closure of bank accounts. The application papers included a copy of an FIC report about 72 suspicious transaction reports that had been filed by South African banks related to the Guptas.

Gordhan survived as Finance Minister for another five months. In late March 2017, Gordhan flew abroad as part of a National Treasury 'investment roadshow'. On the 27th, the same day Gordhan landed at Heathrow to begin the roadshow, Zuma allegedly met with senior leaders of the South African Communist Party (SACP), during which he intimated that he intended to dismiss Gordhan. Zuma allegedly referred to an intelligence report that claimed Gordhan was conspiring with foreign forces against the South African government.

Upon his hasty return to South Africa the next day, Gordhan met with ANC secretary general Gwede Mantashe. Mantashe told him that Zuma had convened a meeting of the 'Top 6 of the ANC', the most senior officials in the party, to inform them that he intended to dismiss Gordhan and replace him with Brian Molefe. Zuma referred to the intelligence report on Gordhan at the meeting.

This was a shocking and depraved idea. Molefe was the ultimate Gupta stooge, who was involved in a succession of questionable decisions while leading both Transnet and Eskom. Molefe, at this time, had quite recently been forced to step down from Eskom after the extent of his connections to the Guptas were exposed by Thuli Madonsela's *State of Capture* report.

The other members of the Top 6 (excluding Zuma) prevailed

upon Zuma not to appoint Molefe, which, as the commission notes, was one of the very rare occasions when the ANC can be said to have done anything to stop state capture. Zuma's second choice, however, wasn't a great deal better. Gordhan's dismissal was announced on 30 March 2017; his replacement was Malusi Gigaba, the former Minister of Public Enterprises.

The commission spent a good deal of time analysing why Gordhan was dismissed. Unsurprisingly, it found he was dismissed in an attempt to push forward state capture. In reaching this conclusion, two factors loomed large in the commission's reasoning. The first related to the intelligence report upon which Zuma relied. Here, the commission turned to the evidence of Dr Dintwe, who was the Inspector General of Intelligence at the time. Dintwe repeatedly asked Zuma to share the intelligence report with him as part of his own investigation into the matter. Zuma failed to do so. The commission explained this by arguing that Zuma must have known the report 'was fake or was simply not credible, and if he produced it, Dr Dintwe's investigation was likely to result in an adverse finding against him or those who had given him the report'.

The second factor in the commission's thinking was Zuma's stated intention to place Molefe in the role of Finance Minister, and his eventual decision to appoint Gigaba. On this, the commission took an extraordinarily dim view. It called the decision to recommend Molefe 'astonishing' and found that Zuma 'must have been determined to give the Guptas direct access to the nation's Treasury before he left office'. When he could not secure support for Molefe, Zuma turned to Gigaba: or, rather, the Guptas turned to Gigaba. 'The Guptas gave President Zuma another one of their friends to be appointed, namely, Mr Malusi Gigaba and he appointed him,' the commission would find.

## The exception to the rule: State capture resisted

Gigaba's appointment, one might have expected, would unleash another wave of aggressive state capture. Yet, as the commission notes, despite being a Gupta associate, Gigaba 'was not able to do much for the Guptas as Minister of Finance'. Whatever plans may have been afoot were thwarted when Cyril Ramaphosa was elected president of the ANC at its December 2017 elective conference.

Within two months of this election, Zuma was forced to resign as President of South Africa, to be replaced by Ramaphosa. Ramaphosa swiftly removed Gigaba and appointed Nhlanhla Nene to his second term as Minister of Finance.

In a strange twist of fate, Nene's return as Minister of Finance was to be short-lived – because of the Zondo Commission. In October 2018, Nene was called to give evidence at the commission, during which he confessed to visiting the Guptas' Saxonwold compound at least six times between 2009 and 2014. Nene apologised to the country for the meetings, and decided to resign a week later.

Nene's admission notwithstanding, the commission would conclude that state capture was effectively resisted at Treasury. This was due to the efforts of Nene, Gordhan and officials like Lungisa Fuzile. 'The country should be grateful to all of them,' the commission noted.

In concluding, the commission took the opportunity to express shocked relief that Treasury had been spared: 'It is almost a miracle that the National Treasury was saved from the tentacles of the Guptas! I shudder to think what would have happened to this country if President Zuma was not forced to move Mr Des van Rooyen out of the National Treasury and if Mr Van Rooyen and his advisors had been allowed to continue in the Treasury.' But tragically, the case of the National Treasury was a rare exception. In other spheres of the state – particular at SARS and in the state security services – the programme of capture succeeded with alarming ease.

## RECOMMENDATION

*The NPA should consider bringing charges of bribery and corruption against Rajesh (Tony) Gupta pursuant to his offer of an alleged bribe of R600m to Mcebisi Jonas so that Jonas would agree to assume the position of Minister of Finance and run it to the advantage of the Gupta enterprise.*

# The capture of SARS

UNLIKE TREASURY, SARS was unable to resist a concerted and pre-planned effort of state capture. The result was a sustained attack on one of the most important parts of the entire state apparatus, which destroyed SARS's ability to tackle the so-called illicit economy – the tobacco smugglers and other criminals that ran South Africa's underworld.

For my money, the capture of SARS and its systematic destruction, aided and abetted by the swanky American consultancy firm Bain, form the most shocking and possibly most damaging case considered by the commission. A state cannot function without a tax authority, and especially one that is at the forefront of disrupting organised crime. The capture of SARS was economic and political despoliation of the highest order.

## The Nugent Commission

During the life of the Zondo Commission, another commission delivered its own findings on SARS – the Nugent Commission. The latter was established to investigate the destruction of SARS under Tom Moyane, the man Zuma appointed to head SARS as its commissioner in 2014. The Nugent Commission's findings were damning. It found that:

- there had been a total collapse of integrity and governance brought about by Tom Moyane's leadership and his campaign to 'restructure' SARS;

- the dismantling of governance at SARS was pursued vigorously by Moyane as soon as he arrived;
- Moyane's tenure had led to the mass exodus of senior staff;
- Moyane instilled a culture of fear and intimidation through a purge of officials; and
- Bain had aided and abetted Moyane in his campaign to 'restructure' SARS.

The Zondo Commission made the decision that it would not disrupt or challenge these findings, although, as the content of its own report makes clear, it seems very unlikely that it would have found much differently. The Zondo Commission, instead, decided to accept and build on the Nugent Commission's findings and, in particular, seek to place the destruction of SARS within the broader context of state capture.

One major difference between the Zondo Commission and the Nugent Commission was the participation of Moyane in the former but not the latter. Moyane refused to engage with the Nugent Commission, did not respond to its inquiries and did not give evidence. Moyane, however, did appear before the Zondo Commission; this gave the commission the advantage of being able to test the evidence of the man at the centre of the dismantling of SARS.

## Zuma, Bain and Ambrobrite

Between 11 August 2012 and July 2014, President Jacob Zuma met a businessman called Vittorio Massone on at least 17 occasions. Massone was, at the time, a senior representative of Bain in Johannesburg. Bain, for its part, is one of the most well-known and 'respectable' management consultancies in the world. It is headquartered in the US. On average, Bain, in the person of Massone, met President Zuma every six weeks over a period of two years.

Massone tried, at various points of the commission's hearings, to say that the meetings were simply marketing meetings to promote Bain to the President. This version was comprehensively disputed by Athol Williams, a Bain employee who was appointed to investigate Bain's conduct in South Africa, and who reviewed its internal documents. Williams would later fall out with Bain, but he refused to let the matter go.

Williams presented the commission with documents from the meetings. They showed that Bain had been preparing plans, shared with Zuma, about making massive structural changes to South Africa's political economy. One of the proposals was to create a 'delivery agency' that could deal with 'execution roadblocks'. The essence of this plan was to set up a centralised procurement agency reporting directly to the President, cutting out all ministerial oversight and involvement. One can only imagine the fortunes the Guptas would have made if Zuma's office had directed government procurement.

On 1 November 2013, during these meetings behind closed doors, Bain entered into a 'Business Development and Stakeholder Management' contract with a company by the name of Ambrobrite. At the time, Ambrobrite had no web presence, no trading history and never filed financial statements. SARS suspected that Ambrobrite's tax certificate was fraudulent. The contract between Bain and Ambrobrite stated that Ambrobrite had access to intelligence and information about leadership and management changes at various state-owned entities (SOEs) and that Bain would benefit from strategic advice. Bain would pay Ambrobrite R3.6m a year. This was the most Bain paid to any of its consultants in the entire world. Bain renewed Ambrobrite's contracts every six months until 2016.

What Ambrobrite actually did was obscure. Ambrobrite was set up by Duma Ndlovu and Mandla KaNozulu. Ndlovu was a TV producer responsible for the popular show *Muvhango*. KaNozulu was an artist. When asked, they claimed that Ambrobrite was an events management company, which may have been at least a partial truth. Evidence led before the commission suggested that one of Ambrobrite's jobs was to organise parties where Bain could meet politicians. Indeed, Ambrobrite organised one such party in September 2013, where Jacob Zuma was in attendance. Athol Williams, when he reviewed the contracts, was of the opinion that Ambrobrite's primary function was to use its proximity to and relationships with politicians to open doors for Bain.

Internal records show that Bain employees were extremely uncomfortable about the relationship with Ambrobrite. In one email, the director of finance at Bain's London office, Geoff Smout, said that 'the whole situation feels very dodgy ... for some reason I do not trust the situation'. Another Bain employee, Wendy Miller, the global head of marketing, questioned whether it would survive the 'sunshine test': if the relationship was made public, would Bain feel comfortable defending it? Massone responded to Williams by commenting that 'it is simply a business development arrangement where these people would inform us if they are aware of changes in the key positions in selected companies'.

## Bain, Moyane and plans for SARS

Bain began working with Tom Moyane in 2013, long before Moyane was appointed the SARS Commissioner, to develop a 'strategic turnaround' plan, which was presented to President Zuma. The commission does not record exactly when the Bain–Moyane consultations started, but notes that in December 2013 Massone's performance assessment recorded that he had been involved in producing a 'high level outside-in "strategic turnaround" document with SARS'. Remarkably, the same performance review predicted that 'the person we prepared it with [Moyane] and who pitched it to the SA President is most likely going to be appointed as Commissioner in the next few weeks/months and Bain will be assisting him should he get the job'.

On 26 May 2014, Bain presented Moyane with a 'First 100 Days Plan', which set out how Moyane would go about restructuring SARS when he got the job. The date of this plan is striking – it would be many more months until Moyane got the job. The document set out a plan to be implemented in three phases: 'keep ball rolling, gain higher ground and take control'. Most notably, the plan included a programme to 'build a healthy sponsorship spine to accelerate change and identify individuals to neutralise'.

Bain and Moyane later tried to claim that the use of the term 'neutralise' was unfortunate, and what they really meant was that there would be a plan to get opponents onside. The commission was having none of it: 'the attempts by Bain and Moyane to explain away the obvious intention behind the use of the words "neutralise" were unconvincing,' it found. 'The clear intention signified in plain language was to identify people within SARS to get rid of.'

During his evidence Athol Williams commented that the level of detail in the Bain planning documents was striking because Bain had no previous tax authority experience. He speculated that Bain was being fed information from inside SARS. The commission identified this insider as Jonas Makwakwa, head of internal audit at SARS. Emails and document reviewed by the commission showed that Bain had multiple meetings with Makwakwa. 'Not only was this illegal,' the commission noted, 'it also meant that Bain had access to confidential information which was not in the public domain.'

## Moyane gets the job – and Bain gets its contracts

The government first publicly advertised for the replacement of the SARS Commissioner in the latter half of 2013, with the final closing date being 13 September 2013. Over 120 people applied for the position. At some point in 2013, Zuma told Pravin Gordhan that he intended to appoint Moyane directly. Gordhan strongly suggested to Zuma that he go through the usual process and submit his preferred candidate to Cabinet to be interviewed. Zuma refused and, on 23 September 2014, Zuma appointed Moyane to the position of Commissioner, as Bain had long already known would happen.

The very next month, SARS issued requests for proposals (RFPs) for an organisational strategy review and redesign of SARS. An RFP is a formal procurement step whereby suppliers are invited to submit detailed bids for government tenders. SARS did this by means of a 'closed tender', which meant that the RFP was not publicly advertised but sent to a selection of bidders chosen by SARS. In January 2015, Bain was awarded the contract. Bain would ultimately be paid R167m for its consultancy services over a period of 27 months.

The commission found that there were serious problems and irregularities with the entire bid. One problem was the need for the bid in the first place. SARS was already a highly functional and high-performing organisation: 'there was no justifiable reason for [SARS] to hire external consultants to perform the stated services'. Bain itself was well aware that it did not actually have the expertise to deliver on the contract. In an email sent on 18 November 2014, Massone commented about the proposal that 'as much as it is "designed" for us … we need to make sure they feel comfortable with the team and our expertise (and we know we can't claim to have done much on the specific topic)'. On this, the commission was scathing: 'Bain knew that they did not have the necessary expertise. They must have thought South Africa did not know this or did not care whether they had the necessary expertise. I think President Zuma and Mr Moyane neither knew nor cared.'

When Bain later established an inquiry into its dealings in South Africa, it appointed the law firm Baker McKenzie, which set up a whistleblower email. Numerous Bain employees wrote to the email address with concerns about the contract. In one email, an employee commented that 'our work there was effectively a sham'. Another claimed that the RFP was based on a draft that had actually been written by Fabrice Franzen, a Bain executive. This was related to the further problem, namely, that SARS had sent a preliminary request for information and requests for references *prior* to the contract being published. Communications prior to the issuing of an RFP were irregular 'in terms of the governing legislation', the commission commented.

But the biggest issue had to do with how the contract was extended. The original RFP sent to Bain and other consultants stipulated that it would be for six weeks of work, for which payment would amount to R2.6m. When the Bid Adjudication Committee at SARS reviewed the bid, about which they expressed concerns, they gave approval on the explicit basis that, if any additional work took place, SARS would have to go back to the market with an open tender.

This was never done. Instead, when the deadline was rapidly approaching, SARS developed a work-around; it declared that the Bain project was an emergency and that Bain was the only consultant that could do the work. 'This was clearly not an emergency,' the commission simply concluded. Adopting this method was thus, in the commission's view, an 'unlawful use' of certain 'deviation' provisions allowed for in Treasury regulations.

The commission found that there was collusion between Bain and SARS employees to get around the legal provisions guiding contract extensions. Emails reviewed by the commission showed that Jonas Makwakwa – who had earlier provided inside information to Bain – had told Bain not to 'worry' about the extension because SARS was 'going to make a plan'. Makwakwa claimed that Moyane himself had 'gone to see' the people in procurement, presumably to intervene on Bain's behalf. The result, the commission found, was that 'there was a flouting of the procurement legislation in order to extend what was originally supposed to be a six-week contract for R2.6 million, into one that lasted 27 months and cost SARS around R164 million'.

## Moyane's reign of terror and that 'rogue unit'

Moyane's appointment led to an exodus of senior and experienced staff. The first casualty was Barry Hore, the chief operating officer (COO) of SARS, to whom 70% of operational staff ultimately reported. He was widely credited as being central to SARS's stellar performance.

Hore was specifically identified in Bain's '100 Days Plan' as somebody to be 'neutralised'. The plan recommended the need to 'test BH [Barry Hore] as the COO'. Hore resigned in December 2014, only a few months after Moyane's appointment. On 3 December 2014, Bain executive Franzen wrote to Massone, saying, 'Goodbye Barry Hore ... Now I am scared by Tom [Moyane]. This guy [Hore] was supposed to be untouchable and it took Tom just a few weeks to make him resign.' In his evidence before the commission, Moyane denied any attempt to 'neutralise' or 'test' Hore, and claimed that there was no acrimony between them. Hore left, Moyane claimed, because he 'wanted his own time'. The commission rejected this version totally: 'Mr Hore's forced departure was part of the execution of the plan.'

Jonas Makwakwa eventually replaced Hore as COO. Makwakwa, of course, was the man the commission found had been leaking inside information from SARS to Bain to help Bain draft Moyane's '100 Days Plan'.

The commission found that Hore's departure was not an isolated incident but part of a pattern. Within a year of Moyane's arrival, five of the most senior SARS executives left. These included:

| Name | Position | Date resigned |
| --- | --- | --- |
| Johann van Loggerenberg | Group executive: enforcement investigations | February 2015 |
| Adrian Lackay | SARS spokesperson | March 2015 |

| Name | Position | Date resigned |
|---|---|---|
| Ivan Pillay | Acting commissioner | May 2015 |
| Peter Richer | Group executive: strategic planning and risk; and acting chief executive: strategy enablement and communications | May 2015 |
| Gene Ravele | Chief officer: tax and customs enforcement investigations | May 2015 |

Again, when Moyane was asked about these resignations, he denied any responsibility. The commission disagreed: 'An essential part of Mr Moyane's 100 Day Plan was to identify individuals that could hamper change and neutralise them. It would appear from the facts that this is precisely what Mr Moyane did. There is no other rational explanation for the sudden departure of so many senior people in such a short space of time.'

Lurking in the background of these resignations were claims and counter-claims of perfidy on the part of the senior SARS executives. According to Van Loggerenberg, SARS's investigations into the criminal economy led to numerous attempts to undermine staff and the institution itself. One of the primary means by which this was achieved was through the creation and dissemination of damning 'dossiers'. The dossiers purported to show that senior staff members were involved in all sorts of wrongdoing. The practice of damning-by-dossier developed precisely at the time that Moyane arrived at SARS, according to Van Loggerenberg, who also suspected that some of the dossiers were being provided to the media by state security agents.

The most notorious hit-job revolved around claims that SARS, under its previous management, had created a specialised investigative unit – the 'rogue unit' – that was, among other things, illegally spying on President Zuma and running a brothel. The dossier alleging the existence of the 'rogue unit' first appeared on 12 October 2014, only weeks after Moyane took over the role as Commissioner. The *Sunday Times*, engaging in what the commission called 'poor journalism', repeated the allegations in more than 30 articles between 2014 and 2016. The 'rogue unit' was in fact a fabrication: the *Sunday Times* would eventually retract the story in totality and apologise, while the High Court would also find the story had no basis.

Moyane's response to the narrative was strange. He never questioned the veracity of the claims. On 16 October 2014, the six implicated executives wrote to Moyane, telling him that the allegations were a total fabrication. They requested an investigation and offered to take polygraph tests. They asked Moyane to institute legal proceedings against the *Sunday Times*. Moyane was unmoved.

Instead, he responded by suspending the executive committee (a senior management body) in November 2014 following a story that the 'rogue unit' was running a brothel. Moyane made no attempt to defend SARS. Remarkably, despite the extent and seriousness of the allegations, Moyane never reached out to any of those implicated to find out their version. He remained totally silent, which the commission considered strange: 'the fact that he kept quiet suggests he knew well where the allegations were coming from'. During Moyane's evidence before the commission, he stood by claims that the establishment of the special investigative unit was unlawful, despite the findings of the courts, which the commission found to be 'telling'.

## Dismantling SARS

Johann van Loggerenberg testified that Moyane used the allegations of the existence of a 'rogue unit' to target senior staff and to push forward aggressively with the 'restructuring' of SARS. Moyane's targets included a highly effective set of investigative and enforcement units grouped together under the Projects and Evidence Management and Technical Support Division (PEMTS). This was headed by Van Loggerenberg. PEMTS incorporated a range of mutually supportive units, which were extremely effective at tackling the illicit economy. By the time Van Loggerenberg left SARS, it was running 87 active cases. One of the most impressive was Project Honey Badger, which tackled illicit tobacco smuggling. In 2011/12 SARS collected

R10.8bn in excise fees from tobacco; by 2013/14 this had increased to R13.1bn, showing a 15% year-on-year growth.

Moyane dismantled PEMTS through restructuring and closed a large number of active investigations. Van Loggerenberg testified that the effect of this was to effectively end a whole range of high-profile projects. He noted that the projects that were closed showed four key similarities. First, they all ended shortly after Moyane's arrival. Second, many of them implicated criminal actors with strong links to politicians (although the commission, somewhat unfortunately, did not name any names). Third, they were all sophisticated and complicated criminal schemes. Fourth, many of them allegedly involved state security operatives.

As a result of the closure of these projects, the effectiveness of SARS in tackling the illicit economy plummeted. So, for example, Project Honey Badger came to a halt sometime in either late 2014 or early 2015. The result was that, in the 2015/16 and 2017/18 financial years, there was a 15% drop in the amount of tobacco excise collected, while the illicit part of the industry flourished.

## Moyane, Gordhan and the Vlok Symington hostage debacle

At the very time that Moyane was dismantling SARS, he was also deeply involved in a criminal case against Pravin Gordhan, with whom he appears to have had an extremely acrimonious relationship. Moyane's involvement in the Gordhan affair, and his creation of an 'extreme climate of fear and bullying', came together in one of the most extraordinary moments recounted by the commission – the infamous 'hostage taking' of Vlok Symington.

To briefly recap, in 2009 Gordhan (then SARS Commissioner) approved an application for early retirement on the part of his Deputy Commissioner, Ivan Pillay. Another SARS executive, Oupa Magashula, was also part of the decision. In February 2016, General Berning Ntlemeza of the Hawks sent Gordhan a list of 27 questions about the Pillay retirement and other matters, which was shortly thereafter leaked to the press. Ntlemeza was ostensibly investigating a criminal complaint filed by Moyane in 2015 with SAPS, which, while not laid against Gordhan, dealt with issues in which Gordhan was involved. In early October 2016, Shaun Abrahams, the head of the National Prosecuting Authority (NPA), announced that charges were being brought against Gordhan and others in relation to the Pillay retirement matter.

Following Abrahams's announcement, the Helen Suzman Foundation and Freedom Under Law wrote to him to protest against the decision because they believed that the approval of Pillay's retirement was lawful. The two organisations attached a 2009 memo that had been written by another senior SARS employee, Vlok Symington. The memo found that the way in which Pillay's early retirement was being handled was lawful, subject to certain conditions. Abrahams would later explain that he had made the decision to prosecute in part because he did not have this 2009 memo. According to the commission, Moyane had had access to this memo since at least December 2014. Abrahams, in later correspondence with General Ntlemeza, questioned why the Hawks had not given him a copy of the memorandum, suggesting that they, too, had had access to it.

In response to the disclosure of the Symington memorandum, Abrahams instructed an NPA employee, Dr Torie Pretorius, to review the memorandum in the light of the NPA's decision to prosecute. Pretorius advised that the NPA should ask certain questions of Symington and that he needed to depose an affidavit in response. Symington was informed of the request by his direct line manager, Kosi Louw. On the morning of 18 October, Symington collected a four-page letter that included Pretorius's questions.

Crucially, as Symington would only later realise, Pretorius's correspondence included a vital attachment: an email written by David Makhapela, a partner of the law firm Mashiane, Moodley and Monama, which was advising SAPS on the matter. The email chain originated with the NPA, went to the Hawks, then Makhapela, and onwards to Moyane. Makhapela wrote that 'on ethical reasons, I cannot be involved in this one, as I hold a different view to the one pursued by the NPA and the Hawks'. In other words, he did not support the criminal charges. Later, in April 2018, it emerged that Makhapela had actually provided Moyane with an opinion on the Pillay retirement matter in November 2014, nearly two years prior to the NPA prosecution and a year before Moyane filed criminal charges. He had advised that there was nothing unlawful about Pillay's retirement.

After collecting the letter with questions from Pretorius, Symington met Brigadier Xaba and Colonel Maluleke of the SAPS in the SARS boardroom and promised to depose an affidavit in response by 1 pm. He then returned to his office. Soon thereafter, Symington was confronted by Mr Titi, Moyane's bodyguard. Titi demanded that Symington hand over the whole bundle of documents. Symington suggested that he return to Xaba and Maluleke to discuss the issue. Xaba then asked Symington to hand over all his documents, and said he would give him a photocopied version of the self-same bundle – most likely, with the Makhapela email removed.

Matters soon escalated. Titi blocked the door of the boardroom and refused to let Symington leave. Symington then called SARS's security and the police to inform them he was being held hostage. The police did not respond after Colonel Maluleke intervened to tell them everything was all right. Distressed and disturbed, Symington then began recording the whole situation, taking a video of the bundle of documents that had been given to him. Only later, when he reviewed the footage, did he realise the real reason for the situation: he had been handed Makhapela's letter. Eventually, Symington was allowed to leave but, as he did so, Titi snatched the documents away from him.

On 31 October 2016, Abrahams dropped the prosecution of Gordhan. In his public announcement, he explained that he was doing so in part because he had become aware of Symington's 2009 memo, which had been in the hands of both Moyane and the Hawks.

Moyane, in his evidence before the commission, would again deny wrongdoing. He alleged that, in fact, the Vlok Symington memo did not find the Pillay retirement lawful. According to Moyane, this was 'the biggest lie ever told in support of unfounded allegations against me'. Reviewing this whole sordid situation, the commission commented:

This saga illustrates an extreme example of the culture of fear and bullying which characterised Mr Moyane's tenure at SARS. It also illustrates the lengths that he went to have certain people, who were obstacles to state capture, removed. Mr Symington described this time as a 'nightmare' time at SARS, and to visibly see the efficiency rate dropping during Mr Moyane's tenure was something he hoped would never happen again.

## Moyane vs Gordhan at the Zondo-dome

One of the most dramatic moments of the entire commission occurred when Moyane was granted the right to cross-examine Gordhan. The questioning was fractious and ill-tempered; Moyane implied that Gordhan was racist and was party to state capture.

The commission dealt with this cross-examination at length in its report. Most of the cross-examination, the commission ruefully noted, 'concentrated on the clear personal animosity between the two men and the alleged origins thereof, which have no direct bearing on state capture. So, too, a lot of what Mr Gordhan testified about Mr Moyane's involvement in state capture was either based on hearsay or on the so-called public narrative. Neither of these sources of information assisted the work of the commission.'

The commission found that the only useful information came from Moyane's line of questioning that claimed Gordhan had no tangible evidence of state capture. In response, Gordhan outlined all the examples he knew of the matter. In this, he explained how Moyane had refused to account to him as the Finance Minister, which Gordhan saw as part of a programme of capture.

Despite the fireworks, therefore, the great battle of Gordhan and Moyane produced results that were far less important, and less truly dramatic, than all the other evidence reviewed by the commission on SARS.

## Conclusion: A clear example of state capture

The commission concluded its report on the capture of SARS by confirming that it was, indeed, a 'clear example of state capture'. The commission found the following:

> The SARS evidence is a clear example of how the private sector colluded with the Executive, including President Zuma, to capture an institution that was highly regarded internationally and render it ineffective.
>
> SARS's investigatory and enforcement capacity presented a hurdle to those involved in organised crime, and was, therefore, a target for those engaged in state capture. The involvement of the media in perpetuating false narratives which discredited

targeted people as well as providing grounds for their removal was a notable feature of the evidence led in regard to the capture of SARS.

SARS was systemically and deliberately weakened, chiefly through the restructuring of its institutional capacity, strategic appointments and dismissals of key individuals, and a pervasive culture of fear and bullying. It is a clear example of state capture ...

The only feasible conclusion is that the organization was deliberately captured and President Zuma and Mr Moyane played critical roles in the capture of SARS and dismantling it in the way it was done during Mr Moyane's term as Commissioner.

## RECOMMENDATIONS

*The state should review all contracts placed with Bain for compliance with relevant statutory and constitutional provisions.*

*Law enforcement should investigate with a view to enabling the NPA to prosecute any person for unlawful conduct in relation to the award of contracts to Bain.*

*The SARS Act of 1997 should be amended to make the appointment of the SARS Commissioner open, transparent and competitive.*

*Tom Moyane should be charged with perjury for providing false testimony to Parliament.*

# The State Security Agency

SOUTH AFRICA'S INTELLIGENCE services have, for the last two decades, been deeply implicated in the fierce factional fighting for control of the ANC and the levers of state power. Dodgy dossiers and nonsense reports have been concocted to spin the oddest and most inane narratives, while spies and spooks, operating with huge budgets not subject to scrutiny, have played fast and loose with the country's democracy.

The commission's investigation into the State Security Agency (SSA) and Crime Intelligence (CI) confirms what many of us had long suspected: the country's intelligence services were up to all sorts of outrageous mischief behind the scenes. Unfortunately, the commission's report on the SSA and CI is written in a somewhat frustrating style. Essentially, the commission starts and ends its report on the SSA by providing a high-level overview of its findings and recommendations. The meat in the middle of the sandwich, which runs to a few hundred pages, is a straightforward description of the evidence given by witnesses to the commission, most of which is reproduced without much commentary. So, while the commission's findings are, ultimately, the most important part of the report, some of the high-level overview doesn't make a great deal of sense when divorced from the content of the evidence.

I am obviously loath to put words in the mouth of the commission, but I also don't want the reader to be left without the important context of what actually happened. To resolve this, I start this chapter by providing my own overview and summary of the evidence that has emerged around the SSA over the last few years, focusing on the results of two high-profile investigations. I then move on to the commission's high-level thematic overview and findings, which will hopefully make more sense in the light of my rapid-fire summary.

One more thing: the commission's report also includes a section on corruption within SAPS Crime Intelligence. The commission found that there was significant looting within the Crime Intelligence unit by, amongt others, General Solly Lazarus and General Richard Mdluli. However, the commission was keen to put this in context: it found that there was no evidence that Lazarus and Mdluli looted CI for any other reason than their own personal benefit. And while this was deplorable, the inference is that the corruption at CI was not part of a broader state capture programme. Because of this, and in the interest of brevity, I have decided not to include a section on CI.

## Background: An agency out of control

The State Security Agency was a beast of Zuma's creation, which he brought into being by means of a 2009 proclamation. As I'll discuss below, this proclamation was almost certainly unlawful. Previously, South Africa's civilian intelligence was split between a number of agencies. Importantly, domestic and foreign intelligence services were housed in their own independent units.

The effect of the proclamation was to amalgamate all South Africa's intelligence agencies into a single body, collapsing foreign and domestic intelligence and communications monitoring into a single mega spy complex. All of this would be overseen by a single director general reporting to the Minister of State Security, a structure that involved a huge concentration of power.

Two of the more notorious directors general who occupied this position of immense power were Dennis Dlomo and Arthur Fraser, against both of whom rafts of serious allegations have been made. The ministers who oversaw the SSA between 2009 and the period of the commission's investigation included Siyabonga Cwele (2009–14), David Mahlobo (2014–17), Bongani Bongo (2017–18), Dipuo Letsatsi-Duba (2018–19) and Ayanda Dlodlo (2019 onwards).

The activities of the SSA were subject to two investigations, about which the commission heard considerable evidence. The first was called the High Level Review Panel (HLRP).[3] This investigation was concluded and published in 2019. The second was an investigation called Project Veza, which, at the time of the commission's hearings, was still active but subject to controversial interference. Both of these investigations provided chilling prima facie evidence of wrongdoing on an industrial scale. The commission indicated on a number of occasions that it held the work of the HLRP in high esteem and agreed with its findings.

The HLRP was appointed by President Ramaphosa in 2018. It was chaired by the long-time ANC stalwart Sydney Mufamadi, who also gave extended evidence before the commission. In broad terms, the HLRP found that the SSA had, since at least 2009, been subjected to profound politicisation and factionalisation, which mirrored the factions in the ruling party. This led to a free-for-all in which the agency completely ignored its constitutional obligations of non-partisanship, and in which considerable state resources were funnelled into covert projects for the benefit of particular political actors.

The HLRP identified two particularly problematic units or organisations within the SSA. The first was the Principal Agent Network (PAN). PAN was a top-secret organisation of undercover operatives and informants. It ran from 2006 to 2011. There was considerable evidence that state resources were stolen on a grand scale through this programme. The second was the Special Operations Unit (SOU), which fell under the effective control of the deputy director general at the time, Thulani Dlomo. Mufamadi explained to the commission that the SOU became a law unto itself. Members of the SOU felt that their reporting lines ran straight to the executive (i.e. the minister and the President) rather than through the SSA structures. Within the SSA, officers senior to Dlomo were cut out of the loop.

The SOU ran a number of hugely problematic projects. One was called Project Construção, which provided VIP protection to various high-profile political actors, displacing the SAPS, which had once looked after this job. The result was the creation of an effective Special Operations Protection Services that provided spy-laden protection to a handful of 'VIPs". Among the VIPs who received

---

3   High Level Review Panel on the State Security Agency, December 2018, https://www.gov.za/sites/default/files/gcis_document/201903/high-level-review-panel-state-security-agency.pdf.

this protection were Dudu Myeni, the chairperson of SAA and close confidante of Zuma; Shaun Abrahams, the National Director of Public Prosecutions; and Collen Maine, the ANC Youth League president.

Another project was called Project Commitment. The HLRP was told by an informant that, under this project, R2.5m per month was meant to be given to the benefit of President Zuma in 2015/16, rising to R4.5m in 2016/17. The informant alleged that the money was routed via the minister at the time, David Mahlobo. While it was reportedly withdrawn in cash, there was, however, no corroborating evidence that the money was actually given to Zuma.

A particularly chilling programme was conducted under the rubric of Project Justice. The HLRP was told that the focus of this project was to try to quash or neutralise the various criminal charges facing Jacob Zuma. This would be achieved by bribing members of the judiciary. The informants who spoke to the HLRP suggested that the money was handled by Minister Mahlobo, who was also said to be responsible for handling the officers. However, there was, again, no independent corroborating evidence to prove that the bribes were paid.

Other projects included:
- Project Wave: a project to infiltrate and influence the media, launched in 2016/17 with a budget of R24m;
- Project Accurate/Khusela: a project to recruit toxicologists at vast expense to test the food and bedding of President Zuma for poison, the most notable achievement of which was to find on one occasion that the sell-by date of certain soft drinks had expired;
- Project Tin Roof: an investigation into the alleged poisoning of Zuma by an ex-wife;
- The Workers' Association: an attempt to create a supposedly grassroots workers' movement to counter the influence of unions in the platinum belt, which was given millions by the SOU;
- Project Academia: an attempt to intervene in the Fees Must Fall protest movement by supporting a 'Young Bright Minds' initiative that would deploy 'patriotic' students into the movement.

The second investigation into the SSA was called Project Veza. This was an internal SSA project that attempted to review the SSA's files and interview witnesses to establish the extent and nature of corruption at the agency. Veza focused on the SOU and, in particular, on the office that directed it: Thulani Dlomo's Chief Directorate of Special Operations (CDSO).

Project Veza was brought to a halt in controversial (and frankly confusing) circumstances in 2021. The Veza team was instructed by the ministry to hand over all its investigative documents to Advocate Muofhe, who, for reasons the commission's report does not clarify, then claimed that the Veza team was actually a 'rogue unit'. The Veza investigators were kicked off the project and denied access to their offices. The commission's own investigations led it to believe that the Veza investigators were not politically motivated. The commission strongly hinted that it believed the Veza project should continue.

The work of Project Veza was explained by a witness given the pseudonym Miss K, who testified to the investigation she had conducted in conjunction with another pseudonymous individual called Witness Y. Miss K's evidence largely confirmed the findings of the HLRP, although it added some useful meat to its bones, especially around money flows. In particular, the Veza investigation, using withdrawal receipts and other documents, estimated that an amount of R1.5bn had been routed via the CDSO for various projects.

In addition to the SOU projects identified in the HLRP, Veza identified a range of other issues. These included:

- the proliferation and mishandling of firearms and ammunition from the SSA armoury;
- the establishment of parallel vetting procedures that bypassed lawful routes to allow the CDSO to issue security clearances to agents of its choosing;
- the creation of a Presidential Protection Unit that drew considerable resources from the SSA.

## The commission's findings

The commission, after reviewing the work of the HLRP and Project Veza, and after canvassing the testimony of a number of other witnesses, set out its 'high-level overview' of findings.

### *The 2009 Proclamation*

As noted above, the SSA was created by means of a presidential proclamation in 2009. This, the commission found, was almost certainly unlawful. The proclamation envisaged a radical restructuring of the agencies, which were codified in law. However, there was no change to the underlying laws until 2013, when the new structure was included in an omnibus General Intelligence Laws Amendment Act. So, for four years, the SSA operated without any basis in law, while the proclamation itself was unlawful for rendering institutional rearrangements in the teeth of the existing legislation.

## Vulnerabilities to politicisation and capture

The commission identified several vulnerable features of South Africa's intelligence architecture which made it susceptible to capture. The first issue was the susceptibility of intelligence agencies to politicisation. In simple terms, this means that intelligence agencies become involved in political contestation and use their powers to achieve specific outcomes. The commission recognised that 'intelligence services are susceptible to politicisation [because] they are valuable tools, the use of which can help cement political power'. The commission noted the evidence of the High Level Review Panel (HLRP). This found that the country's intelligence functions had become directly embroiled in factional political infighting and that huge resources had been used and stolen under the cover of secrecy.

The second risk area related to the need to separate specific functions: political oversight, administration and operations. Under the system set up in 2009, the director general was responsible for administration, while his deputies were responsible for operations. The Minister of State Security was responsible for political oversight. But the evidence showed that, in fact, these clear lines of division were not kept in practice: the executive, through the minister, frequently got involved in operations.

The commission also noted that the amalgamation of all the intelligence structures into a single department, under a single director general, created an intense concentration of power in the hands of one person. Moreover, 'resources became increasingly concentrated in the hands of a few individuals. The evidence shows how these individuals abused civilian intelligence to promote illegitimate interests.'

The third potential vulnerability had to do with potentially lax financial controls and accountability mechanisms. The secrecy provisions around intelligence services meant that it was possible, and indeed easy, to engage in all kinds of questionable and deeply problematic expenditure. Indeed, the commission found that 'the evidence reveals that internal controls relating to operational expenditure were usually breached or bypassed with impunity'.

Finally, the commission noted that there was a profound weakening of oversight over the SSA, which was illustrated by a number of examples. The first was that the Auditor General, responsible for auditing all government expenditure, did not scrutinise spending within covert operations. The second related to the operation of the Office of the Inspector General of Intelligence, which is tasked with investigating and reporting on potential issues within the SSA. However, the Inspector General's office was entirely funded out of the SSA budget and relied on the SSA entirely for its operational needs. This totally undermined the independence of the office.

The third example related to the oversight role that was supposed to be played by the Joint Standing Committee on Intelligence (JSCI) in Parliament, which is supposed to scrutinise and hold the SSA to account. The evidence reviewed by the commission showed that the JSCI was largely dysfunctional for most of the period after 2009.

## Preventing investigations into the Guptas

After identifying the various vulnerabilities that plagued the SSA from 2009 onwards, the commission then moved on to addressing specific themes or items from its investigations, which it placed under the remarkably anodyne heading 'Certain findings'. The first finding related to the commission's inquiry into the cessation of investigations into the Guptas.

Three key witnesses gave evidence on this topic: Ambassador Jeff Maqetuka, who served as the first director general of the SSA; Ambassador Moe Shaik, the head of the foreign branch in the SSA; and Gibson Njenje, the head of the domestic branch. Together, they testified that, by at least 2011, there were serious concerns about the influence of the Guptas over the President. This was crystallised when Fikile Mbalula told a sitting of the ANC's NEC that he had been told of his appointment as Minister of Sports by a Gupta brother prior to being told by the President.

All three believed that the story had profound national security implications, and that a deeper investigation was warranted into how the Guptas had come to hold this information; the commission, for its part, agreed that there was probable cause for an investigation to be launched. However, the three claimed that their investigations, which had just begun, were stopped through the intervention of Siyabonga Cwele, who was then the Minister of State Security. All three also testified that, when they approached Jacob Zuma about the issue, 'it was clear from what he said and his body language that he disapproved of the investigation'.

Cwele denied that he had any role in stopping the investigation. But the commission was unconvinced. It found that the 'probabilities were overwhelming' that he had done so. This further meant that Cwele was guilty of involving himself directly in the operations of the SSA, thus violating the sanctity of the division between operations and political oversight.

Zuma, too, was the subject of an adverse finding in this regard: the commission found that 'President Zuma did not want the Guptas to be investigated'. And while he had not given 'express instructions' to halt the investigation in his conversation with the three intelligence heads, 'he said enough in the meeting with the trio to make it clear to them that his view was that there was no justification for the investigation and, in his view, it should not be pursued'.

## Executive and ministerial involvement in operations

The commission found the 'evidence was overwhelming' that the two ministers overseeing the SSA during Zuma's presidency – Siyabonga Cwele and David Mahlobo – involved themselves repeatedly in the internal operations of the SSA.

David Mahlobo's role in the SSA was highlighted for particular opprobrium; not only did he involve himself in operations, he also directed them. Mahlobo was found to be involved in a range of covert operations under Project Justice and Operation Commitment. A letter discovered by the commission with the title 'Projects approved by the minister' showed that R120m had been set aside in the SSA's budget for 'Minister's Projects'.

## Illegal operations by the SSA

The commission found that there was evidence of a quite stunning array of illegal operations at the SSA:

- SSA money was withdrawn on the instruction of Minister Ayanda Dlodlo (who succeeded David Mahlobo) and used for the comfort of Umkhonto we Sizwe (MK) veterans travelling to the ANC's 8 January celebrations in Rustenburg in 2016;
- A member of the SSA (codenamed Dorothy) testified that the SSA provided financial and logistical assistance at the ANC's 54th national conference at Nasrec in 2017;
- A number of operations were conducted to try to influence grassroots opinion in favour of the ANC among 'coloured people' in the Cape;
- The Special Operations Unit of the SSA, especially under Dlomo, operated as a 'law unto itself', launching a vast number of illegal operations.

## Cash is king

The commission heard extensive evidence that large sums of cash were withdrawn against the SSA's budget, with almost no known controls over where that money was spent. These withdrawals could run into millions of rand at a time. Record-keeping was basically non-existent, and there was 'no proper verification to determine for what purpose the money withdrawn was actually used and whether the intended recipient in fact received the money'.

One witness testified that on at least three occasions, she had witnessed millions in cash being delivered to Minister Mahlobo, which was then counted in front of her. In one notable encounter, Mahlobo was said to have received cash amounting to R4.51m. However, somewhat frustratingly, the commission was not able to make a particular finding about where this cash might have been spent.

## The abuse of secrecy

The commission found that there were a number of serious abuses of the secrecy provisions that protected the SSA from scrutiny. The most notable example of this related to the quashing of criminal investigations on the grounds of national security and, in particular, the closure of investigations into the Principal Agent Network (PAN). Various investigations indicated that huge amounts of money had been stolen or laundered through the PAN network; there have also been persistent hints that PAN operatives may have been interfering in politics.

The commission heard evidence that the Hawks were in the process of investigating the PAN programme, but that the investigation was halted at the instruction of Siyabonga Cwele. The agent at the Hawks who was given the instruction – General Njenje – claimed that Cwele had told him that Jacob Zuma wanted to stop the investigation. Zuma allegedly claimed that prosecuting the director general in charge of the PAN programme – Arthur Fraser – would be a threat to national security. The commission did not find that Zuma had issued the instruction, but it did find that it was probable that Cwele had told Njenje this in his discussions.

## Theft and loss of firearms

The SSA maintained an armoury of firearms and ammunition at a site at its Musanda complex in Pretoria. One witness testified that guns and ammunition were issued to people who had no clearance, or even competence, to handle guns; they also testified that this had been done on the instruction of Dlomo. At some point, Arthur Fraser, the DG, issued an instruction for all arms to be returned to the armoury; a large number of rifles and sub-machine guns failed to be returned or accounted for.

## The abuse of vetting

The commission found that Thulani Dlomo, one-time deputy director general of the SSA, established an unlawful parallel vetting system. He was found to have recruited a person external to the SSA to conduct the vetting procedures. Remarkably, individuals vetted by Dlomo's parallel scheme were granted security clearances.

Even where vetting was done through the proper channels, abuse was rife. The most notable example cited by the commission was the case of Dr Dintwe, who was appointed the Inspector General of Intelligence in 2017 for a five-year term. In this role, Dintwe attempted to investigate the notorious spymaster Arthur Fraser. When Fraser found out about the investigation, he withdrew Dintwe's security clearance. Dintwe had to turn to the courts to have his security clearance certificate restored.

## Irregular recruitments

As one would expect in the free-for-all of corruption and fraud in the SSA, irregular appointments were rife. There was little evidence that any objective criteria were applied to recruitments into the SSA. Indeed, the primary motivation for appointments was, according to the commission, nepotism or factionalism. Evidence was heard that certain ministers (who remained unnamed) had intervened to appoint family members.

## Questionable intelligence reports

The commission was at pains to highlight the extraordinarily damaging impacts of dodgy dossiers and intelligence reports. Five reports, in particular, were identified for specific critique. The first was the so-called Mdluli report, named after General Richard Mdluli, the head of Crime Intelligence at the time. Shaik, Njenje and Maqetuka testified that, when they approached Zuma about the Guptas, he responded by referring to the Mdluli report, which alleged a plot to topple him. All three had already rejected the report, yet Zuma insisted that he believed it was accurate. Shaik, in particular, understood that Zuma's continued belief in the Mdluli report showed he no longer trusted the three intelligence chiefs then in place.

The second report was a discredited Crime Intelligence report; this one also involved Mdluli. It claimed that there was a sophisticated plot to remove Mdluli from the SAPS. Again, this report appears to have been believed by Zuma in the teeth of the opinion of Shaik and colleagues.

The third report was referred to, briefly, in the previous section on the National Treasury. This claimed that, during a trip to the UK, Pravin Gordhan and Mcebisi Jonas planned to meet with foreign handlers to organise 'regime change' in South Africa. It was allegedly on the basis of this report that Zuma recalled both Gordhan and Nene from the trip. Dr Dintwe attempted to investigate the report. He discovered that the only person who had a copy was Zuma. When he approached Zuma to discuss the report, Zuma failed to share it, only obliquely hinting that he would discuss the matter further at some undisclosed time.

Dintwe also discussed two further reports. In one, it was alleged that Gauteng Hawks head General Shadrack Sibiya, Independent Police Investigative Directorate head Robert McBride and the private investigator Paul O'Sullivan were plotting to overthrow the government. In the other, it was alleged that the head of the Hawks, General Anwar Dramat, was involved in the unlawful rendition of foreign nationals. Both reports were proved to be untrue, but not before Dramat and his alleged co-conspirator, General Sibiya, were charged with the offence. All reports were of dubious provenance and even more questionable quality.

## The failure of the JSCI

Parliament's Joint Standing Committee on Intelligence (JSCI) is one of the primary accountability mechanisms in preventing intelligence abuses. But, the commission found, the JSCI failed to function in any meaningful way at all in the period from 2009 onwards. For example, it took the JSCI until September 2021 – twelve years after the fact – to note the unlawfulness of the 2009 proclamation that created the SSA.

The position of Inspector General of Intelligence was not filled between December 2009 and April 2010 or again between March 2015 and March 2017. The JSCI was responsible for identifying, interviewing and nominating candidates. The commission blamed the JSCI for failing to act swiftly to fill this vital position, the result of which was to create considerable scope for wrongdoing.

## The bizarre relationship between the Auditor General and the Inspector General of Intelligence

The siphoning of funds from the SSA was facilitated, at least in part, by the fact that there was almost no financial oversight. The Auditor General, empowered to investigate and audit every government department, could not properly audit the SSA because large amounts of information were classified and were withheld from him.

Because of this, the Auditor General attempted to instruct the Office of the Inspector General of Intelligence to conduct audits. This was because the Inspector General would have access to classified material. But this was clearly unsatisfactory as the Inspector General was not an auditor. The result was, as the commission notes, a 'box-ticking exercise without proper analysis'.

# PART TWO

# The Capture of State-Owned Enterprises

*The systematic looting of state-owned enterprises (SOEs) was the meat and potatoes of state capture. It was at SOEs that contracts could be conceived, manipulated and executed to direct scarce public resources into the pockets of the Gupta enterprise. And, whatever you might say about the Guptas, they were extremely effective and efficient at inserting themselves in multiple SOEs at the same time, getting paid vast sums for doing very little.*

*Because the Guptas were working across multiple SOEs simultaneously, the order in which I approach them is a bit arbitrary. Nevertheless, I have opted to foreground the three biggest SOEs that were targeted upfront – Transnet, Eskom and SAA. And, within them, I start with Transnet, not least because it was this report that contained some of the most combustible evidence of how the Guptas were handing bags of cash to the civil servants who swayed contracts in their favour.*

*A forewarning: the first chapter on Transnet is the longest in this book by some way. Once you've seen just how many irregular deals were done there, you'll understand why.*

# Transnet

TRANSNET WAS, OF ALL the SOEs, the largest site of state capture. In calculations that I performed for the commission, and the commission quotes in its introductory comments on Transnet, I found that contracts worth R41.204bn had been irregularly awarded to companies linked to the Gupta enterprise and Salim Essa. This was equal to 72.21% of all the cost of state contracts that were linked to the Guptas.

## The processes that enabled the capture of Transnet

The commission's final report into Transnet devotes a considerable amount of time, upfront, to discussing how internal governance processes at Transnet were changed to facilitate corruption, and identifying which senior staff members were mostly responsible for the mass looting that followed.

The single biggest governance change at Transnet was the creation of a new entity called the Board Acquisition and Disposal Committee (BADC). The BADC was a subcommittee of the Transnet board and became central to many corrupt contracts. I've always found it bleakly funny that its acronym was BADC, which I always read to mean 'the Bad Committee'.

The BADC was created in 2011 as part of a profound change in how Transnet undertook procurement. Prior to 2011, the Transnet board was not directly involved in procurement, and did not have any delegation of authority – a fancy phrase for permission to contract and spend – for procurement. The BADC changed all of this: under the 2011 Delegation of Authority Framework, it was empowered to approve approaches to the market and conclude contracts equal to R500m. The amount the BADC could approve increased regularly; in 2012 it was increased to R2bn, while the full board could approve amounts above this. By 2016 the BADC could approve contracts worth R3bn. The Delegation of Authority Frameworks that were adopted by Transnet also simultaneously increased the amounts that could be approved by the group chief executive officer (GCEO) and group chief financial officer (GCFO). In 2013, for example, the authority for the GCFO increased to R750m and for the GCEO to R1bn.

In layman's terms, this all meant that a small handful of people – the GCEO, GCFO and members of the BADC – oversaw and effectively controlled a good portion of the 'high value tenders' approved by Transnet. And this is where most of the dodgy decisions were made. As the commission noted: 'many of the irregularities that attended [high value tender] procurements between 2011 and 2017 took place within the BADC or at the instance of the CGEO and GCFO'.

## *Zuma, Hogan and the battle to appoint Transnet's group CEO*

The commission traces the beginning of state capture at Transnet to 2009 and, in particularly, the election of Jacob Zuma. Zuma appointed Barbara Hogan, a struggle stalwart and wife of the ANC veteran Ahmed Kathrada, as his first Minister of Public Enterprises. Hogan testified that, from the start, Zuma was obstructive and recalcitrant. This was particularly true in relation to Hogan's attempts to use her powers as minister to appoint a new group CEO following the resignation of Maria Ramos in 2009.

After Ramos resigned, the Transnet board set about finding a replacement. After a round of interviews, the board put forward Pravin Gordhan as its only recommendation. But, shortly after this, Gordhan pulled out of the running as he was about to be appointed Minister of Finance. After a further extensive round of interviews, the board recommended the appointment of another highly qualified candidate, Sipho Maseko.

In so doing, the board rejected the application of a man who would become central to the capture of Transnet: Siyabonga Gama, who had been the CEO of Transnet Freight Rail (TFR) since 2005. TFR was part of the broader Transnet group. Shortly after Gama was overlooked, 'false reports', as the commission called them, started featuring in the media. The reports claimed that Gama was the victim of an anti-transformation cabal of white no-goodniks who had instituted investigations into Gama to sideline him.

According to Hogan, in June 2009 Zuma told her that he did not support the appointment of Maseko; Zuma, instead, wanted Gama as GCEO. The problem with this, in addition to ignoring the board recommendations, was that Gama was facing serious allegations of wrongdoing. He was suspected of offences in relation to the award of a contract to General Nyanda Security Services. General Siphiwe Nyanda was a member of Zuma's Cabinet, prior to which he had been in business with Fana Hlongwane – the Arms Deal 'agent' who, as we have seen, was the person who facilitated and attended the meeting at which Mcebisi Jonas was offered a bribe by Tony Gupta. Zuma, incidentally, would deny he supported Gama, although the commission, after hearing his version, rejected it as a 'complete fabrication'.

Hogan tried to force the issue. In July 2009 she sent a 'decision memo' to Zuma recommending the appointment of Maseko. The memo also included an extremely detailed account of the allegations against Gama. Hogan concluded the memo by saying that if there was no further movement on the issue, she wanted the 'shareholder Minister' (herself) to oversee the procurement in order to 'immunise' the process from further controversy. Zuma would later acknowledge that he received the memo. Hogan testified that, despite this, Zuma never responded.

Hogan pushed again, sending an urgent letter to Zuma on 25 August 2009. She asked that her 'decision memo' be placed before Cabinet for discussion so that she could ask for Cabinet approval for the appointment of Maseko. Zuma, this time, responded, but refused to put the memo before Cabinet. Instead, he asked to be supplied with a list of three preferred candidates for him to consider. Hogan testified that she was later told that Zuma had instructed the Cabinet secretary to ensure the memo was not presented before Cabinet.

In late August, at the same time that Hogan was imploring Zuma to put the matter before Cabinet, disciplinary charges were formally levelled against Gama and on 1 September 2009 he was suspended on full pay. His disciplinary hearing took placed over 14 days between 13 January and 25 February 2010 and was chaired by the highly respected advocate Mark Antrobus SC.

Antrobus found Gama guilty on all three charges, including that he had authorised an irregular contract at an ultimate cost of R95m to Nyanda's security company, which was considerably more than the R10m he was allowed to approve. Gama had cancelled the original open tender and approved its award on 'confinement' – basically without any competitors. Antrobus found that Gama had approved the confinement without reading the underlying contract and had failed to investigate irregularities in the cancellation of the open tender process. In another contract to buy 50 'like new' refurbished locomotives, the board had required that the contract stipulate that all local work on the contract be done by Transnet Engineering. Gama failed to ensure that this criterion was included in the contract. Indeed, Gama admitted that he had failed to read the contract at all or to make sure that the board requirement was included. As a result, on 28 June 2010, the chairperson of the inquiry recommended Gama's dismissal. He did so because he believed that his conduct on each of the three charges was, on its own, sufficient for dismissal. Gama was duly dismissed on 29 June 2010.

Hogan testified that Zuma had intimated that he would not do anything to appoint a new GCEO until Gama's disciplinary hearing was concluded. With that done, Hogan now tried to have a new board appointed so that it could start choosing a new GCEO by placing a memorandum, dated 27 October 2010, before Cabinet. Four days later, on 31 October 2010, Hogan was called to a meeting with President Zuma and ANC secretary general Gwede Mantashe, and told she was being redeployed as the ambassador to Finland. Hogan declined the position and shortly thereafter resigned as an MP.

Hogan was replaced by Malusi Gigaba the following day, 1 November 2010. He would hold the post until 25 May 2014. The commission's own matter-of-fact summary of Gigaba's relationship with the Guptas is hard to beat for punchiness and brevity:

Mr Gigaba in fact knew all the Gupta brothers and their mother, and was especially a close friend of Mr Ajay Gupta (whom he would visit at Sahara Computers) and made regular visits to the Gupta Saxonwold compound while he was Minister of Public Enterprises. His special advisor, Siyabonga Mahlangu, was tasked with managing the Guptas and was a buffer between Mr Gigaba and Mr Ajay Gupta so as to not confuse the roles of friendship and business. He permitted Mr Mahlangu to travel with President Zuma's son, Duduzane Zuma, to a Gupta wedding in India. The trip was paid for by Sahara Computers and Mr Mahlangu was paid his salary in his absence. Mr Gigaba attended the notorious Gupta wedding at Sun City, and the Guptas were invited to his wedding.

Not long after, Gigaba proposed a slate of new Transnet board members, which was approved by Cabinet on 8 December 2010. One of the most notable changes was the removal of the only rail specialist on the board – a Mr Raman – and his replacement with Iqbal Sharma. Sharma would later chair the BADC and act as one of the key movers behind state capture in this position while, simultaneously, being business partner of the Guptas' key lieutenant, Salim Essa. Gigaba would later try to get Sharma appointed as the chairperson of the board, but he was, fortunately, blocked from the position. Media articles at the time speculated that there were fears that Sharma was too closely associated with the Guptas.

The new Gigaba-appointed board was chaired by Mafika Mkwanazi. Mkwanazi would act as the GCEO for about three months until the appointment of the man who would really deliver for the Guptas: Brian Molefe.

## In comes Molefe

In January 2011, the new Transnet board appointed a Nominations and Governance Committee and hired a recruitment agency to fill the GCEO position. In early February 2011, nine candidates, including Molefe, were interviewed. Iqbal Sharma was the person who nominated Molefe; he also sat on the interview panel. The end result of this process was that three people were recommended to Gigaba, including Molefe. The highest scoring candidate was Dr

Mandla Gantsho. However, the board, in defiance of clear ministerial guidelines, failed to identify their preferred candidate, which, on the basis of the scoring result, should have been Gantsho.

Gigaba should have gone back to the board and asked for their preferred candidate. He did not do so. Instead, Gigaba recorded a memorandum, dated 14 February 2011, in which he requested that Cabinet approve the appointment of *his* preferred candidate, Brian Molefe. Cabinet was never told that Gantsho had scored higher in his assessment. Cabinet approved the appointment on 16 February 2011.

Throughout its reports, the commission would make a great deal about an incident that had preceded Molefe's appointment: in December 2010, before the GCEO position was even advertised, the Guptas' newspaper *New Age* predicted Molefe's appointment as GCEO. This was before Molefe could even have applied for the role. The commission concluded, repeatedly, that this prediction was made, and was so accurate, because the Guptas themselves either ensured or at least approved Molefe's appointment as GCEO.

Molefe had had a relationship with Ajay Gupta for several years prior to his 2011 appointment. And, upon his becoming GCEO, this relationship deepened. The commission estimates that Molefe visited the Gupta compound approximately 50 times in the four years that he served as GCEO of Transnet. The effect of all this, the commission noted, was that 'Mr Gigaba (a friend of the Guptas) was instrumental in the appointment of Mr Molefe (another friend of the Guptas), with his appointment having been predicted in the newspaper owned by the Guptas, and initiated by Mr Sharma (another Gupta associate)'.

## The resurrection of Siyabonga Gama

Despite the damning conclusions of the disciplinary hearing that led to the dismissal of Gama, he would soon be rehabilitated. The rehabilitation started under Mkwanazi, the board chair appointed by Gigaba. In a meeting sometime in early November 2010, Gigaba asked Mkwanazi to ask the board to review the fairness of Gama's dismissal. Gama had, after his dismissal, referred his case to the Transnet Bargaining Council. He initially claimed his dismissal was unfair; he subsequently amended it to claim that dismissal was too harsh a sanction. Gigaba believed that Gama's dismissal was too harsh because white employees had committed more serious acts of misconduct and weren't dismissed, and for a second reason that is too technical to explain here but was the height of inanity.

In December 2011, a month after this meeting, the new Transnet board was appointed with Mkwanazi as chairperson. To make matters more complicated, in late December the Public Protector wrote to Transnet saying that she was investigating claims that Gama had been unfairly dismissed. To deal with the Public Protector inquiry, Mkwanazi enlisted the help of Siyabulela Mapoma, who was then the Transnet general manager of legal services. Mapoma would testify before the commission that Mkwanazi had made it clear to him that his job was to secure Gama's reinstatement. Mapoma had assumed the instruction ultimately came from Zuma. Of course, Mkwanazi would deny making any mention of Zuma, while Gigaba would further deny that he had given any instruction to Mkwanazi.

Matters then unfolded in an extremely complicated manner. The gist is that Transnet had originally instructed the law firm Bowman Gilfillan to advise on Gama's appeal. A Mr Todd from Bowman reviewed the case and wrote a report that found that Transnet's case was strong and that Gama would lose the appeal. So, simultaneously but before the Todd opinion was completed, Mkwanazi appointed a second legal advisor, Sibusiso Gule of Deneys Reitz, on the suggestion of Gigaba's Gupta-linked advisor Mahlangu. When questioned, Mkwanazi admitted he had appointed Deneys Reitz because it was likely that Bowman's advice would be that Transnet would win.

In the event, Gama's case never came properly before the Transnet bargaining body. Instead, on 10 February 2011, Gama signed a draft settlement agreement. At this stage, there was no legal advice to support a settlement with Gama. It was only a few days later that Deneys Reitz was asked to write a 'two-pager' explaining the settlement to the board. The opinion that was received was remarkably vague. Nevertheless, on 16 February 2011, the board met to consider the Todd report, the Deneys Reitz two-pager, and the draft agreement. The board decided that Gama's dismissal was too harsh a sentence, and gave a reason that the commission found was not even passably logical.

According to Mapoma, he was called by Mahlangu sometime

between the 16 February board meeting and Gama's eventual settlement. He testified that Mahlangu had put pressure on him to finalise Gama's settlement as 'No. 1 wanted to get it done quickly'. Mapoma claimed he reported this to Mkwanazi. Mahlangu later admitted he had taken the call but denied its content.

In the event, on 23 February 2011, Transnet and Gama entered into a formal settlement agreement. Gama was reinstated as the CEO of TFR. All employment benefits due to him since his dismissal were paid: this amounted to R13m. In addition, Transnet agreed to cover 75% of Gama's legal costs following his failed attempt to obtain a High Court interdict to stop his original dismissal. Gama's attorneys were paid more than R4m, which the commission thought was highly questionable.

After reviewing this complicated saga of bureaucratic wrangling, the commission found that Gama had been reinstated as a result of a political decision. A 'conspectus' of the evidence

strongly indicate[d] that political interference was probably at play. Mr Mapoma's conclusion at the time, that the complete capitulation in the settlement negotiations arose from an instruction to reinstate Mr Gama, which he understood to have come from President Zuma, is the most plausible account. There is simply no other credible explanation for this level of indefensible decision making ... Mr Gigaba probably did not simply request Mr Mkwanazi (and the board) to review the fairness of the dismissal, but instead probably required Mr Gama to be reinstated.

The commission's recommendations on the Gama matter were forthright. The commission first held that, considering the role Gama later played in enriching the Guptas, the conduct of Gigaba and Mkwanazi 'gives rise to a reasonable suspicion that the crime of corruption may have been committed'. As a result, the commission recommended further investigations. Second, the commission recommended further inquiries to establish whether the board, the GCFO and the GCEO had violated the Public Finance Management Act (PFMA) by agreeing to the settlement agreement.

While the commission made no recommendation about Zuma,

it did conclude that 'the evidence of the role played by Mr Gigaba, President Zuma and Mr Mkwanazi in the Gama saga, and the likely benefit of Mr Gama's reinstatement and subsequent promotion for the Gupta enterprise, may provide a reasonable basis to conclude that these individuals participated in the affairs of and were associated with the Gupta enterprise'.

## The Gupta dream team

The appointments of Gama (CEO of Transnet Freight Rail), Molefe (Group CEO) and Anoj Singh (Group CFO) ensured that Transnet's most senior management would be Gupta allies and supporters. The appointment of Iqbal Sharma to the BADC only strengthened the reach of the family.

The links between these four and the Guptas were firm. Molefe, as noted above, was a frequent and repeated visitor to the Gupta compound. His appointment as GCEO was predicted by the Guptas' *New Age* newspaper before the position was even advertised. In January 2016, Gama met Salim Essa in Dubai shortly after Gama had approved a highly irregular payment to the company Trillian, which was 50% owned by Essa. The commission heard what it called 'compelling evidence' that Gama's Dubai hotel bill was paid for by the Guptas' Sahara Computers.

Singh had similar connections. Singh's girlfriend, Selina Naik, left Transnet in 2014 to go and work at Sahara Computers between 2015 and 2017. Her boss was Ashu Chawla, who was the Gupta enterprise's functional COO. Evidence showed that Singh visited the Gupta compound. Although Singh tried to downplay the number of times (he admitted 12 visits in four years for 'religious and cultural functions'), his driver placed him there more often. Between April 2014 and June 2015, Singh took six trips to Dubai, 'all of which were arranged and probably paid for by the Gupta enterprise'. In several cases, Singh's bills were settled by either Sahara or Salim Essa, who was also in Dubai at the same time as Singh, and was once on the same flight as he. This, of course, somewhat undermined Singh's own attempts to minimise any relationship he had with Essa. Most strikingly – particularly in light of what I turn to next – Singh accumulated R19m in a current account over three years by spending almost nothing of his own salary. 'This indicated he had other sources of money besides his salary,' the commission inferred.

Iqbal Sharma, for his part, shared mutual business interests with Essa during the period in which he served on the Transnet board and for the two years he acted as the chairperson of the BADC between August 2012 and November 2014. Essa was a director of a company called VR Laser Services and another called Elgasolve (both of which would be embroiled in issues at Denel). In February 2013 Sharma declared a 50% shareholding in Elgasolve, which in turn owned 74.9% of the shares in VR Laser. In 2014, Elgasolve held 80% of the shares in a company called the National Agricultural Development Project (NADP). Both Sharma and Essa were directors of NADP from November 2013 and were listed as active directors on 13 April 2021. Thus, Sharma, the chairman of the most important procurement body at Transnet for two years, was simultaneously in business with Salim Essa.

Additional appointments in 2014 brought a new crop of senior executives with links to the Guptas. On 26 May 2014, following the general election, Lynne Brown was appointed the Minister of Public Enterprises. She oversaw a reshuffle of the board in December 2014. After a number of non-executive directors resigned, they were replaced by Richard Seleke and Stanley Shane.

Both Seleke and Shane were connected to the Guptas or Salim Essa. In 2011, for example, Tony Gupta had recommended that Free State MEC Mxolisi Dukwana appoint Seleke to a senior position. Shane, meanwhile, served as a director of Transnet until June 2017 and as chairperson of the Transnet Second Defined Benefit Pension Fund. During this period, Shane was director of a company called Integrated Capital Management (ICM), through which he was involved in the creation of the company Trillian, which was led by Salim Essa and Eric Wood. My investigations for the commission revealed that ICM was a beneficiary of a dodgy payment related to a heavily manipulated Transnet contract; Gupta companies benefited from the same corrupt deal.

Another senior executive with Gupta links was Garry Pita. Pita served as the acting CFO of Transnet and, in this role, approved a corrupt payment of R93m to Trillian in December 2015. Pita was appointed the GCFO on a permanent basis on 1 February 2016. During this time he met Essa at the Gupta compound to discuss how contracts could be ceded from Transnet's consultants Regiments to Essa's company Trillian. He attended functions at the Gupta compound on a few occasions. He also admitted to meeting Essa on unspecified dates at the Gupta compound, at Essa's offices in Melrose Arch and at the Parreirinha restaurant in Turffontein.

Rounding out this cast of rogues was Phetolo Ramosebudi, who was appointed Transnet's treasurer in March 2015. As I'll show later, Ramosebudi served as the treasurer of Airports Company South Africa (ACSA) between 2007 and 2011, moving to SAA in the same role between January 2012 and February 2015, when he left to join Transnet. The commission found that Ramosebudi developed a 'corrupt relationship' with Regiments while at ACSA, and received large payments from Regiments for his own benefit. Ramosebudi would oversee the award of over R50m in payments from ACSA to Regiments.

Considering this cast of characters, it is somewhat unsurprising that staff members who tried to resist the capture of Transnet hardly fared well. One example was Mathane Makgatho. She resigned as head of Group Treasury in November 2014 after opposing several questionable contracts, in particular Transnet contracts with Regiments. After extended conflict with Singh, she came to feel unsafe, and believed she was under surveillance and that her car had been tampered with.

## The cash bribes

The raft of extraordinarily manipulated contracts placed by Transnet, which I deal with immediately hereafter, simply has to be understood in the light of the incendiary evidence of three witnesses before the commission. All three were drivers and close protection agents; all were granted anonymity when they testified before the commission; all claimed that the Guptas had handed bags of cash to Transnet's senior executives.

Witness 1 (W1) implicated Brian Molefe. He claimed that he was extensively threatened before his testimony. W1 provided close protection and driving services for Molefe from 11 February 2011 to April 2014. He detailed multiple meetings between the Guptas and Molefe in Saxonwold, including 15 trips recorded in his travel logbook. W1 recalled that on at least one trip, Gigaba was also present at the Gupta compound.

W1 testified that Molefe had a light-brown backpack; Molefe, indeed, turned up to give evidence with the backpack and held it up for the commission to see. Molefe also had a sports bag. W1 testified that he sometimes saw Molefe leaving meetings with the Guptas with a full sports bag, whose contents he could not always identify. However, on one occasion recalled by W1, Molefe attended a meeting at the Transnet boardroom, during which he asked W1 to collect a cell phone from the car. He found a backpack in the boot filled with bundles of R200 notes. W1 raised the matter with Molefe's assistant because he believed it was a security risk.

W1 also said that he was frequently sent to make cash deposits on behalf of Molefe at banks near the Carlton Centre in Johannesburg. Molefe, under oath, admitted that he did send W1 to make cash deposits. But, Molefe claimed, these cash deposits related to a burial society in which he played a role. Molefe was unable to produce any records of the burial society. He also, remarkably, declined to cross-examine W1.

The commission, after reviewing this evidence, the role Molefe played at Transnet in favouring the Gupta enterprise, and his general lack of credibility, found that there were 'reasonable grounds to believe that Mr Molefe may have committed the crime of corruption by accepting a gratification to act in violation of his duties'.

The commission then moved on to the testimony of Witness 3 (W3). W3 implicated Brian Molefe, Anoj Singh, Garry Pita and Malusi Gigaba. W3 had originally worked for Gigaba in 2005 and 2006 when he was Minister of Home Affairs. In 2013, after a stint in the private sector, he was seconded to Gigaba between July and December 2013, during which period Gigaba was the Minister of Public Enterprises. He was subsequently assigned to Singh in July 2014 until Singh moved to Eskom, after which he worked for Pita.

W3 testified that he took Gigaba to the Saxonwold compound approximately six or seven times. During the visits, he also saw Molefe, Jacob Zuma and others implicated in state capture such as Matshela Koko. W3 confirmed that Gigaba habitually carried large amounts of cash and used it to buy expensive clothes and pay restaurant bills. On one occasion, W3 found bundles of R200 notes in Gigaba's boot, which he suspected came from the Guptas. The commission found that, based on W3's evidence and all the other evidence implicating Gigaba, there were 'reasonable grounds' to believe that Gigaba may have been involved in corruption and that he participated in, or was associated with, the Gupta enterprise.

W3's evidence became more explicit when it came to Singh, to whom he was assigned after Gigaba. W3 testified that he took Singh to the Saxonwold compound more than ten times. During some of these visits, Singh would emerge with a full sports bag, which W3 suspected was full of cash – because Singh gave him cash from the bag. W3 estimated that he drove Singh between six or seven times to a facility called Knox Vault, which was based around the corner from the Guptas in Killarney. As I'll discuss in more detail in relation to Alexkor, Knox Vault was owned by a business partner of Kuben Moodley, an Essa associate in charge of the company Albatime.

Singh leased safety deposit boxes at Knox, as did Kuben Moodley and Garry Pita. When questioned, Singh admitted that he had maintained four deposit boxes at Knox, one for himself and one each for his wife and small children. The commission then confronted Singh with records from Knox that showed he had hired successively larger boxes over time, eventually needing eight to hold his deposits.

Singh, of course, denied the claims. One of his rebuttals was that, while he did visit Knox Vault, he did so in his own private car during worktime. But this fell flat when 'undisputed evidence' was disclosed that Singh left his car at Transnet during the week, when he used his driver's services, and only drove his car home at the weekend. Singh was also unable to explain why, if W3 had never driven him to Knox Vault, W3 had become aware of Knox Vault. In fact, the commission first learned of Knox Vault from W3. Under questioning, Singh tried to claim that W3 must have learned about the Knox boxes from the commission's investigators – that, in effect, the commission was part of a fraudulent scheme to incriminate Singh. You can imagine how well that went down.

W3 also testified to an extraordinary incident that took place at the Three Rivers Lodge in Vereeniging in July 2014. He said that he drove Singh there to attend a conference. While sitting in the car park, two Chinese men walked into the lodge with two suitcases, one maroon and the other black. Later in the afternoon, Singh asked W3 to come into the building, where he encountered Singh, Molefe and the two Chinese men. Singh told W3 to take the 'very heavy' maroon suitcase to the car; shortly thereafter, he saw Molefe's driver put the black suitcase in Molefe's boot. A few days later, W3 found the maroon bag in the boot of the car while parked at the Transnet parking lot. When he opened the (now lighter) suitcase, it contained rolls of R200 notes. Both Singh and Molefe denied the account. But on this incident, and on the other evidence put forward by W3 about Singh, the commission believed W3's version was more plausible. Accordingly, the commission again found that there were reasonable grounds to believe that Singh and Molefe had committed corruption.

The last person implicated by W3 was Garry Pita. This evidence was less incriminating: W3 never saw Pita leave the Saxonwold compound with cash. However, he did testify that he took Pita to the compound on multiple occasions; he also drove Pita to Knox Vault six times, and saw Pita retrieve a sports bag from his boot to take into the Knox building. He also drove Pita to meet Essa at a restaurant in Turffontein at least 15 times.

Pita admitted to the commission that he did have boxes at Knox Vault, and that W3 had driven him there. He also confirmed that he had, indeed, taken a sports bag into the building. Pita, however, claimed that he was storing the records of his mother's restaurant in Killarney Mall (opposite Knox). The commission found this 'doubtful' because his mother sold the restaurant in October 2014, and Pita leased his first box in June 2015. Pita maintained he kept the boxes to hold the records during ongoing negotiations related to the sale of the business, which the commission found to be implausible.

Regarding Pita, the commission found that, based on this evidence and the extensive evidence that Pita had made decisions that benefited the Gupta enterprise, there were 'reasonable grounds' to believe he had received cash payments as a quid pro quo. The commission recommended further investigations to establish whether Pita should be prosecuted for corruption.

The final anonymous witness was Witness 2 (W2). W2's evidence was complicated by the fact that he had an acrimonious and complicated relationship with Gama, whom he implicated. W2, who drove for Gama between May 2012 and December 2017, testified that he took Gama to the Saxonwold compound on four occasions, none of which were officially recorded. W2 testified to seeing Molefe at the compound.

W2 gave evidence about three particularly notable incidents. First, in November 2016, during one of the visits to the Gupta compound, Gama came out and told W2 to expect somebody to bring a bag. Shortly thereafter, somebody, who W2 thought might have been a Gupta family member, gave him a bag to put in the boot. After this, W2 drove to the Maslow Hotel in Sandton, where they met with Transnet Engineering head Thamsanqa Jiyane. Gama told W2 to move the bag into Jiyane's car. While he was doing this, W2 opened the bag to find it full of cash.

The second incident took place on 13 June 2017, when W2 picked up a bag from Salim Essa at Melrose Apartments, and then drove to fetch Gama at a hotel. They then drove to Gama's girlfriend's house in Bryanston. Upon getting there, Gama opened the bag and, with W2's help, counted out approximately R1m in cash. Gama gave half to his girlfriend and R50,000 to W2. Gama took the rest of the cash with him to his home in Midrand, to which W2 had driven him. W2, to corroborate his story, presented the commission with printouts of his travel history stored with Google Maps. The commission ultimately found that W2's version of events on this score should be 'accepted as true'.

The final incident took place in July 2017, when W2 drove Gama to Melrose Apartments to meet Essa. Gama went in and then returned with a plastic bag, which he put in the boot, and then told W2 to drive him to a friend in Sandhurst. While waiting there, W2 looked in the plastic bag to find bundles of R200 notes secured with elastic bands. W2, again, attached his Google Maps history.

When reviewing all the evidence, the commission sounded a note of caution because of the obvious hostility between W2 and Gama. Nevertheless, the commission found that, on the totality of evidence, including the clear pattern of cash payments made to other Transnet officials, there were 'reasonable grounds' to believe that Gama 'may have committed the crime of corruption in relation to these payments'.

With these bombshell findings, the commission then moved on to describe how vast sums of money were spent by Transnet on contracts that were aggressively and systematically manipulated by Molefe, Gama and Singh – and how some of these contracts earned the Gupta enterprise billions in kickbacks and other dodgy payments.

## The GNS/Abalozi contract

One irregular contract the commission examined was that with GNS (General Nyanda's security outfit, which later came to be called Abalozi), for the provision of security services to stop cable theft. This contract was awarded to GNS in 2008 on 'confinement', i.e. without any competitive bid. This was somewhat strange as the contract had originally been on open tender. GNS was paid a total of R95.5m over two years and two months, a payment facilitated by two extensions to the original contract.

Towards the end of 2009 or early 2010 (the date is not clear), Transnet opted to cancel the contract because serious irregularities and misrepresentations had come to light. Two Transnet employees were dismissed in March 2010 as a result. The disciplinary process found that the problems with the contract were profound. For one thing, GNS had no employees, was not registered for PAYE, and wrongfully used subcontractors to do its work. The open tender process was, itself, wrongly cancelled, the confinement was improper, and the price paid to GNS was excessive for the services delivered. GNS had, moreover, plagiarised its statement of supposed expertise from the websites of foreign service providers. On 1 July 2010, after GNS refused to provide information to confirm that its subcontractors had actually performed any work, the company was blacklisted by Transnet for five years. The blacklisting also targeted GNS's directors and any associated company.

On 27 October 2010, Transnet filed a claim for the recovery of R95.6m paid to GNS (now called Abalozi) on the grounds that the contract was void due to illegality and misrepresentation. In response, Abalozi filed four counter-claims. It argued that, in fact, Abalozi was owed R93.7m in damages because Transnet's findings had led Abalozi to lose other business, and was due R6m in compensation for unfair defamation, a further R88m for the reimbursement of claimed expenditure and R300m in damages for lost business due to the blacklisting.

GNS/Abalozi's case may have seem hopeless in the light of what Transnet had found in March 2010. But, as the commission notes, 'after Gama's reinstatement as CEO of TFR in early 2011, there appears to have been a concerted effort to withdraw the litigation'. This effort dragged on over three years. It involved the writing of two reports – one by a Transnet legal employee called Mr Silinga, and another by the law firm Harris, Nupen, Molebatsi (HNM) – that argued, in fact, GNS had provided services. Both used methodologies that the commission found were unsustainable.

The commission was clear: the GNS/Abalozi contract stipulated very clearly that GNS was contracted to provide 'warm bodies' on the ground to protect Transnet assets. And GNS/Abalozi could provide no evidence to prove this: 'the agreement [between GNS and Transnet] was entirely about the deployment of specified human resources. Not a shred of evidence has been produced by GNS/Abalozi in the last 13 years which establishes that any person was deployed by GNS/Abalozi to perform the tasks contemplated in the contract'.

Following a submission by Silinga to Molefe, Molefe agreed to withdraw the blacklisting of GNS/Abalozi on 10 April 2013. A year later, in May 2014, the 'erroneous' HNS report was presented to Transnet's Risk Committee. On this basis, it recommended that the litigation against GNS/Abalozi should be withdrawn. This led to a protracted negotiation process, and eventually Molefe signed a deed of agreement on 4 August 2014, without any input from Bowman Gilfillan, which was advising Transnet on the litigation. Under the terms of the settlement, Transnet agreed to pay 'all the legal costs incurred by Abalozi, its directors and the co-founders of GNS on an attorney and own client scale'.

The settlement did not fix an actual amount as payment in settlement. But with this very generous settlement in hand, GNS/Abalozi tried to argue that it should be paid a settlement fee of R40m. It felt this was fair because, according to their own calculations, they had suffered damages of R1.4bn; this included a remarkable claim for R700m for defamation and 'pain and suffering'. The commission, when reviewing the settlement, was clear that it did not provide for payments for these sorts of claims; it found that, in reality, the only thing Transnet agreed to pay was legal costs, which the commission estimated would have come to no more than R200,000 at that time.

Nevertheless, on 30 January 2015, Silinga wrote a memo to Anoj Singh, the Group CFO, to request a payment of R20m in final settlement. Molefe approved, and Singh authorised the payment, which was made on 30 January 2015. The commission was damning of Molefe's approval, which he had given without any legal advice. The commission understood Molefe's subsequent testimony to also imply that he had granted the approval 'without a full examination of the evidence supporting the additional claims. He could point to no memorandum or other documentary evidence upon which he allegedly relied to take the decision' to settle. This was a serious dereliction of duty on Molefe's part: 'Mr Molefe seemed more intent on advancing the interests of GNS/Abalozi than that of Transnet.' The commission recommended, as a result, that further investigations be done to establish whether Molefe should be prosecuted for violations of the PFMA.

## The 95 locos contract

Between 2011 and 2014, Transnet went on a veritable spending spree, buying thousands of train locomotives to use on its freight lines. The decisions and contracts were bedevilled by an extraordinary array of irregularities. They were also an absolute godsend for the Gupta enterprise: according to my calculations, which the commission relied on, the Gupta enterprise would earn over R7bn in kickbacks from the contracts. Having spent 15 years investigating grand corruption, I thought I was immune to shock. But I'm still gobsmacked and appalled every time I think about the scale of these kickbacks.

The first deal was for the purchase of 95 locomotives (snazzily shortened to 'locos' by the commission and others, an affectation I adopt here). The process leading to the 95 loco deal was started in April 2011, very shortly after Molefe's appointment at GCEO and Gama's return to TFR; the board approved a Locomotive Modernisation Plan in the same month. In August 2011, Gama submitted a memorandum to the BADC on the affordability of the programme, the upshot of which was that the BADC approved the immediate acquisition of 138 locos (43 diesel and 95 electric).

At the end of August 2011, the board approved the acquisition of the 138 locos for approximately R3.6bn. It recommended that the 43 diesel locos be bought by confinement, and the 95 electric locos be bought on a 45/50 split in 2012/13 and 2013/14 respectively. The board recommended an open bid process. About five weeks later, on 24 October 2011, the chairperson of the board, Mkwanazi, wrote to the Minister of Public Enterprises (Malusi Gigaba) to request approval for the 95 locos purchase; this was required under the PFMA. Gigaba approved the request on 21 December 2011 to buy 95 locos at an estimated cost of R2.7bn.

The bid process started when Transnet issued requests for proposals (RFPs) on 6 December 2011. The closing date for the bids was originally 28 February 2012, but this was extended by Gama to 17 April 2012. Procurement rules forbid executives to engage with bidders during a bid period. But that didn't stop Transnet's executives. On 16 December 2011, Garry Pita wrote to Wang Pan, the deputy director of the Overseas Business Division of China South Railway (CSR). Pita at the time was the group chief supply chain officer. He opened his letter by saying that Brian Molefe had informed him that Molefe had met Wang Pan in early December (which Molefe admitted in testimony), and that CSR had expressed an interest in the tender. Pita took the opportunity to 'advise' CSR that the tender had been announced.

On 19 January 2012, Wang Pan wrote to Molefe outlining CSR's credentials and then said that a CSR delegation intended to visit South Africa to take part in a compulsory briefing session. Pan asked whether Molefe would meet with him directly, and facilitate site visits and meetings with other technical staff. Molefe replied the same day, and informed Pan that he had forwarded his email to Gama, who would 'process and respond' to Pan's request. '[Molefe] did not object to CSR's attempt to gain preferential access prior to the closing of the bids,' the commission wryly noted. In the light of the requirements of Transnet's procurement manual, the commission held that 'the communication between CSR and the officials of Transnet was thus inappropriate and affirms that CSR may have been favoured as a potential bidder'.

It is not clear whether any meetings such as Pan proposed ever took place. But what was interesting about this exchange was that, as investigators from the law firm Fundudzi later found, Pan had forwarded this letter to Rupesh Bansal, a Gupta associate. Bansal then forwarded the letter to the Gupta company Oakbay and to Suchi Bansal at the Worlds Window Group (WWG). WWG worked closely with the Guptas at this stage and, as I'll discuss below, would play a role in laundering the kickbacks that CSR paid to the Gupta enterprise. This 'indicat[ed] possible involvement and influence by individuals linked to the Guptas at this early stage,' the commission noted.

And, as it turned out, CSR's bid *was* helped along. By 17 April 2012, nine bidders had submitted offers. All bidders were supposed to submit certificates to show BBEEE, tax and VAT compliance; this was mandatory. CSR, however, had no South African subsidiary, and so it couldn't have obtained a certificate. CSR should have been immediately excluded. It is not clear from the commission's report why it wasn't.

Despite this major lapse, CSR was allowed to be evaluated in the next stage. The evaluation was done by what was called the Cross-Functional Evaluation Team (CFET), a body full of technical and other experts, who had been appointed by Gama. Only bidders who scored 60% or more in the first evaluation were allowed to proceed. Three bidders met this threshold. CSR, which was awarded a score of zero for BBEEE compliance, did not make the cut. CSR, at this point, should have been out of the running.

So, on 6 June 2012, Gama wrote to Molefe, pointing out that one local bidder did not have a BBEEE certificate, while CSR had no South African office, resulting in its exclusion. Gama then proposed two options; one was to proceed as planned, while the other was to remove BBEEE compliance from this stage of the bidding and instead consider it only at the very end of the bidding process. Molefe approved the second option on 8 June 2012, and the BADC approved the alteration of the terms of the formal 'request for proposal' the following month. This was remarkable: the BADC was choosing to fundamentally change the requirements of the bid in the very middle of its evaluation.

The result of this intervention was that, after removing the BBEEE requirement, CSR's score shot up to 69%, thus passing the minimum threshold. CSR could thus move on to the next stage of the procurement. CSR was the only foreign bidder that benefited from this change. Having been granted a reprieve, CSR duly established a South African office called CRRC E-Loco Supply (Pty) Ltd with four black South African directors. Thus, by the time Transnet considered BBEEE credentials again (during 'phase 3' of the procurement), CSR could now be given a decent BBEEE score.

Gama, when he testified before the commission, was dismissive; he said that the change made no real difference because all the bidders'

BBEEE credentials were eventually evaluated. It made no difference, he said, whether it was done at the beginning or the end. 'His view is indisputably wrong', the commission found. 'More likely, he devised his so-called option 2 to accommodate and favour CSR.' Indeed, the result was that, because of Gama's option 2 suggestion and Molefe's acceptance of it, 'CSR was inappropriately favoured ... when it should have been rightfully disqualified. CSR's non-disqualification served the state capture agenda and ensured that the planned 20% kickback to the Gupta enterprise negotiated by Mr Essa remained possible'.

The third phase of the evaluation commenced in August 2012; by then the field had been winnowed down to Siemens, Bombardier and CSR. CSR emerged the winner with the highest score, and in late 2012 CSR and Transnet signed the 'Locomotive Supply Agreement' contract. CSR had won.

But this was not the end of the irregularities with this contract. In total, CSR would be paid R3,432,869,565 by Transnet between December 2013 and December 2018. This was R700m more than had been originally estimated and approved by Gigaba. No evidence could be found to show that this increase was approved by the minister or the Transnet board.

To rub salt in the wounds, CSR would experience significant delays in supplying the locos. Calculations by the law firm MNS suggested that Transnet could, and probably should, have levied late penalties amounting to R1.7bn. This was never done. The commission, which found the evidence on the late penalties 'incomplete', recommended further investigation to establish where the failure to recoup late penalties may have amounted to a PFMA violation by the Transnet board.

## The 100 locos contract

The next contract considered by the commission was the purchase of a further 100 locos, again from CSR. The decision to purchase them derived from the fact that Transnet's huge capital expenditure programme – the 1,064 locos deal – had suffered delays. This meant that there was an urgent need to acquire 100 locos to serve on Transnet's coal export line that ran between the Ermelo coalfields and Richards Bay.

Thus, on 13 October 2013, Francis Callard, a senior TFR engineer, submitted a motivation for the accelerated purchase of 100 Class 19E electric locos. Most importantly, Callard argued that the urgency required that TFR buy the locos on confinement from Mitsui African Rail Solutions, at an estimated cost of R3.871bn. Callard justified buying from Mitsui for pretty sound reasons: TFR was already operating 110 of the same locos on its coal line, and they were doing the job adequately. Transnet crew and drivers were already trained on the locos, and, because there was no need for any redesign, the Mitsui production line could fire up quickly and start producing locos in short order.

On 20 January 2014, Callard produced an updated business rationale. Two days later, he received an email from Lindiwe Mdletshe, a TFR employee. She attached a revised version of the business case, which made wholesale changes; the most notable was that the preferred supplier be changed from Mitsui to CSR. It's not quite clear who actually produced the amended business case. Gama testified that he never directed changes to be made and had assumed that it was Anoj Singh's initiative. Singh denied that he had made any changes directly but then conceded under questioning that it was possible he had asked a subordinate to do so 'on the direction of Mr Molefe'.

The following day, 23 January, Callard attempted to raise issues with the revised memorandum with Gama and Thamsanqa Jiyane, a Transnet Engineering executive. Callard was worried that the whole rationale for the procurement was being undermined because the CSR locos would not be used alongside the existing coal line locos. Initially, Gama appeared receptive and pushed back on a request from Singh to sign the revised memo. But, following a meeting with Molefe and Singh the next day, Gama relented, and seemingly agreed not to raise any issues.

The result was that, on 24 January 2014, the BADC was presented with the business case. The BADC meeting was chaired by Salim Essa's erstwhile business partner, Iqbal Sharma, and attended by Molefe, Singh and Pita with Gama and Jiyane in partial attendance. The BADC approved the business case and resolved to recommend to the board the purchase of 100 locos at an estimated cost of R3.8bn. A special board meeting convened later that day – attended by Molefe, Singh and Gama – accepted the recommendation: CSR would get the contract.

The commission was damning of the decision to go with CSR. One of the key rationales for the original confinement to Mitsui was the need to buy locos that could be used on a particular coal line and that would be delivered quickly. Yet CSR was asked to supply Class 20E locos, which would require huge modifications to make sure they worked alongside Mitsui's Class 19E locos. Indeed, Transnet would eventually pay an additional R347m for modifications to CSR's trains.

Moreover, the original requirement in the 2013 business case was that the locos be delivered within 12 months – so during 2014. But, when Transnet and CSR signed on the dotted line, CSR agreed to deliver the locos only between June 2015 and November 2015. The commission found that 'the delays negated the entire raison d'être of the project. The confinement to CSR was flawed in concept and execution … If no good grounds for confinement existed, Transnet should have resorted to an open tender. Instead, key individuals resorted to a confinement with the aim of inappropriately favouring CSR, most likely with the intention to favour the Gupta enterprise.'

Sadly, there was more. In terms of the agreements signed with CSR for the 100 locos on 17 March 2014 (the same day Transnet signed similar agreements on the 1,064 deal), Transnet agreed to pay an eye-watering 60% of the total contract price upfront; typically, Transnet would pay 10% of a contract upfront. The result was that Transnet paid CSR R1.32bn before receiving a single train. This suggested that 'CSR was unduly favoured and that Molefe and other officials involved in concluding this contract acted in breach of their fiduciary duties and in contravention of section 50 and 51 of the PFMA,' the commission commented.

And, as with the 95 locos deal, the 100 locos deal also came with a much bigger price tag than anticipated. The original board approval in January 2014 was for a purchase price of R3.871bn. Five months later, Molefe was forced to ask the board to approve an increase in price to R4.84bn, just under R1bn more. Transnet would ultimately pay R5,159,831,654.92 for the 100 locos themselves, the delivery expenses and the costs of 'operationalisation' – all for urgently needed trains that were delivered late.

## The 1,064 locos deal

This deal is perhaps the most notorious – and certainly the biggest – contract subject to state capture. Its roots lay in Transnet's adoption of what it called a Market Demand Strategy (MDS) in 2011. The innocuous name somewhat downplayed an enormous capital investment and expansion programme worth R300bn that would massively increase Transnet's capacity. A good portion of this spend would be focused on expanding the locomotive fleet operated by Transnet Freight Rail – Siyabonga Gama's patch.

Between 2011 and 2012, Francis Calland, the TFR engineer, worked on producing and developing a business case for the purchase of 1,064 locomotives at an estimated cost of R38.6bn. The plan was to purchase 599 electric locomotives and 465 diesel locos. Ultimately the electric and diesel loco contracts were split so that two suppliers would be selected in each category, giving a total of four suppliers. The result was that, when the final contracts were signed in March 2014, CSR was contracted to provide 359 electric locos, Bombardier to supply 240 electric locos, China North Rail (CNR) 232 diesel locos and General Electric 233 diesel locos.

The board approved the issuing of a request for proposal in July 2012. This was somewhat strange as the board only approved the business case on 25 April 2013. It was only on 3 August 2013 that the shareholder minister – Malusi Gigaba – granted his approval for the whole contract to proceed.

The commission's investigations found at least 15 different issues or profound irregularities with the way the 1,064 procurements were concluded. In the interests of brevity, readability and everyone's sanity, I focus on perhaps the most extraordinary of all problems – the unjustified increase in the price of the contracts.

When the board approved the business case for the 1,064 deal, the estimated total cost (ETC) was R38.6bn without so-called hedging costs, forex escalations and 'other price escalations'. Hedging refers to the practice of trying to protect against unfavourable exchange rate developments, although, for our purposes, this is not really important. When the hedging and other costs were included, the price, as eventually approved by the board in May 2014, leapt to R54.5bn.

But this was a fabrication – and an audacious one at that. The original business case, dated 7 March 2012 and approved by various Transnet committees in March and May the same year, stipulated a total ETC of R38.146bn, *including* hedging costs. Callard and a number of other witnesses before the commission testified that the ETC figure of R38.6bn already priced in hedging and escalations. Correspondence from McKinsey – which acted as transaction advisors – also showed that the R38bn cost included hedging and escalations.

Strikingly, the commission's investigations found multiple versions of the business case. A version dated 29 April 2013 – after the board had already approved the business case – stated that the ETC only excluded borrowing costs. A final version dated 30 April deleted this, and instead inserted the line that the R38.6bn excluded 'the potential effects from forex hedging, forex escalations and other price escalations'.

The metadata on the document (a sort of digital fingerprint) showed that the final version had been edited on the computer of Yusuf Mohamed, a Transnet employee, on the morning of the 30th. Mohamed admitted that he amended the business case on the instruction of Anoj Singh. He said that Singh had told him to do so in order to bring the business case in line with the board resolution on 25 April. The commission speculated that, in order for any of this to make sense, there was a possibility that the board resolution had also been changed, after the fact, to show that the board had approved a version of the business case that didn't actually exist at the time.

Further evidence was presented that made a highly compelling case that the R54bn cost was bogus. In 2018, Fundudzi, a law firm hired by Transnet to review the transactions, used calculations by Callard to confirm that the R38bn cost included hedging. Another calculation was performed by Alister Chabi, an actuary appointed by another law firm, MNS, which had also been asked to review and audit the 1,064 purchases. Chabi performed an extensive recalculation using all the available data. His calculations showed that the R38.6bn must have included hedging costs. Indeed, the commission found that Chabi's calculations 'leave no doubt' that the ETC of R38.6bn *did* include hedging costs.

In essence, what happened was that key people at Transnet

misstated and inflated the cost of the transaction. The result was that in May 2014 the board approved an increase in the ETC from R38.6bn to R54.5bn – for no good reason. The commission speculated that this massive increase in price may have been implemented in order to finance the extraordinary kickbacks that were paid to the Gupta enterprise.

The 1,064 deal led the commission to make a whole range of recommendations that individuals be investigated for wrongdoing, including fraud and corruption. The details are given in the 'recommendations' section at the end of this chapter.

## The Gupta kickbacks

The systematic and repeated irregularities in all the contracts awarded to CSR and CNR (which amalgamated in 2014 to become a new single entity called CRRC) have to be understood in the light of the overwhelming evidence that the Gupta enterprise earned billions in kickbacks from these deals. In my evidence before the commission, I presented extensive evidence about how these kickbacks were paid; this evidence was accepted, in full, by the commission. In support of these claims, I included four key sets of documents.

The first set was a series of 'business development agreements' (BDAs) that were entered into between CNR, CSR and CRRC (when the two amalgamated) and companies either connected to the Guptas or controlled directly by Salim Essa. The BDAs set out how these companies would be paid a jaw-dropping 20% to 21% of the total price paid to CNR/CSR/CRRC by Transnet. This amounted to more than R7bn, against a total amount of R26.237bn paid to CNR/CSR and CRRC for the contracts they won.

The second document was discovered in the GuptaLeaks emails: an Excel spreadsheet that was saved with the name 'Final CSR 2015 Workings'. The spreadsheet was sent to Ashu Chawla in 2015 from the email address infoportal@zoho.com. The commission's investigations concluded that this address was controlled by Salim Essa. Essa's email to Chawla forwarded an email written by Rupesh Bansal (a director of the Worlds Window Group) to an address controlled by Zhang Minyu, a CSR employee who directed CSR's Indian subsidiary. The Excel spreadsheet set out, in quite extensive detail, the amount of the kickbacks that CSR and CNR were due to pay on the loco contracts, and how much had already been paid.

The third set of documents comprised HSBC bank transaction records for four companies: JJ Trading (JJT), Century General Trading (CGT), Tequesta Group and Regiments Asia. Both Tequesta Group and Regiments Asia were formed in Hong Kong in 2015; both listed Salim Essa as their sole director. The HSBC transaction records, which were initially leaked to the media but then confirmed by the commission by subpoena, showed that CRRC paid over $150m to the two companies.

The final set of documents consisted of a small selection of Habib Bank statements for Tequesta and Regiments.

Together, these documents painted a lurid picture of extraordinary corruption. This took place in two rough phases. In the initial phase, CNR and CSR signed its 'business development agreements' with either JJT or CGT. JJT was to receive the kickbacks paid on the 359 and 100 loco contracts, which were equal to 21% of the total contract value. CGT was to receive 20% of the value of the 95 locos contract.

JJT and CGT were both controlled by the Worlds Window Group, a metal trader based in India. In my submissions to the commission, I provided a raft of evidence emanating from the GuptaLeaks that the Guptas and the Worlds Window Group had been in business since at least 2010, and that WWG helped the Guptas launder funds. The 2015 Workings Excel document indicated that, while the BDAs were signed with CGT and JJT, and the kickbacks paid to them, they were only supposed to retain 15%; the remaining 85% was to be paid to the Guptas. In essence, CGT and JJT were paid a 15% fee to act as the primary money launderers. Notably, HSBC bank records secured by the commission for CGT and JJT showed that they had received payments from the Chinese manufacturers and that they had also made onward payments to companies controlled by the Guptas in Dubai.

But by 2014 the Guptas and the Worlds Window Group had fallen out. As a result, CGT and JJT were kicked to the kerb and replaced by Tequesta Group and Regiments Asia. Tequesta and Regiments Asia were paid directly by CRRC.

Using all this evidence, which I considered in the light of a stellar audit performed by amaBhungane, I calculated that CNR/CSR/CRRC had paid $275,608,209.23 in kickbacks on these contracts, equal to R3,400,558,015 (I give a much more detailed accounting in the later chapter on money flows). I further calculated that, based on the BDA agreements, the Guptas were due to receive a further R3,768,046,193.40. It was not possible to confirm definitively that the kickbacks were paid – we simply didn't have the bank records – but I argued that it was highly likely they were paid, not least because CRRC was paid in full by Transnet. When all was added together, I thus calculated that a total of R7,168,604.208.40 in kickbacks was likely to have been paid on the 95, 100 and 359 loco deals.

## The CNR/BEX relocation contract

In February 2014, in the middle of the 1,064 negotiations, Transnet instructed PricewaterhouseCoopers (PwC) to review whether Transnet Engineering, the Transnet subsidiary that actually produced stuff, could effectively contribute to building or assembling the locos that were being bought. The PwC report fretted that putting all the assembly lines for the four types of locos in one place could create various bottlenecks. It thus recommended that two of the four assembly lines be set up in Durban; these would be the lines assembling the diesel locos built by CNR and BT.

While this report would be heeded by Transnet, it was something of a botched job. When CNR signed the contracts in March 2014, it stipulated that it would indeed assemble the trains in Durban. But its original bid, and the price it agreed with Transnet, were based on the cost of assembling the trains in Gauteng. So, in March 2014, Transnet asked CNR's local subsidiary, CNRRSA, to provide an estimate of how much it would cost to assemble in Durban rather than Gauteng. On 11 March 2014, CNNRSA wrote to Garry Pita and Lindiwe Mdletshe stating that the additional cost to use Durban would be R9,755,600, although CNRRSA also claimed there might be a 'considerable amount of immeasurable financial losses' incurred by relocating to Durban, but didn't explain what these vague losses might be.

No evidence could be found of any response to this letter. The next development in the story that could be found in Transnet's records was an unsigned proposal attached to a letter sent by CNRRSA to Transnet dated 1 February 2015. This proposal included a schedule that claimed the costs would be in the region of R318.7m. The commission could find no evidence that this was discussed with anyone at Transnet.

A few months later, on 25 April 2015, CNNRRSA appointed a company called Business Expansion Structured Products (Pty) Ltd (known as BEX) to act as an intermediary on this issue. BEX was a shell company with a sole director, Mark Shaw, who was appointed on 15 April 2015. BEX was appointed by CNNRRSA despite CNNRRSA's minority shareholders raising objections and, at a later stage, alerting the authorities.

This agreement was based on an unsigned BDA that had been distributed by email the previous month. This BDA, the commission commented, 'bears significant resemblance' to the BDAs that CSR signed with Essa's companies Tequesta and Regiments. The essence of this BDA was extraordinary. It stated that CNNRRSA and BEX had agreed that the 'benchmark costs' for the move would be R280m excluding VAT. If BEX, however, got Transnet to pay more than this amount, this excess would be paid to BEX. The BDA provided a handy example: if BEX succeeded in getting Transnet to pay R650m, BEX would be entitled to a fee of R370m.

When BEX and CNNRRSA finally signed the 25 April 2015 agreement, the 'benchmark cost' was increased to R580m. So, for BEX to earn money, it would have to get Transnet to agree to pay more than R580m. The total effect of the contract was therefore that CNNRRSA would pay BEX, a shell company with one director and no history, to get Transnet to agree to huge fees for the relocation, which were most likely not justified by the real costs that would be incurred by CNNRSSA. And BEX would be motivated to get the costs increased as much as possible so as to increase its own cut.

BEX was remarkably successful. On 15 May 2015, about three weeks after BEX and CNNRRSA signed their agreement, Transnet's Lindiwe Mdletshe sent a memorandum to Gama. It motivated for a new process of negotiation to conclude an agreement for the increased costs of relocation. The maximum cost that could be agreed was R669,784,286, a figure remarkably similar to the R650m that had been quoted as an example in the BEX–CNNRRSA agreement. The memo was recommended by Ravi Nair (then the acting CEO of TFR), Anoj Singh and Silinga (group executive: legal and compliance), who had also been involved in the GNS/Abalozi settlements.

The memo recommended that Singh, Jiyane (then CEO of Transnet Engineering), Pita, Silinga and Mdletshe conduct the negotiations. In the first meeting between the team, CNRRSA and BEX, CNRRSA proposed a relocation cost of R719,090,548, but, with a highly generous and thoughtful 10% discount, this could be cut to R647,181,494. The day after the meeting, Pita, who had attended, wrote an email to the other members of the negotiating team, including Yousuf Laher. Pita's email raised serious reservations about the costs. Laher concurred, saying much of the pricing made no sense. The commission was unable to find evidence that any member of the negotiating team was ever told about, or ever tried to ask, why the relocation costs had rocketed from R9.8m in March 2014 to over R700m.

On 22 July 2015, Mdletshe distributed a revised proposal from CNNRRSA, which was ultimately adopted. Under the terms of this proposal, the total cost was recorded as R669,784,286; with a 10% discount this fell to R602,805,858. But, in a very generous offer, Transnet would pay 50% of this amount upfront (R301,402,929) and the remainder on a monthly basis over 24 months. Two memos setting out these costs and requesting approval were distributed by Mdletshe. They were recommended by Ravi Nair, Singh, Pita, Silinga and Jiyane. Gama signed the memorandum the following day. The effect of these memoranda was that the total value of CNR's contract to provide diesel locos was increased from R9,947,116,464 to R10,549,297,958 to take into account the increased relocation costs.

In the end, Transnet paid only R368.89m for the relocation costs (the 50% upfront cost plus VAT). Shortly thereafter, CNRRSA paid BEX R76,585,630.42 on 25 September 2015. Using bank records subpoenaed by the commission, I was able to discover that BEX paid out the funds it received in four streams. One stream ended up paying R9m into the account of Integrated Capital Management, one of whose directors at the time was Stanley Shane, a Transnet board member. A further R33.73m was paid to Confident Concepts, a Gupta family company.

The commission's findings and recommendations were straightforward: a whole host of people should be investigated for PFMA violations and for corruption.

## The financial advisors: McKinsey, Regiments and the Gupta enterprise

Regiments, a financial advisory firm headed by Eric Wood that included a range of subsidiary and partner firms, was a major beneficiary of state capture. When Eric Wood parted ways with Regiments, taking a handful of employees with him, he did so to form a new set of companies called Trillian. Trillian was set up with Salim Essa – the 50% shareholder – although, in a sense, this was as much a new development as a formalisation of the income Essa's companies earned from Regiments.

Their services were of the abstruse and abstract kind – financial modelling and advice. Somewhat fittingly, the ways in which they scored off state capture was similarly complicated and technical; so much so, in fact, that it is sometimes hard to describe. As a result, I've opted here to give a broad overview and some highlights rather than a blow-by-blow account.

The essential takeaway is that, between 2012 and 2016, Transnet contracted with four companies to provide it with financial advice and contract guidance: the US firm McKinsey, Regiments, the US firm JP Morgan, and Trillian. The first primary partner used by Transnet was McKinsey, which, at the insistence of Transnet, partnered with Regiments. In 2014, McKinsey would 'cede' – hand over – all its contracts with Transnet directly to Regiments. When Wood left Regiments to form Trillian with Essa, Transnet contracts soon followed. McKinsey's interactions with Regiments were led and overseen by Vikas Sagar.

The commission found that it was reasonable to conclude that McKinsey had contracted with Regiments because it knew Regiments would get its contracts between 2012 and 2015. This was confirmed by McKinsey's own investigation, which, in turn, led the firm to pay back the huge fees it had earned from Transnet.

The most important contract granted to McKinsey and Regiments was to provide transaction advice on the 1,064 deal. But, in reality, McKinsey and Regiments were scoring loads of contracts: a total of eight, for a total value of R2.2bn. Importantly, in six of these contracts, Regiments diverted huge sums to two companies: Homix and Albatime. Homix, as I discuss later, was controlled by the Gupta enterprise; Albatime was controlled by Kuben Moodley, an associate of Salim Essa. Albatime was, among other things, used by the Guptas as a laundry vehicle when the Guptas bought Optimum coal mine.

All the eight contracts with McKinsey and Regiments were awarded on confinement, without an open tender. Four of the eight contracts won by McKinsey–Regiments were approved by Molefe over just four days between 31 March 2014 and 3 April 2014, with a total value of R619m. These four contracts were awarded, moreover, on the basis of a confidential confinement, which meant that a whole range of procurement steps were not performed. In all these four contracts, Homix and Albatime were appointed the so-called supplier development partners.

McKinsey was well aware that the contracts it was getting with Regiments involved huge payments to Homix and Albatime. In June 2014, for example, Regiments emailed McKinsey a spreadsheet. This provided a detailed breakdown of fees that Regiments would pay to Homix and Albatime; the spreadsheet set out payments of over R100m at the time. McKinsey would later confirm to Parliament that neither Homix nor Albatime performed any services in any project in which McKinsey was involved.

Anoj Singh, too, was well aware of the arrangements. On 18 May 2015, Regiments forwarded a document called 'Advisory Invoice Tracking' to Singh. The spreadsheet detailed a reconciliation of the payments Regiments had received from Transnet and the corresponding payments it made to Homix, another company called Chivita (an alternative to Homix) and Albatime. This very same spreadsheet was also shared with Garry Pita on 5 August 2015, after Pita had taken over the position of group chief financial officer from Singh.

The fee arrangements with Homix/Chivita and Albatime were straightforward. The fees were split on a 45/50/5 basis: Homix/Chivita would get 50% of the fee paid to Regiments by Transnet, Albatime would get 5%, and Regiments would retain 45%. In the 2015/16 financial year, Regiments paid R274.15m to Homix/Chivita and Albatime. This included over R100m from fees that Regiments earned on contracts it shared with McKinsey.

## The financing of the 1,064 contracts
The extraordinary number of irregularities in the Regiments and

Trillian contracts can be seen in two examples: the arrangements around the China Development Bank (CDB) loan and the rand-denominated Club Loan.

In August 2012, Transnet's board approved taking out a $1.5bn loan from CDB. This loan was to be used to cover, in part, the purchase of locos from CNR and CSR. The remainder of the required financing would be raised through a loan with a consortium of South African lenders (this was called the Club Loan, in reference to the fact that it was a 'club' of lenders that loaned the money).

It was only in March 2014, however, that Transnet started negotiating in earnest with the CDB; this was the same month that Transnet signed the contracts to buy 1,064 locos from CSR, CNR, Bombardier and General Electric. In its original proposal, CDB offered the loan at an interest rate considerably above what Transnet normally paid. In order to resolve the situation, Singh and the head of Transnet's Treasury, Mathane Makgatho, travelled to China in July 2014. If you recall, Makgatho was one of the honest civil servants identified by the commission who was pushed out of Transnet under Singh and Molefe.

When Makgatho returned from China, she was shocked to learn that CDB had been communicating directly with Regiments, and that Wood had been leading a parallel negotiating process with CDB. This was highly inappropriate as it was Transnet Treasury, and not Regiments, that was empowered to negotiate the loan. Singh would later claim that he got Regiments involved because he felt that Treasury was failing to negotiate a favourable rate.

In August 2014, Makgatho was copied into an email from CDB to Eric Wood at Regiments. This showed that Regiments was negotiating the price of CDB's loan. Makgatho quickly wrote to Molefe and Singh and pointed out that Transnet Treasury had been negotiating since April. Molefe responded by calling Makgatho and Singh into his office for a meeting, after which he then set up another meeting in Melrose Arch between Transnet and Regiments. The meeting was attended by Singh, Molefe and Makgatho for Transnet, and Eric Wood and Niven Pillay from Regiments.

At the heart of the meeting was a proposal that had been put forward by Regiments about how the loan could be priced and concluded. Molefe and Singh urged Makgatho to accept Regiments' model. But Makgatho was not convinced; she thought the offer was way too expensive. Makgatho further recorded her discomfort about Regiments' involvement in an email to Molefe sent soon after, in which she warned him that 'the fact that Transnet's biggest ever transaction is being negotiated and decided by outsiders (Regiments) is a cause for concern as it exposes the company to undue risk'.

Matters reached a head in late August. Makgatho compiled a memorandum in which she set out her concerns with the CDB loan and detailed the costs and conditions. She sent this to Molefe, asking him to pass it on to the board. Makgatho was particularly concerned that the board might be given misleading information about the true cost of the loan. A week later, Singh wrote his own memo, in which he argued against the points raised by Makgatho, and which he also wanted to be shared with the board. Molefe merely 'noted' Makgatho's concerns. Singh then made a PowerPoint presentation to the board about the cost of the loan, based on an analysis provided by Regiments. The commission found that the presentation was factually incorrect in several respects; the board, as a result, was not given a true picture of the cost of the loan.

Based on Singh's presentation, on 4 June 2015 the board approved the signing of the loan agreement with CDB for $1.5bn. The interest rate that was agreed to was significantly higher than what Transnet usually paid; it was a 'very expensive loan', according to the commission.

By this time, Makgatho had already left; she resigned in November 2014. She was replaced in the role of treasurer by Phetolo Ramosebudi, who as treasurer of Airports Company South Africa, had received gratifications from Regiments. In late April 2015, Ramosebudi wrote a memo to the BADC. This recommended that Transnet officially appoint Regiments, by confinement, for transaction advisory services for the 1,064 contract. He recommended that Regiments get a success fee of R166m for, among other things, assisting with the CDB loan. This in effect amounted to giving Regiments a last-minute contract so that it would be paid a success fee on a loan that would be approved a week later. Ramosebudi's proposal was supported by Pita, Singh and Gama.

The memo was approved the following day by the BADC. On 3 June 2015, the day before the CDB loan had even been approved, Regiments submitted an invoice to Transnet in connection with the

CDB loan. Regiments invoiced an amount of R166m plus VAT, or R189.24m. This was paid to Regiments on 11 June 2015. Of this amount, R147,607,200 was paid to Albatime, which then paid R122m to Sahara Computers, the Gupta's IT company.

The payment of any sort of success fee was absurd, and not just because the CDB loan was a bad deal. Regiments, at the time of the CDB deal, had already been appointed as a transaction advisor on the 1,064 deal, and was being paid accordingly. The contract that Regiments signed envisaged that Regiments would provide the sort of services it provided on the CDB loan. So, simply, Regiments was already being contracted and paid for its work on the CDB loan. The additional contract, which led to the R166m fee, effectively paid Regiments a second time for a job it was already supposed to be doing.

The commission also heard evidence from Dr Jonathan Bloom, who was tasked with reviewing the Regiments deals. He examined how the R166m success fee was calculated. He found that Regiments had used a calculation that led to a massively inflated success fee; the fee that Regiments should have earned, if the usual methodology was employed, was R63m, not R166m. Of course, as Bloom also confirmed, Regiments should not have been paid any success fee, because it had already been paid to provide these services.

Similar problems bedevilled the so-called Club Loan, which was marked by nonsensical reasoning and procedural violations that, in the interest of sanity and brevity, I don't unpack here. The key takeaway from the Club Loan was that Trillian, which had just been formed, and which had no capacity to do work on the Club Loan, and did none, was paid R93.48m as a fee for its 'help'.

So, not only were the 1,064 loco contracts themselves massively corrupt, involving billions in kickbacks to Gupta companies; but the very expensive and prejudicial loans that Transnet took out to pay for the contracts were also used to pay fees to the Guptas. The 1,064 deals – indeed, all the loco deals – involved an orgy of corruption that, in my long career in investigating grand corruption, is second only to the Arms Deal in scale and sheer audacity.

## The Manganese Expansion Project
The Manganese Expansion Project (MEP) was unique in that,

despite the best efforts of Salim Essa and Anoj Singh, the pressure they brought to bear did not totally derail the contract. The MEP was first contemplated in 2009 to meet increased Chinese demand for manganese. It was anticipated that it would proceed in two parts: phase 1 and phase 2. The approval for the MEP as a whole was granted in October 2012 by the board with an estimated cost of R2.4bn. Phase 1 was to be managed by Transnet Capital Projects.

In January 2013, Molefe sought and received BADC approval for the project to proceed. This project included a R220m contract for project management and engineering services. Because the contract was less than R250m, Molefe had the delegated authority to approve a confinement. In August 2013 he awarded the contract on confinement to a company called Hatch, which had already been working on parts of the project since 2011.

The commission's investigations found that, two weeks prior to Molefe's approval, the terms of the contract had been amended by Anoj Singh. The amendments required that 50% of the contract be spent on supplier development. In layman's terms, this meant that Hatch would effectively have to use a new and emerging supplier for 50% of the contract's value. Singh's amendment increased the supplier development portion from 30% to 50%.

As it turned out, by this time Hatch had already been subject to undue pressure. In July 2013, Hatch executive Henk Bester received a call from Nalen Padayachee of a company called PM Africa; they agreed to meet at the Hatch offices. When Padayachee arrived, he was accompanied by Dave Reddy from another company, DEC Engineering. According to Bester, Reddy told Henk Bester that they knew all about the confinement, which at that stage was private. Reddy further told Bester that 'number 1' wanted Hatch to partner with PM Africa and DEC and to make them supplier development partners. Bester believed that 'number 1' was Anoj Singh.

This hunch seemed to be confirmed when Bester approached the senior manager of Transnet Capital Management, Rudie Basson, to tell him about the meeting. Bester recalled that Basson told him that Singh had originally wanted the confinement contract to specifically stipulate that Hatch had to use PM Africa and DEC. Basson and his colleagues had to disabuse Singh of this notion. Singh, of course, denied issuing any instruction. But the commission then confronted

Singh with WhatsApp conversations between him and another TCP manager, Gerhard Bierman. In the messages Bierman was clearly informing Singh that it would be inappropriate to name specific subcontractors. Singh eventually conceded before the commission that, while he didn't instruct anyone, there was 'a request from me to co-hire two companies'.

Hatch continued to meet PM Africa and DEC over the following months, and on one occasion Padayachee intimated that the confinement would not proceed unless Hatch worked with them. Despite this, Hatch refused to relent, and successfully called their bluff: the contract was approved in August 2013 without Hatch agreeing to use the two companies.

More pressure was applied, however. Following Molefe's approval, Hatch had to enter into more detailed negotiations to confirm the full content of the contract. In October 2013, Hatch was unexpectedly called to a meeting with Garry Pita. This was strange as Pita had, until then, had no involvement in the contract, which did not fall under his division. The meeting was attended by Bester and another Hatch executive, Alan Grey. Singh, who was supposed to attend, failed to show up. Pita informed Bester and Grey that he had been instructed to talk to them about the supplier development part of the contract. Hatch responded by saying that he would only appoint PM Africa and DEC if he received a written instruction from Transnet, which, of course, Transnet could not do. The meeting then became 'heated', and Pita allegedly told Bester that he must do as he was told. Again, Hatch refused to budge.

On phase 1 of the project, the commission would hold that there were reasonable grounds to believe that Reddy and Padayachee had committed corruption offences under PRECCA; this was because they effectively told Hatch that if Hatch offered them gratification – the SDP contracts – they would influence the procurement in their favour.

However, this was not the end of the story. In April 2014, Transnet went to market to advertise contracts for phase 2 of the MEP. These contracts would be more valuable, equal to somewhere between R700m and R1bn. The contracts would require at least 45% of its value to be assigned to supplier development and that 30% (potentially as part of the 45%) be subcontracted to small businesses. For various reasons, Hatch tendered as part of a consortium called H2N.

A little prior to this contract being advertised, Hatch asked Reddy to set up a meeting with Singh. Hatch was concerned because it was not being paid on invoices it had submitted on a different project. A meeting was arranged in Melrose Arch.

Henk Bester, Craig Sumption and Craig Simmer represented Hatch at the meeting.

When Bester arrived, he was approached by Salim Essa, who said he was there to meet them with Singh. After Essa checked if the restaurant was 'clean', he called Singh, who arrived a few minutes later. The meeting soon went off track as Essa started telling Hatch to appoint DEC as a supplier development partner or subcontractor. Bester left the meeting with the impression that Essa was actually Singh's boss. Singh denied that the meeting took place at all, claiming it was fabricated. He couldn't, however, explain why Bester and his colleagues would think it had occurred.

Soon thereafter, Reddy called Bester again to tell him that Essa had requested a follow-up meeting at Melrose Arch. This was attended by Reddy, Bester and Essa. During the meeting, Essa suggested that Hatch include 'his' company in their bid, although he did not identify which company was 'his'. By then, Hatch had already submitted its bid and could not include any more companies. Essa, according to Bester, was undeterred, and continued to press Bester. Essa told Bester that he (Essa) had a lot of power: that he was actually in control of the budget of the project and that, if H2N originally provided R80m for supplier development in its proposal, Essa would ensure that Transnet eventually increased this to R350m. Essa also offered Bester the tender documentation of H2N's competitors.

In one of the more notable exchanges, Essa tried to illustrate his influence and reach by bragging about his inside knowledge. He told Bester that the newspapers would imminently announce the appointment of Molefe as the head of Eskom, and that 'we' were responsible. Essa never explained who the 'we' was that he referred to, but Bester testified that he came to believe that this meant the Guptas. The prediction, as we'll see in the next section, turned out to be right.

To Hatch's credit, at no stage did it give in to the pressure, and it refused to cut Reddy's and Padayachee's companies into the action.

On the basis of this evidence, the commission found that there were reasonable grounds to suspect Essa of corruption. This was because Essa effectively offered Hatch the contract in return for Hatch paying a gratification in the form of giving contracts to a company identified by Essa. The commission, too, found that there were reasonable grounds to believe that Singh, Reddy and Padayachee were also guilty of corruption for their conduct in respect of phase 1 and phase 2 of the project.

## Neotel and Homix

Prior to 2007, Transnet's huge IT infrastructure was managed by two entities, both of which were Transnet subsidiaries, Arivia and Transtel. Arivia maintained all the hardware and software, while Transtel provide network services like cabling and routers. Transnet decided to sell both entities to the private sector. The effect was to privatise critical infrastructure, and to create de facto private monopolies in the process. Margaret Thatcher would have been proud. The network services operated by Transtel were sold to Neotel in 2007; the data centre was sold to T-Systems. Both companies would subsequently become involved in corrupt arrangements with the Guptas to keep these privileged positions.

In 2012, Transnet employed an outside company to review its IT assets and networking arrangements. The review recommended that the network contracts be put out for competitive tender. In June 2013, Transnet thus issued requests for proposals (RFPs) on the network contract. The total value was R1.5bn over three years, with an option to extend the contract to five years at R2.5bn. Five bidders responded to the RFPs including Neotel and T-Systems; for this bid, T-Systems partnered with an SOE called Broadband Infraco, of which Salim Essa was a notable director.

After the first round of evaluation, only Neotel, Didata and T-Systems made it through. But there were two problems that would later rear their heads. The first was that the outside consultant Transnet used, which recommended the network service go out to tender, was a company called Detecon. Detecon was a subsidiary of T-Systems International, which raised conflict of interest issues around the involvement of T-Systems South Africa in any bid. The second problem related to T-Systems' final score. After this first phase of evaluation, T-Systems scored 69.93%; this was just short of the 70% that all bidders needed to score to make it through to the next round. Luckily for T-Systems, its score was 'rounded up' to 70%, which got it through. But this was in fact not allowed; regulations in place stipulated that rounding must be done to two decimal places. T-Systems' score should thus have been rounded only to 69.94%, which, of course, would have knocked it out of contention.

After the 70% threshold was applied, further evaluations were done on the three bidders. Neotel emerged in first place with 90 points, Didata in second with 75.37 points and T-Systems with 65.35. In an effort to try to get over the line at the last minute, T-Systems made an unsolicited offer to discount its bid by R248m. This offer was rightly ignored. The evaluation team recommended the award to Neotel and, in late October 2013, the acting GCEO, Mrs Sharla Chetty, approved the issuing of a letter of intent to Neotel and letters of regret to T-Systems and Didata.

Shortly thereafter, however, Garry Pita intervened. He told Gerhard van der Westhuizen, who would be part of the negotiation team, not to issue the letter of intent. Pita claimed that Singh had given him this instruction and that Singh, in turn, was acting on the instructions of Molefe, who wanted to review the letter after he returned from a trip abroad.

In November 2013, Molefe convened a meeting with Singh, Van der Westhuizen and two other executives. Molefe told the meeting that he did not support the award to Neotel and listed a whole series of reasons. Van der Westhuizen initially tried to push back but, as he told the commission, he came to believe that pushing too hard would not work and would be bad for his future career at Transnet.

When he testified before the commission, Van der Westhuizen indicated that he believed that the relationship between T-Systems and Broadband Infraco, of which Essa was a director, may have affected Molefe's thinking. Molefe denied any knowledge that Essa was a director. But Molefe also denied knowledge of something even more profound: T-Systems had, at this time, already ceded large parts of another contract it had with Transnet to the company Zestilor. Zestilor was owned by Salim Essa's wife and was eventually paid hundreds of millions of rand as a result. In simpler terms, T-Systems was already in bed with Zestilor, a Gupta enterprise company.

Molefe's 'ignorance' was striking; after all, it was Molefe who had signed the agreement on behalf of Transnet that pushed contracts to Zestilor in the first place.

Following the meeting with Molefe, Singh instructed Van der Westhuizen to draft a new memo that would overturn the award to Neotel. The memo was signed by Molefe and then sent to Singh and Pita in late November. It raised a range of concerns with Neotel; it also placed weight on the last-minute discount offered by T-Systems, which had been rightly ignored by the evaluators at the time.

The commission was damning of the decision to overturn the award to Neotel for two reasons. First, it was totally inappropriate for Molefe to rely on T-Systems' last-minute offer of a discount as this gave the company an advantage over other bidders, who were not given the same chance to review their own prices. Second, the entire approval process was based on the BADC delegating decision-making authority to the GCEO, who, at the time, was Ms Chetty. She had already made a decision – to issue the letter of intent to Neotel. Molefe did not have the power simply to take the decision again. As the commission noted, 'the BADC did not delegate the approval authority … to Mr Molefe personally, but rather to the holder of the post'.

Nevertheless, in the teeth of these problems, on 20 November 2013 Transnet sent letters of regret to Neotel and others, and a letter to T-Systems announcing it was the preferred bidder.

The award of the contract to T-Systems created all sorts of headaches. The biggest was that when Transnet privatised Transtel, it sold all of the equipment it was using to Neotel. When Transnet tried to buy this equipment back from Neotel, it was rebuffed. Transnet was also told that some of the equipment was now out of date and needed to be replaced; Neotel wasn't going to replace this equipment now that it had lost the contract.

The result was that Transnet needed to get hold of a whole bunch of new IT equipment. So, in February 2014, Van der Westhuizen sent a memo to Singh asking for approval to buy new network equipment from the US IT giant Cisco. The maximum value of the purchases would be R305m. T-Systems agreed that it would reduce its own tender by the same amount so that Transnet didn't end up paying double.

But, to add complexity to this whole situation, Transnet could not buy the Cisco equipment directly. This was because Cisco had entered into an exclusivity agreement with Neotel. So, essentially, Transnet, by taking the network contract away from Neotel, was forced to buy new Cisco IT equipment from and through Neotel, the company it had just jilted. Awkward.

On the very same day that Van der Westhuizen wrote his memo to Singh, Taufique Hasware Khan wrote a seemingly unsolicited letter to a senior Neotel employee, François van der Merwe. Khan represented the company Homix. He was also a director of several other shell companies that the Guptas would use to receive and launder state capture money. Khan's letter to Neotel advised it of 'an opportunity at Transnet that we have been working on for some time'. This 'opportunity' was the Cisco replacement deal. Homix offered to provide unspecified 'advisory services' to Neotel for the deal, in return for a fee equal to 10% of the contract value.

What advisory services Homix could provide was distinctly unclear, not least because Transnet was already obliged to buy all Cisco equipment from Neotel because Neotel held the exclusive licence over Cisco equipment sales. Nevertheless, the following day, 22 February 2014, Van der Merwe wrote back to Khan, attaching a letter of acceptance that provided for them to enter into a detailed written agreement.

When this letter was raised with Transnet's Van der Westhuizen at the commission, he was somewhat surprised. He had never met anyone from Homix during the entire Cisco deal. More to the point, he had no idea how this unknown company had found out about the approval for the deal on the very day it was approved, and before anyone outside Transnet had been alerted to its approval.

In the event, Neotel did pay a fee of R30.3m (excluding VAT) to Homix in connection with the Cisco transaction. The commission could find no supporting documentation for this transaction. It is also not entirely clear what Homix actually did to earn this fee, and the commission does not explore this point. Nevertheless, the commission found that there were 'reasonable grounds' to believe that Khan at Homix, Van der Merwe at Neotel, and 'perhaps others' had committed the offence of corruption in relation to the contract.

Using documents provided to me by the commission, I was able to calculate that Neotel was ultimately paid R345m by Transnet in relation to the Cisco contract.

Things soon took an unexpected turn. In April 2014, Transnet's auditors reviewed the award of the network services contract to T-Systems. They found that T-Systems should have been disqualified for the two reasons I already noted: because of the potential conflict of interest through the involvement of Detecon and the whole rounding-off issue. They also questioned Molefe's authority to revoke the award.

The result was that, after consulting with T-Systems, Molefe took the decision to reverse the award of the contract to T-Systems. Molefe approved this decision on 6 June 2014. The following month, Singh and Molefe wrote to the BADC to explain why T-Systems would no longer be designated the preferred supplier. T-Systems, for its part, accepted the revocation, clearing the way for Neotel to contract with Transnet for the network services contract.

Reviewing this procedural horror show, the commission was damning of Molefe. It found that there were 'strong reasonable grounds' to believe that he had violated the PFMA; it also found that Molefe's 'lack of honesty and integrity' in relation to the award to Transnet would be of 'evidential value' in proving that he was acting as part of the Gupta enterprise.

With T-Systems out of the picture, Transnet and Neotel entered into lengthy contract negotiations in late 2014. By December 2014 matters had reached a stalemate, partially because Transnet wanted to include a clause that would allow it to buy Neotel's equipment if, in a few years, it was decided not to renew the contract with Neotel. One can see the problem here. On the one hand, Transnet wanted to avoid another situation where it was unable to buy back the equipment it needed to function. On the other, when the contract came up for renewal again, Neotel would be in a much stronger bargaining position if it could retain ownership of the IT equipment that Transnet would need to use.

Senior employees from both sides became involved to try to resolve the issues, including the CEO of Neotel, Sunil Joshi. Anoj Singh from Transnet also became actively involved. Meetings took place on 8, 11 and 13 December 2014. During the meeting on the 11th, Singh and Joshi went into a private 'breakaway' session; its content was never disclosed to Van der Westhuizen, Transnet's commercial negotiator. It was at the meeting on 13 December that all of the issues were finally ironed out.

Unbeknown to Van der Westhuizen, on 12 December 2014 – the day before the deal was concluded – Khan of Homix wrote a letter to Neotel's CEO Sunil Joshi. Khan's letter recorded that Homix had, on the day the letter was sent, engaged (presumably with Neotel) in the negotiations, which Khan reflected had 'reached an impasse'. Homix offered to help resolve this impasse, in return for which it would be paid a 2% fee on the big network services deal (equal to R36m), and a further fee of R25m for the part of the contract that related to the sale of assets.

The commission dismissed the idea that Homix could have realistically performed any legitimate services. 'It seems improbable that services of Homix to the value of R61m were either necessary or rendered in the 24 hours from Homix's proposal to the conclusion of the [deals]'. All the same, Neotel agreed to contract with Homix, and Homix was duly paid R41.04m (R36m plus VAT) on 27 February 2015, allegedly for its role on the network services contract.

The Neotel–Homix deal would provide one of the more important insights into the extent of state capture. This was because, in 2015, Neotel's auditors Deloitte raised concerns with the payments made to Neotel, which they suspected of being facilitation payments. They were not persuaded by Joshi's arguments to the contrary, or the intervention of Ashok Narayan, an employee of Sahara and one of the Guptas' most trusted lieutenants. Presumably attempting to avoid an adverse audit filing, Narayan wrote to Joshi setting out the services that had been performed by Homix and why it deserved its fee. Narayan claimed that Homix had provided negotiation 'levers' (and all sorts of other nonsense business jargon) to justify the payment. Narayan's intervention, when it became public, confirmed the Gupta enterprise's control and influence over Homix and its involvement in the corruption at Transnet.

Another intervention is also worth noting. By May 2015, Neotel's board was sufficiently moved to appoint Werksmans, the law firm, to investigate the transaction. Shortly thereafter, the chairman of Neotel's board received a letter from Siyabonga Gama, who had just been appointed GCEO of Transnet. Gama claimed that Transnet was 'comfortable and confident of the veracity of its procurement process'.

He also said that Transnet itself often used business consultants to 'navigate complex financial, technical and commercial aspects of the transaction', and then noted that Transnet was aware that Neotel had used Homix in the same way. The commission's response to this intervention was damning: 'In saying this about Homix, Mr Gama exposed his dishonesty. Homix was a shell company, with which Neotel was engaged in fraudulent and corrupt activity to the detriment of Transnet. Yet, Mr Gama essentially vouched for it.'

Unsurprisingly, the commission would find on this matter that there were reasonable grounds to believe that Neotel executives, including Joshi, Van der Merwe and Steven Whiley (who also approved payments), were engaged in corruption, and, through the payments made to Homix, 'participated in the conduct' of the Guptas' racketeering enterprise.

## The dodgy T-Systems IT contract

The commission's last substantive discussion about dodgy Transnet contracts focused on yet another IT contract, one where once again Molefe tried to advantage T-Systems. As we have seen, when Transnet privatised all its data and network services, T-Systems was allowed to buy Arivia, and was thereafter contracted to provide the services Arivia used to supply. These included the provision of various IT data services, equipment rental and maintenance of Transnet's primary data centres. Transnet awarded T-Systems a contract for these services in January 2010. Despite repeated attempts to have the contracts reviewed or cancelled, T-Systems would eventually be granted five extensions on the 2010 contract running until 2019. T-Systems was paid R4.8bn in this period.

Although the commission does not look into all the repeated renewals that were given, T-Systems' remarkable fortune in retaining Transnet's business for so long must be seen in the light of its other relationships. In particular, in late 2014, after T-Systems was informed that it might lose its contract, it agreed to 'cede' some of its contract to Zestilor. This meant in effect that Zestilor would deliver the services and get paid. Zestilor was owned by Salim Essa's wife, and would be paid hundreds of millions of rand from this arrangement. Simultaneously, T-Systems agreed to enter into a supplier development agreement with Sechaba, another

Gupta enterprise company. The result was that Sechaba was paid to perform services for T-Systems in fulfilment of the Transnet contracts. Sechaba received over R300m from T-Systems between February 2015 and December 2017.

In 2015, Transnet instructed an Irish specialist, Gartner, to review the services provided by T-Systems. This led to a redrafting of the technical requirements and specifications, which, in turn, led Transnet to issue a new request for proposal on this transaction in November 2015. As it would eventually turn out, Transnet made such a mess of this process that T-Systems' contracts would have to be renewed many times until 8 March 2019.

In the first half of 2016, Transnet conducted its first phase evaluation of all the bidders who had put forward bids. The result was that seven bidders were found to have met the required technical standards. These included T-Systems, Ubuntu Technologies and Gijima Holdings.

In the middle of this evaluation process, Transnet appointed a group chief information officer (GCIO), who was responsible for Transnet's IT. Ms Makano Mosidi was appointed to the position and, as a result, the tender process came under her portfolio. By the time she joined, the evaluation process had reached an advanced stage (step 7 of phase 2, to be precise). By this stage, the bidders that remained had already been reviewed and found to have met the minimum requirements on all sorts of things. Most importantly – for reasons that will be become apparent shortly – they had all met the minimum technical, risk and financial requirements.

In June 2016, during this process, Mosidi, the new GCIO, received an email from Garry Pita. He recommended that Transnet should shortlist only two bidders: T-Systems and Ubuntu. Pita argued that they were the two cheapest bidders and had received the best scores so far. Mosidi, however, pushed back: she was worried that in these sorts of tenders, unforeseen events could lead to the withdrawal of bidders at a late stage. She advised shortlisting four bidders just in case.

Gama, for his part, disagreed with the suggestion: it was 'adialectic', he sniffily pronounced, 'to think negotiating with more will save more time and money'. Whatever was meant by this, Gama's response ensured that Transnet would thus only shortlist two bidders. Mosidi responded by pointing out that due diligence had not yet been done, and this could raise issues. This turned out to be remarkably prescient as, a month later, Ubuntu withdrew its bid. The result was that Gijima, which had previously been ranked third, moved into second place and was added to the two-company shortlist. It was now a straight shoot-out between T-Systems and Gijima.

Between July and August 2016 two processes ran simultaneously – a due diligence exercise and an evaluation of the best and final offers of Gijima and T-Systems. Gijima proved to be the best bidder on this ground: it offered the cheapest bid and was given a score of 99%. T-Systems was awarded a final score of 85.07%. At this point, it would seem that T-Systems was all out of luck.

However, following the due diligence, Pita and another senior Transnet executive prepared a memorandum that motivated for the appointment of T-Systems rather than Gijima. They argued that the due diligence process had revealed various risks inherent in Gijima's bid. These risks were also reviewed by the very snappily named Cross-Functional Evaluation Team (the technical boffins who reviewed the detail of contracts), who also believed that Gijima's bid presented risks.

In September 2016, Mosidi was presented with a full file of all of the evaluation material. But she was perturbed. She felt that it was very strange for risks in relation to Gijima to be raised at this late stage. Indeed, by this point, Gijima and T-Systems had already passed their technical evaluations, which is precisely why they were allowed to proceed to the best and final offer stage. Mosidi was called to a meeting at the Carlton Centre to conclude the process and confirm T-Systems as the preferred bidder. While Mosidi eventually signed the memorandum, she appended a note saying that she thought that the risks could be mitigated and that Gijima could deliver on the contract. Mosidi would, in addition, write a lengthy response to the various risk issues, which she gave to the executive manager in Gama's office.

At about the same time, on 5 October 2016, a letter started circulating within Transnet. It was signed by a group of 'Concerned and Proud Transnet Employees'. The contents of the letter strongly suggested that some of its authors were from the technical Cross-Functional Evaluation Team. The letter alleged, among other things, that the risks associated with Gijima had been manufactured to help T-Systems.

In October 2016, as this letter was doing the rounds, Mosidi met Gama at a hotel in Johannesburg where they discussed the tender. Mosidi claimed that Gama told her to get her facts straight, as getting in the way of a tender could be a 'life-endangering process'. She took this to be a threat. Gama, for his part, denied this, although he did say that he may have told her that interested parties might conduct surveillance on officials overseeing procurements. The commission itself was somewhat equivocal about this interaction, and made no outright finding as to which version it preferred.

Over the next few months, many engagements were held where the risks were discussed both with Gijima and internally. In February 2017, two memoranda were drafted, showing that there was still heavy contestation about the issue. One memorandum, written by Pita, who was then the GCFO, recommended T-Systems. The other, written by Mosidi, recommended Gijima. Gama then stepped in and told them to sort it out. Mosidi must have been very persuasive as, on 8 February 2017, Pita agreed to sign a memorandum recommending the appointment of Gijima.

The BADC, however, came to T-Systems' rescue. On 13 February 2017, the committee considered the recommendation. Stanley Shane, whose company had received R9m from the BEX–CNR kickbacks discussed above, chaired the meeting. The BADC rejected the recommendation to appoint Gijima and, instead, recommended to the board that T-Systems be appointed. The meeting was unedifying, to say the least. 'The transcript of the meeting discloses a degree of irrationality and adverse animus or bias against Gijima on the part of some members of the BADC.' Shane's interventions, the commission found, were particularly 'troubling', as was that of other members.

One member, Zainul Nagdee, illustrating a total lack of understanding of what was happening, complained that Gijima had been given too many chances to mitigate risks. My investigations for the commission revealed that Nagdee's company, Lechabile Technologies, which he operated with his son, was used to receive money from state capture-related contracts via the convoluted money-laundering network used by the Guptas. This suggested that Nagdee was either laundering money for the Guptas or was himself the beneficiary of state capture corruption.

Strikingly, when the High Court later reviewed this contract at the request of Transnet, it would also conclude that the conduct of the BADC was extraordinary; it wondered whether its decisions were driven by 'extraneous considerations'.

The BADC's recommendations were recorded in a memorandum sent by Gama and Pita to the board on 15 February 2017. This recommended the appointment of T-Systems for a period of five years with an option to extend for a further two. A week later, on 22 February 2017, the Transnet board agreed, and awarded the contract to T-Systems.

The following month, Gijima decided to kick up a stink. It appealed to the Transnet procurement ombudsman, who then referred it to the Treasury. In late July 2017, Treasury wrote to Transnet to confirm its conclusions: the contract should have been awarded to Gijima. Echoing the arguments of Mosidi, Treasury found that all the technical and risk issues should have been identified in the actual tender documents upfront.

Eventually, on 27 September 2017, the Transnet board decided to set aside the award to T-Systems. Transnet also referred the issue to the High Court, and asked that the court grant an order declaring the award to T-Systems null and void, and mandate the appointment of Gijima. On 28 December 2018, the High Court delivered a stinging judgment that confirmed that the award to T-Systems was unlawful.

In considering all this, the commission found that there was prima facie evidence that Shane and Nagdee, in particular, had favoured T-Systems and may thus have violated the PFMA. The commission, however, stopped short of declaring a reasonable basis to conclude that Gama, Shane or Nagdee was guilty of corruption – mostly because there was no direct evidence that they received gratification in connection with T-Systems. Nevertheless, the commission thought that their conduct would be of 'evidential value' (or, in layman's terms, worthy of note) in establishing whether they formed part of the Gupta enterprise.

## The other dodgy deals: ZPMC and Liebherr Cranes

Two further transactions took place at Transnet that benefited the Gupta enterprise. The commission did not specifically investigate the procurement processes behind them; as a result, it did not dedicate sections of its report to discuss them in any detail. I dealt with the two transactions – the purchase of cranes from ZPMC and Liebherr

Cranes – in my evidence before the commission. The commission commented that my evidence 'indicates that these transactions were tainted by corruption and contributed to the illegal flow of funds to the Gupta enterprise'.

The first contract was awarded to the Chinese company ZPMC, for which it was paid R877.81m. Importantly, ZPMC had entered into a business development agreement with JJ Trading in June 2011. JJ Trading, of course, was used to receive and distribute kickbacks from other loco deals. Documents found in the GuptaLeaks – transaction ledgers shared between key Gupta lietenants and Tony Gupta – recorded movements into and out of bank accounts operated by the Guptas in Dubai. The ledgers showed that between 22 December 2011 and 30 January 2014 these Dubai companies were paid at least $3,987,103 (about R34m) by ZPMC.

The second contract was placed with Liebherr on 17 February 2014. Transnet paid Liebherr R841.1m under the contract. The Dubai ledgers disclosed in the GuptaLeaks showed that Liebherr paid $3,232,430.88 to a Gupta company in Dubai called Accurate Investments. The payments were made between 22 July 2013 and May 2014, and were thereafter laundered to a range of other Gupta companies. The commission confirmed that Accurate Investments was nothing more than a shell used to receive money for the Guptas. The commission commented:

> It is difficult to conceive of any legitimate payments that could have been made by Liebherr to a 'sales agent' in respect of a cranes contract that ought to have been awarded by a fair, competitive and transparent process in accordance with the requirements of Section 217 of the Constitution. If there was any legitimate reason for these payments to Accurate Investments as a 'sales agent', Liebherr could have been expected to place evidence before the commission but it declined to do so.

# RECOMMENDATIONS

| The loco kickbacks | |
|---|---|
| Person/Companies | Should be further investigated for potential: |
| Salim Essa, Regiments Asia, Tequesta Group, JJ Trading FZE, Century General Trading FZE, 'relevant functionaries' of CSR Zhuzhou Electric Locomotives, CNR and CRRC | Corruption under PRECCA<br><br>Racketeering and offences related to proceeds of unlawful activities under POCA |
| Regiments contracts with Transnet as supplier development partner, incl. fees paid to Essa and Moodley companies | |
| Regiments Capital, Eric Wood, Salim Essa (and any company controlled by him), Kuben Moodley (and any company controlled by him) and Anoj Singh | Fraud and corruption under PRECCA<br><br>Racketeering and offences related to proceeds of unlawful activities under POCA |
| Receipt of gratification by individuals (the cash bribes) | |
| Brian Molefe, Anoj Singh, Siyabonga Gama, Garry Pita and Thamsanqa Jiyane | Corruption under PRECCA<br><br>Racketeering and offences related to proceeds of unlawful activities under POCA |
| Cash bribes at Three Rivers Lodge | |
| Brian Molefe and Anoj Singh | Corruption under PRECCA |
| Singh's Dubai travel paid for by Guptas | |
| Anoj Singh | Corruption under PRECCA |

| Gama's stay at Oberoi Hotel (Dubai) paid for by Guptas | |
|---|---|
| Siyabonga Gama | Corruption under PRECCA |
| Reinstatement of Siyabonga Gama | |
| Board members of Transnet as of 23 February 2011 | Violations of the Companies Act with a view to recover R17m paid to Gama |
| Any relevant person | Fraud in relation to payment of R1.39m on 16 April 2105 by Transnet to Langa Attorneys |
| Jacob Zuma, Malusi Gigaba, Mafika Mkwanazi | Corruption under PRECCA and/or racketeering under POCA |
| GNS/Abalozi contract | |
| Brian Molefe | Violation of PFMA |
| 95 locos contract | |
| Brian Molefe and Siyabonga Gama | Violation of PFMA and/or racketeering and/or offences related to proceeds of unlawful activities under POCA |
| Transnet board in place at time of LSA between Transnet and CSR | Violation of PFMA |
| 100 locos contract | |
| Brian Molefe, Anoj Singh, Thamsanqa Jiyane, Siyabonga Gama | Violation of PFMA for failing to disclose material information to the board |

| | |
|---|---|
| *Any relevant Transnet official* | *Violation of PFMA for advance payments to CSR* |
| *Any member of board or Transnet official* | *Violation of PFMA for condoning R740m price increase* |

| *1,064 locos contracts* ||
|---|---|
| *Any official of Transnet* | *Violation of PFMA for deviating from instruction note of National Treasury and PPPFA regulations* |
| *Brian Molefe, Anoj Singh and Siyabonga Gama* | *Fraud and/or violation of PFMA in relation to misstatement of estimated total cost* |
| *Anoj Singh* | *Fraud in relation to email to Malusi Gigaba related to misstatement of estimated total cost* |
| *Any official of Transnet* | *Violation of PFMA for adjusting prices of CSR in relation to Transnet Engineering* |
| *Anoj Singh and Thamsanqa Jiyane* | *Violation of PFMA in relation to approval of batch pricing* |
| *Any member of Transnet negotiating team* | *Corruption under PRECCA or violation of PFMA in relation to excessive advance payments to CNR and CSR* |
| *Anoj Singh* | *Fraud in relation to mispresentation to board regarding net present value* |
| *Any member of board and/or Transnet official* | *Violation of PFMA by agreeing to price increase of locos* |

| CNR–BEX relocation contract | |
|---|---|
| *Majority directors of CNRRSA, BEX, Mark Shaw, Integrated Capital Management, Confident Concepts and any associated people* | *Corruption under PRECCA; racketeering and offences related to proceeds of unlawful activities under POCA* |
| **Bombardier relocation contract** | |
| *Siyabonga Gama and Ravi Nair and members of Transnet Negotiating Team* | *Violation of PFMA by agreeing to fees of R1.2bn for relocation to Durban without good reason* |
| **The financial advisors** | |
| *Brian Molefe, Anoj Singh, Eric Wood, Regiments and any associated person* | *Corruption under PRECCA, and racketeering and offences related to proceeds of unlawful activities under POCA, and violation of PFMA in relation to R79.23m paid by Transnet to Regiments on 30 April 2014* |
| *Siyabonga Gama* | *Violation of PFMA for contracting with Nkonki for R500m* |
| *Anoj Singh* | *Violation of PFMA in relation to recommending Regiments' proposals in relation to loan interest rate calculations* |
| *Anoj Singh* | *Violation of PFMA in relation to recommendation to board to approve $1.5bn CDB loan* |

| | |
|---|---|
| *Siyabonga Gama, Anoj Singh, Regiments, Eric Wood, Kuben Moodley, Albatime and Sahara Computers* | *Corruption under PRECCA, and racketeering and offences related to proceeds of unlawful activities under POCA, and violations of the PFMA in relation to payment of success fee of R189.24m to Regiments, which was on-paid in part to Albatime and thereafter to Sahara Computers* |
| *Siyabonga Gama, Phatelo Ramosebudi, Garry Pita, Eric Wood, Salim Essa, Trillian and Albatime* | *Corruption under PRECCA, and racketeering and offences related to proceeds of unlawful activities under POCA in relation to payment of R93.84m to Trillian and on-payment to Albatime in amount of R78.48m* |
| *Phetolo Ramosebudi and Eric Wood* | *Corruption under PRECCA, and racketeering and offences related to proceeds of unlawful activities under POCA in relation to discount or reduction on price payable for Range Rover Sport vehicle* |
| *Phetolo Ramosebudi, Garry Pita, Regiments Capital, Regiments Fund Managers, Eric Wood, Stanley Shane and any other associated person* | *Corruption under PRECCA, and racketeering and offences related to proceeds of unlawful activities under POCA, and violations of PFMA in relation to payments to Regiments for interest rate, cross-currency swaps and credit default swaps* |

| Manganese Expansion Project | |
|---|---|
| *Nalen Padayachee and Dave Reddy* | *Corruption under PRECCA for attempting to become SDP suppliers to Hatch* |
| *Salim Essa and Anoj Singh* | *Corruption under PRECCA, and racketeering under POCA for attempt to secure inducement to influence contract award to Hatch* |
| Neotel and Homix | |
| *Taufique Khan, Homix, Neotel, François van der Merwe* | *Corruption under PRECCA, and racketeering and offences related to proceeds of unlawful activities under POCA regarding payment of R34m to Homix by Neotel* |
| *Neotel, Sunil Joshi, François van der Merwe, Taufique Khan, Homix and any other associated person* | *Corruption under PRECCA, and racketeering and offences related to proceeds of unlawful activities under POCA regarding payment of R41.04m to Homix and the promise of a further payment of R25m by Neotel* |
| T-Systems' IT contracts | |
| *Stanley Shane and Zainul Nagdee* | *Violation of PFMA by unjustifiably favouring T-Systems on spurious grounds* |

# Eskom

THE CAPTURE OF ESKOM was one of the more complete and incontrovertible cases of state capture. Following their success in manipulating every tender in sight at Transnet, Brian Molefe and Anoj Singh were sent to Eskom to continue in this vein. They were supported by a board that was so packed with Gupta associates it was almost farcical. The result was a slew of dodgy contracts that poured billions of rand into the bank accounts and cash-carrying hold-alls of the Gupta enterprise – all of which contributed to the grand failure of Eskom and its adoption of widespread load-shedding and power cuts that continue to blight the lives of all South Africans.

## Eskom's 2014 board

The Gupta enterprise's capture of Eskom started in at least 2012. As I'll show in much more detail later, Eskom was a major sponsor of the lamentable TNA business breakfasts broadcast on SABC2, which earned the Gupta enterprise close to R2m per episode. The sponsorships were driven and facilitated by two Eskom CEOs, Brian Dames and Collin Matjila.

But the capture of Eskom was supercharged in 2014, facilitated, in large part, by the Guptas' influence at the Department of Public Enterprises (DPE). The commission notes that, between 2010 and April 2014, Malusi Gigaba served as the Minister of Public Enterprsies. Evidence led by his ex-wife, which the commission found credible, suggested that Gigaba became increasingly wary of the Guptas towards the end of his period as minister, and started screening and avoiding their calls.

In April 2014, Gigaba was removed and reappointed as the Minister of Home Affairs: a definite demotion in terms of prestige and clout. Gigaba was replaced by Lynne Brown. The commission noted that, if the Guptas had enough power and influence to get Zuma to do all sorts of things, it was reasonable to believe that they had the power to influence Zuma's appointment of Brown. And, indeed, Brown was a 'Gupta minister', according to the commission, who acted in their interest on a number of occasions, and appointed members to the boards of SAA, Transnet and Denel that were clearly unsuited for the role and were linked to the Guptas or other corruption scandals.

Cell phone records show that between November 2014 and March 2015 Lynne Brown was in regular contact with Salim Essa, the Guptas' main lieutenant. It was during this period – in December 2014 – that Brown appointed a new board to oversee the management of Eskom. Most of the appointees had never served on a board before; many claimed to have applied for the position because they had seen public advertisements. The commission, however, showed that the primary qualification of the majority of the 2014 board intake was their connection to the Gupta enterprise. I have provided, in the accompanying table, a summary of the commission's evidence about these connections.

Remarkably, of the 2014 board intake (and the two board members appointed in March 2015), only two did not have connections of some kind to the Guptas, according to the commission. These two directors were Pat Naidoo and Norman Baloyi. Baloyi was singled out by the commission as the only member of Eskom's 2014 board who resisted the dismissal of four key Eskom executives – part of the first phase of the capture of Eskom.

| Board member appointed in December 2014 | Connection to Guptas and other material facts |
|---|---|
| Nazia Carim (11 December 2014 – 1 July 2016) | Wife of Salim Essa's cousin. No previous experience of serving on a board. Communicated six times with Tony Gupta and twenty times with Salim Essa between May 2012 and 30 June 2017. She claimed that her calls with Essa were to do with other matters, including seeking legal advice for Duduzane Zuma. |
| Mariam Cassim (13 March 2015 – 2017) | Cellphone records show that Cassim had ten calls with Tony Gupta and Ajay Gupta between March 2015 and December 2015. Cassim did not testify before the commission, but deposed an affidavit saying the calls were merely for networking purposes to congratulate them on various business successes. The commission rejected this version as implausible, as her calls were timed with key developments in the capture of Eskom. |
| Romeo Khumalo (11 December 2014 – 12 April 2016) | Khumalo was the CEO of Vodacom at the time. He shared a directorship in Ujiri Technologies with Salim Essa. Between 11 January 2013 and 15 February 2016, Khumalo spoke on his cell phone with Tony Gupta 58 times, with Essa 80 times, and Atul Gupta four times. The commission accused Khumalo of doing everything in his power to avoid giving evidence. |

| Board member appointed in December 2014 | Connection to Guptas and other material facts |
|---|---|
| Zethemba Khoza (11 December 2014 – 19 January 2018) | Cellphone records show that Khoza communicated with Essa six times between 28 March 2015 and 5 November 2016, and twice with Tony Gupta. |
| Venete Jarlene Klein (11 December 2014 to 2017) | Klein owned a company called Centuria 400 (Pty) Limited. In my report to the commission following my money trail investigation, I found that Centuria had been paid R150,000 by a company called Saamed Bullion, which was a money-laundering entity used by the Guptas to move state capture money abroad. Klein denied any knowledge of the links between Saamed Bullion and the Guptas. |
| Giovanni Michele Lombardi (25 May 2015 – 19 January 2018) | Appointed without any shortlisting process. His CV was sent to Essa's notorious 'Business Man' email address prior to his appointment, suggesting he was vetted by Essa. However, there was no direct evidence that he was a Gupta plant. |
| Chwayita Mabude (June 2011 – 23 June 2017) | Mabude was the director of Innova Management Solutions, which was actually managed by the Gupta enterprise. Innova was paid funds by the Free State government, which was then laundered to Gupta enterprise companies in South Africa and Dubai. |

| Board member appointed in December 2014 | Connection to Guptas and other material facts |
| --- | --- |
| Viroshni Naidoo (11 December 2014 – 2017) | Wife of Kuben Moodley. She also served as the part-time advisor to Minister Zwane. In declarations to the board in February 2016 and May 2016, she declared income from Albatime, which was controlled by Moodley. This was extraordinary – as I show below, during this exact time, Albatime was used by the Guptas to launder state capture funds to buy Optimum coal mine, which was also funded by irregular payments made by Eskom. She had no previous experience of serving on a board of an SOE. |
| Dr Ben Ngubane (11 December 2014 – 12 June 2017) | Served as a director in the company Gade Oil and Gas, of which Salim Essa was a prior director. At Eskom, the commission found that he communicated with Essa on at least two occasions through the infamous 'Business Man' email address. |
| Mark Vivian Pamensky (11 December 2014 – 25 November 2016) | Pamensky was a director in the Gupta flagship companies Oakbay Resources and Shiva Uranium. He was also a director of Yellow Star Trading (alongside Salim Essa) and BIT Information Technology (of which Kuben Moodley was a prior director). During period between 31 January 2008 and 21 June 2017 he communicated 1,169 times with Essa, 106 times with Atul Gupa, 43 times with Tony Gupta, and twice with Duduzane Zuma. Pamensky attended the infamous Sun City wedding. |

| Board member appointed in December 2014 | Connection to Guptas and other material facts |
|---|---|
| Zola Tsotsi (board chairperson, 2011 to December 2014 and again from December 2014 to March 2015) | Tsotsi testified that during his prior stint as Eskom board chair, he was summoned three times to Saxonwold and asked to assist the Guptas. He claimed he did not. The commission would find that he had presented a list of people to serve on various Eskom board subcommittees to Lynne Brown; this list had been sent to him by Salim Essa. However, Tsotsi was eventually removed seemingly at the behest of the Guptas for his refusal to assist them with sufficient alacrity. |

## The dismissal of the four executives

On 11 March 2015, the Eskom board suspended three executives; the following day, the same happened to a fourth. The four executives were Tshediso Matona (the group CEO, who had served only five months in the role), Ms Tsholofelo Molefe (Financial Director), Dan Marokane (Group Executive: Group Capital) and Matshela Koko (Group Executive: Technology and Commercial). The commission found that these suspensions were part of a plan to replace non-compliant executives who may have resisted state capture. The only exception was Matshela Koko, who was reappointed after a period of time. The commission would find that Koko was central to a number of state capture cases; it also suggested that Koko's suspension was a ruse designed to 'ensure that, when later, the Guptas used him, there would be no suspicion of his association with the Guptas'.

The commission dated the beginning of the plan to 25 February 2015. Ms Matsietsi Mokholo testified before the commission; she was acting director general of the DPE at the time. According to her, Jacob Zuma called her, explaining that he had tried and failed to reach Lynne Brown, told her that, as acting DG, she must ensure that the 2014 board's first meeting, due the next day, was postponed. She called Zola Tsotsi, the board chair, who also received a phone call from Zuma. Tsotsi admitted that it was on this basis that the meeting was suspended.

The commission found that Zuma had purposely and unlawfully interfered in the operation of the Eskom board: the President simply did not have the power to determine when the board could or couldn't meet. Most importantly, the commission found that Zuma was a 'critical player' in a plan by the Guptas to delay the meeting to make possible the replacement of Zola Tsotsi as board chair with Dr Ben Ngubane, who it was believed would be more pliant than Tsotsi.

The board meeting was ultimately postponed until 9 March 2015, with a second held two days later. Much happened in this period. On 6 March 2015, SAA board chairperson Dudu Myeni held a meeting with Nick Linnell. As I'll discuss later, Myeni was the ghastly chair of SAA who was closely connected to Zuma. During her period at SAA, Linnell provided advice and conducted a 'review' of the entity. Linnell testified before the commission that Myeni told him that he needed to travel urgently to Pretoria to meet Zuma.

Linnell and Myeni duly travelled to Zuma's official residence on the same day, where they met. She told him that Zuma, who incidentally failed to turn up at the meeting, was concerned about the performance of Eskom, and wanted an in-depth investigation into its running. Myeni had recommended Linnell. A meeting with Zuma was eventually convened on 8 March 2015, attended by Linnell, Myeni and Zola Tsotsi. Myeni explained to the meeting that Linnell had led an inquiry at SAA and she wanted him to do the same at Eskom. Tsotsi testified before the commission that Myeni made it clear that, in order for the investigation to take place unhindered, Eskom would need to suspend certain key executives whose conduct would form part of the investigation.

Both Linnell and Tsotsi testified that Zuma (JZ) eventually joined the second half of the meeting. And while he did not seem particularly engaged, it was clear he was aware of its purpose. Tsotsi recalled that JZ told him to sound out the board; Linnell recalled that JZ told them all 'to go and do it'. Linnell was a quick worker: that evening, he started drafting resolutions and pre-suspension memos, which he sent to a law firm to vet, and to Tsotsi.

The following day, 9 March 2015, the board convened for its first meeting. Tsotsi explained to the board that JZ had met with him and directed that an inquiry be held into Eskom. The board members were concerned that Tsotsi was not being truthful, and complained they were being rushed into a decision. They requested that they hear from the minister, Lynne Brown. A meeting was set down for this purpose two days later, on 11 March.

Prior to the 11 March meeting, a number of extraordinary interactions took place. On 10 March 2015, Matshela Koko called three Eskom officials and employees: Suzanne Daniels, an Eskom legal chief who worked closely with Koko, Abram Masongo and Ms Nonkululeko Dlamini. Koko asked that all three attend a meeting with him at Melrose Arch. Dlamini did not attend, as her direct boss, Tsholofelo Molefe (who was shortly to be suspended), would not release her.

Both Daniels and Masongo testified that they met with Koko at an office at Melrose Arch. They were joined by Salim Essa. During the meetings, Essa and Koko explained that the board would shortly suspend certain executives, including Koko himself. Koko was, apparently, unruffled by the mention of his name in this regard. Masango was told that three of the executives would not be allowed to return, while Koko himself would eventually get a reprieve. Masango testified that Koko told Salim Essa during the meeting that Masango could be appointed to act in the position of group CEO, thereby filling one of the suspended positions. Masango would later identify the office in which they met at Melrose Arch during a site walk-through: it was the office of Trillian, Essa's and Eric Wood's state capture vehicle.

Dlamini, after explaining that she could not meet at Melrose Arch during the day, testified that she met Koko that evening at a KFC or McDonald's outlet. Koko informed her about the forthcoming suspensions, and asked her to send her CV, so that she could be considered for an acting position.

Koko, of course, later denied the substance of all the meetings. The commission was totally unconvinced. Not only would it be remarkable that three individuals separately testified to the same sort of interaction, but all these versions were further corroborated by the evidence of witnesses with whom they met and discussed matters on the same day. Koko's denials were thus dismissed as a 'fabrication' by the commission.

The board met again on 11 March 2015. Matona testified that he was presenting a turn-around strategy when he was interrupted by the arrival of Minister Lynne Brown. Shortly thereafter, the board decided to approve the suspension of the four executives. Notably, Brown included suspending Tsholofelo Molefe, a move that had only been previously discussed by Essa. The commission believed that Brown was thus fulfilling a plan hatched and directed by Essa. The four executives were issued with suspension letters the same day.

As Koko had predicted in his meeting with Masongo, three of the executives never returned to Eskom. Matona originally lodged a dispute with the CCMA, but he was then called to a meeting with JZ. Matona testified that JZ apologised, saying that he had 'got in the middle of a spaghetti' at Eskom, but that he was still valued. JZ asked Matona to continue working in government, and he was duly appointed the head of the secretariat of the National Planning Commission.

Tsholofelo Molefe and Dan Marokane received no such niceties. Despite their repeated attempts to meet with the board, they were rebuffed or, when they did meet with board representatives, were effectively told they were no longer welcome. Ultimately Matona, Molefe and Marokane left Eskom after being granted significant exit packages. Matona was paid R6m, plus contributions to the Government Employees Pension fund which would give him ten years' worth of employment to his pension figure. Marokane was paid R6,237,634.44, plus unspecified pension earnings. Molefe was paid R8,178,362.86, again with additional unspecified pension earnings.

And there was one more kicker: the in-depth investigation into Eskom, which had supposedly necessitated the suspension of the executives in the first place, was to be conducted by the law firm Dentons. But, six weeks after it received the instruction, in late April or early May 2015, Dentons was told to stop its investigation. This was prior to Molefe being removed from Eskom. No in-depth investigation was ever concluded.

## Completing the takeover: Removing Tsotsi and Baloyi, welcoming Molefe and Singh

Zola Tsotsi would not survive much longer, either. Tsotsi testified that he believed he was in the cross hairs of Lynne Brown from at least February 2015. The day before the State of the Nation address, Tsotsi was called to a meeting with Brown where she accused him of interfering in management decisions. A few hours later, he was summoned to meet Tony Gupta in Constantia, Cape Town. Tsotsi claimed that Tony Gupta accused him of being insufficiently supportive of Gupta projects, and threatened that he could ensure his removal.

Almost immediately after the suspensions were completed, board members began criticising Tsotsi. Ironically, members accused Tsotsi of failing to consult them about the intended inquiry and the appointment of Nick Linnell, despite having frequently sought Linnell's advice on the suspension of the four executives.

Over the next two weeks, Tsotsi met with the board on a number of occasions, and was informed it had lost confidence in his chairmanship. Tsotsi eventually succumbed to pressure and resigned on 30 March 2015. The commission found that the charges levelled against him at the time were largely bogus. Tsotsi was replaced by Ben Ngubane as acting chairperson.

The commission's investigations revealed that the Guptas knew about Tsotsi's removal in advance, and helped the process along. On 19 March 2015, the board was due to meet Tsotsi and ask him to step down. Prior to this meeting, Nazeem Howa sent Salim Essa a draft copy of a board statement announcing Tsotsi's removal – before any decision had even been made by the board. The statement was not released then, as Tsotsi pushed back, but a modified version of the statement was eventually published when Tsotsi jumped ship.

Another target was Norman Baloyi. As noted above, Baloyi was one of the December 2014 intake. However, unlike the rest, he had no notable connections to the Guptas. He was also the only board member to question the suspension of the four executives, as well as raise queries about the charges against Tsotsi. Baloyi had also asked why one notable high-value tender – a dodgy contract award to T-Systems, which was employing Gupta companies as its partners – did not come to the board for approval. Baloyi was removed by Lynne Brown in April 2015, only a few weeks after Tsotsi left.

Just less than a month after the four executives were suspended, Lynne Brown announced that the man who had led Transnet to the benefit of the Gupta enterprise would now take over Eskom: Brian

Molefe. Molefe was seconded from Transnet to Eskom as acting group CEO on 20 April 2015. He was appointed in the position full-time in October 2015. Soon after his appointment in April 2015, he made it known that he wanted to be joined by his right-hand man at Transnet, Anoj Singh. Singh duly transferred to Eskom at some point in July or August 2015 (the commission noted that the documentation was ambiguous about the exact date this was actually confirmed). Singh was appointed Eskom's chief financial officer.

The commission found that Molefe's and Singh's appointments completed the capture of all key positions at Eskom and of the governance structures around it. Jacob Zuma, it commented, did what the Guptas wanted. So too did Minister Lynne Brown. The board was largely constituted of people with connections to the Guptas. And now the organisation's two most powerful executive positions would be filled by Molefe and Singh, who had already proved their relentless drive to fix contracts to the benefit of the Guptas. As the commission lamented: 'South Africans thought that the ANC government was in control of Eskom but it was not. It had relinquished control to the Guptas and those people the Guptas wanted. The ANC and the ANC government should be ashamed this happened on its watch.'

## The acquisition of Optimum coal mine

Molefe's arrival was timed just right for him to guide and ensure one of the most infamous examples of state capture: the purchase of Optimum Coal Holdings (and Optimum coal mine) from Glencore. This story is a little complicated; but the key takeaways are simple. First, Glencore was put under huge pressure by Eskom and other Gupta associates to sell the mine. Second, Eskom went out of its way to pay Tegeta, the entity that bought Optimum, a highly irregular 'prepayment' to help Tegeta when it lacked funds to complete the purchase. Finally, an examination of the flow of funds used to buy Optimum shows that most the money used by Tegeta to buy the mine emanated from state capture.

The Optimum story had a long background. In January 1993, Eskom signed a coal supply agreement with a company called the Trans-Natal Coal Corporation and Trans-Natal Colliery. These would eventually be renamed Optimum. The companies would supply Eskom with coal to power the Hendrina power station. The mines were important to Eskom as a railway had been built that allowed the mined coal to be delivered directly to Hendrina nearby. After various changes of name and buyouts, Glencore, the massive energy and resource multinational, bought Optimum Coal Holdings (OCH), which owned the renamed Optimum Coal Mining (OCM). Glencore completed its acquisition by March 2012.

Glencore faced a serious problem. By the time the mine was bought, the coal seam was 30 kilometres from where it was first mined. This required a hugely long conveyor belt to carry the coal, but as a result the coal dropped and tumbled repeatedly, breaking into smaller pieces. The outcome was that the coal produced in 2012 was of very different quality from that produced in 1993. The original 1993 agreement allowed Eskom to levy fines for failure to meet quality requirements, while the various clauses about increases in costs underestimated the long-term cost requirements of the mine. In simple terms, by 2013 Eskom was paying Optimum less than it was costing Optimum to mine and deliver the coal. By July 2013, Optimum was losing R150/tonne, equivalent to R829m per year.

Optimum thus requested Eskom to enter into what were called hardship negotiations that would allow the original contract to be renegotiated to keep OCM a going concern. This led to a series of agreements and compromises but, most importantly, by early 2015 it looked as if Eskom and Optimum were on the way to negotiating a mutually suitable settlement. In March, an expert report recommended the price paid by Eskom be increased to a level that would allow Optimum to recoup its costs; in mid-April, an Executive Procurement Committee approved the settlement and cost increase in principle.

Molefe was appointed the GCEO of Eskom on 20 April 2015, five days after this meeting. His appointment changed everything. On 23 April 2015, a mere three days later, the board was asked to consider the March 2015 settlement agreement. It simply resolved to defer the matter entirely to Molefe's control.

Molefe took an extremely hard line. He told Glencore that he would not renegotiate the contract. On 10 June 2015, he sent a letter to OCM setting out his position. He would hold OCM to the original 1993 agreement, even if it led to OCM losing money. He would also hold OCM liable for a massive R2.17bn penalty, which he said was due immediately. This penalty was hugely controversial: the original 1993 agreement allowed Eskom to levy penalties for quality or delivery failures. But Eskom's own lawyers were not entirely sure that the penalties were being correctly calculated. In any event, by demanding the penalty be paid immediately, Molefe was putting huge pressure on OCM and its survivability. When Molefe appeared before the commission, he provided numerous reasons for why he adopted this hard-line stance. The commission, in brief, found most of them were not credible.

In the immediate wake of Molefe's hard-line stance, the Guptas started making their moves. On 1 July 2015, KPMG approached Glencore to inform the company that there was an undisclosed buyer interested in OCM. Glencore objected to the buyer's identity being hidden, and it was duly revealed that the approach was being made by the Gupta flagship, Oakbay. By 25 July 2015, Oakbay concluded a non-disclosure agreement with Glencore/OCM so that it could get access to more information.

Bang in the middle of all this, on 16 July 2015, Eskom issued OCM with a demand that the R2.17bn penalties be settled immediately. Partially as a result, by August 2015, the writing was on the wall, and OCM and OCH went into business rescue – basically, they handed control over to specialists who would either dispose of assets to settle debt or guide the company to stability.

Further pressure was placed, or was attempted to be placed, on Glencore and OCM. In September 2015, Molefe and Ngubane met with the Minister of Mineral Resources, Ngoako Ramatlhodi. Ramatlhodi testified that Molefe and Ngubane pressed him to suspend all Glencore's mining licences, and that when he asked for time to consider, Ngubane became angry and said he would brief JZ. Molefe and Ngubane denied this recollection; but the commission believed Ramatlhodi. Not long after, on 22 September 2015, Ramatlhodi was summoned to meet JZ in Pretoria. He was informed that he was to be moved to the Department of Public Enterprises and out of the Department of Mineral Resources (DMR).

Ramatlhodi was replaced with Mosebenzi Zwane, whom the commission characterised as 'a Gupta minister'. Indeed, his connections and involvements with the Guptas are legion, as this book shows. Zwane, for example, was involved in the award of the Vrede dairy farm contract to Estina, which was then looted by the Guptas. He would also eventually lead the so-called Inter-Ministerial Committee to investigate the closure of the Guptas' bank accounts, which amounted to little more than an attempt to intimidate South Africa's banks for the Guptas' benefit. When Zwane went over to the DMR, he appointed advisors with impeccable Gupta pedigrees, including Kuben Moodley and Malcolm Mabaso. Zwane would end up playing a role of his own in the Optimum coal mine affair, as we'll see below.

Following Ramatlhodi's dismissal, negotiations between Oakbay and OCM resumed, although other suitors now began expressing interest. Molefe, the commission found, did the best he could to scare them off. One interested party, Phembani Group, was told by Molefe that Eskom would not consent to them buying OCM unless Phembani paid the full R2.17bn in penalties. This was particularly remarkable in the light of the fact that, when Tegeta eventually did take over OCH, these penalties were swiftly reduced to R500m, of which Tegeta ultimately ended up paying about R120m.

On 12 November 2015, the business rescue practitioners and Oakbay/Tegeta signed a term sheet – basically a skeleton agreement – that cleared the way for Tegeta to acquire Optimum. The deal looked increasingly certain. But then, during November 2015, Clinton Ephron, a director of OCM and OCH and CEO of Glencore's South African coal business, received a call to attend a meeting with an official from the DMR by the name of Joel Raphela. The meeting was duly held on 24 November at Melrose Arch. It was attended by Raphela, Matshela Koko and representatives of both Oakbay/ Tegeta and OCM/Glencore. Koko informed the assembled meeting that Eskom would now only consent to the deal being concluded – Eskom had potential veto power – if OCH sold *all* its assets to Tegeta, and not just OCM. This included the extremely valuable Richards Bay coal terminal and another coal mine, Koornfontein.

On the same day, a representative of Zwane's office placed a call with Ivan Glasenberg, the global CEO of Glencore. Glasenberg was told that Zwane would be visiting Switzerland and wanted to meet him. The meeting was duly scheduled for 1 December 2015.

A day after the meeting and phone call, Ajay Gupta contacted Ephron to make an offer of R1bn to buy OCH. The next day, Ephron informed Ajay Gupta that this was not enough as it would not settle OCH's debts with South African banks. On the same day that Ajay Gupta was refused, the Department of Mineral Resources issued instructions to Glencore and OCM to stop all mining activities.

David Msiza, a chief inspector at DMR, testified before the commission that the instruction to shut down Glencore's mining operations came from Malcolm Mabaso, Zwane's advisor, who claimed that there were health and safety concerns. Msiza recalled that, the following week, Kuben Moodley and Mabaso, Zwane's advisors, had told him that they wanted to be involved in the way the inspections would be conducted, and that Zwane would be the person to decide if the injunctions were lifted. Zwane, unsurprisingly, denied this account, but he was hardly helped in his attempt to deny pressuring Glencore if one considers his later conduct in Switzerland. The injunctions on Glencore would only be lifted on 9 December.

Matters then gathered further pace. On 1 December 2015, while Glencore's licences were suspended, Matshela Koko hosted a meeting at Eskom with the business rescue practitioners and two representatives of OCH, including Clinton Ephron. Koko was informed by Ephron that Glencore, presumably responding to the pressure placed on it by the suspension of its mining licences, had decided to take OCH out of business rescue. Glencore would also honour all the original Eskom contracts until 2018, despite this entailing a loss to Glencore. Koko initially responded by saying he was satisfied as Eskom would continue to buy coal at a favourable rate with no threat to the security of the supply.

At the same time as this meeting, Mosebenzi Zwane met Ivan Glasenberg in Switzerland. Zwane used the meeting to urge Glencore to sell OCH to the Guptas. Zwane claimed before the commission that he did so because he was worried that if OCH closed, there would be extensive job losses. But this simply made no sense: by that time, Glencore had decided to keep OCH open and subsidise it so it could honour its agreements with Eskom. Glasenberg claimed that he informed Zwane of this fact at the meeting.

After this meeting, Glasenberg contacted Ephron, who was just exiting the Koko meeting and took the call in the Eskom parking lot. Glasenberg told Ephron that Zwane had indicated that Tony Gupta wanted to meet Glasenberg in Switzerland the following day, and wanted Ephron there. Ephron jumped on a plane.

The meeting was attended by Zwane, Salim Essa, Tony Gupta, Glasenberg and Ephron. Zwane attended the first half of the meeting, seemingly so that he could give his imprimatur of support for the Guptas. Notably, Zwane introduced Essa as one of his advisors. Following this intervention, Zwane departed, and the remaining parties hammered out a deal: Glencore would sell OCH for R2.15bn, with Glencore agreeing to put in additional funds to settle outstanding debt. At the commission Zwane again defended his decision to attend the 2 December meeting, and bat for the Guptas, on the basis that he was worried about job losses. The commission disagreed: 'on the probabilities', it found, 'he sought to assist the Guptas'.

After the meeting in Switzerland, Zwane boarded a private jet with the Guptas to travel to India. Zwane claimed that he had a throat issue that required specialist treatment, and that the Guptas recommended a good Indian doctor. Records obtained by the commission showed that, following his Indian sojourn, he travelled with the Guptas to Muscat, the capital of Oman, where the Guptas paid for his chauffeurred 7-series BMW. The commission found that Zwane's flight from Delhi to Muscat had been charged to the Guptas.

By 10 December 2015, the pressure on Glencore had paid off: Tegeta entered into a sales agreement to purchase all OCH's assets. Now all the Guptas had to do was find the money.

But, before we move on to this, one further thing should be noted. The commission was particularly perturbed by the fact that, during the negotiation process, Mark Pamensky, Eskom's board member who also served as a director of Oakbay, reached out to Ajay Gupta to provide him with unsolicited advice about negotiation strategy. Pamensky told him that if he was required in Dubai at any moment, he would be there in a flash. And while the commission found that Pamensky did not necessarily violate any laws in doing so, it was indicative of both Pamensky's own attitude to his job at Eskom and the extent to which the Eskom board was concerned with the Guptas' financial welfare.

## The R1.68bn guarantee

The agreement to buy the mine was subject to what were called suspensive conditions: in non-legalese, these are things that have to be done before the contract takes full effect. In this case, the sale was reliant on a number of things, including approval from Eskom and the Department of Mineral Resources. It also required payment of the full amount by a certain date. But, most importantly, approval for the transaction had to be given by the so-called consortium banks. These were the banks that held OCH's debt. They had to be satisfied that the new owner of OCH would have the funds and wherewithal to pay back the debt or continue to service it on an ongoing basis.

By the time the contract was signed, the Guptas didn't have all the cash they needed to pay the final sales price, and they didn't have the capital to hand which they could present to the banks to convince them that they could repay the debt. What the Guptas thus needed – and would be given by means of multiple irregularities – was some sort of guarantee from a credible backer (like Eskom) that Tegeta would have access to capital to settle the purchase price and the debt.

Luckily for the Guptas, they could rely on helpful Eskom officials to fix this for them – before Tegeta had even signed the final contract to buy OCH. On 4 December 2015, Koko instructed Suzanne Daniels to write a letter to the director general of the DMR for help. The letter implied that there was a risk of OCM being liquidated, which was untrue. The DG at DMR at the time, Dr Thibedi Ramontja, received a letter asking for his signature, which he claimed came from Zwane's office. The letter responded to the 'urgent' liquidation issue by promising to rapidly ensure the transfer of mining licences. Most importantly, the letter recommended that Eskom buy a year's worth of coal upfront. While Ramontja claimed he signed the letter, he did not date it, and he did not send it out of DMR. Yet somehow the letter ended up at Eskom.

On 7 December, Daniels was called by Ngubane, who asked her to draft an urgent round-robin resolution, which would call for Eskom to purchase R1.68bn of coal upfront. The drafting of the resolution was a highly collaborative affair: the commission found evidence that it had been put together with Anoj Singh's input; he in turn had sent it for comment to Eric Wood and Mohamed Bobat of Regiments. Wood also got input from Salim Essa. A review of the draft changes showed that one of the big alterations was to remove the fact that PFMA approval was required from the minister.

The result was that, on 8 December, Eskom sent a round-robin resolution to the board asking for urgent approval, by midday the next day, of the plan to buy R1.68bn of coal and make the payment upfront. The commission found that the resolution contained numerous misleading statements, including the false claim that the purchase was urgent because the coal was needed to avoid load-shedding. The resolution was approved the following day, on 9 December 2015 – the day *before* Tegeta had even signed the final purchase agreement with OCH.

The following day – 10 December – the OCH sales agreement was signed. On the same day, Anoj Singh decided to convert this approval for an immediate R1.68bn prepayment into a bank guarantee. The guarantee was to the effect that Tegeta could draw down any amount of the R1.68bn when required – it was a commitment to pay Tegeta whenever it needed money, in order to fulfil the coal sales agreement. This was remarkable as Tegeta did not yet even own the mine.

The drafting of this guarantee agreement was similarly collaborative. The original draft appears to have emanated from the 'Business Man' email address controlled by Essa, which was sent to Koko. Koko sent it to Daniels, who got a law firm to vet the agreement. Once this was done, the vetted version was then sent by Daniels to Koko and Singh, from there to Eric Wood, and from Wood to Essa. Remarkably, this agreement included its own suspensive condition, namely, that Eskom would not require Tegeta to deliver any coal until the end of March 2016. In effect, this negated the entire purported rationale of the prepayment, which was to buy Eskom coal urgently.

Singh signed the guarantee without getting any board approval. Indeed, neither Singh nor Daniels told the board at all that the prepayment had been converted into a guarantee. The commission noted that the PFMA made it explicit that the issuance of guarantees like this required board approval. Moreover, the board was only entitled to approve a guarantee equal to R750m, after which it required ministerial approval. Of course, no ministerial approval was even sought. So, in short, the issuance of the guarantee violated the PFMA and was unlawful – and all of this was done before Tegeta had even taken control of the mine!

With the guarantee now approved, Ravindra Nath, a key Gupta employee, wrote to the Bank of Baroda. He informed Baroda about the guarantee and asked the bank to supply a letter confirming that Tegeta had the funds to complete the purchase. This was duly issued by the bank. And now Tegeta could present the Eskom guarantee and Baroda's letter to the consortium banks to convince them that Tegeta was liquid enough to complete the purchase. As it would turn out, this was not true.

Farcically, Tegeta then refused to let the business rescue practitioners or the consortium banks retain a copy of the Baroda letter. They were allowed to see it but not keep it to check its bona fides. The result was that, despite all this noise and thunder and irregularity, the consortium banks did not approve the transaction on the basis of the Baroda letter or the Eskom guarantee. Instead, this matter resolved itself when Tegeta paid the full asking price, which then removed this as an issue.

## The outrageous R659m prepayment

As the deadline approached to transfer the full price to complete the purchase, the Guptas faced a serious problem: they simply did not have the money at hand to complete the purchase. Indeed, on 4 April 2016, Salim Essa called OCH's Clinton Ephron to tell him that Tegeta was R600m short. Essa asked Ephron whether this amount could be paid after the purchase was done using the revenue earned from the mine. Unsurprisingly, this was rejected. So too was an attempt to ask the consortium banks to grant Tegeta a short-term loan of R600m; a request that was rejected on 11 April 2016. The result was that Tegeta had only a handful of days to find R600m: the final payments had to be made to OCH's lawyers on 14 April 2016.

As these attempts to raise funds were playing out, Tegeta's Ravindra Nath contacted Dr Ayanda Nteta, who was then the acting director for Eskom's Fuel Sourcing Division. Nath made a verbal offer on 8 April 2016 for a prepurchase deal whereby Eskom could purchase coal upfront with certain discounts applied. At no stage prior to the approval of this purchase did Tegeta or Nath make the offer in writing, nor did Tegeta ever provide a rationale or motivation for why Eskom should take up the offer.

On the basis of this verbal offer, Eskom's most senior employees worked themselves to death over a weekend to make it happen. On 10 April, Nteta submitted a draft resolution to Daniels to approve a prepurchase of R500m, which would eventually balloon to R659m. Nteta and Daniels then collaborated to draft the resolution, which was to be submitted to a special and urgently convened board Tender Committee meeting on 11 April 2016. The draft resolution was submitted for signature on the same day; it was duly signed by Koko, Dr Nteta and one Vusi Mboweni.

The submission to the board Tender Committee included a motivation for why the deal had to be done urgently. As Tegeta had made no effort to make this argument itself, it was entirely a construction of Eskom's officials, especially Daniels. The submission argued that Eskom urgently needed to procure coal to supply to its Arnot power station, which it claimed was running short of coal. This was simply not true.

First, the submission itself explained that, despite this urgency, OCH would source the coal supplied under the contract from its export coal seam. In other words, the 'urgent' coal deliveries could only be made *after* the coal had been mined by OCH. It did not have coal simply waiting around to be delivered. So there was no way the coal could be delivered urgently.

Second, there just wasn't any urgent demand at Arnot. When Dr Nteta appeared before the commission, she was confronted with Eskom's April 2016 Supply Plan. This made it clear that there was no anticipated shortfall over the winter months at Arnot station, which Nteta conceded. Another witness – a senior Eskom official, André van Heerden – presented an affidavit to the commission. Van Heerden was Eskom's senior manager of integrated planning, and was responsible for planning coal deliveries and levels. Van Heerden explained that there *had* been a risk of a coal shortfall identified in December 2015. However, this was based on a risk of industrial action in January 2016, which never materialised. Moreover, he confirmed that the Arnot station had 'healthy' supplies of coal until September 2016 and would only be in trouble in October 2016.

The only conclusion to draw, the commission found, was quite simple: 'Eskom paid for coal it did not need; certainly not immediately or urgently. Dr Nteta and her colleagues acted in concert to deliberately include information in the submission that was calculated to mislead the board Tender Committee or the reader.' Remarkably, Tegeta's first formal written offer, on its own letterhead, was only emailed by Nath to Nteta on 12 April 2016 – the day *after* the prepayment had already been approved. And, as it turned out, this was not even the final version. It was only on 29 April 2016 that Nath sent a final version of the written offer with certain changes to Nteta. He only did so because Nteta needed a document to provide to her seniors to support the payment.

The board Tender Committee approved the submission for the prepayment at a meeting at 9 pm on 11 April 2016. The meeting lasted all of 28 minutes. At no stage did the minutes reflect why the meeting was held urgently, when the same committee was due to meet two days later on the 13th. The 11 April 2016 meeting was minuted. However, the commission found that the minutes had been put together after the fact. This was because, during the meeting, certain issues were raised that were only dealt with the following day. The minutes had to be edited to make it look as if these issues were resolved in the meeting itself. The result was that the 'minutes were fabricated, after the fact, in order to create the impression that the board Tender Committee had applied its mind during the meeting, which was not the case'.

All that was left was for the final signatures of Singh and Koko, which they appended to the agreement on 13 April 2016. The agreement required that payment be made on the same day by 2 pm. And, indeed, the payment was made with extraordinary swiftness by Eskom that afternoon. In order to do so, Eskom's officials had to manipulate its computerised supply chain systems to get the payment through on what were effectively false pretences. The commission commented that 'in order to make this possible, a series of required governance processes were skipped, mid-level managers bypassed and false information fed into Eskom's financial management system together with various manual overrides to force it to trigger a payment'.

Lurking in the background of all of this wrangling and irregularities was a key fact that nobody appeared to be paying any attention to: in early April, prior to the approval of the prepayment, the Guptas and their companies, including Tegeta, received letters from South Africa's Big Four banks saying that they intended to close their bank accounts owing to reputational and other concerns. So, while Eskom was bending over backwards to make the purchase happen, Tegeta and other Gupta companies were facing the very real prospect of losing their primary transactional banking facilities.

This was only acknowledged on 13 April 2016, when Singh and Koko appeared before the board Tender Committee to give final approval to the prepayment. Singh apologised to the committee, explaining that he 'forgot' to tell them there were actually concerns about the long-term viability of Tegeta because of the bank account issues. When Singh was asked about this at the commission, he denied he had ever issued this apology or raised this issue. Too bad for him that the commission had an audio recording of the meeting, which proved that Singh had, indeed, made this point.

## Screwing South Africa just a little bit more

The commission was absolutely clear in its final findings – the R659m prepayment was predicated entirely on helping Tegeta buy OCH when it simply did not have the cash to do so. But the Guptas did not just rely on Eskom's generosity to buy OCH. As I will show later, my own calculations indicated that most of the capital used to buy OCH actually derived from state capture. My analysis suggested that of the over R2bn paid by Tegeta to purchase the mine, R1.8bn derived from fund flows linked to state capture, which were laundered through a series of complicated loan-backs to allow the Guptas to buy OCH with the money it stole from South Africa.

In March 2017, just under a year after the purchase of OCH by Tegeta, Tegeta and Eskom reached a settlement agreement regarding the R2.15bn penalty claim against OCH by Eskom. Remember that Molefe, in particular, was utterly insistent that Glencore pay this full penalty. The board Tender Committee, when it reviewed the issue, gave approval for a settlement amounting to not less than R500m. Even this was ignored. Instead, according to the settlement agreement, Tegeta would only need to pay R255.4m, in the teeth of the Tender Committee's resolution that the settlement be *at least* R500m. The settlement agreement was signed by Koko, Singh and Daniels. It was never forwarded to the full board for approval. 'On the evidence heard by the commission all these three officials were working with the Guptas and their associates,' the commission commented.

Tegeta was given 20 months – from April 2016 to December 2018 – to pay the settlement amount. In the end, Tegeta only made payments on the penalties until January 2018. The following month, the mine was put into business rescue and the Guptas effectively absconded from the country. The closure of the Guptas' bank accounts was cited as the reason for the collapse of Tegeta and OCH. The commission calculated that, by the time it went into business rescue, Tegeta had paid just less than half of the amount, and still owed Eskom R133.7m.

The closure of Optimum mine, which flowed directly from the criminality and malfeasance of the Gupta enterprise, was an utter disaster for Eskom. Hendrina power station was entirely dependent on the mine for its coal supply, which stopped abruptly, and it was left immediately short of 400,000 tonnes of coal. Eskom was forced to divert coal meant for other stations to Hendrina. This disrupted the entire national coal supply and reduced Eskom's overall coal stockpiles dramatically. In addition, the coal delivered to Hendrina now had to be delivered by truck, instead of directly from OCM's conveyor belt, which had its own huge knock-on effect on the price.

## The Brakfontein debacle: The Guptas score big

The Guptas controlled other mines in South Africa, one of which also supplied coal to Eskom: the Brakfontein Colliery, which was owned by Tegeta.

The Guptas had been trying to obtain Eskom coal contracts from at least 2011 onwards. They offered to supply Eskom with coal from two collieries, Vierfontein and Brakfontein. Both were unsuitable suppliers. Vierfontein was bedevilled with environmental issues. Brakfontein, at the time, also lacked a water licence, which was a mandatory requirement for any supplier to Eskom. Brakfontein would only get its water licence in December 2014.

Tegeta returned to Eskom in May 2014 to make another unsolicited offer. Despite the fact that Brakfontein had no water licence at the time, Eskom started negotiating deals with Tegeta. Another problem was that, while load-shedding allowed Eskom to consider unsolicited offers, they were supposed to be forwarded to Eskom's Supplier Development Department for vetting, after which they would be added to a supplier database. This was never done.

Following extensive and procedurally problematic negotiations, Eskom entered into a coal supply agreement on 10 March 2015 to supply 13.9m tonnes of coal to Eskom from Brakfontein over ten years between April 2015 and September 2025. For this, Tegeta would be paid R3.7bn. The date of this agreement was, of course, significant: the following day, Eskom suspended its four executives, including Koko. Koko, at the time, was overseeing the contract as it fell within his remit, and he would be required to sign it off. One Eskom employee at the heart of the negotiations, Johann Bester, would testify to the commission that he believed the signing of the contract was rushed so that it could be completed prior to Koko's suspension.

Coal is mined from long deposits called seams, which can run kilometres long. The coal supply agreement envisaged that Tegeta would supply coal from two seams at Brakfontein, which it would 'blend' into a single product. The two seams were the Seam 4 Lower (S4L) and Seam 4 Upper (S4U). The importance of this was that, throughout the negotiations with Tegeta, Eskom had raised concerns about the quality of the coal from Brakfontein. In particular, Eskom tests had shown that the coal from the S4U did not meet quality requirements for use in key power stations. The 'blended' product also failed because of the inclusion of the S4U coal. In effect, the only coal Brakfontein could supply that would be of use to Eskom – or at least meet its specifications – was the coal from S4L. Despite this, the contract envisaged that Brakfontein would supply the 'blended' product.

This was not the only problem with the whole process. The commission notes that at no stage was any financial assessment made of Tegeta's financial viability. This was striking as, the month after the contract was signed, KPMG gave Eskom an opinion that Tegeta was not financially sound enough to be granted such a big contract. There was thus a real risk that Eskom would be receiving key strategic supplies from a company that might not last very long – and, indeed, Tegeta did go bust in 2018.

In addition, Tegeta held a mining right (issued by the DMR) until only October 2020. So unless Tegeta could get it renewed, the mining licence would expire before the end of the contract. Brakfontein had, admittedly, secured a mining right for a new portion of the mine (called Brakfontein Extension), but this had not yet been mined and none of the coal had been tested for quality.

The contract signed in March 2015 had an important suspensive condition: the coal supplied by Brakfontein had to be subject to a 'combustion test' by the end of the month. This would test if the coal would burn correctly in Eskom's coal burners. This was never performed; previous tests, concluded in June 2014 and October 2014, months prior to the signing of the contract, showed that the coal was of insufficient quality to supply Majuba, the primary target power station.

This issue was resolved by means of a contract amendment signed on 12 May 2015. This effectively waived the combustion testing requirement, and said that Eskom would not require such tests before the coal was supplied.

Despite all this, Tegeta wrote to Eskom on 19 June 2015 to make a new offer: Tegeta wanted to increase the amount of coal it supplied by 200,000 tonnes a month, which it would supply from Brakfontein Extension. In response, Dr Nteta (who was involved in the prepayment fiasco mentioned above) replied to Ravindra Nath, the Gupta employee who made the unsolicited proposal. The letter confirmed that a meeting had taken place to negotiate this outcome, and recorded that Eskom was in agreement in principle. This letter did note that all new supplies would have to be subject to combustion tests.

On the same day Nteta sent this reply to Nath, Nath forwarded it to Tony Gupta. Shortly thereafter, Nath wrote to Nteta saying that the letter Nteta had written was insufficient and had to be amended to satisfy Tegeta's 'bankers'. In effect, Nath and Tegeta were telling Eskom what to write and what to agree. Nath provided a new copy of the letter, which, most notably, removed the requirement that combustion tests be performed and the stipulation that Eskom stations would only accept coal from Tegeta if needed. The new letter was duly signed by Johann Bester the next day. Bester claimed before the commission that he could not remember signing it. And while the commission made no specific finding on Bester, it did note that an earlier Fundudzi investigation had recommended that Bester be investigated for potential PRECCA violations.

## The testing farce

Between March 2015 and April 2015, Eskom used a company called SGS Services SA to test Brakfontein's coal. It then moved to a new company, Siboniswe Coal Services, which tested the coal between May 2015 and August 2015. Siboniswe repeatedly reported during this period that Brakfontein's coal was not compliant.

On 1 July 2015, Dr Mark van der Riet, a coal specialist, was seconded to Eskom's Primary Energy Division (PED). He was asked to assist PED in managing Eskom's coal supplies. Dr Van der Riet testified that his quality assurance staff were concerned about the quality of Brakfontein coal, which had been deteriorating from July 2015, just as Eskom started buying additional coal from Brakfontein. The practical result was that, when coal was delivered to Eskom, approximately 50% of the deliveries had been rejected.

Tegeta was furious, and in August 2015 a senior Tegeta manager, Jacques Roux, complained directly to Koko. Roux complained that Siboniswe's tests were problematic, and that some 'white lady' had told Tegeta that the samples would only be approved if a bribe was paid. When the commission asked the director of Siboniswe about it, he was perplexed: no such person worked at the company. The commission would ultimately find that the allegation was 'likely a ruse' developed by Koko and Roux to get rid of Siboniswe, which was repeatedly failing Brakfontein's coal.

Mr Masuka, the director of Siboniswe, testified before the commission that he had been subject to intimidation and threats by Koko. He claimed that he was called into a meeting at Koko's office to interrogate him about the results. Koko accused Masuka of 'fighting with the Guptas', which surprised Masuka greatly as he had no idea who they were.

While this was all happening, Dr Van der Riet and three of his colleagues were progressing with their investigation of the deterioration in Brakfontein's coal quality. They completed their investigation in late August and presented their results to Koko and Daniels: the coal was, indeed, deteriorating in quality. On 28 August 2015, this finding was additionally verified after samples had been sent to the South African Bureau of Standards (SABS) for testing. The report, which Dr Van der Riet delivered to Koko on the 28th, showed that 29 out of the 30 samples tested by SABS had failed the quality control tests. This was even worse that Siboniswe's results, which had failed 15 of 30 samples.

This was clearly a disaster for Tegeta and for Koko. So, in his infinite wisdom, Koko ordered that yet another sample be taken. Koko told Dr Van der Riet that he and a colleague would be allowed to witness the testing to verify the results. But then, later that day, Koko reversed his instruction, saying that they should not witness the testing. And then, even later that day, Koko called Dr Van der Riet, telling him that the new sampling had been cancelled by Tegeta. While Koko denied this call, the commission found his denials were not credible.

Despite the fact that the testing was supposedly cancelled, Koko was provided with a new progress report the following day, showing the results of the new test. This report now claimed that the Brakfontein coal was, in fact, totally above board and fit for purpose. The test was, of course, not witnessed by anyone at Eskom, which, as Dr Van der Riet explained to the commission, meant that they were of dubious reliability.

The writing was on the wall for Dr Van der Riet and his colleagues. On 31 August, the day after, he was told to hand over the whole of his investigative file to Koko. Van der Riet testified that the investigative file included CCTV footage and an affidavit showing that on 30 August, the day the new results were delivered to Koko, Tegeta's Jacques Roux and a colleague had forced their way into SABS's offices and confronted staff about the tests. The CCTV footage and the affidavit were subsequently lost.

On 1 September 2015, Dr Van der Riet went to the Eskom offices to hand over the file, which he gave to Vusi Mboweni, who reported to Koko. During the meeting, Van der Riet was handed a letter suspending him and his three colleagues. The letter came from Koko, despite the fact that Van der Riet and his colleagues reported to Mboweni. The commission found that the most reasonable conclusion was that the suspensions were made by Koko to thwart their ongoing investigations.

On the same day, presumably in an attempt to look even-handed, Koko ordered that coal supplies from Brakfontein be suspended. But the suspension was lifted only days later, which had the effect of finally terminating any investigation into the coal quality.

But there was one final kicker. On 6 September 2015, two days before Koko would lift Brakfontein's suspension, another test was conducted by an Eskom lab of Brakfontein's coal. The technician found that the coal from Brakfontein tested on 6 September 2015 was of vastly different quality from that tested on 29 August: recall that it was this test, which was unwitnessed, that found the coal to be of suitable quality. The technician concluded that, in fact, the coal used in the 29 August test could not have come from the same source – it was not actually from Brakfontein. So, the only time that Brakfontein passed a test, it did so by using coal from a totally different mine.

The commission heard extensive evidence from many Eskom employees who alleged that severe pressure was placed on power stations to accept poor quality coal from Brakfontein. One of these witnesses was Gert Opperman, who testified that Koko had placed pressure on him to get Majuba to accept poor quality coal from Brakfontein.

The testing issue was 'resolved' in October. Koko ordered that all Brakfontein tests would now have to be completed by an Eskom lab situated in the Kendal power station. At the time, the Kendal lab did not have the requisite independent certification – it only received it two years after Koko's instruction in October 2017. The Kendal test results were much more to Tegeta's liking: between October 2015 and Tegeta's collapse in 2018, Kendal failed only 3% of Brakfontein's stockpile.

And this was not even the end of this story. On 8 August 2016 Vuyisile Ncube, who was Opperman's manager, made a submission to the board Tender Committee. The submission motivated for the procurement of a further 10.8m tonnes from Brakfontein Extension. This would have increased the value of the R3.79bn contract by a further R2.9bn. Luckily, the request was forwarded to Treasury, which rejected the application because of concerns over quality. Indeed, when the coal from Brakfontein Extension was tested again independently in November 2016, it was found to be unsuitable for a good number of Eskom's stations.

## The cost of Brakfontein
According to the commission's calculations, Eskom ultimately paid Tegeta R1,260,022,596.75 for coal supplies from Brakfontein to the Majuba power station. But this was not the only cost. Between October 2016 and September 2017, Brakfontein seriously underdelivered on its coal requirements. And when Tegeta was placed in business rescue in February 2018, the coal supply stopped

altogether. Eskom calculated that, between February 2018 and December 2018, Tegeta should have been subject to non-performance penalties of R531m.

Throughout the life of the Brakfontein contracts, the poor-quality coal and delivery failures threatened the viability of Majuba power station, one of the most important power-generating units in the country. At one stage, Majuba's stockpiled coal supplies fell to less than ten days: the absolute minimum to ensure ongoing delivery and safety was forty days. Most of this shortfall was due to Brakfontein's failure to deliver.

Of course, when Tegeta went under, this caught Eskom short once more. Eskom was only able to procure new coal supplies to fill the gap left by Brakfontein in October 2018, nearly eight months after Tegeta's business rescue. The Brakfontein deals thus did not just cost inordinate amounts of money – they posed a serious threat to the energy stability of the entire country.

## Friends reunited: Singh, Molefe, McKinsey, Regiments and Trillian

As we saw previously, McKinsey, Regiments and Trillian made an absolute killing from dodgy contracts at Transnet that were largely overseen by Anoj Singh and Molefe. When Singh and Molefe took over the reins at Eskom, the money started flowing once more.

As with Transnet, the contracts awarded by Eskom to McKinsey, Regiments and Trillian, and the irregularities attendant on them, were extraordinarily complicated. To cut through this, what follows here is a very high-level overview of the events that took place.

McKinsey and Regiments were awarded two large contracts by Eskom after Molefe and Singh took over. The first was called a master services agreement (MSA). The commission heard evidence that McKinsey began negotiating the Eskom MSA with Molefe and Singh just after Molefe was appointed and while Singh was still working at Transnet.

The MSA was awarded to McKinsey on 17 December 2015 by means of an acceptance letter, following a board Tender Committee approval in October 2015 to negotiate for the conclusion of the MSA on sole-source basis. The MSA included four 'streams' of work that were grouped together under this overarching structure.

Extraordinarily, work on the MSA began without any contract being signed by Eskom and McKinsey. This was only signed in late September and early October 2016, by which time the contract had already been cancelled and Eskom had paid out a final fee.

The process of approving and awarding the MSA was highly irregular. One of the most important issues was the way in which the funding was structured. The MSA was concluded on an at-risk basis; effectively, McKinsey and Regiments would be paid a percentage of the 'savings' or efficiencies that their work generated for Eskom. There was no cap placed on this fee. The fee structure envisaged that McKinsey would be paid 70% of the fee, while Regiments would receive 30% of the fee.

This entire fee structure was unlawful: a National Treasury note, which was basically an extension of the PFMA, provided that consultants could only be appointed on a fixed-fee basis. Any deviation from this required approval from the director general of the National Treasury. Of course, at no stage was this approval sought or granted, despite Singh, Koko and others being repeatedly told that this was a mandatory requirement.

Because of this issue, the acceptance letter sent to McKinsey in December 2015 included a bizarre and largely unintelligible provision. After parsing its tortuous legalese, the commission found that the effect of the provision was that, if National Treasury raised issues with the contract in the light of this lack of approval, Eskom and McKinsey would endeavour to renegotiate the entire contract.

Other problems bedevilled the contract. In July 2015, Koko returned from suspension, and started becoming involved. The commission found that Koko, on his return, began sending internal Eskom documents to Essa's 'Business Man' email address. This included an email setting out Eskom's entire negotiating position. Suzanne Daniels, meanwhile, testified that when Koko returned from suspension, he was in possession of a document that he said was part of his instructions from his 'principals'. The document listed a range of Eskom projects and put a 'revenue' figure next to each.

A Regiments employee testified that the firm frequently put precisely these sorts of documents together to estimate how much it could earn on different projects. The inference, of course, was that Koko was being told what contracts would make their way to Regiments and what it would earn from them. Koko made handwritten notes on the document, and conceded when testifying that they were in his handwriting. Among Koko's notes was a scrawled 'Zetlor', most likely referring to Zestilor, which suggests that Koko was aware of some sort of plan by which Zestilor – a Gupta company controlled by Essa's wife – would get money from Eskom.

Things became openly farcical in February 2016, when Eric Wood left Regiments to form Trillian alongside Salim Essa. The plan was that Trillian would simply take over Regiments' part in the MSA contract (and another contract I'll discuss below). McKinsey, however, never approved this plan. Indeed, in March 2016, McKinsey wrote to Eskom and Trillian saying that it did not want to contract with Trillian because there were concerns about Salim Essa being a 'politically exposed person'. McKinsey, in short, was snubbing Trillian.

Trillian's supporters within Eskom acted swiftly and ruthlessly. In June 2016, Eskom's Steering Committee (Steerco) convened a meeting chaired by Anoj Singh. Singh now raised concerns with how McKinsey's MSA contract had been awarded on a sole-source basis. The commission called this a 'complete farce' – Singh was now raising concerns about the sole-source issue when it was Singh and Koko, in particular, who were central in getting the contract awarded on this basis. Steerco decided that the McKinsey MSA would have to be terminated.

The commission was absolutely clear about what was really happening: 'It is reasonable to conclude that the termination was underpinned by these executives' disappointment by McKinsey's decision not to subcontract their friend's [Salim Essa's] company, Trillian; and set about to devise another means of channelling money to Trillian.'

Two days after the Steerco decision, a submission was made to the board Tender Subcommittee requesting approval to cancel the contract, to negotiate a final fee, and to find ways to redirect the contracted work. The fact that Eskom was even thinking of paying McKinsey any sort of fee was remarkable considering that there was not even a contract in place at the time.

Eskom ultimately agreed to settle with McKinsey and Trillian.

The settlement was equal to R1.8bn. The commission noted that the methodology used to calculate this fee was obtuse and arbitrary. Between August 2016 and February 2017, Eskom paid just under R1.6bn to McKinsey and Trillian under this settlement agreement. McKinsey was paid approximately R1.1bn while Trillian pocketed the rest. The amount earned by McKinsey from this settlement was ten times what McKinsey had ever previously earned at Eskom.

The payment to Trillian was, frankly, insane. McKinsey had explicitly rejected any partnership with Trillian. The firm had no contract with Trillian at all, while Trillian had no contract with Eskom. The commission, on this basis, delivered one of its most scathing findings in all its work: 'The payment to Trillian was unconscionable and constituted corruption of the highest order. The officials at Eskom who pushed for payments to be made to Trillian knowing that Eskom had no contract with Trillian and McKinsey had not appointed Trillian as its SDL should hang their heads in shame and face the full wrath of the law.'

If this was not enough, the commission's investigations found that Eskom had been advised to withhold payments to McKinsey and Trillian in December 2016. In November 2016, Eskom hired a set of international consultants, OWM, to review the work under the MSA. OWM was concerned about how the fees were calculated. It also raised concerns about the overall legality of the contract, urged Eskom to get legal advice, and advised Eskom not to make any further payments until the legal advice was received. OWM provided its final report in December 2016 making these recommendations, which were then simply ignored when they were placed before the board Tender Committee.

Trillian also earned handsomely on the other contract that Eskom awarded to McKinsey, the so-called Eskom Corporate Plan contract. This contract emerged from an unsolicited proposal sent by McKinsey that ended up on the desk of Koko. It offered McKinsey's help with certain financial work that fell outside the MSA. A submission to the board was duly prepared by Koko and Singh for the board chair, and on 10 September 2015 the board resolved to appoint McKinsey on a sole-source basis. The fee was set at R101,733,124.80 for eight months of work. As with much of Regiments' and McKinsey's other work, the commission heard evidence that all the services provided under the contract could have been performed by Eskom's internal treasury and financial management units.

One of the requirements of the contract, stipulated by Eskom, was that McKinsey needed to work with a supplier development partner. McKinsey nominated Regiments, although it never signed any sort of subcontracting agreement to this effect. Regiments soon fell away after the creation of Trillian, and the latter then sought to insert itself in the contract. Of course, as we saw earlier, McKinsey ultimately rejected Trillian as a supplier development partner.

On 3 February 2016, Trillian Management Consulting invoiced Eskom for work on the corporate plan, equal to R30.6m. At the time, Trillian had only two employees doing any work on the contract. The invoice was sent by Trillian's financial director, Tebogo Leballo, to Anoj Singh. The invoice included a cover letter from Trillian's Bianca Goodson (who claimed it was signed electronically without her knowledge) explaining that, because Trillian was small and had cash-flow problems, it wanted to be paid directly by Eskom. This was because Trillian feared it would take too long to be paid by McKinsey after McKinsey had been paid by Eskom. This was obviously nonsense: McKinsey had explicitly rejected Trillian and most likely had no intention of ever paying the firm.

On 14 April 2016, Trillian was paid R30.6m for its 'work' on the corporate plan (the very same day that Tegeta paid its final amounts to acquire OCH). As with the payment on the MSA, this was both irregular and unjustified, as Trillian had no contract with McKinsey and no contract with Eskom.

The commission, on reviewing the totality of the evidence about the MSA and corporate plan, placed the blame for all the irregularities and wrongdoing at the feet of a number of key Eskom officials. Singh, Molefe and Koko were explicitly identified as being the central players involved in the conceptualisation and furtherance of a scheme to capture Eskom for Trillian's and McKinsey's benefit. The commission also found that four other parties were implicated: Edwin Mabelane (the chief procurement officer), Prish Govender (a senior financial executive), Suzanne Daniels and Zethembe Khoza.

## Crisis averted: The Huarong financing deal

Another deal considered by the commission involved negotiations between Eskom and a company called Huarong Energy Africa (HEA). HEA sought to provide Eskom with loan and financing provisions. Ultimately, the deal was not concluded, largely because of the intervention of the head of Eskom Treasury, André Pillay. Pillay was concerned about the deal and its probity, and eventually succeeded in getting National Treasury to kill the deal. Pillay had until then been at loggerheads with Anoj Singh and Eskom's new CEO in 2017, Sean Maritz.

The HEA–Eskom negotiations were problematic for several reasons. But two were particularly serious. The first was that, in March 2017, following a whole series of negotiations, Anoj Singh approached Pillay and told him that HEA was eager to start moving the deal forward, and wanted Eskom to sign what was called a 'term sheet'; this was, in simple terms, a document setting out the nature of the transaction, the fees that would be paid, and other ancillary matters.

Importantly, Singh wanted to sign a draft of the term sheet that would remove previous draft clauses that made the term sheet non-binding. And, indeed, Singh did sign the term sheet with these clauses removed on 14 March 2017. Singh failed to refer the term sheet to Eskom's legal department for any sort of review. He later tried to argue that the term sheet he had signed was not binding. But this was patently ridiculous, as the first paragraph stated that 'this term sheet shall create legally binding obligations on each party and shall be in full force upon its signature'. Importantly, the term sheet included a stipulation that HEA would be due a large payment of fees upon the initiation of the deal.

Singh left Eskom before the contract was concluded, but the deal was taken up with gusto by the new Eskom CEO, Sean Maritz. Again, after much negotiation, meetings and board discussion, Maritz took much the same route as Singh: he agreed to sign a further agreement called an asset loan framework agreement (ALFA), which potentially bound Eskom to the deal and for the payment of fees to HEA. Maritz signed the ALFA in December 2017.

Presumably because the term sheet was signed, HEA was clearly of the opinion that it was due to receive its upfront arrangement fees.

So, on 21 November 2017, HEA submitted an invoice for $21.8m for payment of these fees. Pillay, as head of Treasury, blocked the payment. But then Maritz, the following month, signed the ALFA, which again emboldened HEA to submit the invoice again.

It was at this point that Pillay decided to approach the director general at the National Treasury, Dondo Mogajane, to raise his concerns with the deal. Shortly thereafter, as a result of this intervention, approval for the deal, which had previously been granted by the Reserve Bank, was revoked.

There was an additional kicker to all of this. HEA was a South African company that was formed specifically to do this deal. HEA had no assets of its own but purported to represent its parent company in China, Huarong. The commission believed that HEA might not even have been able to raise the money that it was intending to loan Eskom. Instead, it concluded that the entire deal was pursued by 'certain Eskom officials' simply in order to create the obligation to pay the $21.8m raising fee. On reviewing the term sheet and other documents, the commission opined that Eskom had got itself into a situation where it would be legally bound to pay the $21.8m, even if HEA did not provide the financing.

The commission found that all those officials who pushed for this fee to be paid (although it did not identify them by name) were potentially guilty of fraud, as they represented to Eskom that the whole arrangement was in Eskom's interests. The reality was that it could have landed Eskom with a massive bill for which it received nothing in return.

## Koko's international travel

The commission concluded its report on Eskom by looking into claims that Koko had received undue benefits from the Gupta enterprise. In late 2015, Koko and his family travelled on holiday to Bali. Thereafter, they travelled from Bali to Dubai, where they stayed at the Oberoi Hotel, the usual haunt of the Guptas. Records suggested that Koko's trip from Bali to Dubai was at least arranged by Salim Essa, and that Koko's Oberoi Hotel bill had been settled by Sahara Computers.

Koko denied the allegation. In his defence, he produced evidence that he had made payments to Thompsons Travel totalling R385,000, of which R383,800 was paid in cash. But all this evidence showed was that Koko had paid for his and his family's visit to Bali, not that he had paid for the trip to Dubai.

The commission sought evidence from Travel Excellence, the travel agent used by Salim Essa and the Guptas. This showed that Essa had contacted Travel Excellence to get them to help Koko and his family obtain visas and make other logistical arrangements.

Koko tried to argue that he had, in fact, paid the Oberoi Hotel bill. But this version, too, was rejected by the commission. Koko presented copies of invoices from the Oberoi that he claimed showed he paid the bills; but the invoices did not actually reflect any payment made by him. Most importantly, the GuptaLeaks quite clearly showed that the hotel had sought payment from Sahara Computers for the stay, and had directed that request to Ashu Chawla.

The inference, of course, was simple. Koko was another of those many officials who had benefited unduly from Gupta largesse; and the Guptas could rely on Koko to involve himself in endless manipulations to benefit them.

## Recommendations

*The NPA should investigate members of the 2014 Eskom board who supported or enabled the suspension of the 'four executives', for potential violations of the PFMA.*

*Serious consideration should be given by Eskom to initiating legal proceedings to recover the R18m paid to three executives to secure their termination, from members of the 2014 Eskom board, except for Norman Baloyi who sought to challenge this process.*

*All those officials who brought pressure to bear on Glencore related to the sale of OCH or were party to the approval of the R659m prepayment and the R1.68bn guarantee were prima facie guilty of theft and should face criminal charges. The recommendation for the proferring of criminal charges is particularly applicable to Anoj Singh and Matshela Koko for their role in arranging the R659m prepayment and the R1.68bn guarantee.*

*The NPA should conduct further investigations into the supply of coal from Brakfontein with a view to the prosecution of Matshela Koko, Vusi Mboweni, Dr Ayanda Nteta and Jacques Roux for PFMA violations and potential corruption under PRECCA*

*The NPA should consider the criminal prosecution for theft or fraud of Anoj Singh and Sean Maritz for their roles in signing the term sheet and ALFA agreement related to the Huarong financing transaction. The NPA should consider similar charges against the director of HEA, Rajeev Thomas.*

*The NPA should conduct further investigations with a view to the prosecution of Brian Molefe, Anoj Singh and Matshela Koko for PRECCA violations flowing from the benefits they received from the Guptas or Salim Essa. These investigations should consider the entirety of the irregularities attendant on Eskom's contracts with McKinsey and the unlawful payments to both McKinsey and Trillian.*

*The NPA should consider investigating members of the 2014 Eskom board for potential PFMA violations for failing to protect Eskom from financial prejudice in relation to the master services agreement and corporate plan contracts awarded by Eskom to McKinsey.*

# South African Airways

SOUTH AFRICAN AIRWAYS (SAA) was one of the big three SOEs (alongside Transnet and Eskom) at which the commission found extraordinarily high levels of dysfunction and corruption. At SAA, the two predominant figures were Dudu Myeni and Yakhe Kwinana. Myeni served as the chairperson of the SAA board from 2012 onwards; Kwinana served as the chairperson of South African Airways Technical (SAAT), a subsidiary of SAA. Together, Kwinana and Myeni were involved in some of the most obviously egregious cases of wrongdoing and corruption uncovered by the commission.

## The move from governance to dysfunction

Between September 2009 and September 2012, the SAA board was chaired by Cheryl Carolus, who had previously chaired SA Tourism and South African National Parks. The group chief executive officer (GCEO) during Carolus's stint as chair of SAA was Sizakele Petunia Mzimela, who served in this position between April 2010 and October 2012.

SAA, under Carolus's leadership, embarked on a turn-around strategy for the airline called the New Growth Strategy. A big part of this was to expand services on the 'East–West Corridor', which would include routes reaching Mumbai and Beijing. The strategy required 'recapitalisation' – new planes, basically. The strategy was presented to Barbara Hogan, the Minister of Public Enterprises at the time, with whom the board had a good relationship. Hogan and specialists within the department approved the strategy.

Just over a month later, however, Hogan was fired as minister and replaced by Malusi Gigaba. Carolus testified that the relationship between the board and Gigaba quickly developed tensions, not least because Gigaba had criticised the board in the press. According to Mzimela, there was a 'breakdown in good governance' under Gigaba.

Both Mzimela and Carolus testified that Gigaba had engaged them on the issue of the 'Mumbai route'. At the time, SAA's primary competitor on this route, Jet Airways, had sought to have SAA cancel its own services, leaving Jet Airways a clear ride. Mzimela and Carolus told the commission that Gigaba and his advisor Solomon Mahlangu (who acted as Gigaba's go-between with the Guptas) had tried to pressure SAA to close down the profitable route.

Both Gigaba and Mahlangu denied the accusation. But the commission was unconvinced, and referred to a meeting attended by Gigaba, Mzimela and representatives of Jet Airways. The Jet Airways reps turned up two hours late to the meeting and then berated Mzimela for not taking their preferred action to close down SAA's route. The commission remarked that it was incredible that a minister would sit around for two hours to wait for reps of a private company and then remain silent while SAA's CEO was being dressed down. This, the commission believed, suggested that Gigaba extended a degree of preference to Jet Airways and that, in the circumstances, it was unsurprising that Mzimela came to believe that he supported closing down the Mumbai route.

Nevertheless, between 2010 and September 2012, SAA operated with moderate success under the Carolus board, turning a small net profit (though operational loss) in the period. But things took a turn for the worse in September 2012, eventually leading to a collapse in the board and the elevation of Dudu Myeni.

The key point of dispute and tension was the issuance of a government guarantee that would underwrite SAA's planned expansion. Without the guarantee, SAA would receive a qualified audit, which would have a cascading effect with negative outcomes. The Companies Act specified that SAA's financial results had to be presented to an AGM within six months of the end of the financial year: the deadline was thus 30 September 2012. For the directors of the board there were also consequences for their own positions if the results weren't filed on time; they could face charges of being delinquent, which would impact on their other directorships. So, SAA had to file its results by 30 September 2012, and, in order to do so in good order, it required the confirmation of the government guarantee.

Early September came and no guarantee was forthcoming. The board proposed, as a result, that it would present its full financial results without the guarantee. Gigaba disagreed, and told the board he was postponing the AGM to 25 September so he would have time to get the government guarantee. Then on the day of the purported AGM, Gigaba cancelled it. Carolus met with Gigaba and explained that many board members were anxious and were threatening to resign if the guarantee did not arrive. Gigaba responded by telling Carolus that, in fact, his staff had already sent the guarantee to SAA and that Carolus's staff had let everyone down.

The following day, unbeknown to Carolus and the board, Gigaba put out a statement in the *Business Day*. He claimed that the AGM would be postponed because SAA had not completed its financial statements. Carolus testified that this was not true: the financial statements were complete and all that was needed was the guarantee.

Gigaba's statement that the guarantee had already been sent was clearly false. In fact, the guarantee, which was eventually agreed by Treasury, was only approved on the 26th and faxed by Treasury to SAA on 27 September. Remarkably, the disclosed correspondence showed that the request to Treasury for approval of the guarantee was only sent on 21 September by the Department of Public Enterprises (DPE), despite the board telling Gigaba at the beginning of the year that they needed the guarantee.

While this was all playing out, Carolus convened a meeting of the board and explained that she planned to resign because of Gigaba's conduct and her lack of trust that he would resolve the guarantee. On 27 September, in the light of Gigaba's statements in *Business Day*, eight of the twelve directors of the board resigned.

## Kona, SAA and the Guptas

Following the resignation of the board, seven new non-executive directors were appointed. Only three members of the Carolus board were retained: Dudu Myeni, Yakhe Kwinana and Lindi Nkosi-Thomas. Vuyisile Kona, already a board member, was appointed the acting chair on 28 September 2012, and then, on 12 October 2012, he was also selected as the acting CEO. Due to concerns about him holding both positions, the board requested Gigaba choose a new acting chairperson. Fatefully, Gigaba chose Myeni, who was appointed on 7 December 2012. She would serve as chairperson of the SAA board for close to five years.

Myeni was close to Jacob Zuma, and served as the executive chairperson of the Jacob Zuma Foundation from 2008 onwards. As I'll discuss later, Angelo Agrizzi, the former COO of Bosasa, told the commission that in 2015 Bosasa started paying Myeni R300,000 in cash a month for the Jacob Zuma Foundation.

As soon as Kona was appointed, he began working on a new turn-around plan. For this, he approached SAA's supply chain management department to ask it to tender for a consultant to guide the process. The best offer was made by Lufthansa Consulting, which was selected by the supply chain team. At about the same time, Kona was approached by Solomon Mahlangu, Gigaba's advisor and Gupta go-between, who, according to Kona, 'insisted' that he meet with the Guptas.

The meeting with the Guptas is dealt with in more detail elsewhere, but the essence was that Tony Gupta, as was his wont, offered bribes to Kona to advance the Guptas' interests. Kona testified that once this was rejected, Tony Gupta asked him about the turn-around consultancy contract. Kona told Tony that the contract had been awarded to Lufthansa Consulting. This made Tony furious. Kona claimed that Tony Gupta quickly called Tshediso Matona, the director general at the DPE, to ask how this had happened. Matona then called Kona to berate him. A few days later, Kona testified, DPE officials told him that they were intending to investigate the award of the Lufthansa contract.

Kona then approached Myeni to tell her about the Saxonwold meeting. Myeni responded by asking what he ate and drank at the meeting, and clearly did not take it seriously. A few days later, perhaps because Myeni had relayed Kona's version, Mahlangu texted Kona, warning him that he was 'compromising the mission'. Kona believed this meant that he was not supposed to talk about the

Guptas. Mahlangu would claim that the 'mission' was actually about getting Kona appointed permanently. The commission, somewhat unsurprisingly, rejected Mahlangu's version and favoured Kona's.

Not long after, the board sought legal opinions on the Lufthansa contract, which alleged that the contract was awarded improperly and that Kona was involved; Kona, needless to say, denied the allegations. Nevertheless, Kona was suspended as acting CEO on 11 February 2013 by Gigaba, and then removed from the board completely on 26 February. Kona maintained his innocence at the commission and claimed that it was his resistance to the Guptas that led to his sacking.

## Myeni's strategy at the commission and her revelation of Witness X

The commission spent a good deal of the next few hundred pages of its report describing the dysfunction and corruption over which Myeni presided. Its findings were informed, in part, by Myeni's strategy when appearing before the commission. Myeni repeatedly invoked privilege, saying that any answer she gave might incriminate her. The commission found that she had abused the invocation of privilege by refusing to answer where questions were innocuous, or did not involve an allegation of criminality, or simply made her uncomfortable. Each time the evidence leaders believed that she was abusing privilege, this was noted.

Following Myeni's sometimes farcical appearance, the commission requested that she return on 5 May 2021 to answer questions in cases where she had originally asserted privilege when she was not entitled to. Myeni failed to attend, whereafter the commission instructed that a charge be laid against her with the police for violating the Commissions Act. Myeni, after this threat, relented and agreed to answer. But, owing to various constraints, the commission did not call her in person but asked her to answer questions on affidavit.

Despite promising comprehensive answers, Myeni's responding affidavit disappointed the commission. It consisted of one-word answers or claims that she had no knowledge of the matters the commission asked about. The commission, unsurprisingly, was of the opinion that Myeni's failure to attend in May 2021 was 'consistent with a witness who will go to great lengths to avoid being questioned', and that her eventual responding affidavit was 'vague and evasive'. The result was that, in many cases, the evidence against Myeni remained uncontested by her.

More seriously, the commission lambasted Myeni for revealing the identity of a witness (Witness X), who had testified on condition of anonymity. As soon as Myeni revealed Witness X's identity, Judge Zondo instructed that a criminal complaint be lodged with the police, but, at the time the commission's final report was published, nothing had happened on this front.

Mr X gave evidence that he had received money from the bank account of Myeni's son, Thalente Myeni. Witness X had no business relationship with Thalente or his business, Premier Attraction. Nevertheless, R3.15m was paid into Witness X's account in late 2015 and early 2016. Thalente instructed X where to pay the money. Some was withdrawn in cash and dropped at Myeni's home; two transfers were paid into an account of which Dudu Myeni provided the details. During his initial responses to the commission investigators, X said that the money was destined for the Jacob Zuma Foundation.

The commission's own investigations established that the money was paid to Thalente's Premier Attraction by a company called VNA Consulting. The latter, meanwhile, had been paid the money as part of a housing project in the Free State. Thalente, when he appeared before the commission, claimed that this all flowed from a business relationship he shared with both VNA and Witness X, despite X's denials. Thalente, however, could produce no documents to prove this and could not convince the commission that this was a reasonable explanation.

The commission recommended further investigations to establish whether there was any 'corrupt relationship' between all of those involved in this sequence of payments, which were redirected to benefit, among others, the Jacob Zuma Foundation.

## Pembroke Capital

With Myeni installed as chairperson at SAA, the incidents of irregularity, corruption and poor governance came thick and fast. The commission's first target was Myeni's conduct around a deal involving Pembroke Capital.

In 2012, the board of SAA had approved the acquisition of twenty A320 narrow-body aircraft. These were to be used to provide capacity for more regional and shorter flights. The deal was done but the financing (the loans used to buy the aircraft) still needed to be finalised. On 27 May 2013, following a procurement process and the withdrawal of the Bank of China, the board resolved to award a contract to Pembroke Capital. Pembroke would be given a contract to finance ten of the twenty aircraft, and a new procurement process would be needed for the remainder.

Kwinana and Myeni were unimpressed. On 2 June 2013, just days after the board had approved the Pembroke deal, Kwinana used a meeting of the board Audit and Risk Committee to start raising issues with the deal; but, as the deal was done, the board decided not to revisit it.

PFMA regulations required that the deal receive approval from the Minister of Public Enterprises. A request for approval was submitted shortly after the 27 May board decision. But then, on 20 June, Myeni wrote to Gigaba, the minister, and told him that the board had made a second decision: only two aircraft would be financed by Pembroke. Three weeks later, Myeni wrote again, saying that the board had made a third decision, this time to revert back to financing ten aircraft with Pembroke.

The commission heard evidence, which it clearly agreed with, that Myeni had never told the board about the second and third letters. In fact, the board had at no stage ever ratified the 'second decision'. It was true that the board secretary had tried to circulate a memo to get this second decision ratified, but this was shot down by the board as a decision had already been made. Members of the board speculated that Myeni had been trying to secure financing on her own, without the involvement of SAA management or the board, although this was not addressed in detail by the commission. Nevertheless, the commission would find that Myeni had materially misled the minister and that this amounted to a prima facie case of fraud.

The board became increasingly frustrated as, despite their resolution on the matter, the transaction was endlessly stalled. In January 2014, the board held a meeting to raise concerns as to why the transaction had not been concluded in the seven months since

May 2013. Myeni did not attend the meeting. The board noted that a big reason for the delay appeared to be because of Myeni's exchanges with Gigaba. The board held a further meeting on 3 April; Myeni again failed to attend. The board resolved that Myeni had to explain herself. She never did.

The failure to conclude the Pembroke transaction diligently and timeously was a disaster for SAA. The airline was forced to pay R800m in pre-delivery payments, which led to a further cash shortfall. Myeni, of course, refused to respond to questioning on her misrepresentations to the minister, citing privilege.

## The collapse of the board

By early 2014, the board was exasperated by the behaviour of Myeni; the Pembroke transaction was only one transgression. It set about trying to get Myeni to account for her behaviour and the minister to intervene. The board requested the Institute of Directors in South Africa NPC (IoDSA), a non-profit organisation that gives training and guidance to corporate bodies, to review the board. Myeni insisted that the evaluations be done in person, rather than electronically. This ended up delaying the finalisation of the board's report for the upcoming AGM on 29 January.

The tension around this issue, and others, led the board to convene a meeting on 22 January, where problems with Myeni's leadership were discussed. The result was that, the following day, all the board members, excluding Kwinana, Nkosi-Thomas and Dr Rajesh Naithani, wrote a letter to Myeni, which was copied to Gigaba. It laid out serious problems with Myeni's leadership. These included undermining the Pembroke deal and instituting forensic investigations into board members in ways that instilled a climate of fear. The board requested that Myeni attend a meeting to discuss the issue. Myeni refused.

On 3 April 2014, the board asked the company secretary to prepare a report about the board's effectiveness. Not surprisingly, the company secretary found that the board was not a coherent team, and detailed the conflict between the board and Myeni. The board adopted the report and wrote to the DPE to request a session with the minister, the board and Myeni. The board had, by this time, received legal advice that it could use the Companies Act to remove

Myeni. Gigaba duly scheduled a meeting. Myeni, again, failed to attend.

In June 2014, Lynne Brown, who had recently been appointed the new minister, convened a meeting with the board. Myeni arrived during the meeting. All issues were aired, following which the minister was provided with a report from DPE officials. It found that the board was completely dysfunctional. However, the board was in for a surprise. In October 2014, it was sent a notice that a special general meeting would be convened to consider removing the seven members who had signed the January 2014 letter. The board members, who believed they had done nothing wrong and that the meeting had already come to a predetermined outcome, decided to resign.

Later that month, as required, Brown appointed a new set of directors. She decided to retain only three members of the previous board, most of whom had already resigned. Brown retained Myeni, Kwinana and Dr Naithani. The commission was excoriating in its criticism of the decision to retain these three in the light of what had preceded it. Brown explained that she decided to retain Myeni and Kwinana to ensure 'continuity'. The commission was scathing in response:

> However, that begs the question: continuity for what purpose? The account by the majority of the board was that Ms Myeni had chaired a hopelessly dysfunctional board and had acted improperly and in breach of her duties. That is not the type of continuity that a Minister should be looking for in an SOE. Continuity could also have been maintained by acting on the complaints of the majority of the board, which may have encouraged them to stay on. The Minister's explanation for failing to deal with or meaningfully investigate serious, fundamental concerns about the organisation's leadership is inexcusable.

Brown appointed two new members to the board, Anthony Dixon and Dr John Tambi. By November 2015, Dixon had resigned, leaving a very tiny board. Indeed, the commission found that this was 'as good as SAA having no board at all',' and was 'scandalous'.

## The Airbus swap and Emirates deals

During the life of the commission, the non-profit group Organisation Undoing Tax Abuse (OUTA) brought a High Court claim against Myeni. OUTA approached the court to have Myeni declared a delinquent director under the Companies Act. In May 2020, Judge Tolmay ordered in OUTA's favour, declaring Myeni delinquent and thereby preventing her from acting as a director. Tolmay found that Myeni was a 'director gone rogue' who was guilty of 'dishonesty, breach of fiduciary duty and gross recklessness'.

The OUTA judgment, which the commission accepted, based its finding on Myeni's conduct in relation to two deals. The first deal was the 'Emirates deal'. Prior to Myeni's chairmanship of the board, SAA operated a code-sharing deal with Emirates; this allowed SAA to buy flight slots from Emirates and resell at a profit. It was very lucrative for SAA, bringing profits of R170m per year. Because SAA could not operate international flights economically, it became imperative to expand the scale of the code-sharing exercise. In 2013, SAA entered into a code-sharing relationship with Etihad, but this was not profitable.

However, in 2015 Emirates approached SAA for an enhanced code-sharing deal, which was extremely beneficial to SAA. The board had secured an external consultant whose report backed the deal, and so it began drafting a memorandum of understanding (MOU). Then Myeni got involved. She raised concerns with the deal and then demanded to meet personally with Emirates executives. A meeting was duly set up in Dubai, which Myeni then failed to attend, to the extreme chagrin of Emirates officials, who felt deeply disrespected. The CEO of Emirates then proposed a second meeting in Cape Town; again, Myeni failed to turn up. SAA executives tried to salvage the deal by signing a non-binding MOU, but, to all intents and purposes, the deal had been killed.

Evidence led before the High Court showed the Myeni was highly obstructive. One executive member received a call from Myeni to say Jacob Zuma had instructed that the MOU not be signed. In July 2015, Myeni attended a meeting with executives and staff; she demanded that all electronic devices be removed, issued nonsensical action points, and prevented the circulation of a round-robin resolution to support the MOU.

The second deal was the notorious Airbus deal. Under this deal, SAA would cancel an old deal that it had struck to buy ten Airbus A320-200s, and replace it with a leasing deal whereby SAA would lease five aircraft directly from Airbus. Finalising this deal was extremely urgent, as the original deal put SAA in a parlous situation. Under the old deal, SAA would be forced to pay Airbus R1bn in 2015. This would have effectively bankrupted SAA and led to the calling in of all sorts of debt – a calamitous development for SAA and the economy as a whole.

The National Treasury had already approved the new leasing deal; all that was missing was a final board resolution. Myeni, however, failed to meet a deadline to produce the resolution. Shortly thereafter, Myeni, Kwinana and Dr Tambi attempted to renegotiate the deal with Airbus. Myeni went so far as to send a letter to the president of Airbus to agree new terms. This new deal was, frankly, insane: it would include introducing a new company, African Aircraft Leasing Company, which would buy the aircraft from Airbus and then lease them to SAA. Although the commission is silent on this aspect, the obvious inference to draw, I believe, is that Myeni sought to insert a new middleman that could earn undue fees from the project. Ultimately, Treasury, under the guidance of Gordhan, had to intervene to save the SAA deal.

## LSG Skychefs and Air Chefs

In July 2015, Mathulwane Emily Mpshe was appointed the acting CEO of SAA, a position she held until November 2015, after which she was replaced by Musa Zwane. Mpshe testified before the commission that Myeni had repeatedly involved herself directly in operational matters, including employee disciplinary matters. She also testified about the outrageous intervention in one particular transaction: the LSG Skychefs deal.

In 2015, a subsidiary of SAA, Air Chefs, was engaged in providing catering in SAA lounges, but there were concerns about quality. As a result, the service went out on a new tender. LSG Skychefs, a subsidiary of Lufthansa but nevertheless a BEE-compliant South African company, was selected. In August 2015, Mpshe notified the board of the deal, which she could approve as it fell within her delegation of authority. She informed the board that Air Chefs would lose only a small part of its business and that LSG had agreed to take over the employment of all Air Chefs staff affected by the change. On 21 August 2015, Dr Masimba Dahwa, the head of SAA procurement, wrote a letter to LSG Skychefs notifying it of the award of the contract.

Ten days later, however, Myeni and Mpshe appeared before the Public Enterprise Parliamentary Portfolio Committee in Parliament. Myeni raised the issue of this award. This led the committee to complain about the appointment of a German company (Lufthansa, the parent company, was German, although, as we have seen, the subsidiary LSG Skychefs was South African). Myeni informed the committee that she was surprised by the deal and did not support it. Mpshe later claimed that, immediately after the meeting, Myeni had berated her for the deal, saying that, by giving it to a 'foreign' company, 'you mean Black people can't cook'.

The day after, Myeni wrote to Mpshe, telling her not to award the contract to LSG; Mpshe responded by saying that the contract award had already been made. The following day, Kwinana piled on further pressure, telling Mpshe to cancel the deal. Kwinana wrote that 'this looks like treason' and that she was going to request an investigation by the Special Investigating Unit.

On 29 September 2015, the board passed a resolution to cancel the contract, and awarded it to Air Chefs instead, without any proper procurement process. The decision was made despite legal advice received by Mpshe to the effect that it had already been legally awarded and cancellation might lead to a legal challenge. In fact, LSG did mount a legal challenge, and customers continued to complain about the quality of the services provided by Air Chefs.

The commission asked both Myeni and Kwinana about the Air Chefs deal. Myeni's and Kwinana's only comment of note was that their intervention was predicated on a desire to 'nurture' Air Chefs like a child. Beyond this, Myeni cited privilege, as was her wont. Kwinana's answers were, in the commission's view, basically nonsense. Indeed, Kwinana was a 'very poor witness', the commission found. 'She continually refused to make the most basic of concessions, even when the evidence presented to show that she was wrong was overwhelming. In the end, this severely undermined her credibility as a witness. She showed herself to be willing to be dishonest under oath simply to avoid having to account for her unlawful and irresponsible conduct.'

Considering the totality of the evidence on the LSG matter, the commission found that both Myeni and Kwinana had 'displayed a wanton disregard for the best interests of SAA' and had 'acted in gross disregard for their fiduciary duty'.

## The fake whistleblowers

The commission's discussion of Kwinana as a witness led it on to another jaw-dropping revelation. In August 2016, Kwinana resigned from the SAA board. She then approached OUTA (which would later have Kwinana's partner-in-crime, Myeni, declared a delinquent director in 2020) allegedly in the hope that it would not cite her in litigation involving Myeni. Kwinana told OUTA that she and Myeni used to go to internet cafes together, where they would fill out false whistleblower reports to target employees they didn't like.

OUTA's staff, perhaps in the knowledge that it would be needed down the line, recorded the conversation, and also produced a transcript. Both were given to the commission. When Kwinana was confronted with the audio and transcript by the commission, she nevertheless maintained that she had never made the claim. While the commission could not tell for certain whether Kwinana had lied to OUTA, it concluded that, on the balance of probabilities, she and Myeni probably did submit these false reports.

## The '30% set-aside' and the disturbing downfall of Dr Dahwa

During his 2015 State of the Nation address, President Zuma stated that 'government will set aside 30 per cent of appropriate categories of state procurement for purchasing from small to medium enterprises, cooperatives as well as township and rural communities'. The SAA board, in its infinite wisdom, interpreted this to mean that 30% of *all* SAA's procurement had to be set aside for BEE companies, and then adopted this as policy. It would come to be known as the '30% set-aside'.

Following the adoption of this policy, SAA began hosting supplier development conferences and roadshows to inform potential bidders about the 30% set-aside. Dr Masimba Dahwa, the head of SAA procurement, testified to the commission that Kwinana and Myeni put pressure on him to make commitments to suppliers at events, without any due process. One of the attendees at the roadshows was Vuyisile Ndzeku of JM Aviation – of whom more below.

Dahwa testified that, following one roadshow, Kwinana simply instructed Dahwa to award 15% of the services involved in two large contracts to all the attendees of the roadshow. The two contracts were then being serviced by Swissport and Engen. Dahwa explained that this was illegal, and that, in addition, he did not see how it would be feasible to award contracts to sixty different companies for the services. Kwinana told Dahwa to instead form a holding company, which, of course, he could simply not do as the chief procurement officer. Kwinana would ultimately form her own company, Quintessential, which attempted to give life to this vision.

Dahwa further testified that Kwinana and Myeni sought aggressively to impose the 30% set-aside, not just on forthcoming contracts, but on contracts SAA had already entered into. Dahwa was told by a senior member of SAA staff that Kwinana had attended a meeting with an SAA contractor, Bidvest. At the meeting, Kwinana told Bidvest that it had to implement the 30% set-aside policy. Bidvest was bemused; it was already BEE compliant and 63.42% black-owned, and, perhaps most importantly, the contract and its terms had already been agreed. Upon getting wind of this, Treasury was forced to write to the acting CEO, Mpshe, to explain what the 30% set-aside actually meant, an understanding which Mpshe shared. Kwinana, however, chose to raise questions with Treasury in a letter that the commission called 'curious'.

In an echo of the 'hostage situation' at SARS described earlier, things became bizarre and disturbing, according to the testimony of Dahwa and Mpshe. On 2 October 2015, Dahwa was called into a meeting with Kwinana in a boardroom at SAA Park. Dahwa testified that Kwinana asked him whether he had made any progress with the 30% set-aside and, specifically, whether he had implemented this in relation to SAA's existing contracts with Swissport and Engen. Dahwa again explained that this was unlawful.

Shortly thereafter, Myeni arrived at the meeting, and picked up the cudgel. Dahwa testified that Kwinana complained about his failure to implement the policy and accused Dahwa of making excuses. Myeni began threatening Dahwa, explaining that she intended to advertise his position. Seemingly out of nowhere, Myeni instructed Dahwa to write award letters to be sent to an entity called Jamicron and Kwinana's brainchild, Quintessential. Jamicron was to be told that it would be awarded 30% of SAA's huge contract with Swissport while Quintessential would be awarded 15% of SAA's contract with Engen.

Dahwa, despite the threats, refused to sign the letter. He testified that he was then instructed to remove his name from the letter, and to replace it with the name of the acting CEO, Mpshe. But Mpshe, too, refused to sign the letter. After Dahwa explained this, Myeni took them all into Mpshe's office, where Mpshe again refused to sign. When Mpshe finally decided to leave, Myeni was alleged to have told Dahwa that the EFF was going to raise a stink about transformation at SAA, and then made a pointed comment about Dahwa's nationality: he is Zimbabwean.

Outrageously, a week later Kwinana wrote to Myeni to complain about Dahwa's behaviour. She claimed Dahwa was 'hell bent on sabotaging and derailing the transformation agenda of the present government', and that he was part of a 'sinister, retrogressive agenda' to defeat transformation. Kwinana concluded by speculating that Dahwa was resistant to transformation because, as a Zimbabwean, he did not share the pain South Africans had suffered during the liberation struggle.

Dahwa testified that, at roughly the same time, he was asked by Myeni to put together a presentation to help MK veterans make bids for contracts at SAA. The meeting was attended by Kebby Maphatsoe, the Deputy Minister of Military Veterans and Defence, and Des van Rooyen. Van Rooyen was, at the time, treasurer general of the MK Veterans' Association, which purported to represent veterans from the ANC's armed wing Umkhonto we Sizwe. Dahwa testified that Myeni dressed him down for simply talking about 'policies and procedures'. Dahwa further claimed that Van Rooyen later organised meetings with him in which Van Rooyen insisted that SAA give security contracts to the MK veterans; Dahwa, for his part, was disturbed that Van Rooyen even knew about the contracts.

The writing was now on the wall for Dahwa, who became increasingly worried after Van Rooyen's influence was seemingly illustrated by his appointment as Minister of Finance. Soon thereafter, Dahwa was accused of disciplinary infractions, which the commission concluded were bogus. Following an attempt at conciliation and then arbitration, Dahwa accepted a six-month pay package and resigned. He testified that, owing to the manner of his dismissal, he remained unemployed and did not receive another job offer for three and a half years, during which time he lost his house.

Mpshe, too, was soon to be axed. On 13 November 2015, not long after the October bust-up in the SAA boardroom, the board resolved that Mpshe be 'removed with immediate effect' as acting CEO, to be replaced by Musa Zwane. Mpshe returned to her position as HR director at SAA, but shortly thereafter she received a letter from Zwane that itemised her wrongdoing and told her to go on leave. Mpshe would be suspended for 22 months. Frustrated that her attempts to resolve the issue were going nowhere, she accepted a separation package in 2018.

## The extraordinary tale of BNP Capital

One of the key witnesses before the commission on the subject of SAA was Cynthia Agnes Soraya Stimpel. Stimpel had worked for ten years as the head of financial risk and analysis for SAA and then acting group treasurer.

Stimpel testified that, by 2015, SAA was in a precarious position. It had a short-term debt of R11bn, which was continually being 'rolled over'; SAA was not unlike a man with huge credit card debt who was paying vast amounts of money just to service the monthly interest. Treasury, displeased, instructed SAA to develop a long-term debt plan. The result was that SAA set about consolidating its short-term loans into long-term loans with a ten-year settlement period. If done correctly, it would have saved SAA R400m in interest payments.

The plan was approved by the board in April 2015, and a request for proposal (RFP) was issued in the same month. The RFP was sent to the Big Five banks in South Africa. Kwinana, however, began questioning why it had been sent only to the Big Five, and not to other providers. The board, after some toing and froing with Treasury, instructed Stimpel to issue a new RFP, this time including other smaller companies among those that would be allowed to bid. Stimpel testified that this was the first time in her knowledge that the board had become so intimately involved in an RFP.

A new RFP was issued on 10 September 2015 with responses due in October 2015. Shortly thereafter, Stimpel had a conversation with Wolf Meyer, who was SAA's CFO at the time. Meyer claimed that a person from a company called First Financial Solutions had told him that 'number 1' had instructed the contract go to them. Meyer had recorded the conversation on a microphone pen.

Meyer testified that the following month he was called into a board meeting and told by Myeni to hand over the microphone pen: he was deeply concerned that Myeni was even aware of its existence. In the light of the incident, and following negative press stories about Meyer, he resigned as CFO. He was replaced by Phumeza Nhantsi, who was appointed acting CFO at the end of November 2015. Nhantsi would play an important role in the unfolding of the BNP deal.

The bidder that scored the highest on the long-term debt RFP was a company called Seacrest Capital, which offered to finance the full R15bn. According to Stimpel, Seacrest then became oddly reluctant to undergo a full due diligence process. Stimpel thus told the board to either accept the Seacrest offer, but only after a due diligence process, or give a smaller contract to the Big Five banks to service an imminent debt need of R4bn.

Things then went full-on nuts. In December 2015, the board decided to reject both recommendations. Instead, it now recommended raising the money from the Free State Development Corporation (FDC), a body that, as later investigations confirmed, was only legally entitled to invest in the Free State. The board resolution gave the new acting CFO, Nhantsi, and the new acting CEO, Zwane, approval to enter into the contract. As it emerged, the FDC offer consisted of a single letter of proposal sent directly to the board by the FDC's Shephard Moyo, in which he explained that the FDC was exploring a new joint venture in the Free State with a foreign investor.

Stimpel, for her part, was never provided with the FDC's letter, and only saw a copy when it was given to her by the commission's investigators. When she was instructed by the board to 'ratify' the appointment of the FDC, she refused, pointing out the whole process was irregular as FDC had not bid as part of the RFP.

When the FDC provided a term sheet (an offer of how much the loan would cost), it emerged that the FDC's partner in the deal was a company called Grissag. Grissag was one of the funders behind Seacrest, the original RFP winner that had resisted due diligence. Grissag was an odd company. Pieter Johannes van der Merwe testified on behalf of Grissag before the commission. He claimed to have formed Grissag in 2014 with a retired Russian national. He testified that both he and the Russian national had previously worked for the Soviet Union.

By April 2016, after Treasury reviewed the deal and confirmed that the FDC had no mandate to do this sort of work, the FDC deal had died. Now the board decided to appoint a transaction advisor to oversee the debt process; Stimpel attempted to object, pointing out that this sort of work was already being done by SAA Treasury. Nevertheless, a new RFP was issued for a transaction advisor. Initially it was suggested that the advisor would, in addition to consulting and advising, also source the loan, but this was eventually removed – for the time being.

Seven bidders responded to the new transaction advisor RFP, including the company BNP Capital. BNP Capital's joint venture partner in the bid was a company called Inline Trading 10 (Pty Limited). It would later emerge that Inline Trading 10 was a car dealership, of all things. SAA's various bid committees nevertheless recommended BNP Capital, despite a total lack of information about Inline Trading 10, and despite the fact that BNP had no consolidated BEE certificate, which was a mandatory requirement.

BNP was duly appointed, but the scope of its contract swiftly changed. On 21 April 2016, the board approved a modification that would allow BNP to both provide advice on the debt deal and source the financing. Soon thereafter, Nhantsi contacted Stimpel and said she wanted her to ratify a decision to award BNP a 3% transaction advisory fee. Stimpel refused, and then went on leave. She told her juniors not to sign the deal, but to no avail; one of her juniors, in her absence, signed off on paying BNP a 1.5% fee, which would have equalled R256m excluding VAT.

Stimpel was told the news by WhatsApp and immediately returned home. She tried her best to prevent any further movement on the deal, but without success. On 24 May 2016, the board approved the decision to appoint BNP as the transaction advisor and also to source funding; the letter of award was sent the following day.

BNP, soon after, wrote to SAA to inform the airline that it had already done loads of work on the deal, and was thus demanding a cancellation fee that would cover its costs. The cancellation fee would be 50% of the transaction advisory fee and 50% of the fee it would charge for financing. This would come to about R128m. SAA was now in the invidious position that it would have to accept whatever financing deal BNP put before the airline, lest it incur the cancellation fee.

And who did BNP Capital suggest supply the loan? None other than Grissag, which had been the joint venture partner in the FDC's offer, and one of the funders behind Seacrest, which had refused due diligence. Grissag provided an extremely onerous term sheet, in which SAA would pay 3% of the total loan as a first fee, and then 1% of every amount SAA withdrew from the loan facility. Together, this would have been an enormous amount of money. Despite every regulation in the book being violated, and despite these horrific terms, Nhantsi signed the term sheet with Grissag at the beginning of June 2016.

Nhantsi gave extensive evidence before the commission, which the commission dealt with in depth. It found that Nhantsi was neither qualified nor suited for the position of CFO. She claimed that she had approved the BNP deal under severe pressure. According to her version, the real player behind all of this was a man by the name of Masotsha Mngadi, who, at the time, worked at Nedbank; Myeni had given Mngadi's number to Nhatnsi and told her to consult with him. Kwinana, in her evidence, claimed that Mngadi was 'Myeni's man'. Mngadi, in turn, was the controlling mind behind Inline Trading 10 – the car dealership that was also BNP's BEE partner. Nhantsi testified that she believed that Myeni may have benefited from the deal, or intended to do so.

There were further layers to this onion. When Kwinana approached OUTA (as we have seen), she told the organisation that Mngadi was close to Myeni's son, Thalente. She had seen Mngadi and Thalente together on multiple occasions. The conversation was, as noted above, recorded: but this did not stop Kwinana from denying in her testimony that she ever said this to OUTA.

Stimpel would not let the matter go and, in the face of repeated violations of logic and good procurement practice, she blew the whistle. She approached OUTA and laid out the problems with the deal. To prove her case, Stimpel sought copies of the BNP deal, and found them on the floor of the office of a procurement advisor. She took the copies to provide to OUTA. Myeni subsequently confronted Stimpel for 'stealing' the documents. Stimpel, not long after, was suspended because she took the documents, and eventually accepted a leaving package of six months' pay and early retirement. She testified that this involved serious financial losses to herself.

OUTA, soon after, announced that it was launching a High Court case to seek an urgent interdict to stop the deal. The day after the announcement, SAA decided to cancel the deal. SAA attempted to save face by claiming that this was because BNP had just lost its financial service provider licence. But, as a final kicker in this mind-bending deal, it eventually emerged that BNP had lost its licence in May 2015, before it had even entered into the deal with SAA.

Nhantsi and Zwane were, for their part, eventually punished for their misconduct. On 19 June 2018, Nazeer Cassim, as part of an SAA disciplinary proceeding, found that both were guilty of gross misconduct.

The commission, in its conclusion on the BNP Capital deal, praised Stimpel for her service and steadfast commitment to good governance. Without her 'unwavering commitment to proper procurement process', the commission found, the BNP deal would most likely have gone through in some form. Sadly, the commission noted, there was nobody like Stimpel around to stop two other profoundly problematic deals that were concluded: the Swissport and AAR–JM Aviation deals.

## Swissport and JM Aviation

In late 2015, the SAA subsidiary SAAT took a decision to conclude a contract with Swissport, which would extend its existing contract for a further five years. Swissport was to be contracted to provide so-called ground handling services, in effect to operate the infrastructure around the movement of aircraft, luggage and other necessities. SAAT's tender had two stipulations: first, that Swissport would have to buy all the equipment to be used on the contract from a BEE vendor and that it would also agree to buy all ground power units (GPUs) in SAA's inventory. GPUs are, basically, big starter batteries that power or start parked aircraft.

Peter Kohl, the former CEO of Swissport, gave an affidavit to the commission. According to his version, Swissport SA was heavily reliant on SAA's business, and, if it failed to get the contract, Swissport SA was likely to be liquidated. In December 2015, Lester Peters, a senior official in global supply chain management at SAA, sent Swissport a draft contract that included a 30% set-aside provision. Swissport and Kohl pushed back, saying that it would not genuinely advance transformation, and was likely to be illegal.

On 10 February, Kohl and Vuyisile Ndzeku met with Kwinana and other officials from SAA. Ndzeku would end up playing a major role in this transaction. At the time, he was a shareholder in Swissport and, simultaneously, a shareholder in a company called JM Aviation. JM Aviation's other shareholders consisted of Ndzeku's family and one member of staff. During the meeting, Kwinana insisted that Swissport sign the draft contract sent by Peters that included the 30% set-aside, and informed Kohl that SAA wanted the 30% to be given to a company called Jamicron, which was run by Daluxolo Peter. Swissport again refused. SAA responded by writing a letter to Swissport indicating that it would, as a result, cancel Swissport's business with SAA. This would have been a calamity for the company.

But the threat never materialised. In March 2016, Swissport signed a new contract with SAA, in terms of which it would subcontract some (but seemingly not a full 30%) of its services to BEE companies. It also agreed to purchase SAAT's GPUs. Under the agreement, SAA got to choose Swissport's BEE partner on the project. This was JM Aviation, which, in addition, would have the privilege of buying SAA's GPUs and selling them to Swissport. Kohl, for his part, claimed that he was unaware that his colleague Ndzeku, while working for Swissport, was also the controlling mind behind JM Aviation.

When Ndzeku testified, he confirmed that he never disclosed his directorship in JM Aviation to Swissport. He also confirmed that he had had frequent conversations with Kwinana about the deal and how to facilitate the award of 30% of the contract set aside to Jamicron, run by Daluxolo Peter. Ndzeku claimed that when he met Kwinana in person, she was sometimes accompanied by Peter. Kwinana told Ndzeku that both she and Myeni wanted Peter and Jamicron to become the empowerment partners.

Swissport landed the contract, in part because it was willing to pay JM Aviation R28.5m, which it did in March 2016, the same month in which SAA agreed the deal with Swissport. JM Aviation then transferred R20m of this amount to Jamicron. Ndzeku testified before the commission that the payment to Jamicron was actually Peter Kohl's idea. Daluxolo Peter, however, claimed that it was entirely Ndzeku's idea and that, moreover, Ndzeku was the person who formed Jamicron and installed Peter as a director. Ndzeku's denials of any involvement fell flat, however, because he was unable to explain why he had also been paid R2.5m out of the R28.5m.

Unfortunately, the commission's description of how the R28.5m was fully disbursed is vague and a little hard to follow. What emerges is that, of this amount, R5m was retained by Kwinana's friend Daluxolo Peter. A further R2.5m was also paid to BMK Attorneys with the reference 'Pete'. BMK Attorneys, at the time, was undertaking the disciplinary hearing into Myeni's enemy Dr Dahwa. Soon thereafter, BMK Attorneys used the R2.5m to buy two luxury cars for Lester Peters – the SAA official who, way back in December 2015, had tried to get Swissport to sign the deal.

JM Aviation would also end up paying both Kwinana and another SAA official, Nontsasa Memela, who was the head of procurement at SAAT. Although it is not entirely clear from the commission's report, these payments do not appear to have derived from the R28.5m paid by Swissport to JM Aviation but from other dodgy deals, which I'll come to shortly.

In any event, the commission took an extremely dim view of Swissport's payment to JM Aviation. It did not make a definitive finding of corruption against Swissport, not least because it was not able to get Kohl to give oral evidence. Nevertheless, the commission was extremely unimpressed that Swissport was unable to provide any evidence that the payment to JM Aviation pertained to any sort of legitimate contract; it was also swayed by the fact that JM Aviation, prior to this payment, was effectively dormant and, when it received the R28.5m, spent none of it on the type of business expenses incurred by an actual enterprise. The commission thus found:

The only reasonable inference to draw from the evidence is that Swissport was in dire straits when SAA terminated its month to month ground handling services contract in February 2016. At that stage, Swissport was not willing to accede to SAA's demand that it part with 30% of the revenue under the agreement. However, it faced liquidation in South Africa if it did not retain the SAA work. It therefore was willing to procure the services of JM Aviation and Jamicron (Mr Ndzeku and Mr Peter) to facilitate the conclusion of the contract with SAA. These parties then paid certain crucial decision-makers at SAAT (Ms Yakhe Kwinana, Ms Nontsasa Memela and Mr Lester Peters) and the contract was indeed awarded to them. JM Aviation and Jamicron then took a share of that payment. If Swissport paid this amount in order to secure the ground handling contract with SAA and knew that it would be used to pay bribes to SAA and SAAT officials, then it committed an act of corruption.

## The sale of the GPUs

As I noted above, one part of the whole Swissport deal was that SAA would sell its ground power units (GPUs) to Swissport. SAA would then lease the GPUs back as needed. On the face of it, this was a terrible deal, because SAA would sell inventory it still needed to use. Indeed, SAA ended up paying R8.4m to lease the GPUs back.

But that was not the only oddity in the deal. SAAT ended up selling the GPUs, not to Swissport, but to JM Aviation. Originally, SAAT had bought the GPUs for R9.1m including VAT in 2015. Not long after, SAAT sold the GPUs to JM Aviation for only R3,392,640. Three days later, JM Aviation sold the same GPUs to Swissport for more than R9m. JM Aviation, as a result, earned R6m in profit in the space of three days.

The SAAT official who was tasked with negotiating the price was JM Aviation was none other than Nontsasa Memela. The commission was frankly disdainful of Memela's evidence before it, which showed that she made no serious attempt to establish the value of the GPUs before they were sold. Memela, as I'll show below, was also a recipient of payments from JM Aviation.

## AAR and JM Aviation

JM Aviation was central to another scandalous contract awarded by SAAT. This was related to the supply of components. The background is that SAAT hired certain components it needed to operate from third-party suppliers. This saved SAAT money because it did not to pay inventory costs. Prior to February 2013, this contract had been served by Air France.

SAAT decided to go to tender for a new contract in February 2013. SAA's Cross-Functional Sourcing Team (CFST), basically SAA's technical boffins, had recommended awarding Air France the contract for SAA's Airbus fleet and Air Israel for the Boeing fleet. Shortly thereafter, however, the tender was withdrawn, and a new tender was issued, this time in October 2014.

Bids were received for the new tender at the end of 2014, and the CFST was in the process of evaluating them. But then, in April 2015, the board instructed the CFST to stop the evaluation because SAAT wanted time to try to negotiate a contract with a company that had not even bid; an American company called AAR. Two months later, the board cancelled the second tender process, and gave approval for negotiations to begin with AAR.

The relationship between AAR and SAAT stretched back to February 2015 when Cheryl Jackson, a manager at AAR, made a proposal to become the components supplier to the acting CEO of SAA, Nico Bezuidenhout. It was clearly favourably received as, between 2 and 8 May 2015, board members Dr Tambi and Kwinana, acting CEO Zwane, and the procurement official Memela all flew at AAR's expense to the US, where they were driven around in limos and wined and dined. The following month, SAAT and AAR signed an MOU that would smooth the way for AAR to provide the services. This was, according to the commission, a violation of the PFMA, as these sorts of agreements required Treasury approval, which was never sought.

Further tenders were issued in 2015 and then subject to withdrawals and caveats. In December 2015, SAA issued its final, fifth, tender on the components deal, which it had been trying to conclude since 2013. AAR submitted a bid; its joint venture partner was JM Aviation.

Despite AAR's close relationship with SAAT's leadership, it was not viewed as the favourite by SAAT's boffins in the CFST charged with evaluation. On review of the bids, CFST recommended that the contract be awarded to Air France. The CFST was particularly concerned that AAR might have been low-balling and offering an unrealistic bid as it had changed its prices during the bidding process. As it later emerged, these concerns were well founded: SAA ended up paying R1.8bn to AAR for services that AAR had claimed would cost around R1.2bn. The CFST's recommendation was approved by another SAA procurement body and then sent to the board for final approval.

On 9 May 2016, SAAT held a special session to discuss the contract. SAAT, whose chairman was Kwinana at the time, rejected these recommendations and instead resolved to award the contract to AAR and JM Aviation. Four days later, on 13 May 2016, SAAT sent the letter of award to AAR and JM Aviation. As part of the deal, SAAT agreed to pay AAR a deposit of $4.3m (about R60m), but this was supposed to be in the form of a credit note, not cash. Despite this contractual nicety, SAAT ended up paying the deposit in cash.

So, SAAT had been trying to sign a contract with a new component supplier since 2013. In the middle of this process, it decided to start working with an American company, AAR, which had not even been one of the original bidders. SAAT ended up issuing a remarkable *five* different tenders, after four had been cancelled for various spurious reasons. Then, when AAR and JM Aviation's bid was considered by the experts, they were rejected, and were only awarded the bid when the expert recommendations were overturned by Kwinana's board. And then AAR–JM were paid a deposit of R60m in cash, when they were only supposed to be given a credit note.

The commission's investigations revealed that all this work to favour AAR (and it did find that both Kwinana and Memela had favoured AAR over other bidders) flowed from a byzantine connection of relationships, which is both too mind-numbing and too dense to unpack here. But the gist of the commission's investigations is that AAR had unofficially worked with an agent called Sibongile Sambo, who worked for the company SRS Aviation. Sambo introduced AAR to the acting CEO Zwane, and also became fast friends with Memela, the SAA procurement official. Through Memela, Sambo met Kwinana. Sambo testified that Kwinana informed her that AAR would need to pay Kwinana and other parties to get the deal. But, after working on the deal for a number of years with AAR, Sambo was cut out at the last minute in favour of Ndzeku's JM Aviation, and she gave extensive testimony to the commission.

## The kickbacks to Kwinana and Memela

Kwinana was paid what appear to be pretty obvious kickbacks by JM Aviation via a company that Kwinana controlled called Zanospark. Zanospark was paid R4.3m by JM Aviation between July 2016 and September 2016. Part of this was sourced from the profit that JM Aviation earned in buying SAAT's GPUs on the cheap and selling them a few days later to Swissport for a R6m profit. The commission's investigations revealed that five days after Swissport paid JM Aviation, the latter paid R2.5m to Ms Hendricks, who was Ndzeku's wife. Hendricks then paid the funds to Zanospark.

Ndzeku, when asked about the payments, claimed that he had paid the money via Hendricks, but that this was part of an investment in Kwinana's Zanospark. He said that Kwinana was to use the money for forex trading. But neither Kwinana nor Ndzeku could provide any evidence to prove this investment relationship, and, after dismissing both their paper-thin defences, the commission found:

> Ms Kwinana was not investing Mr Ndzeku's money for him. The money she received from JM Aviation and Ms Hendricks was for her ... Ms Kwinana has failed to give any plausible explanation for why as the Chairperson of SAAT and a board member of SAA it was lawful and appropriate for her to have received payments from an entity, and persons affiliated with it, that was a supplier to SAAT. The payments were, therefore, probably corrupt payments because they were made in exchange for decisions, in which Ms Kwinana was involved, that benefited the entity that made the payments.

JM Aviation also paid Memela: in this case, JM Aviation paid R2.5m towards the purchase of a R3.8m house for Memela's benefit in the Johannesburg suburb of Bedfordview. Memela had previously been denied finance to purchase the property. The payment was made on 5

May 2016, only four days prior to AAR–JM Aviation being selected for the components tender, and at the very same time that Memela had been tasked with negotiating the sales price on the GPUs

The commission was spun an entertaining yarn about why JM Aviation had made a payment for Memela's benefit. This payment was made to Memela's attorney, Ms Lindelwa Mbanjwa, who then used it for the Bedfordview sale. Both Ndzeku and Memela claimed that Ndzeku had bought a house from Memela's mother in 2015, and that the R2.5m payment was to cover the cost of this sale. Ndzeku presented documents to try to prove this story. This included an affidavit that was supposedly deposed by Memela's now-deceased mother, to which she was supposed to have attested in 2015 or 2016. In the midst of all of this was an additional property purchase, which was eventually abandoned, in which Memela was going to buy a property from Kwinana's investment company, Slipknot.

The story fell apart spectacularly when the commission began pointing out a series of improbabilities in Ndzeku's version. Ndzeku eventually crumbled and admitted that the affidavit supposedly signed by Memela's dead mother was, indeed, a forgery. He also admitted that the purchase agreement he presented showing he was buying Memela's property was not signed in 2015, as he suggested, but in 2019. Ndzeku claimed that the whole thing was a ruse fabricated by Ms Mbanjwa. Memela, in response to this, stuck to her story, but to little avail: one by one, the commission punctured her explanations and excuses. Kwinana also fared badly, as it emerged that the whole Slipknot agreement was also most likely forged.

After showing that Memela was involved in multiple ways in the AAR–JM Aviation components tender and the sale of the GPUs, and after eviscerating the versions put forward by Ndzuku, Memela and Kwinana, the commission found as follows:

> In the end, the evidence presented to the commission shows clearly that Ms Memela received payment of R2.5m from JM Aviation to facilitate the JM Aviation/AAR components tender and the sale of the GPUs. It also shows that Ms Memela, Ms Kwinana and Ms Mbanjwa conspired to try to hide their corrupt activities by fabricating agreements after the commission of their corrupt activities. This type of conduct calls for prosecution.

## SAA, Regiments and Ramosebudi

As we saw with the sections on Eskom and Transnet, Regiments made a killing from contracts it got with SOEs. SAA was no different.

Regiments had a key ally at SAA: Phetolo Ramosebudi, who served as the SAA treasurer from January 2012 until February 2015, after which, as I've already noted, he was appointed treasurer at Transnet. Prior to his stint at SAA, Ramosebudi was treasurer at Airports Company South Africa (ACSA) from 2007 until 2011.

It was while at ACSA that Ramosebudi developed a 'corrupt relationship with Regiments Capital', as the commission bluntly stated. Between 2010 and 2013, he issued invoices in the name of his brother to Regiments totalling R9,132,490.39. Ramosebudi sent the invoices to either Eric Wood or Niven Pillay, both partners at Regiments Capital. While Regiments did not pay the full amount invoiced, the commission was able to confirm that they did pay R5,173,103.66 to Ramosebudi or entities linked to him. Ramosebudi, when confronted by the commission, offered no explanation, and cited privilege against self-incrimination.

The commission found that the payments from Regiments Capital to Ramosebudi seemed to be 'a corrupt quid pro quo for Mr Ramosebudi's role in allowing Regiments Capital to extract more than R50 million in gratuitous payments from ACSA'. The commission identified four times when Regiments was paid these 'gratuitous fees', all of which are so complicated they require their own book.

The key to these transactions was that Regiments, which was supposed to be representing the best interests of ACSA, was simultaneously working with the banks offering loans to ACSA to generate fees. The commission was particularly critical of Nedbank, and two of its employees especially: Mario Visnenza and Moss Brickman. The commission could not make definitive findings on Nedbank because it ran out of time to call the bank to account; it nevertheless indicated that there was evidence that Regiments and Nedbank worked together to increase the fees that both would be paid by ACSA.

Ramosebudi took his proclivity for assisting Regiments with him to SAA, and was involved in a particularly problematic deal. In November 2013, SAA issued a tender for financial advisors who could 'unlock' working capital (whatever that means). The contract was awarded to McKinsey, which had partnered with Regiments. While McKinsey denied any knowledge of Regiments' problematic dealings, it did agree to repay SAA when the commission approached the firm with evidence. McKinsey repaid over R12.4m to SAA on this deal.

The bid was subjected to extreme manipulation. The commission noted that Ramosebudi had sent Wood key information about the forthcoming contract a month prior to the bid even being issued. Ramosebudi asked Regiments to comment on the scope of the contract and the evaluation criteria; Regiments supplied changes and comments, which were integrated in the tender. A week after Ramosebudi shared these documents and invited Regiments' comments, Ramosebudi invoiced Regiments for R375,606, which was eventually paid to one of Ramosebudi's companies. So, in simple terms, Ramosebudi was allowing Regiments to literally write the terms and conditions of the bid that it would eventually win and, within a week, he was invoicing Regiments.

Ramosebudi went even further in helping Regiments win the deal, according to the commission. During the bid evaluation process, Ramosebudi told Eric Wood that the bid committee evaluating the deal – on which Ramosebudi sat – had a maximum approval authority of R100m. The McKinsey and Regiments' bid had included an 8% fee which, when applied, might have pushed their fee over the R100m threshold. Ramosebudi told Wood to cap the fees, which Regiments duly did, reducing it to just over R80m. When Regiments wrote to the bid committee to say it was reducing its fees, a conscientious official argued that the other bidders should also be allowed to review their offers. The commission found that Ramosebudi successfully pressured the official to let the matter go.

The Gupta enterprise lurked behind a good deal of Regiments' contracts with many SOEs, and the case of SAA was no different. The commission's investigations revealed that in March 2015 SAA paid McKinsey just over R12m. Regiments invoiced McKinsey for almost exactly half of the fee McKinsey received, which was duly paid. Of the amount to Regiments, just under R2.5m was paid to Homix and a further R312,075 to Albatime, both of which were entities that formed part of the extended Gupta enterprise. Ramosebudi was asked, during his evidence, whether he knew payments to Regiments were being paid on to companies involving Salim Essa and Ashok Narayan, the publicly identified controlling mind of Homix. Ramosebudi refused to answer the question.

## The failure of the auditors: PwC's calamitous conduct at SAA

SAA appointed PwC and Nkonki to audit the SOE from 2013/14 to 2015/16. They were paid a total of R69,780,888 for this work. The commission found that this was irregular expenditure because SAA and PwC–Nkonki were technically required to get the approval (or concurrence) of the Auditor General every year the services were renewed. This was not done. The fact that PwC failed to pick this up gives a flavour of how it conducted the audits of SAA.

In late 2014 and early 2015, PwC joined forces with Yakhe Kwinana's audit firm, Kwinana and Associates. They jointly bid for three contracts from SAA and were awarded one, for which Kwinana's company was paid over R6m in 2016. PwC was supposed to conduct a conflict of interest check. The usual standard was to check whether the work it performed with a joint venture partner equalled more than 5% of the partner's revenue. Kwinana and Associates' standard was 10%. With little justification, PwC changed its own standard to 10%.

Kwinana's daughter Lumka Goniwe told PwC that Kwinana's firm had a revenue of over R50m in 2015, and that it expected the fees from the contract to equal only R4.2m (although they came to over R6m in the end). On this basis, they passed the 5%–10% threshold check. But when the commission approached SARS, it turned out that Kwinana's firm had declared a turnover of only R10.5m. The commission was, after some investigation, unable to untangle whether Kwinana's firm had misled SARS or if Kwinana's firm had misled PwC. The commission thus recommended that SARS consider investigating Kwinana and Associates' tax filings.

For the entire period in which PwC and Nkonki audited SAA, they issued unqualified audits. In layman's terms, this meant that PwC and Nkonki had not identified any irregular or unsupported expenditure; a remarkable finding in the light of the orgy of corruption the commission uncovered.

In 2016/17, the Auditor General took over SAA's audits. The AG's first audit was a total about-turn on PwC's and Nkonki's previous efforts. The AG reported a qualified audit with significant findings of concern; in a sample of 140 contracts the AG reviewed, it found that 121 were irregular or non-compliant in some way, equal to R6.6bn out of an expenditure of R7.6bn. Considering how different their findings were, the Auditor General's office then undertook a review of PwC–Nkonki's audits to see if they could be relied on: in short, they couldn't. The Auditor General, as a result, was forced to redo PwC–Nkonki's audits.

The commission heard the testimony of Pule Joseph Mothibe, the PwC partner responsible for SAA's audit. The commission grilled Mothibe about PwC's work. In one case, the Auditor General and the commission found that PwC–Nkonki had given one deal a clean audit, even though it had access to none of the tender documents. 'It is baffling how PwC could have reached any conclusion about compliance – and not note a scope limitation on their findings – in circumstances where there were no supporting documents,' the commission commented.

In the period when Mothibe was on the stand, he was also being investigated by the Independent Regulatory Board for Auditors for potential professional misconduct in relation to the auditing of SAA. In July 2020, after he had given evidence, Mothibe consented to IRBA making an order against him of non-compliance for failing to identify problems in SAA's audits from 2014 to 2016. In the process, Mothibe effectively confessed on PwC's behalf. The commission was, again, unimpressed that PwC had failed to come clean earlier: 'It should not have taken two more years, and a Commission of Inquiry, to achieve this level of accountability from an entity like PwC.'

The commission laid a good deal of the responsibility for the capture of SAA at the door of SAA's auditors. Reviewing PwC's and Nkonki's failure to properly audit the Air Chefs contract, the commission was of the view that if 'SAA's auditors [had] just done their job and the correct attention had been drawn to this unlawful decision, some of the devastating events of the next months at SAA may well have been different'.

The most jaw-dropping example of negligence related to the R1.8bn Swissport contract described earlier. The commission's investigations established that PwC–Nkonki failed to audit the Swissport contract *at all*. PwC–Nkonki decided not to include the Swissport contract in the sample of contracts that it would audit that year. This was particularly remarkable because there was considerable media attention given to the Swissport deal at the time, which should have raised red flags.

Not PwC–Nkonki: when the audit file for 2015/16 was reviewed, there was no evidence that the auditors had done any form of media search as part of their compliance checks. The commission was, again, scathing: 'Had [PwC–Nkonki] done their work properly, had they been doing adequate media reviews in 2015 and 2016, they would have come across these red flags. Had they read board minutes and resolutions with an enquiring mind and a concern to identify irregular expenditure, then this contract would not, and could not, have escaped scrutiny.'

By contrast, when the Auditor General's office reviewed the Swissport contract after the fact, it declared irregular expenditure amounting to R362m, and recommended a further investigation into JM Aviation.

## Why was Myeni not stopped?

In reviewing all the evidence about SAA, the commission sought to answer a very simple question: why was Myeni allowed to remain as chairman until 2017, long after the extraordinary litany of irregularities had started entering the public domain?

On 24 August 2016, the day after Kwinana resigned from the SAA board, Cabinet held a meeting to discuss how the SAA board could move forward. The Cabinet minutes reflect that Pravin Gordhan, of all people, motivated to retain Myeni for a further two years. Fortunately, she was only kept on the board for a single year.

The commission asked Pravin Gordhan to explain this decision and, in assessing his version, was clearly unimpressed by the overall reasoning put forward. But, in the end, the commission generally found that the version presented by Gordhan, in at least one respect, was likely true: Myeni had been kept on the SAA board, long after she should have been removed, at the insistence of Jacob Zuma. This was also the view of Nhlanhla Nene, who, as we have seen, had tried to persuade Zuma to sack Myeni in 2015.

The commission was not able to ask Jacob Zuma about Gordhan's version because he refused to testify any further after two and a half days on the stand: 'he did so in order to avoid having to answer questions in the commission about matters such as this,' it commented. 'He knew he was not going to have answers to many of the questions that were bound to be put to him.'

In the light of Gordhan's and Nene's version, and the failure of Zuma to give a response, the commission thus found that, notwithstanding serious reservations about Myeni's conduct held by Treasury, 'the former President insisted that Ms Myeni be retained in her position at any cost, and with complete disregard for the welfare of SAA. His Cabinet followed suit and voted to retain her beyond 2016.'

## Fast money at SA Express

The last contract that the commission probed had to do with the SAA subsidiary, SA Express. In about 2014, the North West Province had begun looking at how to develop and expand the use of its regional airports in Pilanesberg and Mahikeng. The proposal was made that North West should place contracts with airlines to run new routes between Mahikeng and Johannesburg, and between Pilanesberg, Johannesburg and Cape Town.

The commission found that the contract was awarded to SA Express in a totally irregular manner. Following a meeting in August 2014 involving several provincial departments, six airlines were invited to submit proposals. Four airlines eventually responded. But the contract was never advertised or put out to tender. Without any competitive procurement process to establish the best bidder, SA Express was recommended by the Department of Transport to the provincial Executive Committee (Exco), which agreed with the recommendation to appoint SA Express. The chair of Exco was the provincial Premier, Supra Mahumapelo. Remarkably, SA Express had quoted a fee of over R100m, while another bidder had proposed a fee of just R4.5m.

Following this shambolic process, the provincial Department of Transport entered into a contract with SA Express for the route. The agreement envisaged that the province would pay out two sets of subsidies. First, it would pay SA Express directly for running the aircraft and flying the routes. Second, it would pay a separate management company, which would be responsible for the 'ground handling' services at the provincial airports. At the time SA Express and the province signed the deal, the management company had not yet been identified.

The agreement envisaged that the North West would pay SA Express R232m between 2015 and 2019, and a further R175m to the ground-handling management company. The commission sought to understand whether the fees charged by SA Express in terms of the agreement could be considered reasonable. For this, it heard the evidence of AM Phiri, who had been the general manager for regional expansion at SA Express between 2010 and 2012. Phiri's analysis, which the commission appears to accept, was that there were a number of instances where the fees charged by SA Express seemed to be excessive.

But it was the payments that the province made to the ground-handling management company that ended up presenting the biggest corruption risk. The company selected for the management was called Koreneka. At the time, it was run by Babadi Tlatsana, who ended up giving extensive evidence at the commission.

According to Tlatsana, she approached SA Express to offer her services, and in the process she came to meet and develop a relationship with Brian van Wyk, the commercial manager at SA Express. Tlatsana testified that Van Wyk suggested that she send a proposal to his private email address. Shortly thereafter, Van Wyk called Tlatsana to tell her she had been selected as the preferred bidder (without any notable competitive process), subject to some important caveats: she would have to employ people suggested by Van Wyk. One of these was Joyce Phiri, who was the mother of Van Wyk's life partner at the time. Van Wyk also insisted that Kekana appoint a new accountant, whom he identified.

Tlatsana claimed that in April 2015 Van Wyk instructed her to open an FNB bank account, and that Van Wyk actually brought the contracts to her office to sign. Tlatsana further testified that, for all intents and purposes, her company was hijacked by Van Wyk, who began directing how money paid to it by SA Express would be managed.

The payments to Koreneka caught the attention of Timothy

Ngwenya, the divisional manager of security management at SA Express. In this role, Ngwenya conducted his own investigation into Koreneka. He testified that, during his investigation, he was contacted by the head of SAA Security and told he would be called by somebody from Luthuli House (the ANC headquarters). This eventually led to an in-person meeting with a man simply identified as Sipho at the Intercontinental Hotel at OR Tambo Airport. Sipho explained that the money paid to Koreneka was in fact destined to be used for ANC expenses. He then offered Ngwenya a bribe of R3m to stop his investigation. Ngwenya refused and ploughed on, for which the commission roundly commended him.

Ngwenya's investigation established that Koreneka had submitted four invoices to SA Express between May 2015 and August 2015 for costs related to 'airport refurbishment', or 'facility security management', or 'airport fire truck lease'. Importantly, none of these services featured in the main agreement signed by the North West Province; equally importantly, Van Wyk was involved in approving at least some of the invoices. The invoices, which were duly paid, totalled over R30m.

Further payments were made directly to Koreneka by the North West Department of Transport. In 2015, it submitted an invoice of R20.6m to the department, which was paid. In 2016, it submitted an invoice of R15.8m, although this payment was halted after the department received legal correspondence from Joyce Phiri, the mother of Van Wyk's life partner.

In about June 2016, Tlatsana contacted Ngwenya. She told him that people at SA Express were interfering with her company and threatened to inform the media. She also said that tensions had begun developing between her and the individuals Koreneka had hired at Van Wyk's suggestion. When Tlatsana tried to push back, Van Wyk threatened to take the contract away from her. And, indeed, Van Wyk did eventually give the contract to another company, Valotech Facilities Management CC, which was paid R15m by the North West Transport Department despite not providing any services. Shortly after receiving the R15m payment, Valotech was liquidated.

Tlatsana decided to give Ngwenya all the documents and invoices she had gathered, as well as copies of recordings she had made of conversations with Van Wyk. Tlatsana gave the same documents and recordings to the commission. Ngwenya's investigation ultimately established that Van Wyk was running an 'elaborate' corruption scheme. Ngwenya duly tried to meet Van Wyk to discuss the issue, and a meeting was scheduled. During the meeting, Van Wyk excused himself and never returned. As the commission recalled, in one of its more memorable lines, 'Mr Van Wyk literally ran from the building and did not come back'.

Tlatsana testified that, by 2015, she had had enough, and she started conducting her own investigation as to where the money paid into Koreneka was going. She discovered that an amount of R9.9m was paid into the account of a company called Neo Solutions. From there, Neo Solutions paid R9.6m to Batsamai Investment Holdings. Batsamai had been formed in November 2014 by Sipho Phiri, Van Wyk's boyfriend. A further R300,000 was withdrawn in cash from Neo Solutions for Van Wyk's benefit.

In late 2015 Koreneka was paid R20m by the North West Province. Tlatsana testified that Van Wyk had been pressuring her to gain access to the funds, though she refused. To 'resolve' the situation, Tlatsana met Van Wyk to discuss where all the money was going. Tlatsana recorded the conversation. Van Wyk claimed that the money from Koreneka was being used to 'take care of people', and then he allegedly drew up a note indicating who had received money. Tlatsana took the note, which claimed that payments had been made to Ministers Lynne Brown and Dipuo Peters, to the MEC and head of North West's Transport Department, and to 'number 1' in the province, Premier Supra Mahumapelo. Van Wyk claimed that Mahumapelo had received R5m until then, and was expecting to receive a further R5m.

The commission was unable to establish if any such payments were made to those on the lists. But it was partially frustrated because, of the funds that went to Koreneka, an amount of R9m was paid into the accounts of a cash-in-transit company, AMFS. This had the effect of turning the R9m into cash, which was effectively untraceable. Kalandra Viljoen, the owner of AMFS, appeared before the commission. The commission found that, based on her evidence, AMFS was essentially playing the part of a bank – but without a banking licence.

Viljoen provided the commission with delivery slips, which

showed where the cash that had been withdrawn had been delivered. All three delivery slips were signed by Van Wyk. Tlatsana was asked to check the signature, and confirmed that it was definitely Van Wyk's, as it was the same as the signature he appended to contracts he had signed.

At this point, however, it appears that the commission's trail ran cold: it was unable, as a result, to trace how the R9m that had been given in cash to Van Wyk was actually spent. The commission thus recommended further investigations by law enforcement.

## RECOMMENDATIONS

*The NPA must address the criminal complaint filed by the commission against Dudu Myeni following her revelation of the identity of Witness X.*

*Further investigations should be conducted into the evidence of Witness X and corruption charges pursued if justified.*

*The NPA should investigate Dudu Myeni for fraud for making false statements to the Minister of Public Enterprises in relation to the Pembroke transaction.*

*Law enforcement must investigate the Swissport contract, in particular the prima facie evidence that kickbacks were paid to Mr Daluxolo Peter, Vuyisile Ndzeku, Lester Peter and Nontsasa Memela, with a view to prosecutions on charges of corruption.*

*SARS should investigate JM Aviation to establish if it was VAT complaint in relation to its receipt of R28.5m from Swissport.*

*In relation to the AAR–JM Aviation components tender, the NPA should 'seriously consider' bringing charges of corruption and other crimes against JM Aviation, the board of SAAT, Yakhe Kwinana and Nontsasa Memela. The NPA should also consider engaging the US Department of Justice regarding AAR.*

*The NPA should 'seriously consider' prosecuting Vuyisile Ndzeku, Nontsasa Memela, Lindelwa Mbanjwa and JM Aviation for their role in disguising the nature of payments made to Memela by JM Aviation.*

*The Legal Practice Council should investigate Lindelwa Mbanjwa and Nontsasa Memela in relation to the 'fraudulent scheme to try to hide the money that was paid as a kick-back to Ms Memela'. The Legal Practice Council should also investigate Ms*

*Mbanjwa's conduct in representing a witness at the commission in circumstances where she may have been conflicted.*

*ACSA should take steps to recover the amounts paid to Regiments Capital under the interest swap transactions it was involved in. The amounts should be recovered from Regiments Capital, Phetolo Ramosebudi, Eric Wood, Niven Pillay and, failing them, Nedbank and Standard Bank.*

*Law enforcement must investigate the ACSA–Regiments contracts with a view to prosecuting Phetolo Ramosebudi, Eric Wood, Niven Pillay and Regiments Capital for corruption; recovering funds from Ramosebudi under POCA provisions; and recovering amounts paid to Regiments by Nedbank and Standard Bank under POCA provisions.*

*Law enforcement should investigate the roles of Mario Visnenza, Moss Brickman and Nedbank with a view to prosecution for corruption, and the recovery of Nedbank's profits under POCA provisions.*

*In relation to the working capital tender awarded to the Regiments and McKinsey consortium, law enforcement should investigate with a view to the prosecution of Phetolo Ramosebudi, Eric Wood, Regiments Capital, Indheran Pillay and Tewodros Gebreselasie (from Regiments) for corruption; and the recovery of funds from Phetolo Ramosebudi to the amount of R375,606 paid to Riskmaths Solutions by Regiments Capital.*

*The South African Institute of Chartered Accountants should investigate Yakhe Kwinana to establish if she has the requisite knowledge and appreciation of her duties to continue to practise as a chartered accountant.*

*SARS should investigate Kwinana and Associates in relation to statements it made about its turnover for the 2016 financial year.*

*All individuals involved in the corruption scheme at SA Express must be 'brought to justice'.*

*Law enforcement should consider bringing charges against Mr Natasen, the operator of the Neo Solutions bank account, on charges of money laundering, and his conduct should be reported to the South African Institute of Chartered Accountants and SARS.*

*The Reserve Bank should investigate whether Ms Viljoen's AMFS operation was effectively operating as a bank without a banking licence, or as a cash-in-transit business that failed to comply with its FICA obligations.*

*The Asset Forfeiture Unit should consider recovering under POCA any amounts flowing from the SA Express matter.*

# Denel

As with other volumes of the commission's findings, the Denel report attempted, in broad terms, to answer the question whether Denel had been subject to state capture by the Guptas. The commission's answer was a resounding yes.

## The rarest jewel: A successful SOE

The commission begins its report on Denel by setting out the history of the company. In 1992, Armscor, the apartheid-era weapons manufacturer and sanctions-busting importer, was split in two. Armscor was retained as the government's agent, effectively acting as a tender board overseeing and assisting the South African military to undertake procurement. Armscor's substantial arms manufacturing capacity was hived off into Denel.

From its formation, Denel struggled financially and often required government bailouts. Between 2011 and 2015, however, things looked as if they were turning around. In 2011, the Denel board was reconstituted under a new chair, Zoli Kunene (this board is referred to as the 2011 board for obvious reasons). In January 2012, Denel appointed Riaz Saloojee, a former Umkhonto we Sizwe soldier, as its group CEO. Between 2011 and 2015, for the first time, Denel turned a small profit. By the time the 2011 board was stood down in 2015, Denel had expanded its business and boasted a promising order book.

## An indulgent interregnum

I should pause to point out that the commission was happy to hold up the virtues of Denel's good corporate governance in the years before capture, but I personally read this with considerable discomfort. Denel is the producer of ordnance that has been used in some of the most devastating conflicts in the world. One of its major customers, Saudi Arabia, is a human rights-violating dictatorship that dismembers journalists and has committed war crimes in its vicious assault on Yemen, which has become the greatest humanitarian crisis of this century.

The commission laments Denel's fall from grace as a paragon of good governance and its collapse into torpor and decline. And while I am equally appalled by the tales of corruption and capture the commission told, and the waste of taxpayer money that this involved, I find it harder to mourn the potential collapse of this business.

Arguably, Denel should have been jettisoned and shut down in 1992 through a progressive swords-to-ploughshares approach, closing a company that was integral to the day-to-day oppression of apartheid. Instead, the decision to save Denel and secure its profitability (which it has almost never achieved) has led South Africa into dark places; first, towards the Arms Deal, the original state capture, which it was believed could be used to insert Denel into global supply chains; and, second, to a situation where South Africa routinely exports weapons to the worst possible people in the world, which both facilitates horrendous crimes and taints South African foreign policy by requiring the state to curry favour with Denel's appalling clients. Perhaps, when it comes to Denel, the government should let this relic pass into history.

## The Guptas' circle

The commission heard that the Guptas and their lieutenant Salim Essa began making moves on Denel long before they secured their first deals. According to Riaz Saloojee, he was contacted by Salim Essa in early 2012. Saloojee initially resisted Essa's approaches but, after pestering, relented. Essa, in conversations, had indicated he wanted to speak to Saloojee about how he could introduce people to Denel to help the SOE win business. Essa, Saloojee claimed, said that the requests came from the 'very top'.

Saloojee's first meeting with the Guptas took place, as ever, at the Gupta compound. Saloojee alleged that Essa picked him up from a coffee shop and drove him to the Saxonwold redoubt. There, Saloojee was introduced to Malusi Gigaba. Saloojee further alleged that, during a brief exchange, Gigaba told Saloojee that 'these people' were Gigaba's friends and that he hoped they and Saloojee could work together, after which he swiftly departed. Saloojee believed at the time – and the commission agreed with his view – that the introduction to Gigaba was designed to create the impression of the Gupta enterprise's political influence and reach.

Saloojee was pestered by Essa following this meeting until he again relented. During this second visit, Saloojee was introduced to Duduzane Zuma and Tshepiso Magashule, Ace's son. Essa informed Saloojee that the Guptas and 'number 1' had supported Saloojee's appointment as Denel CEO in 2012. Following this heart-warming endorsement straight from the mouth of criminal kingpins, Saloojee was told that the Guptas wanted to do business with Denel and, in particular, help Denel expand its business in Asia. This prefigured the creation of Denel Asia, which I talk about below. Seemingly to the Guptas' and Essa's chagrin, Saloojee was noncommittal and told the assembled state capturers that they would have to work through the proper channels.

Saloojee was called to genuflect before the Guptas once more in the latter half of 2012. At this meeting Tony Gupta revealed his famous subtlety and patience by admonishing Saloojee for the fact that Denel was one of the only SOEs that wasn't supporting the Gupta newspaper *New Age*. He also said Saloojee was 'not cooperating' and that he didn't want to have to 'elevate it further'. As Tony Gupta then escorted Saloojee out, he asked his visitor why he 'didn't take money' when everybody else did. Saloojee indicated that he was not open to bribery and again reiterated that the Guptas needed to work through proper channels.

On Saloojee's version, he decided that he needed a buffer between himself and the Guptas to put an end to the interminable Saxonwold visits. He thus introduced the Guptas to a man who would come to play a major role in the capture of Denel: Zwelakhe Ntshepe. At the time, Ntshepe was Denel's business executive for marketing development. Saloojee warned Ntshepe that he had to follow due process in all meetings. Considering the commission's later findings, Saloojee's introduction of Ntshepe to the Guptas with a simple admonishment strikes me as remarkably naive.

## The acquisition of VR Laser

VR Laser was a laser-cutting business, primarily involved in using lasers to cut metal sheets into highly specified shapes for military vehicles. These cut-outs – doors and other items – would be provided to a second party that would then weld them onto the vehicles. VR Laser's services were critical to the success of Denel's biggest and most risky project – Project Hoefyster. Hoefyster involved the design of military infantry vehicles called Badgers. Denel invested hugely in this project, upon which its fortunes largely continue to rest.

The Guptas were put in the position to buy VR Laser with the help of Ntshepe. During a trip to the Dubai Airshow, Ntshepe had a conversation with one of the co-owners of VR Laser, J Jiyane (who held shares with his wife). Jiyane reminded Ntshepe of a prior conversation they had had in which he mentioned he was looking to find a partner to invest in VR Laser. Ntshepe introduced Jiyane to Essa, and the ball got rolling. Jiyane maintained that he was never made aware that Essa was connected to or acting for the Guptas.

The Guptas initially bought 74.9% of the shares in VR Laser, for which they paid R72m; the deal was concluded in 2013. This shareholding was held by Elgasolve, of which Iqbal Sharma and Salim Essa were directors, effectively holding the company on behalf of the Gupta enterprise. The property on which VR Laser operated – a massive site – was also bought by Elgasolve but was placed into a new corporate entity.

The Jiyanes were soon jilted. In their discussions with Essa, he had promised that Jiyane would take over the position of CEO and have a real say in the future of the company. As soon as the Guptas took over, the promises were broken. Instead, the Guptas' go-to lawyer, Pieter van der Merwe, was made CEO. The Jiyanes, frustrated, eventually sold their shares in 2014.

This was a key step in the capture of Denel, according to the commission. It ultimately found that the entry of Essa and the Guptas into VR Laser was 'conceived for the purpose of using VR Laser as a vehicle to achieve the capture of Denel'.

## The Guptas' first score: The 'hulls' contract

In 2014 a debate began to rage within Denel about which suppliers should be used to produce critical components for the Hoefyster

Project, in particular the hulls of the Badgers. The hulls were the body of the vehicles onto which a turret – the unit housing the guns and gunner – would be welded. At the time, Denel's supplier of hulls was Land Mobility Technologies (LMT). LMT was owned by Denel. It had been bought in 2011, as it was seen as 'mission critical' to the Hoefyster supply chain. LMT was part-owned by Pamodzi Holdings, LMT's BBEEE partner. This relationship would become part of the controversy surrounding the hulls contract.

Officials within Denel began arguing that LMT's work was substandard and that it could not be trusted to produce the hulls. This was particularly the view of Stephan Burger, the CEO of Denel Land Systems (DLS). DLS was the entity which had previously contracted with LMT for it to provide turrets for the Badgers. Burger argued that LMT's work was so poor that if they were awarded the contract for the manufacture of hulls, the lives of those using the Badger would be at risk.

Following intense disputes, mediated in part by Saloojee, it was decided to put the hulls contract out to closed tender. Requests for offers (RFO) were sent out to three potential suppliers: LMT, DCD Dorbyl and VR Laser. For VR Laser, the contract was a major opportunity to expand its business and make it indispensable to Denel. VR Laser emerged victorious from the evaluation process with an extremely slim 0.76% margin of victory. VR Laser and DLS entered into the hulls contract on 28 November 2014.

The commission found that the entire process was irregular, for a number of reasons. First, during the scoring process, both DCD Dorbyl and LMT were given a nil score for the BBEEE component, which counted 20% towards the score. LMT was given a nil score because its BBEEE certificate had expired. The commission called this an 'extraordinary result' because most people in Denel should have known that LMT had a very public BBEEE partner – Pamodzi Holdings – which had bought into and invested in LMT a number of years previously.

Second, the commission found it irregular that VR Laser was allowed to revise its original price, which was R97m higher than LMT's bid. Neither LMT nor DCD Dorbyl was given the same opportunity.

Third, the commission found it was not fair that LMT had been unable to answer criticisms of its technical capacity. This referred to the fact that, during the evaluation process, the officials visited Patria, the Finnish partner in the Hoefyster Project. Patria backed VR Laser and did not rate LMT's work. The commission believed it was unfair that LMT was not able to answer or respond to these criticisms.

Of particular concern was that two senior officials who were in charge of the probity of procurement for Denel had both opposed the award because they believed that the procurement process was flawed. These two officials, Celia Malahlela and Dennis Mlambo, would end up playing a key role in trying to oppose state capture at Denel.

The commission did not, however, find that the award of the hulls contract to VR Laser was necessarily due to state capture or that the Guptas played an obviously detrimental role. Instead, it believed that Denel executives had taken the view that VR Laser was the better supplier (with some justification) and they wanted to get the deal done as quickly as possible. But this led to Denel cutting corners and taking shortcuts that violated procurement law.

## The Guptas and their cronies take control

In mid-2015 the contracts for the 2011 board came to a conclusion. The incoming Minister of Public Enterprises, Lynne Brown, was responsible for deciding whether the members of the 2011 board would be retained or replaced. This should, arguably, have been a no-brainer: the 2011 board had pushed Denel into profitability and had secured clean audits from the Auditor General. But nobody has ever accused Lynne Brown of having a brain.

Brown opted to take an axe to the majority of the 2011 board. In the position of chairperson, Brown appointed Daniel Lungisani Mantsha. The commission's rage at this appointment is barely disguised. A cursory background check would have confirmed that Mantsha had previously been struck from the roll of advocates. A publicly available judgment confirming his dismissal found him guilty of a range of serious offences and financial impropriety. Kgathatso Tlhakudi, the deputy director general at the DPE, confirmed in testimony that no vetting procedures were performed on Mantsha or members of the incoming 2015 board.

Manthsa, the commission found, had other qualifications: a close friendship with the Guptas. 'Mr Mantsha must have been chosen by the Guptas,' the commission found. It recounted how Mantsha, like so many other officials, was whipped away to enjoy the 'fleshpots of power' in Dubai on the dime of Sahara Computers. Mantsha's version – that Ashu Chawla had paid for the travel through Sahara Computers on the understanding that Mantsha would pay him back – was dismissed with contempt by the commission.

However, obstacles to the capture of the board remained in place in the form of 'three executives'. The first was Riaz Saloojee, who was retained as CEO; in September 2015, Minister Brown privately informed Saloojee that she was delighted with his performance to date, but this support quickly evaporated. At a meeting the board members began enthusing about the potential of expanding into India, which was the Guptas' long-term endgame for Denel. Saloojee suggested caution, thereby irking the new board members in his view. It certainly could not have helped dispel the notion that he would be obstructive to the state capture agenda. The two other executives in the firing line were the chief financial officer, Fikile Mhlontlo, and the company secretary, Elizabeth Africa. Evidently a decision was made at a high level that these three executives had a fatal flaw, namely, something approaching respect for procedure and law.

And thus on 21 September 2015, Saloojee was called to a meeting with the newly constituted Audit and Risk Committee of Denel, which was now staffed with the 2015 intake, to explain an acquisition undertaken by the 2011 board: the purchase of Land Systems South Africa (LSSA), later renamed Denel Vehicle Systems. Mhlontlo and Africa were called into similar meetings. The Audit and Risk Committee was now headed by the Ntshepe, the man whom Saloojee introduced to the Guptas, and who quickly became one of the Guptas' 'witting agents' of state capture at Denel.

The purchase of LSSA is a long and winding story. Suffice it to say that the acquisition had received the approvals of the Department of Defence, the Defence Force, the Minister of Public Enterprises, the Reserve Bank and the Competition Commission. The incoming 2015 board decided, however, that the LSSA acquisition was flawed and irregular. On 22 September 2015, the day after he had been forced to defend himself in front of the Audit and Risk Committee, Saloojee was handed a letter accusing him of defrauding the government by means of the LSSA acquisition. Mhlontlo and Africa receive similar missives. The following day, 23 September 2015, the three were again hauled before the Audit and Risk Committee. This time the committee offered the three executives a three-month pay package if they tendered their resignation.

All three of the executives declined the offer, instead demanding a disciplinary process expedited through arbitration. All felt that they could defend their conduct. All were suspended pending the disciplinary proceedings. Ultimately, no proceedings were ever concluded, despite the repeated pleas of the three executives. Following a long period of stalemate, all three accepted huge payouts. Saloojee was paid a handsome R2,661,383; Mhlontlo was paid an astonishing R8,445,765.35. The total package paid to Africa was undisclosed by the commission, but it did confirm that she received an 'ex gratia' payment of R1.642m. For an SOE that had serious balance sheet issues, paying out these sums of money, just to rid it of political enemies, was extraordinary.

The story of the three suspensions had a remarkable twist. The 2015 board had appointed the law firm Dentons, assisted by Grant Thornton, to investigate the LSSA acquisition, presumably with the hope that the findings could be used to get rid of the executives. Dentons was asked to both review the project as a whole and comment on the 'findings' of the Audit and Risk Committee, which had been used to draw up the effective charge sheets against the three executives.

The Dentons reports did not give the LSSA acquisition a totally clean bill of health; it found certain procedural questions that needed to be resolved. But, most importantly for this story, it found that the Audit and Risk Committee's findings were totally wrong and false. Simply put, Dentons cleared the three executives of the charges that were formulated against them by Denel, and for which they were suspended.

Here's the twist. On 14 December 2015, Saloojee was presented with the 'charges' against him. Three days later, on 17 December, the acting company secretary accidentally sent a letter to Saloojee, which the commission described as 'astonishing'. The letter had been received by the acting company secretary from Mantsha, Denel's captured chairperson, prior to Saloojee receiving his 'charge sheet'. Mantsha's letter instructed the secretary to draft the charge sheet and also to write to Dentons to say its report was rejected. The secretary was further instructed to inform Dentons that Denel expected a new report within 30 days, and 'kindly direct them to provide information to support the charges [against Saloojee]'. Mantsha ended his letter by telling the secretary to 'withdraw' the Dentons report and ensure that it was not circulated.

In simple terms, Mantsha had received Dentons report. But that report cleared the three executives of the charges raised by the Audit and Risk Committee. So Mantsha instead rejected the report and did everything in his power to ensure that nobody saw it.

The commission's view on this was clear: 'the suspensions were, on the evidence of this letter, a hatchet job. The suspensions were, literally, weaponised, to serve a corrupt purpose.' Moreover, the commission found, the three executives were removed so that they could be replaced by 'officials considered more likely to carry on the very schemes of wrongdoing that were contemplated by those who had worked to oust the three employees'.

One quick note of exception: the commission would find the entire 2015 board responsible for these hatchet job suspensions, except for one person, Nonyameko Mandindi. She alone had opposed the appointment of Dentons and had raised her concerns about the suspension of Saloojee with Mantsha. Her interventions were ignored.

## Making the Guptas indispensable

On 3 March 2015, the Executive Committee (Exco) of Denel Land Systems (DLS) held a meeting to discuss a radical idea: giving VR Laser a single-source contract to supply all of DLS's needs when it came to the 'fabrication of structures'. This meant only one provider – in this case, VR Laser – would be contracted to provide the service. Most importantly, there would be no competition or tendering for the contract. The potential for abuse is obvious: without competition, especially when contracts are awarded for lengthy periods of time, the contractor is under no pressure to offer the most competitive prices or to provide the best possible services.

A key player in pushing for the award of the contract was Stephan Burger, the CEO of DLS. He had previously championed the award of the hulls contract to VR Laser, as we saw, and was willing to break procurement regulations to push it through. Burger adopted much the same attitude in this contract, and was roundly criticised by the commission as a result.

The process of awarding the contract faced initial stiff resistance from Celia Malahlela, the executive manager of supply chain management at DLS. It was Malahlela, as you may recall, who had raised objections to the award of the hulls contract. As part of the procurement process, Malahlela was instructed by another DLS manager to send a letter to the Denel group CEO asking for approval. She did so but attached her own opinion in the form of a supply chain note, in which she recommended that the contract should go out on tender. She also raised an issue with the duration of the contract: she suggested that it should be for a maximum of three years, not the remarkable ten years originally envisaged. As the executive in charge of company procurement, this should have been an influential opinion.

But Malahlela's recommendations were ignored, and on 19 May 2015 DLS and VR Laser signed an agreement by which VR Laser was appointed DLS's sole supplier for a full decade. Considering the importance of the contract, this effectively made VR Laser an integral and indispensable part of Denel's supply chain, guaranteeing it a rich source of income, without any competition, for ten years.

The contract faced post-facto challenges too. In October 2015, the DLS executive appears to have realised that the VR Laser contract was irregular from another perspective. The Denel group had adopted a supply chain policy in 2014 for undertaking good procurement. The policy stated that no contract should be awarded to any outside contractor if the services could be provided internally. This policy could only be ignored with the express permission of the group executive in charge of supply chain policy. That executive was Dennis Mlambo, who had previously, together with Malahlela, attempted to challenge the hulls contract.

Mlambo, it turned out, had never been asked to give his approval, which made the entire contract irregular. The response of the DLS executive was bizarre and extraordinary: it decided, on a whim, that because the VR Laser contract had already been entered into, it must take precedence over Denel's procurement policy. The commission's anger at this decision is palpable: two paragraphs are given over to expressing the absurdity of the decision in several formulations.

To compound matters, the DLS board decided to resolve the issue by simply telling Mlambo of its decision, not seeking his approval. But DLS's executive asked Malahlela to inform Mlambo. No doubt because she had already raised concerns with the contract, she instead asked Mlambo to approve the deviation from policy. Mlambo, of course, refused. Mlambo was then approached, once more, by Burger, who tried to persuade Mlambo to sign a memorandum granting retroactive approval; Mlambo rejected this memorandum.

In the end, those executives pushing the VR Laser contract were able to rely on the services of the Guptas' ally, Ntshepe. Mlambo later discovered that Ntshepe had overridden Mlambo's rejection, which he had recorded in writing in the October 2015 memorandum that originally asked for his approval. Ntshepe simply wrote 'approved' under the memorandum, which was taken as sufficient to deal with those thorny things called rules. The commission found Ntshepe's decision 'irregular', not least because he did not have the power to countermand Mlambo. The commission, upon questioning Ntshepe about this, found that he 'failed to give any acceptable reason to his own involvement in approving the DLS Single Source Contract awarded to VR Laser'.

One final problem was raised by the commission. In his original evidence, Burger, the CEO of DLS, had argued that he had the appropriate authority and approvals to sign the single-source contract with VR Laser. The commission, however, found otherwise. Burger argued that he was empowered to enter into the contract – a memorandum of agreement – on the strength of a memorandum that had been signed by Saloojee in April 2015.

However, this memorandum had *not* approved the award of the contract; it had only approved the decision for Denel to open negotiations with VR Laser and potentially enter into a memorandum of understanding. The difference between a memorandum of understanding and a memorandum of agreement is vast: the former is not a contract and simply commits parties to working together in good faith, while the latter is a legally enforceable contract which, in this case, committed Denel and VR Laser to the deal for ten years.

## The Denel Vehicle Services (DVS) and VR Laser single-source contract

By the end of 2015, the capture of Denel was virtually complete, and so a different division of Denel, Denel Vehicle Services, sought to engineer yet another long-term, single-source contract for VR

Laser. The initial driving force behind bringing VR Laser into the company was Ntshepe. Jan Wessels, who was then the COO of the Denel group, testified that he was approached by Ntshepe during the November 2015 Dubai Airshow. Ntshepe instructed Wessels to work with the CEO of Denel Vehicle Systems – Johan Steyn – to establish a relationship between DVS and VR Laser 'as a matter of priority'. Ntshepe informed Steyn simultaneously that he should start taking steps to enter into a memorandum of agreement with VR Laser that mirrored the single-source MOA that had been granted by DLS. The commission believed that Ntshepe moved with such speed in order to impress the Guptas.

This deal also faced pushback. Wessels, then second-in-command to Ntshepe, tried to persuade Ntshepe that the deal was a non-starter. He argued that the work that was going to be given to VR Laser was already being performed in-house at DVS and was, indeed, part of its core business. Giving the contract to VR Laser would kill DVS's own units. Ntshepe rejected the objection out of hand, and told Wessels to proceed with a contract.

Steyn was equally perturbed by the deal, and raised the matter with Wessels. On the strength of their joint concerns, Wessels wrote to Ntshepe on 17 November 2015, setting out a lengthy list of reasons why the deal should not proceed. Ntshepe responded on the same day in jaw-dropping fashion. He simply told Wessels that his email was 'too long' and that his concerns were unfounded.

Wessels's opposition to the deal would end his career at Denel. Shortly after his email to Ntshepe, the latter told him that the Denel chairman and Gupta ally, Mantsha, had instructed that Wessels should no longer be able to attend Denel board meetings. As Wessels was increasingly sidelined, he requested a move to a separate Denel division, from which he resigned in a final act of frustration in August 2016.

And so, a month after Wessels's last valiant attempt to push back against Ntshepe, DVS signed its own single-source contract with VR Laser. Like the one it had just scored with DLS, this contract was also awarded to VR Laser for a full decade, inserting VR Laser into the income stream and supply chain for Denel for ten years.

## Denel Asia

The commission then moved on to discuss Denel Asia. This was, simply, a proposed joint venture through which Denel and VR Laser would market Denel products across the Middle East and Asia. It would be facilitated by the creation of a joint-venture vehicle in Hong Kong. This had been one of the Guptas' long-term ambitions.

The Denel Asia venture ultimately never came to fruition, though hardly for want of trying. The decision to pursue the venture was put into action in October 2015, the month after the appointment of the 2015 board. The incoming board wrote first to the Department of Public Enterprises and then to the Minister of Finance, asking for approval under PFMA to enter into the joint venture. Officials from both departments raised objections to the proposal, which were sent to Denel and Lynne Brown as DPE minister. The officials never received a reply from the minister or the director general at the time, Richard Seleke.

It appears that Denel also received no response from either department. This meant that Denel was able to use a specific provision of the PFMA to attempt to argue that the project was effectively approved. The PFMA provision states that a state entity can move ahead with a project of this type if it does not receive a response to the request from the Department of Public Enterprises within 30 days.

Following much toing and froing, the joint venture was finally buried by Treasury. But Denel's captured board was having none of it. And so on 23 March 2017, Denel took the Minister of Finance (then Pravin Gordhan) and National Treasury to court, asking for an order that the PFMA application be approved. Denel's legal papers were signed by none other than Ntshepe, who, by then, was acting CEO of Denel.

Fortunately, this court application has been withdrawn, and Denel Asia no longer threatens resurrection.


## Findings

Based on all this evidence about Denel, the commission found that

- The existence of state capture at Denel had been established, and that this capture was effected via VR Laser for the benefit of the Guptas;

- The appointment of the 2015 board was highly problematic and involved the appointment of individuals who were manifestly unsuited to the job;
- The appointment of the 2015 board by Minister Lynne Brown, and its deleterious behaviour, illustrate the problem of politicians being able to appoint senior management of SOEs;
- The hulls contract and the two single-source contracts were awarded irregularly in breach of section 217 of the Constitution.

## RECOMMENDATIONS

- *The state should seek to establish a body responsible for the identification, recruitment and selection of the right kind of people for appointment to the boards of SOEs, and for the appointment of CEOs and CFOs.*
- *A new statutory offence should be created that makes it a criminal offence 'for any person vested with public power to abuse public power vested in that person by intentionally using that power otherwise than in good faith for a proper purpose'. The offence should carry a prison sentence of 20 years and fines equal to a maximum of R200m.*
- *Mantsha and members of the 2015 board had prima facie shown themselves to be unfit as company directors due to their role in the suspension of the 'three executives'. The government should ask Denel, DPE and/or the Companies and Intellectual Properties Commission to investigate and bring proceedings against Mantsha and any executive shown to have 'abetted' him in relation to the suspension of the three executives, with a view to having them declared delinquent directors.*
- *The Legal Practice Council should be made aware of Mantsha's conduct so as to determine whether he remains fit to be admitted to the roll of advocates (he had been readmitted at some unknown time after his initial removal).*
- *Law enforcement should conduct investigations in order to establish if violations of the PFMA took place in relation to the hulls contract and the two single-source contracts.*

# SABC

ONE OF THE MORE in-your-face examples of state capture was the Guptas' capture of the SABC. Indeed, their success in looting the state was announced loudly through the broadcasts of the infamous New Age business breakfasts. *The New Age* (*TNA*) was the Guptas' flagship newspaper. The business breakfasts featured soft-ball interviews with a long list of cabinet members, which served mostly to confirm the paucity of talent at the upper levels of government. Sponsored lavishly by other SOEs, the breakfasts were also broadcast at SABC's expense, and earned TNA Media over a million rand per episode. For this, the Guptas merely had to put on a show that had all the pizazz, glamour and substance of a monkey farting through a trombone.

The Guptas, of course, also made their own move into the TV news space, creating their lamentable and often comically inept TV station, ANN7. Evidence heard by the commission showed that *TNA* and ANN7 were of particular interest to Jacob Zuma, who proudly confirmed his involvement in conceptualising the station.

## Zuma, ANN7 and the testimony of Rajesh Sundaram

In considering the capture of the SABC (which was achieved through both Gupta media vehicles, *TNA* and ANN7), the commission spent considerable time discussing Zuma's involvement in the creation of and support for both. Zuma testified before the commission over two days between 15 and 17 July 2019. During his testimony, Zuma freely admitted to his role in the conceptualisation of *TNA*. He testified that the Guptas were his friends, and that he believed the ANN7 project would be to the benefit of the country. To his mind, existing media were on the whole 'very biased' and 'just critical' of the government. Zuma thus approached the Guptas while president of the ANC and, according to his version, asked whether they could 'try a business – a media business – because you are comrades'.

Sometime later, they returned to inform him of the decision to launch a newspaper, but noted that they lacked a name. Zuma provided them with a list of the ANC's various publications in exile, including *The New Age*, which Zuma claimed they 'loved'. 'We were very happy', Zuma noted, when the paper was finally launched and off the ground.

The 'success' of *TNA* prompted Zuma to think even bigger, and he decided to 'push them further'. 'What about a TV channel?' he asked the Guptas. If they were in doubt, Zuma told them: 'I am sure your TV thing can be successful and they agreed.' ANN7 was launched in August 2013. It was owned by Infinity Media, part of the broader Gupta enterprise web of companies.

Zuma, for his part, saw nothing wrong with his involvement in ANN7: 'I thought it was a good thing that they did. There was no law broken there. There were no wrong things done. I discussed with business people many things when I was still in the government. Even suggest certain things can you not do in your business. This was a normal kind of interaction. So they established this and indeed ANN7 brought fresh air in the country in terms of reporting.'

Zuma's engagement with the Guptas around ANN7 went much deeper than his description, according to Rajesh Sundaram. Sundaram was employed as an editor at ANN7 in its earliest days. He resigned just shy of four months after his first employment in protest at what he saw as shoddy content and editorial problems. Sundaram wrote a book – *Indentured* – that described his experience of moving from India to South Africa to take up his position at ANN7, and the various interactions he had with senior Gupta figures. He also testified before the commission, where he confirmed the facts in his book on oath. Sundaram's evidence was unique in that it was the only first-person account of the Guptas present in the same room as Zuma, and how that relationship played out.

Sundaram described attending four meetings with Jacob Zuma, alongside a moving cast that included the Gupta brothers, Ashu Chawla, Nazeem Howa, Duduzane Zuma and the editor of *TNA*, Moegsien Williams. Three of the meetings took place at Zuma's official residence: on 22 June 2013, a Sunday in July 2013, and during the first week of August 2013. A fourth took place at the ANN7 offices two weeks prior to its launch.

The meetings followed much the same pattern: a Gupta brother or Nazeem Howa would make a presentation to Zuma to ask for his feedback. Sundaram was struck by how lax security was on his arrival; he was similarly alert to how much Zuma was treated like a stakeholder or shareholder in the enterprise, being given information beyond what an ordinary interested party might receive. Sundaram testified that Ajay Gupta had told him that it was Zuma who had come up with the name – Africa News Network. The '7' had been appended to ANN when it emerged that this highly original name was, in fact, already taken.

During the first meeting, Sundaram recalled Zuma being given a sneak preview of the channel's graphics and design, as well as a detailed hard-copy presentation that Sundaram had put together. His recollection suggested an eagerness on the part of Ajay Gupta to seek the approval of Zuma for things like the logo design. Zuma, for his part, used the meeting to opine on the mix of programmes of ANN7, asking that content be 'served fresh' rather than having repeated bulletins, as was the practice of eNCA.

The second meeting focused far more closely on the editorial content of the station. Zuma was shown copies of the channel's visual 'identity', which he had asked to see a number of times. Zuma then offered his opinion on the editorial approach ANN7 should take: it should not simply be a publicity channel for the ANC, but should present opposing views to appear credible. This would be balanced by the 'good news' about the country and government that other media outlets ignored. Zuma was also asked for his opinion about journalists and presenters. The name of Jimmy Manyi, who the commission found had been irregularly appointed as the head of the Government Communication and Information System (GCIS) at Zuma's insistence, was bandied about; Zuma offered to speak to him about hosting a talk show.

Sundaram was again struck by the 'intensity' of Zuma's interest, which was like that of a full shareholder. After the meeting, Sundaram asked Nazeem Howa why Zuma was paying the channel so much attention. Howa's response was remarkable:

> I later asked Nazeem why President Zuma insisted on lecturing us on editorial and personnel matters. 'Don't you know? Hasn't Laxmi ji[4] told you already? He has a big say in this venture. His son Duduzane holds 30 per cent in the company. His involvement is very critical for the first year of our operations. If we are able to get government advertisements, we will be able to break even in the first year,' he told me.
>
> If this were true, it would explain a lot, and it felt as though everything was falling into place. The news channel I was heading would be a pro-ANC, pro-Zuma channel that was promoted and run by not only people close to President Zuma but by President Zuma himself. If Nazeem had his facts straight and Zuma held the shares through his son, he would be projected positively in the news bulletins. In this scenario I could see how he would use his position as president to ensure government advertising for the station. It also seemed, if this was the truth, that there was a clear conflict of interest as his son had a stake in not just the Gupta-owned newspaper but also the proposed television news channel.
>
> As a 30 per cent stakeholder, his son would get 30 per cent of the profits earned from the revenues the president was helping them generate.

The commission was clearly intrigued by the idea that Duduzane's share in the company was, in reality, held for the benefit of his father. It noted that Duduzane only attended one of the three meetings in which his father offered advice, guidance and approval, and that his involvement was minimal. Although the commission made no outright finding, it commented that Jacob Zuma's avid interest and his son's relative lack of involvement 'certainly gives rise to the suspicion that the real shareholder was President Zuma and not Mr Duduzane Zuma'.

---

4    'Ji' is a phrase often used in Indian communities as a sign of respect or of some sort of close asssocation.

Sundaram's evidence covered more than just his meetings with Jacob Zuma. He also described any number of interactions that illustrated the reach and power of the Gupta family and the way they controlled aspects of the state. When Sundaram was sorting out his visa, for example, he was told that the Guptas had a special arrangement with the High Commission. Sundaram was given a two-year, inter-company visa without attending a single interview and despite the fact that he was not actually transferring between two related companies. Sundaram also noted that the Guptas were frequently informed of impending visits by officials from the Department of Labour; this allowed them to relocate any employees without compliant visas. Atul explained this arrangement to Sundaram by casually noting that 'it does not cost money to buy loyalty of an official in SA. All it takes is a free meal or drink.'

The commission was clearly disturbed by the arrogance of the Guptas in the exercise of their power, and the nature of the relationship between the family and JZ. In one of its most memorable comments, the commission lamented how easily and cheaply senior officials, including JZ, assisted the Guptas:

> It is most painful to learn that someone from another country who came to our country and did the things that the Gupta family members did to us as South Africans in this country came to the conclusion that South African officials not only can be bribed but that they can simply be bribed by a free meal or a drink. That's how low the Guptas thought of us as South Africans. It must be because of the experience they gained from those South Africans with whom they had intimate dealings. Among them is obviously Mr Jacob Zuma. I cannot help but remember Mr Hlaudi Motsoeneng's evidence in regard to the SABC and MultiChoice contract because in his evidence Mr Motsoeneng told the commission how he enjoyed curry at the Gupta residence.

## Zuma and the Executive Ethics Code

The commission, after considering the totality of the evidence about the involvement of JZ and Duduzane in *TNA* and ANN7, concluded that Zuma acted in violation of the Executive Ethics Code and the Constitution.

The Executive Members' Ethics Act was published in 1998. It flowed from paragraph 96 of the 1996 Constitution, which required that Cabinet members and deputy ministers act in accordance with a code of ethics. Among the requirements are that members may not use their position or any information they receive to enrich themselves or improperly benefit another person, or put themselves in a position where there may be a conflict of interest. The Act also indicates that these officials must also refrain from 'acting in a way that may compromise the credibility or integrity of their office or of the government'.

According to the commission, JZ's relationship with ANN7 and *TNA* violated these provisions in the Constitution and Executive Ethics Code:

> There can be no doubt that in acting as he did, in relation to the *TNA* and the ANN7 TV station, President Zuma acted in breach of the Executive Ethics Code. He, as President, abused his office for his own benefit, that of his son and that of his friends, the Guptas. He placed himself in a situation of a conflict of interest and abused his position as President of the country...
>
> The members of the Gupta family had used their close relationship with President Zuma to facilitate and extend their business interests from India to South Africa. The extension of Infinity Media and the birth of the ANN7 demonstrate the broadening of such interests.
>
> President Zuma had enabled the extension of such business interests for the benefit of his son, Mr Duduzane Zuma. The Gupta family and in turn the President's son, Mr Duduzane Zuma, benefitted from the relationship that the Gupta family had with President Zuma in that they entered into contracts with various State organs and, in particular the SABC, to the detriment of other potential competitors who operated within the same media space.

## The capture of the SABC: The business breakfasts

As I'll discuss in much greater detail later, TNA Media received considerable sponsorship for its business breakfasts, which consisted of execrable and unctuous interviews with Cabinet members and officials. Both Transnet and Eskom sponsored the business breakfasts. Eskom signed three contracts between April 2012 and 2014, in which it provided combined 'sponsorship' of over R50m, with every breakfast receiving over R1m in sponsorship. Simultaneously, Transnet paid an astonishing R122m to sponsor the breakfasts between 2012 and 2017, also at about R1m per show. This was clearly a massive money-spinner for the Guptas. Sundaram would testify that he was told that TNA Media made at least R1.8m per show.

The business breakfasts were broadcast on SABC 2. Remarkably, the commission was told by SABC's Lulama Mokhobo, the SABC group CEO from February 2012, that the SABC was not even aware that Transnet and Eskom were sponsoring the Breakfasts. Equally remarkably, Mokhobo testified that, while the business breakfasts were already being broadcast before she took over, there was no sort of contractual arrangement between the SABC and TNA Media. Mokhobo thus sought to create a contract to regularise this relationship. In March 2012, the SABC entered into a contractual arrangement to broadcast the business breakfasts for 36 months. The contract was signed by Mokhobo and Hlaudi Motsoeneng, who served as the CEO of the SABC from 2011 and 2013, during which time he was embroiled in any number of scandals.

The commission found that the contract between the SABC and TNA Media was clearly to the advantage of the latter. TNA would not contribute any funds towards SABC's costs, which were substantial. SABC was on the hook for the cost of the broadcast, including the cost of camera crews; it also gave TNA the time slot, which was itself a valuable commodity. In return, TNA was required to arrange the interviews, the venue and catering. SABC was granted rights to broadcast the programme and could use 33% of the venue space for sponsorship materials. TNA retained the rights to rebroadcast the footage as well as edit it for promotional purposes.

Exactly how much that all cost the SABC was somewhat unclear. Mokhobo testified that she had determined that approximately R20,326,980 had been spent by the SABC in facilitating these events. The commission also heard evidence from Yolanda van Biljon, an SABC employee, that the SABC had spent R4,268,887 (excluding VAT) on the broadcasts between 2011 and 2017. The commission ultimately recommended that this amount of just over R4m be recouped from TNA, suggesting that it placed more value on this estimate.

The commission did not spend any time engaging with the process by which the contract was entered, although it did note that SABC continued to broadcast the business breakfasts after the period covered by the contract. It does not seem any amendment or extention was contracted for. The commission found that the contract was irregular, and was 'created for the benefit of TNA Media and/ or members of the Gupta family to the detriment of the mandate of the SABC and the Public'. The commission also recommended that Hlaudi Motsoeneng and Mokhobo be investigated for potential breaches of the PFMA for their role in signing the contract on SABC's behalf.

## The theft of SABC's archival footage

The second tangible instance of the capture of the SABC was the transfer of huge amounts of archival footage from the SABC to ANN7. The SABC held an internationally unique and extremely valuable collection of footage, including rare film of the ANC and the struggle. The archive was, in cultural terms, invaluable; in money terms, it was worth millions, if not tens of millions, of dollars. It was also a key revenue stream for the SABC, as broadcasters paid significant fees for the right to broadcast any material from the SABC archives.

Josias Johannes Scott was the SABC employee overseeing the sale of SABC archive footage, and he gave evidence before the commission. He testified that he was summoned to Hlaudi Motsoeneng's office, where he was asked to explain how archival footage was ordinarily transferred. Motsoeneng told him somebody would be in contact soon to discuss the matter. Scott was then contacted by Nazeem Howa, who asked for a meeting. Howa indicated that he wanted to transfer approximately 2,000 minutes of archival footage (about 33 hours' worth).

Scott then met with his manager, Jimi Matthews, the chief executive of news. Matthews approved a deviation from their usual price: SABC would charge R70/minute for the transfer, instead of the usual R100/minute. Scott testified that an employee of ANN7 then worked with his junior to transfer 1,982 minutes of archival footage, although ANN7 was invoiced for 2,000 minutes. Infinity was ultimately invoiced R159,600 for the transfer.

Scott's version was disputed by Sundaram. Sundaram testified that, in fact, the SABC had transferred over 100 *hours* of archival content to ANN7, for which SABC was mostly not paid by ANN7's holding company, Infinity Media. Sundaram was told by the Guptas' Indian partner in the ANN7 venture, Laxmi Goel, that ANN7 had bought the 100 hours from SABC 'for peanuts'. Sundaram recalled that an ANN7 employee visited the SABC archives every day for a month to transfer the tapes and that, by the time this employee left the country, he had copied at least 60 hours. The ANN7 employee then digitised the archive to store it on ANN7's servers. This would give ANN7 a significant advantage over the SABC, which had not digitised the material; this meant the SABC could take hours or days to find images for broadcast, while ANN7 could find it immediately.

Sundaram further recalled an astounding comment made by Howa:

> We are paying them a lump sum to get this footage. We have got a very sweet deal with them. The people at the SABC can be bought for a meal or a drink; they are willing to give away their treasure trove of historical footage for peanuts. They have a clause in the contract that says that we will have to also pay them a 'per second' fee every time we air the footage we have taken from them but they are so stupid, how will they be able to tell what is their footage? How can they audit our use? We will get all their footage forever at just this one-time cost.

Sundaram's version was given credence by an astonishing admission made by Scott. Usually, when footage was transferred, the SABC made sure that the copied footage had a 'burnt-in' time-code. This is, practically speaking, a line usually at the top or bottom of the footage, which would record the running time and source of the material. This was the primary means by which the SABC could protect its property: the 'burnt-in' time-code could not be removed from the footage. So, if anybody broadcast that footage, it would include the time-code: this would provide proof of its origin and allow the SABC to invoice for the broadcast rights. Broadcast rights are considerably more expensive than the cost of transfer: potentially thousands or tens of thousands of rand per minute.

Scott admitted that, when the footage was transferred, it was done *without* the burnt-in time-code. ANN7 was simply given a copy of the raw footage, which it could broadcast without any evidence that it was from the SABC archives, and it could do so unblemished. Scott was asked why he did not use the time-code: his response was that when he did once approach ANN7 about how they had used certain footage (27 minutes' worth), they agreed to pay the SABC for the rights. Nevertheless, the commission recorded that Scott 'conceded that by simply relying on what ANN7 told him he could have deprived SABC of income. He agreed that the method he adopted was not a commercially viable method as testified by Mr Sundaram.'

The commission also heard evidence from Nakedi Ramoshaba, who was employed by ANN7 as its senior archivist from April 2014. She went on to work for Afrotone Media Holdings, which bought the ANN7 archive when it took over the station. Ramoshaba confirmed that, when she arrived at ANN7, the SABC content was on the archival system. When she tried to ask for details of licences and copyright documents for the SABC material, she was rebuffed and silenced.

While a minor story in the grand scheme of state capture, this story seems to me particularly aggravating, not least because of my former life as a historian and heritage consultant. The material held by the SABC was of extraordinary historical significance and cultural value. It was simply handed to the Guptas to use, effectively for free and without control. And all of this would be used in furtherance of a scheme to corrupt the country that had been saved from apartheid by the very people appearing on SABC's film stock. It was perverse.

## Digital migration and Faith Muthambi

The commission spent considerable space in its report on the SABC and the issue of digital migration. In simple terms, this referred to the long-running plan to transition all TV and radio services away from the old-school radiowaves-and-antenna system towards a digital system. This would, in effect, mean that every person in South Africa who wanted to watch TV or access other SABC services would need to install a set-top box (like a DSTV box or, if you're as old as me, an M-Net decoder).

One controversial aspect of this process concerned encryption: would the signal sent to the set-top boxes be decrypted or encrypted. If they were encrypted, the signals would be scrambled. Whatever device received them would need to have a matching encryption key to unscramble the signal. If they were decrypted, the signals would go out without any scrambling or protection; any type of set-top box or TV could pick them up and show them, without the need for any matching encryption key.

The commission's investigation focused at length on the ongoing negotiations between SABC and MultiChoice around these issues, and how SABC negotiated that it would get to include its own news channels on MultiChoice's platform. Despite the complaints of ex-CEO Mokhobo, the commission ultimately found that there was no corruption or wrongdoing in the engagements between MultiChoice and SABC. As a result, I do not describe them here.

However, one aspect on which the commission did find was the actions of the Minister of Communications, Faith Muthambi. The commission's investigations on this matter flowed from an original inquiry by OUTA into the GuptaLeaks. The GuptaLeaks showed that Muthambi was in frequent contact with Tony Gupta or Ashu Chawla; her correspondence was also forwarded to Duduzane Zuma. The correspondence mostly focused on government policy regarding Sentech (a state-owned signals broadcaster) and the whole set-top encryption issue. Muthambi, as Minister of Communications, was quite obviously in charge of a portfolio whose work would impact on the Guptas' media interests.

The most problematic exchange of emails dealt with the powers falling under the Minister of Communications. On 17 July 2014, Muthambi forwarded a draft presidential proclamation to Ashu Chawla, who sent it on to Tony Gupta. Under the draft proclamation, certain powers and responsibilities were to be moved from the Minister of Communications to the Minister of Telecommunications. Some of these powers and responsibilities included issues dealing with digital migration and encryption. In essence, if the proclamation was passed, Muthambi would lose control of these issues to the

Minister of Telecommunications, Siyabonga Cwele. Muthambi also sent a further document to Ashu Chawla explaining the effect of the proclamation; this was then forwarded to Tony Gupta and then Duduzane Zuma.

Most importantly, on 29 July 2014, Muthambi emailed Chawla, ahead of a Cabinet meeting the next day, a memorandum that she had sent to Minister Cwele in which she outlined her concerns with his plans around digital migration. The commission found that this was 'a gross violation of Cabinet confidentiality'. Later, Muthambi shared a further draft proclamation with Chawla, which was then discussed with a number of individuals at the SABC. The commission found that Muthambi's emails to the Guptas amounted to 'an abuse by Ms Muthambi of her office. There is no reasonable explanation for communications of this nature between a Minister and members of the Gupta group who control a television station subject to her regulatory jurisdiction.'

The commission also referred to the decision of the courts to remove Hlaudi Motsoeneng as the COO of SABC. Although the commission did not discuss these rulings in any way, it found that Motsoeneng's 'gross abuse of power at the SABC', which included diverting resources to the Guptas via the business breakfasts, had most likely been sanctioned by Muthambi and Zuma. The commission believed that her conduct in relation to Motsoeneng warranted further investigation by the NPA.

The commission's attitude to Muthambi was hardened by her appearance before it. Muthambi denied that there was anything wrong with her communicating with the Guptas, who were merely interest stakeholders in the media space, according to her version. The commission attacked this lustily, noting that Muthambi failed to include any other stakeholders in these discussions. On this basis, it found that Muthambi had shared confidential information so that she could use her allies, the Guptas, to ensure that President Zuma protected her powers:

> In these circumstances the finding we make is that Ms Muthambi unlawfully shared that confidential information with the Guptas and their associates. It is quite clear that she was doing so in order to get the Guptas to talk to their friend, President Zuma, to ensure

that she had certain powers as Minister of Communications. That means that, like Mr Mosebenzi Zwane, Ms Lynne Brown and Mr Malusi Gigaba, who were Gupta Ministers, she, too, was a Gupta Minister.

## RECOMMENDATIONS

*The NPA should investigate Faith Muthambi for potential violations of PRECCA regarding her conduct in relation to Hlaudi Motsoeneng and the benefits accruing to the Guptas from Motsoeneng's decisions.*

*The costs incurred by the SABC for the Business Breakfast broadcasts (R4,268,887 excluding VAT) should be recovered from TNA and/or other Gupta companies.*

*Parliament or other bodies should consider promulgating a specific offence related to abuse of office.*

*Law enforcement agencies should investigate Hlaudi Motsoeneng and Lulama Mokhobo for potential violations of the PFMA in relation to the contract between SABC and TNA establishing the TNA business breakfasts.*

# The New Age

IN 2010, THE GUPTAS launched their own newspaper, *The New Age (TNA)*, which operated under their media company TNA Media. It had been given the imprimatur of support by Jacob Zuma. As we saw in the previous chapter, Zuma went so far as to testify that he had encouraged the Guptas to launch the paper.

The problem with *The New Age* was that most people didn't want to read it; its survival and profitability were based almost entirely on government expenditure, either through advertising or through subscriptions. *TNA*'s other revenue stream, discussed in the previous section, was the lamentable New Age Business Breakfasts, in which government ministers were soft-soaped live on SABC. All of this was achieved through, and was symbolic of, Gupta-led state capture.

## The dismissal of Themba Maseko and the capture of GCIS

The commission's terms of reference required it to make findings on the dismissal of Themba Maseko, which had also been the subject of an inquiry by the Public Protector. Maseko had served as the director general and CEO of the Government Communication and Information Service (GCIS). GCIS's primary function was to relay news and information about government initiatives, and to provide an access point to search for government data. It also operated an enormous advertising budget, used to pay newspapers to both advertise government positions and raise awareness on matters of importance to the government.

Maseko testified that during September or October 2010, he received a cellphone call from Ajay Gupta, who wanted to discuss a new project. Maseko already knew Ajay Gupta as he had met him at meetings of BrandSA, of which Ajay Gupta was a board member and which fell under Maseko's command at GCIS. Although initially reluctant to meet, Maseko eventually relented, and an appointment was set up for a meeting at the Saxonwold compound.

Maseko testified that, on the day of his meeting with Ajay Gupta, he received a phone call from Jacob Zuma. After some pleasantries, Zuma said, in Zulu, 'My brother, there are these Gupta guys who need to meet with you and who need your help. Please help them.' Maseko informed Zuma that he was already on the way to meet Ajay Gupta, and Zuma signed off by thanking him for his cooperation. Maseko was 'taken aback' by the phone call. He wondered if the phone call had been initiated by the Guptas 'to demonstrate their power and influence over the upper echelons of government'.

Maseko met Ajay Gupta shortly thereafter. According to Maseko, Ajay told him he was aware that the government spent about R600m a year on various media platforms. Ajay explained that he wanted all this expenditure to be transferred to the benefit of the media company that the Guptas were just forming. Maseko was struck by the accuracy of the figure quoted by Ajay Gupta. The R600m amount would have been known only to insiders at the GCIS, which had oversight of the totality of media requests made by various government departments.

When Maseko pushed back, to explain how procurement worked and to point out that the GCIS merely acted on behalf of other government departments, Ajay Gupta objected. Maseko recalled that he 'proceeded to tell me my job is to go and identify, collect and allocate all the communication budget amounts in the various departments to his company'. Further, if any minister or department was recalcitrant, Ajay Gupta told Maseko, he would 'personally summon and deal' with them. In Maseko's interview with the Public Protector, he recalled asking Ajay Gupta how he could wield so much power. Ajay explained that he had regular meetings with President Zuma, at which he could bend Zuma's ear.

Maseko left the meeting angry and defiant: he would not be strong-armed into potentially corrupt arrangements to help the

Guptas. He reached out to a large number of senior ANC and government insiders to tell them of the meeting, including Collins Chabane (the Minister in the Presidency), Deputy President Kgalema Motlanthe, Essop Pahad (the former Minister in the Presidency) and the Reverend Frank Chikane. Chikane confirmed before the commission that the conversation did indeed take place.

Maseko next heard from the Guptas on a Friday at the end of 2010 while he and his wife were on their way to a golf tournament. The first contact was made through a Gupta employee, who asked Maseko to attend a meeting the following working day – a Monday – at 8 am, to discuss government advertising in *TNA*. Maseko testified that he agreed to meet, but that they would have to call on Monday to schedule a proper appointment. The Gupta employee insisted, but Maseko refused: the call ended 'unceremoniously', in Maseko's words.

An hour later, Ajay Gupta contacted Maseko, beginning his conversation in a hostile tone. Ajay told him that he would not 'tolerate' any nonsense and then demanded that the meeting take place the next day – a Saturday. Maseko pushed back and explained he would not be spoken to so rudely; he admitted to using an 'expletive' in the phone call. Ajay responded that, in the light of Maseko's reluctance to assist, he would approach Maseko's seniors. Maseko, for his part, informed Collins Chabane of the conversation the following week.

Maseko testified that he received a call from Chabane in late January 2011 asking him to attend a meeting in person, to which he agreed. At the meeting Chabane reluctantly relayed the news that Jacob Zuma had instructed him to dismiss Maseko. Chabane indicated that he did not agree with the decision, and undertook to help Maseko to ensure that he was placed in another senior government position.

Maseko's removal from the post was announced at a Cabinet meeting two days later, on 2 February 2011; Maseko was slated for a new position within the Department of Public Service and Administration. Jimmy Manyi was named as Maseko's replacement. Maseko claimed that he was unaware of his move until the Cabinet had made the announcement.

When Zuma testified before the commission, he completely and totally rejected the evidence that he had instructed Chabane to remove Maseko. Zuma speculated that Chabane may have had a conversation with a separate government minister, and then noted that 'at times people use the name of the President', implying that Chabane may have used Zuma's name for his own reasons.

Collins Chabane passed away in 2015; he was thus unable to testify. The commission therefore sought other means of corroboration, one of which was the testimony of Abednigo Hlungwani, the private secretary to Chabane at the time. Hlungwani, who claimed to have received threats the day prior to his testimony at the commission, recalled a private call between Zuma and Chabane shortly before Maseko's sacking. He also testified that he had had a private conversation around the same time in which Chabane told him that Maseko was to be replaced.

Another witness to come forward was Brett Simons, who had previously worked at the GCIS. In January 2014, Simons was seconded to Chabane's office. Simon testified that Chabane told him in person that Zuma had been the person who issued the instruction for Maseko's firing. This was also the recollection of Ronald Shingane, an advisor to Chabane between 2009 and 2013: he noted that Chabane had told him about Zuma's instruction as well.

On reviewing this evidence, and after a discussion about whether proper processes were followed in redeploying Maseko, the commission found:

> there is absolutely no doubt that President Zuma did, indeed, instruct Minister Chabane to fire Mr Themba Maseko or move him from his position as DG and CEO of GCIS. There is also no doubt that in giving this instruction, President Zuma was giving effect to the wishes of the Guptas or was complying with their request or instruction to him to remove Mr Maseko because he had refused to co-operate with them.

Zuma's evidence was rejected as a 'dishonest version' and a 'fabrication' deployed by the ex-President to 'avoid accountability for a decision that he took'.

The commission was also disturbed by the evidence about the way Jimmy Manyi was moved into the position at GCIS. At the time of the appointment, Manyi was at the Department of Labour; the minister at the time in the department could not recall ever being approached about Manyi's transfer. The transfer was effectively conducted by the Minister for Public Service and Administration, Richard Baloyi.

The nub of the issue was whether Manyi's appointment as head of GCIS was presented for discussion and approval before Cabinet. The documentary evidence showed that it was not. Baloyi, while denying that he acted with any undue motive, nevertheless acted with speed and in ignorance, which the commission believed must have been because he was fulfilling a presidential instruction: 'Thus, as in relation to the transfer of Mr Maseko, it may be concluded on a balance of probabilities that Minister Baloyi acted in haste in effecting the transfer of Mr Manyi, without due attention to lawful and proper procedures, in order to assist in securing forthwith the practical outcome that the President required.'

## What did the Guptas get from Manyi's GCIS?

In short: a very large amount of money. As noted above, Manyi was appointed as the head of GCIS on 2 February 2011. He held the position for just over 18 months, departing in August 2012. During this period, the GCIS made its largest ever monthly payment to *TNA*, just short of R6m. This was almost double the size of the next largest amount, which was paid in December 2015. In the financial year from March 2011 to 28 February 2012, the GCIS spent R6.39m on *TNA*. This was the second-largest outlay by the GCIS on a media house; only the *Sunday Times* received a greater share of government spending. At the time, there was no evidence about *TNA*'s readership figures and its circulation numbers had not been certified. This amount leapt to R8.2m in 2012/13, and continued growing, eventually reaching just under R10m in 2014/15.

Manyi, who testified before the commission, was evasive when he was asked how the GCIS could spend so much money on *TNA* when there was no evidence anyone was reading it. Manyi eventually denied any accountability for the expenditure, claiming that GCIS merely implemented the wishes of other government departments. The commission was unconvinced, and delivered a damning verdict on Manyi's conduct:

Mr Manyi was correct that GCIS was an 'enabler department' under his watch, but not in the sense that he meant it. GCIS was an enabler of state capture during Mr Manyi's tenure. Had it not been for the fact that Mr Manyi was moved in to replace Mr Maseko, the GCIS would likely have resisted the Guptas' incessant pressure on government departments to divert their media spend to their business

## TNA and Eskom

Eskom concluded three contracts with TNA Media between 2012 and 2014:

- The first, signed in April 2012, was for R7,185,628.74. This contract was concluded between TNA Media and Eskom's media agent, the Media Shop. Of this, R4m was for ad spend in *TNA*, and the remainder was sponsorship for six TNA business breakfasts that were broadcast on SABC 2.
- The second was concluded in November 2012, this time directly between Eskom and TNA. The contract was for an additional four business breakfasts at a total cost of R4m.
- The final contract – again signed directly between Eskom and TNA – was signed in 2014. Under this contract, Eskom agreed to pay R43.2m to TNA to sponsor 36 TNA business breakfasts.

The commission heard evidence from two key people close to the award of the contracts. The first was Chose Choeu, the divisional executive of corporate affairs at Eskom from June 2010 until December 2018. Choeu reported directly to the CEO; at the time of the first contract, this was Brian Dames. The second was Pieter Pretorius, who was responsible for strategic marketing at Eskom. Pretorius reported to Tshepo Moreme, who in turn reported to Choeu. Eskom's sponsorship programme fell under the responsibility of strategic marketing.

Choeu testified that the first contract, placed in April 2012, came about after a TNA employee, Jacques Roux (whom you will remember from the Brakfontein coal story), contacted Eskom asking for a meeting to discuss advertising in March 2011. After some delays – during which CEO Brian Dames was informed of the controversy around TNA – Eskom convened the meeting in August 2011. The meeting was attended by Atul Gupta and Roux for TNA and Dames and Choeu for Eskom. According to Choeu, Dames, without any due process, committed Eskom to contracting with TNA on the spot.

Shortly thereafter, Pretorius was approached to put together a proposal for Eskom to sponsor the business breakfasts. He rejected the idea out of hand, as Eskom could only sponsor events with a proven track record. Pretorius explained this to Choeu and to Nazeem Howa, the CEO of TNA, at a meeting at Eskom's office. Pretorius testified that Choeu approached him sometime after this meeting and explained that 'it is an instruction. It comes from the Minister. Brian Dames had told us you will do this.' Choeu denied this version. He admitted that he told Pretorius about Dames's commitments to TNA in their earlier meeting, but said Pretorius had not raised any concerns. Gigaba, for his part, denied he issued any instruction. The commission, after reviewing the evidence, found Pretorius's version more persuasive.

In March 2012, Choeu emailed Pretorius telling him to 'close the deal' on the TNA business breakfasts as part of Eskom's '49M campaign', which aimed to educate South Africa's 49 million citizens on energy conservation. Shortly thereafter, Roux pitched the proposal alongside Pretorius. Pretorius, however, was concerned that TNA's proposal was far too large, and asked Eskom's media agency, the Media Shop, to come up with something smaller. At the end of March, the Media Shop sent a proposal to Pretorius, along with a note that recorded that Pretorius's boss, Moreme, had impressed on the agency the importance of the contract. The contract was signed the following month.

This contract was manifestly irregular for a whole host of reasons, but two are particularly striking. First, all sponsorships over R50,000 had to be approved by a formal sponsorship committee. This was never done. Second, Eskom was bound to deal only with established media houses whose circulation figures had been audited by the Audit Bureau of Circulations (ABC). *TNA*'s circulation was never audited.

The second contract, awarded later that year, was also irregular, according to the commission. This contract, as noted above, was signed directly between Eskom and TNA, largely because this allowed TNA to be paid more quickly. The contract was signed on Eskom's behalf by Choeu.

One key requirement for ongoing sponsorships was that Eskom was supposed to conduct an evaluation of the previous sponsorship's success and impact. This evaluation was not done. And while this contract was referred to the Sponsorship Committee, its recommendations were mostly ignored: of the ten members of the committee, eight voted against the sponsorship, while only two, including Choeu, backed the proposal.

Choeu admitted before the commission that this second contract was irregular and also confirmed that he was aware that questions had started being asked in Parliament about the business breakfasts. Nevertheless, he cited pressure from CEO Dames and Minister Gigaba to continue the sponsorships as part of the 49M campaign.

The third contract was also bedevilled by irregularities. On this occasion, the proposal remedied the failures of the second contract by including an evaluation of the success of Eskom's previous sponsorships. But the figures included in the evaluation were misleading; there was, in fact, no real information about the success or otherwise of the sponsorships. Choeu testified that he included this in the proposal to help it succeed.

Pretorius was tasked with putting together a presentation for the Sponsorship Committee. To his credit, Pretorius's presentation explicitly recommended against awarding the third, and largest, sponsorship contract to TNA. Pretorius cited the negative press around the business breakfasts and the lack of any audited circulation figures for *TNA* as key reasons.

Pretorius's presentation, however, was never sent to the Sponsorship Committee. Indeed, the entire contract was not sent to the committee. Instead, it was simply handled directly between Choeu and the newly incoming CEO, Collin Matjila. The third contract was signed directly by Matjila in April 2014.

## The ratification: Regularising the irregular

Not long after this contract was signed, a whistleblower approached Eskom's Audit and Risk Committee (ARC) to report the irregularities. As a result, Eskom's ARC appointed the firm Sizwe Ntsaluba Gobodo (SNG) to investigate the contract. Any ratification of the contract would be held in abeyance until SNG concluded its investigation.

Zola Tsotsi, Eskom chairman between 2011 and 2015, testified that he was called to a meeting with Tony Gupta at the Sahara offices in Midrand. Tsotsi claimed that Tony Gupta had expressed his concern at the SNG investigation and wanted Tsotsi to 'make it go away'. While Tsotsi later said he did not intend to help the Guptas, the commission noted that, on 16 October 2014, Tsotsi instructed Eskom's company secretary to ask that SNG not release its report until he had had a chance to speak to SNG's CEO and chairman. The commission believed this conduct was 'suspicious', not least because Tsotsi was one of only two people who were retained on the next Eskom board, which, as the commission had already established, was effectively appointed at the instruction of Salim Essa and the Gupta enterprise.

Not long after, the Public Protector, Advocate Thuli Madonsela, wrote to Tsotsi. She explained that her office was already conducting its own investigations into the business breakfasts. Madonsela expressed her dismay at the fact that the third contract had been signed by Matjila despite her ongoing investigations. She implored Tsotsi to ensure the third contract was not ratified until she had, at the very least, published her findings on the two other contracts.

SNG presented the results of its investigations to the ARC at the beginning of November 2014. ARC forwarded the SNG's findings to the board. These concluded that the contract was irregular because Matjila had exceeded his delegation of authority. It also found that the guidelines for approving sponsorships had not been adhered to and, most outrageously, the contract was missing an early termination or exit clause that would have given Eskom the right to end the contract. The commission's investigations revealed that the clause was removed by Choeu after a complaint from Nazeem Howa.

At the next Eskom board meeting at the end of the month, the SNG report was discussed. On the basis of the SNG findings, the board hired a second firm, Ledwaba Mazwai, to advise on the impact of Matjila's irregular conduct with respect to the contract and his own employment. The Mazwai report was a bit of an oddity. On the one hand, it pointed to irregularities in the contract award. On the other, it suggested that the board could still choose to ratify the contract, in the teeth of these irregularities, if the board felt the contract represented good value for money.

The board met again on 8 December 2014 to discuss the various findings. Ultimately, in the midst of other potential good governance violations, the board came to the conclusion that the 'contract was a bad one' and that it was not to the benefit of Eskom. Another board member at the time testified to the commission that what the board actually meant by this was that the contract was poorly drafted and potentially irregular, but not that Eskom had achieved no value. Tsotsi, however, confirmed that it was the board's intention that the incoming board would be informed of all these matters.

The commission, for its part, was absolutely clear that the business breakfasts were a farcical waste of money for Eskom. It found that *TNA* was under no obligation to display Eskom sponsorship. All that Eskom received was ten complimentary seats to the business breakfasts; and because the reputation of the events was so poor, Eskom struggled to fill them. 'There was no or negligible value for Eskom in sponsoring the TNA business breakfasts,' the commission confirmed.

Only three days later, on 11 December 2014, an entirely new board was appointed. This board, as we have seen, was a horror show of Gupta goons and puppets. Based on the previous board's decision, this incoming board was supposed to have been informed about its predecessor's reservations about the contract. However, the handover report to the new board made no mention of them. Tsotsi explained to the commission that the minutes of previous board meetings should have also been included in the handover pack, but they had been 'inadvertently' omitted.

Sometime between January and February 2015, a circular was sent to board members. It sought approval from the board to ratify the contract. The circular, however, was factually incorrect and misleading in a number of ways. On the issue of whether Matjila exceeded his delegation of authority, for example, the circular recorded that there was a 'difference of opinion' on the matter. It failed to disclose that the opinions were held by a respectable audit firm, on the one hand, and by Collin Matjila, on the other. The round robin even went so far as to omit the contract itself, which meant that board members were being asked to ratify a contract they hadn't seen. Nevertheless, the board approved the circular and ratified the contract, without even meeting in person to do so.

The commission was absolutely blistering about the entire affair. Tsotsi was excoriated for failing to explain to the incoming board members that the round robin was full of errors and flaws. It also noted that, in the context of Tsotsi's own engagements with the Guptas, there was a real possibility that he had tried to 'sweep the contract under the rug' by getting it ratified. And even if that wasn't the motive, 'he acted negligently and in contravention of his fiduciary duties'.

The commission therefore found:

> This contract was concluded because two individuals, Mr Choeu and Mr Matjila, were determined that they would conclude it, regardless of the law and the legal obligations they had to Eskom. The board failed dismally in the exercise of its duties and ratified the contract to make the administrative inconvenience of an 'irregularity' go away and they never bothered to take any further action against those who had originally committed Eskom to this expenditure.

## Eskom and TNA subscriptions

Originally, Eskom subscribed for 30 copies of *TNA* a day at a cost of R25,148 per year. This was then increased to a subscription of 2,000 copies per day at a cost of R1.3m per year. By comparison, Eskom only subscribed to 140 copies of *Business Day* per year at R319,000. The commission heard evidence from Ms Wadja, the head of communications, that she was instructed by Choeu to increase the subscription amount.

Choeu denied the allegation. However, the commission then presented Choeu with a letter that he had written to Wadja, containing the very instruction. Choeu duly conceded the point, and then eventually admitted that he had originally wanted 4,000 copies to be bought and for R7m to be spent on the subscriptions.

'When this conduct is viewed alongside the role he played in committing Eskom to the business breakfasts, it is clear that Mr Choeu saw fit to put the interests of TNA ahead of those of Eskom,' the commission noted. 'This makes one ask the question: What was in it for him that he could look after the Guptas so well at the expense of Eskom, his employer?'

# TNA and Transnet sitting in a tree: L.O.O.T.I.N.G.

TNA Media would make an absolute killing at Transnet, too. Between 2012 and 2017, Transnet spent a truly astonishing R122,809,526.70 sponsoring the business breakfasts. A further R24,872,200.16 was paid to TNA to sponsor 'The Big Interview'. This consisted of a profile and interview with a high-flying individual. There was no Transnet branding, and the topics covered had nothing to do with Transnet specifically. The value to Transnet was non-existent.

As with Eskom and GCIS, the Guptas exerted pressure behind the scenes to get their way. This was the evidence of Mafika Mkwanazi, who, as you will recall, was implicated by the commission's Transnet report in the irregular reinstatement of Siyabonga Gama. Mkwanazi served as the board chair between December 2010 and December 2014, and as the acting CEO from December 2010 to February 2011.

Mkwanazi was approached by Tony Gupta in the brief period in which he acted as the CEO. He testified that he received a call from Tony in January 2011, shortly after his appointment as acting CEO, asking him to come to a meeting. He also told Mkwanazi that he had got Mkwanazi's number from Malusi Gigaba. Gigaba denied this, but the commission found his denials unconvincing.

Mkwanazi duly met with Tony Gupta at the Saxonwold compound. Duduzane Zuma was also in attendance. After explaining that Jacob Zuma was a personal friend, Tony Gupta said that he wanted between 30% and 50% of Transnet's R1bn marketing media spend to be directed towards TNA. This figure was wildly off the mark; Transnet's budget in this regard was R27m in 2010 and R95m in 2011. Mkwanazi rebuffed the approach, and explained that TNA would have to go through the proper channels. Tony Gupta then repeated his closeness to Jacob Zuma, saying that they spoke once a week, and that Zuma even sang his signature song, 'Umshini Wam', to the delight of the Gupta brothers.

Mkwanazi was concerned that, if the friendship was genuine, it was being abused by the Guptas. He testified that he asked Duduzane if Tony Gupta's description of the Gupta–Zuma relationship was accurate. Duduzane confirmed that it was. This was the only thing Duduzane said in the meeting.

Mkwanazi decided that he needed a second meeting with Tony Gupta, but this time in the presence of somebody from the

Department of Public Enterprises. He was duly joined by Solomon Mahlangu, Gigaba's advisor and Gupta go-between. Mkwanazi, for reasons I cannot quite decipher, stated that he wanted to have a witness to the demands that Tony Gupta was making.

The second meeting took place two weeks later, most likely at the end of January 2011. Tony Gupta and Duduzane attended the meeting, as did Mahlangu. Mkwanazi testified that he used the meeting as an opportunity to explain to Tony Gupta, once again, that proper procurement processes had to be followed; Tony apparently accepted the explanation without further comment. Mahlangu remained silent throughout.

Tony Gupta may have shown unexpected magnanimity because he knew that Mkwanazi was not going to be around for very long. Indeed, only a few weeks later, in mid-February 2011, Brian Molefe was appointed CEO of Transnet, displacing Mkwanazi. A few months later, in May 2011, Gigaba submitted a Cabinet memorandum to remove Mkwanazi as the chair of the board, and argued that he should be replaced by Iqbal Sharma. Cabinet disagreed. Nevertheless, Mkwanazi testified that he thought this attempt may have been linked to his failure to meet Tony Gupta's expectations.

TNA started receiving contracts from Transnet shortly after Molefe was appointed CEO, and with his direct involvement. The first coup was to gain sponsorship for 'The Big Interview', for which Transnet received nothing of any notable value. The two motive forces behind this were Brian Molefe and Mboniso Sigonyela, who was the general manager of Transnet group corporate and public affairs, which included responsibility for advertising and sponsorships.

The Guptas' earliest attempts to get sponsorship for 'The Big Interview' took place in December 2011, when Jacques Roux emailed a proposal to Transnet's media agency (called, creatively, The Agency). An independent expert who advised The Agency and Transnet rejected the proposal, noting that it was incredibly expensive and that TNA's circulation had yet to be audited.

Nevertheless, in the teeth of this advice, Sigonyela produced an internal memorandum for Brian Molefe to support the sponsorship of 'The Big Interview'. The memorandum claimed that TNA was a 'key publication' targeted by Transnet, and that it would allow Transnet to 'send key messages to our stakeholders'. How Transnet could achieve this when it had no editorial control and failed to even have its logo on 'The Big Interview' was a mystery. Both Molefe and Sigonyela signed the memo, and the first contract followed shortly thereafter.

An employee reporting to Sigonyela, Mr Jackson, provided evidence to the commission. He noted that he had raised various issues with the proposal. Sigonyela, however, was adamant, and demanded that Jackson stop delaying the progress of the sponsorship. Jackson testified that he had never faced such a level of pressure from Sigonyela before.

Another witness was Ms Palesa Ngoma, a communications specialist at Transnet. She testified that she was instructed by Sigonyela to write supportive memoranda justifying further sponsorships of 'The Big Interview'. She wrote six in all.

The commission found that all the 'Big Interview' sponsorship contracts were irregular 'in that they did not follow the ordinary processes set out (albeit informally) in Transnet. It is also clear that the spending was wasteful and fruitless expenditure as Transnet derived no value from it. No transparent and competitive processes were followed by Transnet in obtaining these services.'

Similar irregularities were attendant on Transnet's sponsorship of the business breakfasts. Daniel Phatlane served as the senior coordinator of stakeholder relations at Transnet from 2011 to 2017. He reported to Sigonyela. Phatlane testified that he first met Jacques Roux of TNA Media in 2011, but only after Roux had already met Sigonyela on a number of days. Sometime thereafter, in September 2011, Roux sent Phatlane the first sponsorship proposal for two business breakfasts at R1.47m. The proposal was a single page, provided no motivation, and did not describe what value Transnet would get from the contract.

Phatlane testified that, despite the shabbiness of the proposal, Sigonyela instructed him to prepare a memorandum to support the sponsorship. Phatlane's memorandum sang the virtues of *TNA* and its role in Transnet's branding and image; Phatlane testified that he was instructed to insert these bromides at the instruction of Sigonyela. The memo was directed to the attention of Siyabulela Mapoma, who was the acting group executive of corporate services. Mapoma, however, rejected the proposal.

Never fear: Molefe was near. Following Mapoma's rejection, Sigonyela prepared another memorandum. This time, however, it was sent straight to Molefe, bypassing the intermediate links on the management chain altogether. By now, the requested sponsorship had skyrocketed: Sigonyela's memorandum (drafted by Phatlane at Sigonyela's instruction) sought sponsorship for 16 business breakfasts at R16m.

Molefe received the proposal on 20 March 2012. He signed it three days later, on 23 March. The deal was formalised in a contract between Transnet and TNA signed on 14 May 2012. As had happened at Eskom, this contract was also missing any early termination clauses.

Not even a year after the first contract was signed, TNA returned with a new proposal, this time for 20 briefings for R20m. This amount, however, exceeded Molefe's delegation of authority for sponsorships. If it was to be approved, it would therefore need to go before the board. The commission believed that a blunt work-around was employed. So when Phatlane created a new supportive memorandum, the word 'sponsorship' was dropped altogether. Instead, the contract's aim was to establish a 'partnership' between TNA and Transnet.

The second deal was codified by means of a 'branding and advertising partnership agreement', which was signed by Molefe on 19 April 2013. The agreement stipulated that Transnet would pay R15m to sponsor fifteen business breakfasts. Notably, this agreement changed the payment terms to favour TNA: payments had to be made within seven days, rather than the usual thirty. Phatlane testified that Sigonyela had confirmed this should be included after TNA applied pressure.

The commission was clear about what it thought of this contract:

This 2013 agreement was clearly irregular. Although it was no different from the 2012 sponsorship agreement, it was recast as a partnership agreement. However, that recasting did not change its nature. It was a sponsorship agreement. Mr Molefe did not have the authority to conclude it as it fell within the authority of the board. Despite this, Mr Molefe went ahead and concluded the agreement, committing Transnet to pay R15 million within

7 days for a service that did not produce any discernible value for Transnet. The expenditure was therefore also fruitless and wasteful.

Three further agreements were ultimately signed by Transnet to support the Big Breakfast. Two were signed by Molefe in 2014 (for R20m) and 2015 (for R21.2m); the third was signed by Siyabonga Gama in 2016 (for R21.2m plus VAT, or R24.168m). Each contract described the relationship as a 'partnership' rather than a sponsorship, avoiding the R10m threshold. All were signed without an early termination clause, or with a termination clause that required both parties to agree to termination before it could be effected. The commission noted that a further payment of R24.168m was made by Transnet to TNA in 2017. This was the same figure that had been paid by Transnet under the previous year's contract. However, the commission 'did not have insight' into what contractual arrangements justified the payment.

The commission, in the light of all this, made a clear and unambiguous finding:

> From the above evidence, it is apparent that Mr Molefe and Mr Sigonyela were directly facilitating the use of public funds for TNA spending. They did not appear to put up any resistance and indeed appeared determined and anxious to ensure that these contracts were concluded (and on extremely disadvantageous terms for Transnet). Mr Sigonyela used threats and intimidation to ensure that his subordinates complied with instructions to advance the interests of TNA. The spend on these contracts was irregular, fruitless and wasteful.

The commission did not, however, lay all the blame at the doors of Sigonyela and Molefe: it also strongly criticised Transnet's internal and external auditors. The commission simply could not fathom how these contracts had passed through any meaningful internal checks.

## SAA: Paying first-class prices for economy-class products

SAA was another target of TNA and the Guptas. Cheryl Carolus, the chair of SAA between 2009 and 2012, testified that SAA was approached by TNA in 2011 seeking advertising spend. The proposal was put through SAA's Bid Adjudication Committee (BAC), which rejected it as it did not meet SAA's business criteria.

Shortly thereafter, Carolus received a call from the director general at DPE, Tshediso Matona, who summoned her to an urgent meeting. He also requested the attendance of the CEO of SAA at the time, Sizakele Mzimela. Solomon Mahlangu, Gigaba's advisor, also attended the meeting. Carolus testified that Matona and Mahlangu tried to convince her of the importance of assisting new entrants to the media market, and to support TNA. Carolus rejected the approach, noting that it was not SAA's job to incubate new companies, but also pointing out that the approach was irregular.

As we have seen, Vuyisile Kona was appointed as the chair of the SAA board in September 2012, and as acting CEO between October 2012 and February 2013. He testified at the commission and claimed that, by the time he took up the position, SAA was already subscribing to *TNA*, but that TNA Media was unhappy with the number of subscriptions. Kona claimed that TNA approached him to push for increased subscriptions. Remarkably (audaciously, even), the approach was made on TNA's behalf by Solomon Mahlangu, according to Kona. Kona explained that TNA would need to go through the normal supply chain structures.

In early November 2012, the Bid Adjudication Committee submitted a new proposal to Kona. It proposed that SAA increase its subscription from 3,000 to 7,000 newspapers per day, which would have cost an additional R2.4m per year. The BAC proposal lacked any reason or justification for the increased number. It also failed to address whether SAA had the money for this increased expenditure; and an SAA operations manager had made a statement attached to the proposal noting that 'there is currently no budget on operations for this'.

Despite these problems, Kona approved the proposal. The commission was clear that this was irregular:

> Mr Kona's approval of the increased subscription with no evidence of effectiveness, circulation, affordability or commercial value, was a breach of his fiduciary duties to SAA and of his obligations under the PFMA to avoid irregular expenditure as

there was no budget to support the increase. It also amounted to wasteful expenditure as there was no information about the commercial value of the subscription to SAA.

What was less clear was the commission's understanding of Kona's role in relation to the Guptas in the light of his approval of this contract. At the end of October 2012, Kona was approached by Solomon Mahlangu and asked to attend a meeting at the Saxonwold compound. Kona duly visited the compund, and on his arrival his cell phone was removed by security. Also at the meeting were Mahlangu, Tony Gupta, Duduzane Zuma and Tshepiso Magashule.

Kona testified that Tony Gupta was the only person to speak in the meeting. The latter 'welcomed' Kona into the 'family', and offered him R100,000 as an introduction. Tony Gupta had somehow caught wind that Kona had not been paid his salary the previous month; Kona was disturbed that Gupta had any knowledge of this. When Kona turned it down, Tony Gupta increased the offer to R500,000. Again, Kona rejected the offer. It was at this point, as we have seen, that Tony Gupta exploded in a rage after finding that the SAA turn-around contract had been awarded to Lufthansa, and even called the DG at the Department of Public Enterprises to complain. Kona, however, claimed that TNA was not raised at any point.

The commission is somewhat obtuse about the impact of this meeting. On the one hand, it took considerable time in its report on TNA to describe the meeting, but it did not ascribe Kona's decision on the subscription issue to this meeting. It also stated that the meeting at the Saxonwold compound came after Kona approved the increased subscription figures, but this seems to be a mistake.

Having gone through both Kona's transcript and his statement before the commission, I believe that he was indicating that the meeting at the Gupta residence took place on the same day he was called by Mahlangu, which was 29 October. The Bid Adjudication memo was dated 6 November. From this, it would be reasonable to ask whether the meeting with Tony Gupta, at which he indicated his political muscle, was a factor in Kona's decision to approve the increase in subscriptions.

Alas, the commission, having made this seeming mistake, simply did not go there.

## RECOMMENDATIONS

*Law enforcement should investigate a possible crime of corruption against Tony Gupta on the basis of Vuyisile Kona's evidence that he was offered bribes of R100,000 and R500,000.*

*Investigations should be undertaken into the role of each board member of the 2015 Eskom board to establish if they played any role in the award of contracts to TNA or were grossly negligent or violated their PFMA obligations in ratifying any contract.*

*Law enforcement should investigate Brian Molefe for potential fraud and/or PFMA violations for his role in signing contracts with TNA while at Transnet.*

*Law enforcement should investigate Collin Matjila for potential fraud and/or PFMA violations for his role in signing contracts with TNA while at Transnet.*

# Alexkor

Alexkor was by far the smallest SOE investigated by the commission; it was also a vivid illustration of how the Gupta enterprise got its tentacles into every nook and cranny to extract its criminal rents.

Alexkor was created in its modern form by the Alexkor Act of 1992. Its primary work is to exploit the mining resources, and in particular the diamond fields and the diamondiferous coastal strip, in the Alexander Bay and Richtersveld areas. In 2003, the Constitutional Court heard a landmark case in which the Richtersveld community demanded the restitution of land that was, at the time, being used by Alexkor. The Constitutional Court confirmed that the land mined by Alexkor had originally been seized from the original inhabitants, and directed that it be returned to the ownership of the community.

In 2007, following the decision, Alexkor, the Richtersveld community and the government entered into a settlement to resolve the use of the land. The result was the creation of a joint venture agreement with a poetic little name that fairly trips off the tongue: the pooling and sharing joint venture agreement (PSJV). PSJV was 51% owned by Alexkor (and thus the government) and 49% by the Richtersveld community. Alexkor retained the exclusive rights to mine the coastline while the diamond deposits on land would be mined by PSJV.

## Gupta associates all the way down

Alexkor, like all SOEs, fell under the control of the Department of

Public Enterprises. In September 2012, Minister Malusi Gigaba appointed Rafique Bagus as the chairperson of Alexkor. The commission noted that Bagus previously worked at the Department of Trade and Industry; what it did not appear to know was that, as my own previous investigations into the Arms Deal revealed, Bagus was a director in a company called Enable Mining.

Enable Mining's other directors were Julekha Mohamed, Jacob Zuma's one-time lawyer, and Chippy Shaik, the brother of Schabir Shaik, who had been convicted for his corrupt relationship with Jacob Zuma, including the solicitation of a bribe for Zuma from an Arms Deal company. Enable Mining was a shareholder in a company called TAN Mining and Exploration. The other shareholder was Ferrostaal, one of the companies that scored the biggest contracts from the Arms Deal.

The Zondo Commission's report found that Bagus's cellphone records showed that he was in frequent contact with associates of the Guptas. Between 2008 and 2013 he spoke on 60 occasions with Iqbal Sharma, and eight times with Ashu Chawla. Between July 2015 and March 2016, he chatted 28 times with Ajay Gupta. He also chatted with Tony Gupta on seven occasions between May 2015 and March 2016. Rounding out this picture, Bagus also attended the infamous Sun City wedding.

In August 2012, Mervyn Carstens was appointed the CEO of PSJV. His cellphone records show that he spoke with the Gupta acolyte Kuben Moodley 97 times between September 2015 and May 2017. He also chatted with Stanley Shane, whose relationship to the Guptas I've already discussed in the Transnet section, on about 10 occasions between February and July 2016.

In October 2013, Zarina Kellerman was appointed as the chief legal officer of Alexkor. She held this position until November 2015. Her cellphone records show that she had a remarkable 479 calls with Kuben Moodley between August 2015 and April 2018. When Kellerman left Alexkor in 2015, she was made an advisor to Mosebenzi Zwane, the ultimate Gupta minister. She was also the secretary to Zwane's so-called Inter-Ministerial Committee which the commission found had attempted to intimidate South African banks after they had closed Gupta bank accounts.

The commission's investigations also established that the recurring nightmare of Regiments was also visited upon Alexkor.

It reviewed considerable emails that suggested that Regiments was looking to contract with Alexkor. At the time, plans were afoot to get Alexkor to diversify into coal, which would be supplied to Eskom. The emails suggested that Regiments sent a draft consultancy agreement to Alexkor to advise on an agreement between Eskom and Alexkor. The commission, however, found that the evidence was sketchy and inconclusive, and it did not seem that the consultancy contract was concluded. The commission thus recommended further investigations into the dealings between Regiments and Alexkor.

## The irregular appointment of Scarlet Sky Investments

The commission heard evidence from a senior consultant from the auditing firm Gobodo, which was appointed by the DPE to investigate allegations of wrongdoing at Alexkor. The most notable target of this investigation was a contract awarded to a company called Scarlet Sky Investments (SSI), whose primary shareholder was Kuben Moodley.

In October 2013, PSJV's Technical Committee raised concerns with how the diamonds mined by PSJV were being marketed. At the time, the marketing was handled by a company called Diamond Marketing Consultants, which had been appointed by Alexkor prior to the 2003 land claim. After a failed trial with another marketer, a request for proposal (RFP) was issued for a new marketing company. The RFP also envisaged that the winning bidder would be involved in what is known as post-mining beneficiation: taking the raw diamonds and adding value by turning them into other products like jewellery.

The RFP, most importantly, required that the winning bidder have licences to conduct the trading and processing of raw diamonds. This was vital because the diamond industry is very closely regulated by the Diamonds Act, which requires that companies obtain diamond trading licences from the South African Diamond Board. Those trading in diamonds without a licence could face ten years in prison.

SSI was one of nine companies to submit bids. SSI's bid was submitted on a letterhead that showed its two directors as Kuben Moodley and Daniel Nathan. The latter was a co-owner of SSI via his company Daniel Nathan Trading (DNT), while Moodley held his shares through a company he controlled called Kimomode.

Carstens, the CEO of PSJV, appointed a third-party company called Gamiso to review the bids. Gamiso recommended three bidders and ranked them in order of preference: Fusion led with 75 points, SSI was in second place with 71.5 points, and CD Diamond came third with 67 points. Crucially, however, Gamiso gave SSI a zero score when it came to the licence requirements because SSI didn't have a diamond licence. Admittedly, Daniel Nathan Trading had a licence, but the Diamonds Act would have prohibited SSI from trading on this licence.

The selection process was finalised at a meeting on 11 December 2014 at Alexkor's office in Johannesburg. The Tender Committee reviewing the bids was made up of three people, one of whom was Rafique Bagus. All three, including Bagus, declared SSI the best bidder. The committee awarded SSI the highest score – five points – on the licensing criteria, even though SSI had no diamond licence. As a result, on 27 February 2015, PSJV awarded the contract to SSI, even though the company had no track record, no experience in trading and cutting diamonds, and – last time for the cheap seats – no diamond licence.

Gobodo's investigation into SSI threw up another issue. The award of the contract to SSI was contingent on a due diligence investigation. The evidence suggested that this was not done. Carstens, the CEO, attempted to argue that he had conducted a due diligence, and pointed to a short email he sent in January 2015. When Gobodo probed Carstens further, he claimed that he had compiled a due diligence report and submitted it to the board. He failed to provide it to Gobodo despite requests. Gobodo's investigations concluded that no due diligence was done and that Carstens had misled the board by claiming otherwise.

One of the more remarkable of the commission's discoveries was that SSI's business address was the same physical address of both Daniel Nathan Trading and Knox Titanium Vault Company. In fact, Knox Vault was owned by Daniel Nathan. If you recall, the commission's investigations into Transnet found that senior executives, including Anoj Singh, had used Knox Vault, and suspected that the vaults were used to store cash bribes paid by the Guptas.

The commission found that SSI conducted approximately R2bn in diamond trading. However, it was all performed by SSI using

Daniel Nathan's licence. The commission indicated that this meant that every single trade performed by SSI was a violation of the Diamonds Act, and strongly recommended further investigation by law enforcement.

SSI was eventually renamed the Alexander Bay Diamond Company (ABDC). After the renaming, ABDC was granted a diamond licence. But the commission suspected that this was itself based on a fraud. The commission reported that Nathan had told the Diamond Board that ABDC was actually a renamed version of his own company, Daniel Nathan Trading, which held a diamond licence. It was on this basis that the Diamond Board agreed to transfer the licence held by Daniel Nathan to ABDC.

## Was Alexkor ripped off?

The commission attempted to dig into the diamond sales to establish if there was any jiggery-pokery around pricing. It heard evidence from a specialist which suggested that the diamonds may have traded at a lower price than they should have, but the evidence was inconclusive. Gobodo's investigation, meanwhile, raised suspicions that some of the buyers of SSI's diamonds may have had links to the Guptas; but this, too, was inconclusive.

The diamond expert did, however, uncover other potential evidence of wrongdoing. He testified that he had reviewed SSI's monthly registers of sales, which have to kept under the Diamonds Act. The registers showed that, at various times, the licence holder was given as DNT, Daniel Nathan Trading House and ABDC. The commission believed that there were reasonable grounds to suspect that these constituted misrepresentations to the South African Diamond and Precious Metals Regulator.

## Alexkor as an example of state capture

The commission concluded its brief report on Alexkor on a cautious note, mostly because it had only been able to conduct a limited investigation. Nevertheless, it found that 'the available evidence nonetheless adds to the body of evidence that some at Alexkor had aligned themselves with the project of the Gupta enterprise. A fuller investigation may well reveal criminal conduct on the part of those involved.'

The ending of the capture of Alexkor took a remarkably long time. In 2019, an administrator was appointed to take over the management of Alexkor and PSJV. It was this administrator who contracted Gobodo to investigate the contract with SSI, which led the administrator to find that the contract was 'questionable from a governance perspective'. It was only in August 2020 that SSI's contract was terminated. At the time of the report's conclusion, Alexkor had applied for its own diamond trading licence.

## RECOMMENDATIONS

*The board of Alexkor should investigate whether Regiments entered into consultancy agreements with Alexkor, the precise nature of any services, and whether Alexkor received full consideration and value.*

*Law enforcement agencies should investigate SSI, ABDC, Daniel Nathan and the directors and employees of SSI, ABDC or any associated company for potential violations of the Diamonds Act.*

*The board of Alexkor should investigate whether the members of the tender committee that selected SSI as the preferred bidder (Rafique Bagus, Dr Roger Paul and Duncan Korabie) violated their fiduciary duties by misrepresenting SSI's compliance with tender requirements.*

*Law enforcement should investigate the three members of the tender committee for fraud or contraventions of the Companies Act for misrepresenting SSI's compliance with tender requirements to the board of Alexkor and/or PSJV.*

*Law enforcement should investigate any director, executive or employee of SSI, ABDC and/or Daniel Nathan Trading for making potentially false statements to the South African Diamond and Precious Metals Regulator to secure the transfer of DNT's diamond trading licence to ABDC.*

*Law enforcement should investigate Mr Carstens and Ms Kellerman for potential fraud for misrepresenting to the board that due diligence was conducted on SSI.*

*The board of Alexkor and PSJV should investigate whether Mr Carstens and Ms Kellerman were in breach of their fiduciary duties for misrepresenting to the board that due diligence was conducted on SSI.*

*Law enforcement agencies should investigate whether Rafique Bagus, Duncan Korabie and Dr Roger Paul (the tender committee) unlawfully acted as board members for PSJV in contravention of a High Court decision related to the lawful constitution of the board.*

*Law enforcement should investigate SSI, Daniel Nathan Trading CC, Daniel Nathan Trading House, Alexander Bay Diamond Company Trading House, ABDC and any directors, employees or executives thereof for violations of the Diamonds Act for making false representations that these companies, which held licences, were trading diamonds when in fact they were traded by SSI.*

*Law enforcement should investigate SSI, or any director or executive thereof, for any offence related to diamonds not accounted for in SSI's register.*

*Law enforcement should investigate SSI, or any director or executive thereof, to establish if SSI underpaid PSJV in relation to a specific diamond sale (Parcel 248).*

*The South African Diamond and Precious Metals Regulator should conduct an inquiry to establish if the buyers of SSI's diamonds held the requisite diamond trading licences.*

# PRASA

The Passenger Rail Agency of South Africa (PRASA) provides services that touch on the lives of millions of South African commuters. It is responsible for maintaining and running South Africa's urban rail networks which, for most working commuters, provide one of the few ways to navigate the remnants of geographical apartheid. Apartheid's spatial planning expelled non-white communities into far-flung dormitory townships; workers living in these townships were, and still are, required to commute incredibly long distances to their places of work.

Corruption at PRASA did not form part of the original Public Protector report that led to the establishment of the Zondo Commission. However, the commission, once it reviewed the public evidence and the materials that were brought to its attention, decided to make it a big part of its investigation. In broad terms, the commission was perturbed by the PRASA evidence for two reasons. First, it noted how attempts to clean up PRASA were resisted and undermined by a range of actors. Second, it was deeply concerned by the scale of corruption at PRASA, which was illustrated by two notoriously corrupt deals: the Swifambo Leasing deal and the Siyangena contract. Both took place under the leadership of the highly controversial group CEO, Lucky Montana.

## Swifambo
On 23 March 2013, PRASA concluded a contract with Swifambo Rail Leasing by which PRASA would purchase 70 locomotives for

R3.5bn. This contract was particularly notorious as the trains that were delivered were totally unsuited to South Africa's rail network; they were too tall to run safely on South Africa's narrow-gauge tracks.

Two years later, PRASA approached the High Court to have the Swifambo contract set aside on the basis of serious irregularities and potential corruption. The application was brought under a new board led by a newly appointed chair, Popo Molefe, who was committed to dealing with corruption at PRASA. On 3 July 2017, the High Court found in PRASA's favour and set the contract aside; the decision was upheld by the Supreme Court of Appeal.

The commission, in telling the story of the Swifambo deal, highlighted the early roles of two parties: Daniel Mthimkhulu and the Spanish company Vossloh España. Mthimkhulu was, effectively, a crony of Lucky Montana; under Montana's leadership, Mthimkhulu rapidly climbed the ranks at PRASA as an engineer. It would later emerge that Mthimkhulu's qualifications were fraudulent. Vossloh España was the company, part of the broader Vossloh group, that provided the locomotives.

In July 2011, Mthimkhulu sent a memorandum to Montana that set out an analysis of PRASA's long-term passenger haulage needs. He claimed that the existing fleet was outdated and that this impacted on PRASA's services. He estimated that PRASA would need to undertake a capital investment programme worth R5bn over six years.

Five months later, PRASA issued a request for proposal for the lease of passenger locomotives. By this stage, Swifambo Rail Leasing did not exist, and only came about when its eventual parent company, Swifambo Holdings (alternatively Railpro Holdings), bought a company called Mafori Finance in February 2012, which it subsequently renamed.

Only six companies submitted bids by the closing date. This included Mafori Financing trading as Swifambo Rail Leasing. Swifambo submitted its bid as part of a joint bid with Vossloh España in February 2012. These bids would have been subject to a first-step compliance check, to see if all the documents needed were submitted. But when PRASA brought its High Court application, it stated that there were no surviving records showing how this was done or who had done it.

In March 2012, PRASA's Bid Evaluation Committee (BEC)

met. According to a later report, the BEC found that Swifambo was the only bidder that met the minimum compliance threshold. On this basis, three months later, PRASA's Corporate Tender and Procurement Committee (CTPC) met in July 2012. Minutes of the meeting show that this committee endorsed the BEC conclusion and recommended that the contract be awarded to Swifambo.

Later that month, the Board Adjudication Committee (BAC) met. It acknowledged the reports of the other committees, and endorsed their findings, recommending Swifambo's appointment. Most importantly, however, the BAC now recommended that the deal proceed on an 'outright purchase' option. The original RFP had envisaged the locomotives would be leased, and the bids were submitted on this basis. Now, however, it was decided that the locomotives be bought. The BAC report was forwarded to Montana. A few days later, after approval by another committee, the board finally approved the appointment of Swifambo. Swifambo was informed of its successful selection on 27 July 2012. And about nine months later, in March 2013, PRASA signed the final contract with Swifambo, by which it purchased 20 Euro 4000 locomotive and 50 Euro dual locomotives.

PRASA's founding affidavit in its High Court application listed a raft of procurement irregularities – so many that the commission decided not even to list them all, choosing instead to highlight the most notable. One of the first irregularities related to how the specifications for the locomotives were drawn up. Under PRASA rules, this should have been done by a committee of three people forming the Cross-Functional Evaluation Team. But, in this instance, the specifications were drawn up by a single individual, Daniel Mthimkhulu. Mthimkhulu's specs were curious: they included requirements that seemed to be tailor-made to meet the locomotives produced by Vossloh, which had partnered with Swifambo. The result, of course, was that Swifambo and Vossloh received considerable advantage in the evaluation process.

A review of Swifambo's bid also found that it did not meet basic requirements of the RFP. For example, bidders were asked to submit tax clearance certificates: Swifambo's certificate had no VAT number, while Vossloh did not submit any certificate. The RFP also envisaged that there would be some local content requirements – that some aspect of the locomotives would be built in South Africa. In fact, the locomotives produced by Vossloh would be manufactured entirely in Spain. Bidders were also asked to show that they had a history of rail leasing and major project management. However, Swifambo Rail Leasing, newly formed, had no such background. Every letter of reference it submitted to support this claim related to Vossloh. However, at this point, while Vossloh was part of the bid, it was not a formal co-bidder, and Swifambo had not signed any contracts with Vossloh – even though Swifambo had admitted that it was entirely reliant on Vossloh to deliver the contract.

PRASA's High Court application also listed all sorts of material problems and irregularities with the document trail leading up to the decision. In certain instances, the minutes did not accord with reality, especially with regard to who attended meetings. In other instances, key documents remained unsigned and undated. In fact, despite the fact that the decision progressed through multiple committees and Montana's office, only a single set of committee minutes and reports was ever signed and properly filed.

A raft of other irregularities were identified, such as the fact that the RFP was only for a lease deal, while the contract was for an outright purchase. But the most obviously absurd part of the entire transaction was that, when Swifambo made its original bid, it offered Vossloh's Euro 3000 locomotive, upon which basis it was evaluated. But it then delivered the Euro 4000 locomotive, which had been designed for European rail networks. They were simply not safe to operate on South Africa's networks as the Euro 4000 was too tall: the Euro 4000 locos were 4.1 metres tall, while the maximum height that could be safely used in South Africa was 3.965 metres.

## The 'bombshell affidavit' and the money flows investigations

In August 2015, PRASA supplemented its founding papers to include a bombshell affidavit submitted by the board chair, Popo Molefe. Molefe claimed that he had been made aware that Auswell Mashaba, the chairperson of Swifambo Rail Leasing, had suffered a crisis of conscience and wanted to come clean. Mashaba told Molefe that he had bid for the locomotives tender after he had been approached by Makhensa Mabunda, an associate of Lucky Montana.

After Swifambo had been awarded the contract, Mashaba was

told by a known fundraiser for the ANC, an Angolan businesswoman called Maria Gomes, that Swifambo had to donate 10% of the contract value to the ANC. Mashaba ended up providing documents showing that approximately R79m was transferred from Swifambo to individuals who Mashaba claimed were supposed to forward the funds on to the ANC.

Mashaba, however, deposed his own affidavit, in which he disavowed aspects of this version, claiming that Molefe's recollection was not entirely accurate. And while he admitted that certain payments were made, he denied that they were made with any corrupt intent. The commission, for its part, sought to call Mashaba to give evidence. In response, Mashaba's attorneys informed the commission that Mashaba did not recognised the 'lawfulness and/or legal validity' of the summons sent to Mashaba by the commission. Mashaba thus failed to testify. The commission duly filed a criminal complaint with the police, which was still being finalised at the time of the commission's report.

The commission spent considerable time setting out the results of two investigations into money flows from PRASA to Swifambo, and from Swifambo onwards. The first was performed by Ryan Sacks, a chartered accountant who was the director of Crowe Forensics. Sacks had been asked by the Hawks to conduct a forensic analysis of the PRASA–Swifambo money flows. Sacks performed an initial analysis – which he called a level 1 analysis – and suggested that he be allowed to move on to a further analysis that would go further in tracing the ultimate disposition of the money. But the Hawks, after receiving this first analysis, never allowed Sacks to continue. The commission would find that the reasons put forward by the Hawks for this failure were nonsensical, and that other considerations might have been at play.

The second investigation was performed by liquidators who effectively took over Swifambo in 2017. The liquidators' report set out details of how money paid to Swifambo by PRASA was spent. Unfortunately, neither report took the money flows analysis to the point where the bombshell affidavit could be verified. Nor was a full funds flow analysis conducted showing the ultimate disposition of all the money, to its very end point.

Nevertheless, certain key facts emerged from both investigations:

a. Swifambo bought the locomotives from Vossloh for €3,657,052 each, and sold them to PRASA for €3,822,900 each. The result was that Swifambo made a profit of €165,848 per locomotive; a total profit of R118m.

b. A review of Swifambo Leasing's account showed that it was basically dormant prior to receiving its first payment from PRASA. It was thus not actually a trading company, and PRASA's first payment to Swifambo Leasing was the first time it received any significant deposits.

c. Between January 2013 and April 2013, Swifambo Holdings operated a call account that paid for basic office costs and other operational expenses equal to just over R1m. Of this, R690,000 was paid for by deposits of Siyaya Rail Solutions, a company controlled by Makhensa Mabunda, Lucky Montana's associate. Evidence led before the commission indicated that Siyaya had itself received contracts from PRASA equal to more than R1bn. The remainder was largely covered by inward payments from Vossloh's South African subsidiary.

d. In total, Swifambo received more than R2.65bn from PRASA, from which it made payments to Vossloh equal to more than R1.8bn. It made further payments of R237,021,909.04 to SARS.

e. Railpro Holdings (the parent company of Swifambo Leasing) made payments of more than R146m to Mashaba or companies controlled by him. He also received a further R22m from Swifambo Leasing. So Mashaba and his companies received R168m from Railpro and Swifambo Leasing.

f. Railpro Holdings made payments of R63m to Mabunda or companies under his control. A further R17m was paid to Mabunda or companies under his control by Swifambo Leasing. Mabunda provided an affidavit to the commission in which he simply 'noted' the payments, and claimed that they were largely for 'services rendered'.

## The Siyangena contracts

PRASA's board under Popo Molefe also sought to overturn a serious of dubious contracts awarded to a company called Siyangena. The contracts were valued at approximately R5.5bn. PRASA submitted its application in 2018. In 2020, the High Court granted PRASA's application to overturn the contracts. The decision was upheld on appeal by the Supreme Court of Appeal in late 2022.

The Siyangena contracts were complicated, and the commission's retelling of them is, at times, obtuse and hard to follow. But the basics were as follows. In 2009, in anticipation of the soccer Confederation Cup, PRASA operated a pilot project to upgrade and develop two stations. The pilot project contracts were awarded to two companies, Intersite and Rainbow. Siyangena was selected as a subcontractor to install 'speed gates' – basically gates that controlled the movement of people through the stations.

PRASA then decided to extend this project as part of its preparation for the 2010 World Cup. Here, however, the contract was not awarded to the two prior contractors. Instead, they went to Siyangena, which would provide gates and other services for an additional five stations. This was described as an 'extension' to the pilot project, and Siyangena's appointment was justified on the basis that it had done work on the previous projects. But PRASA had had no original contract with Siyangena, which was a subcontractor to the two others. The decision to 'extend' the contract with Siyangena amounted to a decision to award it a contract without any procurement process. While the original budget for this 'extension' was around R300m, Siyangena was eventually given a contract worth R1.9bn: this was called 'phase 1'.

PRASA's High Court application placed Lucky Montana at the heart of this process. Other PRASA employees, in particular Luyanda Gantsho, raised issues with the manner in which the contracts were being placed, and with the cost and quality of the items being procured. Montana, however, directed Gantsho to proceed and contract with Siyangena, which Gantsho then did. The High Court noted that there was evidence that Montana had met privately with Siyangena's CEO, Mario Ferreira, while this was all taking place.

Not long afterwards, PRASA decided to steer additional work to Siyangena. The R1.9bn phase 1 contract was now 'extended' into a 'phase 1 extension', which would involve Siyangena installing hardware at a further 12 stations. There was no procurement process involved in the decision at all. This extension was valued at R350m.

In 2013, PRASA decided to expand the scope of its upgrade programme awarded to Siyangena, which was now tasked with upgrading an additional 100 or more stations. Siyangena was awarded work equal to R2.5bn under this extension, now called 'phase 2', in June 2014. The High Court would find that phase 2 was bedevilled with the same irregularities that pertained to the other awards: a lack of proper procurement processes, a lack of competition, and, in this case, the shaping of specifications and requirements so that Siyagena's bids were favoured. Montana was centrally involved, once again.

## Montana's property empire

PRASA's application to have the Siyangena contracts overturned included additional bombshell allegations: that Lucky Montana and his colleague Gantsho (who had been involved in the award of the contracts) had been engaging in property deals with Siyangena. In order to discover the extent of wrongdoing, the commission appointed an investigator, Clint Oellermann, to examine Montana's property dealings.

Oellermann's report noted that, between August 2014 and October 2014, Montana was involved in the purchase of three properties valued at over R36m (a fourth property transaction – which involved Montana selling a property – also took place around this time). These dates were notable: it was in June 2014 that Siyangena was awarded the phase 2 Project, and in September 2014 PRASA agreed to a further addition to this work equal to a further R800m.

Oellermann and the commission investigated four property transactions: three purchases and one sale. All the purchases were funded through arrangements made by the lawyer Riaan van der Walt. Van der Walt represented, among others, Siyangena and other companies associated with Siyangena's CEO, Mario Ferreira. Van der Walt was the sole director of a company called Precise Trade, which was involved in all the property transactions. The overall conclusions reached by Oellermann were summarised by the commission as follows:

> Mr Montana was central to each of the purchases, but attempts were made to conceal his link, even in respect of the one property that was eventually transferred into his name. Despite this,

and the fact that all the properties were fully paid for, on the documents that Mr Oellermann has been able to get his hands on, Mr Montana himself appeared not to have paid even a cent towards the purchases.

Most of the finance for the purchases was made available by Mr Van der Walt, through an Investec Bank account in the name of Precise Trade. In a letter to his erstwhile codirectors, Mr Van der Walt suggested that quite large amounts of money flowed into Precise Trade's account from 'TMM' [TMM Holdings (Pty) Ltd], an entity linked to Mr Ferreira.

The four property transactions can be linked as follows:

a. Precise Trade purchased a house owned by Montana in Parkwood, Johannesburg. Precise Trade paid Montana R6.8m. This was R3.3m more than Montana's own bankers had valued the property only 20 months earlier.

b. After Montana expressed interest in a house in Waterkloof in Pretoria, it was eventually sold to Precise Trade for R11m. However, when the previous owner handed over the keys to the property, she did so to Montana.

c. After Montana's trust company made an offer to buy a property in Sandhurst in Johannesburg, it was ultimately bought by Precise Trade for R13.9m.

d. Montana purchased a house in the wealthy Johannesburg suburb of Hurlingham for R13.5m (of which R2m was an upfront deposit and R11.5m the remaining purchase price). The R2m was paid from Precise Trade's Investec account. The remaining R11.5m was paid by a company called Midtownbrace. Midtownbrace was directed by Andrew Wagner, who told the commission that he had been introduced to Montana by Van der Walt. Wagner said that Midtownbrace agreed to pursue an 'investment' with Montana, after which Midtownbrace paid the full R11.5m towards the property. The property was transferred to Montana thereafter.

Reviewing all the above, the commission concluded:

These payments were made at a time when PRASA was concluding contracts with Siyangena. As has been noted above,

Mr Montana played a role in those decisions. Mr Montana placed himself in a conflict of interest. While on the one hand PRASA was concluding business contracts with Siyangena, he should not in his personal capacity have been involved in any business transaction with Siyangena or entities or individuals connected with Siyangena because Siyangena or those entities or individuals connected with Siyangena could do favours for him so that in turn he could influence PRASA to do favours for them or he, acting in his official capacity as GCEO of PRASA, could remember that Siyangena or people or entities connected with Siyangena had done favours for him in his personal capacity and reciprocate through PRASA. He ought not to have played any role as he was conflicted.

## Resistance to the clean-up of PRASA

The extraordinary plethora of irregularities attendant on the Swifambo and Siyangena transactions provided the background to the second primary theme explored by the commission in relation to PRASA: the extent to which attempts to clean up the agency were resisted and actively undermined at various levels of government.

In this regard, the commission was particularly concerned by the detailed evidence presented by Popo Molefe. On 1 August 2014, a new PRASA board was appointed, of which Molefe was the chair. Molefe testified that he and the board were aware of the importance of the agency, and wanted to do all they could to improve the lives of its users. However, the board members were soon struck by the extent to which their attempts to get PRASA on track were resisted. Lucky Montana was identified as a particularly recalcitrant obstacle.

In 2015, not long after Molefe had taken up his role, a draft version of a Public Protector report on PRASA was distributed to the board; this was eventually published as *Derailed* in August 2015. The report found that PRASA was run abysmally, and highlighted Montana's role in this regard. The report also identified the Swifambo and Siyangena contracts as irregular, on which basis the board then sought to have their award overturned (and at which they eventually succeeded, albeit many years later).

Molefe had hoped to receive the support of his political seniors in pursuing his clean-up mission, but his hopes were dashed. Soon after he was told about the allegations of Swifambo money being funnelled to the ANC, he approached the ANC Top 6 and was granted a meeting. Molefe asked that the ANC back his board in unravelling the corruption of the Montana era, and specifically raised the fact that Montana had been attacking the board in public. He asked that the ANC come to the board's defence should any future attacks be made. The Top 6 pleaded for time to consider the issue and suggested a follow-up meeting. No follow-up meeting was ever held. Unsurprisingly, Molefe felt that the Top 6 and the ANC as a whole did nothing of note to protect the board during this period. As I'll show later, the commission would be particularly scathing of this meeting when it reviewed the role of the ANC in state capture.

Molefe testified to another disappointing meeting, this time with Jacob Zuma, which took place about a week after his meeting with the ANC Top 6. In mid-2015, Lucky Montana stood down from his position as GCEO. In public statements, after he left, he claimed that he would be willing to return to assist PRASA with its various challenges. Molefe's board was not interested, to say the least. Regardless, in August 2015, Molefe was invited to a meeting with Zuma and Minister in the Presidency Jeff Radebe. Minister of Transport Dipuo Peters was also invited, as was Montana, although Molefe was not made aware of this ahead of the meeting.

Montana, Peters, Molefe and Radebe all gave their own versions of what happened at the meeting. The testimony conflicted in various ways. The commission, after considering all of these versions, drew a few conclusions. It found that, even if this was not the intention of the meeting, Zuma attempted to use the occasion to argue for Montana's return to PRASA. Molefe then invited Zuma to address the board as to why they would do so. But, because the meeting ran late, Zuma fell asleep and it was disbanded inconclusively. The key takeaway, however, was that Zuma had indicated that, despite the public acrimony between Montana and PRASA's board, and evidence of Montana's mismanagement, he wanted Montana's return.

Other bodies became actively hostile and uncooperative. One of these was the Parliamentary Portfolio Committee on Transport. During hearings in Parliament in August 2016, ANC members on the committee attacked Molefe for publicising the claims that some of the Swifambo money reached the ANC. They also accused the board of over-paying Werksmans, the law firm that PRASA brought in to try to review PRASA contracts for wrongdoing. Molefe testified that he believed that the PRASA board had effectively been vilified by Parliament.

Molefe also claimed that the Minister of Transport, Dipuo Peters, was obstructive. He said she had intervened in ways that prevented the board from choosing a new CEO after Montana's departure. Peters had insisted that the CFO, Collins Letsoalo, take over on an acting basis; when this was formalised, Letsoalo apparently clashed with the Werksmans investigators who were looking into historical contracts. Molefe further claimed that Peters had attempted to get the board to abandon the Werksmans investigations altogether. Peters denied the allegations.

What was uncontested was that the relationship between the board and Peters deteriorated badly. In March 2017, a letter from Peters was read out during a meeting of the Parliamentary Portfolio Committee on Transport. The effect of the letter was to dismiss the entire PRASA board. Molefe's board was forced to approach the High Court to stop the process. The board members won their challenge and were reappointed.

Soon thereafter, Peters was replaced as Minister of Transport by Mkhacani Joseph Maswanganyi, who had served on the parliamentary portfolio committee that had been so hostile to Molefe's board. Molefe claimed that the board made numerous attempts to meet Maswanganyi but were rebuffed. And while Maswanganyi did not immediately oust the board, he failed to appoint new directors after a handful of resignations. The effect was that the board could not reach a quorum and became dysfunctional. Molefe's board ended in July 2017.

The commission commented on Molefe's evidence that

neither the ANC leadership, the National Executive nor the Portfolio Committee on Transport wanted to assist this board in its fight against corruption at PRASA. This board was on its own in fighting corruption at PRASA. The then President, President Jacob Zuma, gave it no support. The then Deputy President of the ANC and of the country, now President Ramaphosa, gave it no support. Indeed, all the Top Six officials of the ANC gave it no support. The Parliamentary Portfolio Committee on Transport was openly hostile to this board. Minister Dipuo Peters became hostile to this board and fired it through a letter read out in the Portfolio Committee on Transport in Parliament when the board went to have a meeting with the Committee. The board had to go to Court to get reinstated. The next Minister, Mr Maswanganyi, was worse. He rendered it dysfunctional.

The commission was also perturbed by the failure of the Hawks in relation to PRASA matters. Molefe testified that as early as April 2017 PRASA had submitted substantial evidence to the Hawks alleging serious wrongdoing in the Swifambo and Siyangena contracts. Yet nothing happened at the time, and nothing continues to happen.

## Continued instability at PRASA

After Molefe's board term expired, only interim boards were appointed. It was only in October 2020 – three years after Molefe's board ended – that a permanent board was appointed. Similarly, PRASA was saddled with a number of acting CEOs; it was only in February 2021 that a permanent CEO was appointed – Zolani Kgosietsile Matthews. The commission was particularly scathing of the way Minister Dipuo Peters had prevented the appointment of a permanent CEO and also of her reasons. Peters claimed before the commission that she refused to appoint a permanent CEO, despite three board recommendations for the position, because PRASA was 'not ready' for a CEO. The commission's disdain for this explanation was evident, not least because Peters ultimately concluded it was nonsense while giving evidence. The commission was also highly critical of Cyril Ramaphosa, who, for two years after he became President, took no steps towards resolving this extraordinary situation.

The commission was extremely concerned about the state of governance at PRASA at the time it published its report in 2022. It noted that, in early 2021, the PRASA board fired three senior executives on the basis that they had been appointed on fixed-term contracts that had expired. However, when the three executives successfully approached the Labour Court, they pointed out that they had never signed fixed-term contracts. Their attempts to get clarity on this point from the board went unanswered. The commission was outraged that, despite this, the board decided to oppose their Labour Court applications. It simply could not fathom why the board was behaving in this manner.

The commission was also concerned about the dismissal of Zolani Matthews, who had been appointed PRASA's first permanent GCEO in February 2021. Only a few months later, the board sought his dismissal. Matthews took the matter to arbitration, which was heard by the respected Judge Nugent (the same judge who had conducted a stinging review of SARS under Tom Moyane). Nugent found that Matthews's dismissal was unjustified. Again, the commission could not understand the board's attitude, considering how long PRASA had experienced ongoing instability.

Based on these developments and others, the commission concluded its report on PRASA by noting that it was left with an 'uneasy perception that there is much about the ills at PRASA that has not yet been uncovered'. The commission was equally concerned that the recent instability at PRASA 'harked back' to the leadership style of Lucky Montana. On this basis, the commission recommended that an entirely new commission of inquiry be established to investigate 'why PRASA was allowed to slide into almost total ruin, who should be held responsible for that and who could have benefitted from that unacceptable state of affairs'.

## RECOMMENDATIONS

*With regard to Swifambo matters:*
- *All Hawks investigations into misconduct at PRASA should be concluded swiftly.*
- *The NDPP should immediately appoint a team to oversee investigations and prosecutions of those suspected of wrongdoing at PRASA.*
- *The NPA should give serious consideration to the prosecution of all those implicated in the award of the Swifambo contract including Lucky Montana, Daniel Mthimkhulu and Chris Mbatha.*
- *The NPA should investigate the roles played Ms Shezi, Mr Khumalo, Mr Mahlobogwane, Mr Nkosi, Mr Magoro, Mr*

*Holele, Mr Mbatha, Mr Mathobela, Ms Motshologane, Mr Bopape, Ms Ngoye, Ms Shezi and Mr Khuzwayo in relation to the BEC and CTPC decisions to award the contract to Swifambo.*

- *The prosecution of Mr Mashaba and Mr Mabunda should be expedited.*
- *The NPA should consider the Sacks report and the liquidators' report to establish if other prosecutions are warranted.*
- *The NPA should consider the prosecution under the PFMA of the board members who approved the Swifambo award, including Mr Buthelezi, Dr Gasa, Mr Khena, Ms Moore, Mr Nkoenyane, Mr Salanje and Lucky Montana.*

*With regard to the Siyangena matter:*
- *All Hawks investigations into this matter should be concluded swiftly.*
- *The NDPP should immediately appoint a team to oversee investigations and prosecutions of those suspected of wrongdoing at PRASA.*
- *Serious consideration be given to the prosecution of Lucky Montana, Mandla Gantsho and Ms Ngubane for the conclusion of the Siyangena contracts.*
- *The NDPP should consider prosecuting board members who approved the Siyangena contracts, for PFMA violations.*

*With regards to Montana's property dealings:*
- *The Hawks should swiftly conclude its investigations into the four property transactions involving Montana, Riaan van der Walt and Precise Trade.*
- *The NDPP should immediately appoint a team to oversee an investigation and possible prosecution of Montana, Van der Walt and Siyangena (and/or its associated companies) for possible contraventions of PRECCA.*

# PART THREE

# The Big Fish[5]

*When the Zondo Commission first started its hearings, it was already a big-ticket item in terms of media coverage. But the public was electrified when Angelo Agrizzi appeared to give testimony before the commission. Over a number of days, he testified to bribery and corruption on a shocking scale involving the already controversial Bosasa group of companies (which I'll call Bosasa for short). Bosasa had for years been linked to dodgy tenders in the prison system, but it had transmuted into an all-purpose tender-getting machine, offering services across multiple fields to many government entities.*

*The commission's investigation largely confirmed what Agrizzi set out: that the leading lights at Bosasa 'ran the entire business operations on the basis of widespread corruption and fraud'. Indeed, 'corruption was Bosasa's way of doing business'. And this corruption and fraud extended its tentacles through the political system, reaching all the way to Jacob Zuma.*

---

5   I am grateful to Liat Davis for her excellent and invaluable assistance in compiling this chapter.

# Bosasa

## The Bosasa group and its key players

BOSASA WAS AN EXTRAORDINARILY successful company. Angelo Agrizzi, who had served as the company's COO from 1999 to 2016, testified that between 2000 and 2016 Bosasa was awarded contracts equal to at least R2,371,500,000 (that's R2.371bn). This may be a significant underestimate; one analysis by the *Mail & Guardian*'s data team, who gained access to Treasury records, claimed that Bosasa earned R12bn from state contracts between 2003 and 2019.[6]

Agrizzi estimated that about R75m was paid in bribes. But this figure excluded the cost of building houses for officials, or buying them cars and installing fancy security systems, or the cost of holidays and travels for which Bosasa footed the bill. Agrizzi testified that, in his experience, every contract awarded to Bosasa of which he was aware was tainted to some degree by corruption. The commission confirmed that, even if a contract wasn't initially corrupt, corruption would start to 'creep in once they had been awarded, to ensure their retention and their extension or renewal'.

Gavin Watson was the major figure behind Bosasa; he was often described as its 'godfather'. Nothing was done without his approval. Partially because of the role of the Watson family in the struggle for liberation, he was well connected politically to senior ANC politicians. Gavin worked closely with his brothers, who took part in the operations of Bosasa, including Valence Watson, Ronnie

---

6    https://mg.co.za/article/2019-02-01-00-the-bosasa-tally-r12-billion/.

Watson and their brother-in-law Mark Taverner. The Watson family, of course, also benefited from the success of Bosasa.

Other notable figures in Bosasa's operations included:

- *Angelo Agrizzi*: Bosasa's COO, who was involved in all aspects of the business.
- *Joe Gumede*: the executive chairperson and executive director of Bosasa Security, who was involved in dealing with human resources, as well as 'fronting' for Gavin Watson in other areas of the business where necessary.
- *Papa Leshabane*: an executive director, head of media and human resources. Leshabane served multiple roles in Bosasa and was particularly responsible for the Lindela contract with the Department of Correctional Services
- *William Daniel 'Danny' Mansell*: the former managing director and major shareholder in Bosasa. Although Mansell left Bosasa after a fight with Watson, he reappeared in 2003/4 as a consultant for Bosasa on some of its more contentious contracts. When Bosasa started to be investigated, he relocated to the US; Bosasa agreed to pay him $7000 a year on condition he never returned to South Africa.
- *Carlos Bonifacio*: the chief accountant at Bosasa.
- *Leon van Tonder*: employed in various positions in Bosasa, Van Tonder would be involved in a plan to delete Bosasa data when it was being investigated for Department of Correctional Services contracts;
- *Andries Johannes van Tonder*: the CFO of Bosasa.
- *Frans Hendrik Steyn Vorster*: a regional head of Bosasa's facilities management services, he was employed in various positions throughout the group.

## Bosasa's cash bribery system

A good deal of Bosasa's bribery payments were made in cash. Because of the scale of the bribes, Bosasa had to develop sophisticated mechanisms to generate a steady stream of cash. This it did by issuing a constant stream of fictitious invoices. Bosasa would, for example, create false invoices from non-existent labour brokers. These would be paid by means of a cheque, which could then be cashed to withdraw money. Over time, Bosasa also cultivated relationships with a network of cash-heavy businesses such as cash-and-carry wholesalers and liquor stores to help it generate cash reserves; this included companies like Equal Trade, Jumbo Liquor Wholesalers and others. These third parties would give Bosasa the cash they generated from sales, and Bosasa would pay them back with electronic transfers.

One example of this was the relationship with Easy Trade. Easy Trade generated substantial cash from the sale of alcohol. The cash was earmarked and delivered to Bosasa's offices. Bosasa would pay it back by EFT. According to the evidence heard by the commission (including video recordings of the cash deliveries), the cash amounts were never less than R100,000; frequently they reached over R1m. Equal Trade would also sometimes invoice Bosasa for various foodstuffs, but these would never be delivered. Bosasa would pay Equal Trade's invoice by means of an electronic transfer, and Equal Trade would deliver Bosasa cash instead of goods. The commission heard that amounts of between R4m and R6m in cash were collected from Equal Trade per month.

Bosasa also provided some services that generated their own cash streams. For example, it ran phone and canteen services at the Lindela Repatriation Centre. Detainees would pay for the services in cash. A portion of these proceeds would not be banked, but instead diverted to Bosasa's offices.

The rivers of cash that lubricated Bosasa's bribery required a substantial infrastructure. The commission found that huge sums of money were stored in walk-in safes and vaults at the Bosasa offices. The vast cash amounts and the warren of safes and vaults were recorded by a Bosasa employee, Leon van Tonder, at the instruction of Agrizzi, and submitted in evidence. Agrizzi estimated that each vault usually held a minimum of R2m, although the amount could exceed R6.5m depending on the year. This was especially true of the 2015/16 period, when Bosasa was paying out a large number of beneficiaries in cash. This included Bosasa directors, who were paid their December bonuses in cash in order to avoid paying tax on the bonuses.

## The capture of Correctional Services
Bosasa's fortunes were made through the capture of the Department of Correctional Services (DCS), which provided the company with its

first mega-contracts. Four contracts were awarded by DCS to Bosasa; these formed a substantial part of the commission's investigations. The contracts were frequently extended and renewed.

Bosasa's success at the DCS relied in large part on the relationship between Gavin Watson and Linda Mti, the Commissioner of DCS and thus its most senior employee. Mti worked closely with a DCS official called Patrick Gillingham, who was first appointed by Mti as a senior procurement officer and thereafter as CFO. The commission found that Gillingham drove the procurement process, which would be approved by Mti.

## The catering contracts

Bosasa began targeting DCS's lucrative catering services in 2003, at a time when the services were not outsourced. Gavin Watson started the process by directing his employee Frans Vorster to get in touch with Patrick Gillingham to start pitching the idea of tendering for the contracts. Vorster was given cash which he put into A4 envelopes and gave to Gillingham at meetings at a restaurant in the Centurion suburb of Pretoria. Gillingham would, in return for this cash, provide details of the DCS kitchens and menus of the food given to inmates.

With this information in hand, Bosasa's Daniel Mansell put together a strategy and presentation for how Bosasa could win a catering contract that had not yet even been decided on. At the end of 2003, Mansell presented the information to senior officials at DCS. A few months later, at the beginning of 2004, Patrick Gillingham made a presentation to senior DCS management about the possibilities of outsourcing the catering services, long before it was even known that this was on the cards. Gillingham's presentation was put together with the help of Bosasa employees.

Bosasa then went on a further deep dig to evaluate DCS. Bosasa employees were given permission to take tours of prisons around the country in 2004. They were told not to wear their Bosasa uniforms to disguise their identity. On the basis of this information, Agrizzi drew up a report of problems in DCS's services and of what the DCS required, which was sent to Mansell and Gillingham. It would later form the basis of the DCS's contract specification: Bosasa was thus literally writing the specs of a contract that it would soon be bidding on.

On 21 May 2004, the invitation to bid was advertised, using the specifications provided by Agrizzi. Agrizzi was tasked with submitting Bosasa's response. As Bosasa had effectively written the contract, it was a mere formality that Bosasa would be selected; and, indeed, in late July 2004, it secured the contract. The contract was initially for a three-year period with an annual value of R239,427,694, for which Bosasa would provide catering services for seven large prisons. Agrizzi would testify that Bosasa fiddled the figures, which meant that it actually earned more than these amounts: in the first year, DCS paid closer to R310m instead of R239m. By the third year, the actual amount paid by DCS had grown to R450m.

The contract soon became even more lucrative. In late September 2004, Gavin Watson instructed Agrizzi to propose to Gillingham that a further seven facilities be provided with services. This was duly done and signed off by Mti on 17 May 2005. The process was clearly irregular: there was no additional tender, and the contract was simply extended outside procurement rules.

The contract was supposed to end in September 2007. But, because the DCS had failed to advertise for a replacement, the contract was extended for another year. The DCS dragged its heels again, and despite a promise made by Mti to Parliament's Portfolio Committee on Correctional Services, the contract was extended for a further six months to allow the department to finalise a new tender process.

It didn't matter much when the contract eventually expired; Bosasa was simply awarded new ones. On 6 January 2009, Bosasa was awarded a new catering contract for another three years. This used the same specifications as the 2004 contract which had been written by Bosasa itself. A further contract was awarded in 2013 (again, a year late) for three years, at a total annual cost of R420m. Bosasa's gross profit margin was an astonishing 40% (its net profit – profit after tax and other deductions – was still an eye-watering 28%).

The commission would hold that all four contracts were irregularly awarded, potentially violating statutory provisions and certainly violating section 217 of the Constitution.

## The access control contract

In November 2004 Bosasa was invited to attend a monthly meeting of the DCS to present on the implementation of the catering tender and to showcase some of the other services it could provide. The meeting was attended by Mti, Gillingham, Agrizzi and a number of Bosasa directors (excluding Gavin Watson and Mansell). Following the meeting, Mti told Watson that there was an access control contract in the pipeline.

Agrizzi was instructed to draft a specifications document for an access control system to be procured by the DCS which would be advertised; as with the catering contract, this allowed Bosasa to effectively draw up the tender specs on which it would then bid. Agrizzi ensured that Bosasa would win by including security aspects that afforded Bosasa a clear advantage over other bidders. And so, when DCS issued an invitation to bid on 4 February 2005, Bosasa had a huge advantage. In around April 2005 the contract went to Sondolo IT, a large subsidiary of the Bosasa group.

Unsurprisingly, the commission ruled that this contract was also unlawful: Bosasa was allowed to draw up the terms and conditions of the contract which it then went on to win. The contract was thus anathema to the constitutional injunction to ensure competitiveness and fairness.

The contract was awarded for two years. However, during its life, the contract was extended in scope to include the provision of control rooms. The value of this extension was over R236m. As with the catering contracts, Agrizzi testified that the costs had been seriously inflated to ensure Bosasa made mega-profits.

## The fencing contracts

In June 2005, Gavin Watson told Agrizzi that the provision of high security fencing at DCS presented a big business opportunity. However, Bosasa at the time had no experience in erecting such fences or indeed the capacity to do so. To resolve this minor inconvenience, Watson purchased a company called Phezulu Fencing, which then went on to win the fencing contracts. The purchase agreement was structured so that the shareholding in the company would only be transferred once any contract had been awarded. Bosasa nevertheless took over management immediately. The entire negotiation was undertaken before any tender had been publicly announced. According to Agrizzi, the plan to acquire Phezulu only took place following a preceding discussion, in which a contract was mooted, between Bosasa and DCS's Mti and Gillingham.

The fencing contracts followed the template of the catering and access control contracts: Bosasa staff gained access to DCS sites to conduct surveys and identify what needed to be provided. Agrizzi claimed that Mansell, by now a consultant to Bosasa rather than a shareholder, was responsible for drafting the bid specifications to provide fencing for 47 different DCS facilities around the country.

The fencing tender was advertised by DCS on 14 October 2005. Phezulu Fencing was awarded the contract about six weeks later, on 29 November 2005. The commission noted that the invitation to bid provided bidders with approximately four weeks to put together their proposals: this was virtually impossible for anyone except Bosasa, which had prior knowledge of its contents. Agrizzi was certain that DCS officials would have been alive to this fact.

The fencing contract was valued at R486,937,910. The value of the contract was then inflated, according to Agrizzi. This was achieved by adding in a separate and parallel maintenance contract. This contract was not put out to tender at all. Instead, it was merely awarded by Phezulu Fencing to another Bosasa company, Sondolo, and the state would carry the cost of the decision.

This contract, too, was ruled unlawful by the commission. It showed that the DCS had failed to implement a fair procurement system as required by the law, while the tender itself violated section 217 of the Constitution. Importantly, the commission also ruled that there was 'prima facie' evidence that other crimes had been committed.

## The 'television contract'

In late 2005, presumably concurrently with or shortly after the award of the fencing contract, DCS's Gillingham reached out to Agrizzi and Mansell about another opportunity: the installation of a centrally distributed television management programme. Importantly, both Mansell and Gavin Watson were told by Gillingham and Mti that the DCS had a surplus in its budget which it needed to spend quickly lest it be taken away by Treasury (and withheld from the DCS budget in future).

The programme would mean that every prison cell or area with a TV could have its channels chosen remotely: this would allow the

DCS to ensure that all inmates could watch ministerial addresses (the example provided by the commission). Although little sympathy is accorded to inmates and convicts, one has to wonder whether forcing them to listen to the ramblings of ministers may have been too severe a punishment.

Again, Bosasa was given all the internal documents that were required to design the system. Agrizzi used them to draw up the contract specifications, once again ensuring that Bosasa would have an in-built advantage over other bidders.

## The DCS officials captured by Bosasa

Lurking in the background of all this irregularity was an extensive network of corrupted officials, of whom the two most important were Linda Mti and Patrick Gillingham.

The commission heard substantive evidence of the benefits Mti received from Bosasa in reward for his role in directing DCS contracts its way. He was given monthly cash payments; he received money to buy luxury clothes; he was gifted golf clubs; his house was built by Bosasa, which also provided fittings and furniture and expensive security systems (the security systems were estimated to cost just over R400,000). Evidence was shown that the purchase of a Volkswagen Touareg was made at the same time that the fencing and access control contracts were awarded.

Agrizzi further testified that Bosasa covered the costs of Mti's family holidays, the education of his children, and even the cost of a security guard posted outside Mti's house. Invoices provided to the commission under subpoena showed that travel booked for Mti and his family between October 2012 and January 2017 cost R1,234,481.11.

Some of the bribery schemes were more complex. Agrizzi testified that Bosasa built a house to Mti's specifications by a Bosasa subcontractor called Riekele Construction. Agrizzi estimated the contemporary value of the property to be between R16m and R18m. The house was registered to a company called Autumn Storm Investments 119. After the house was built, DCS put out a tender to build a rental home for the National Commissioner. Riekele won the tender and moved Mti into the house. The Department of Public Works then paid rent to Autumn Storm Investments. The brainwave was that the rental amounts would ultimately be paid to Mti's benefit – although this was stopped when Bosasa started receiving controversial media coverage.

In the light of this evidence, the commission found that Mti breached the Constitution and the PFMA in his role in awarding contracts to Bosasa. This included wrongdoing in his own role and the strong probability that he was complicit in PFMA violations caused by Gillingham. The commission also stated that the 'evidence reveals that Mr Mti facilitated the awarding of tenders to benefit himself and his family' in contravention of PRECCA, and that there was a prima facie criminal case against him in this regard.

Gillingham was the second most notable figure. He was found to be integral to the award of DCS contracts to Bosasa. In exchange, the commission found, Gillingham received numerous benefits in the form of cars, properties, holidays and cash payments. Gillingham would, for example, receive R47,000 a month in cash, paid regularly on the 25th. Gillingham was also gifted an international holiday once a year paid for by Bosasa. The Watsons' brother in-law Mark Taverner was also involved in providing furnishings for Gillingham (and Mti).

Gillingham requested that Bosasa build him a house – this was duly done by Riekele. Rubbing salt into the wound, Bosasa accounted for this as a legitimate business expense, which was most likely an unlawful representation made to SARS. Bosasa also helped Gillingham's legal fees when he got divorced, and then paid the R2.2m divorce settlement when it was reached. In 2010, following an investigation by the Special Investigating Unit, Gillingham resigned in the light of disciplinary measures brought against him. Bosasa covered his legal fees for the disciplinary hearing, and when Gillingham did eventually resign, Bosasa paid him R110,000 a month.

As with Mti, the commission found that Gillingham violated PFMA regulations, and that he had done so in order to benefit himself and his family, suggesting further PRECCA offences.

Agrizzi testified that another eight DCS officials received regular payments from Bosasa, including Josiah Maako, Maria Mabena, Shishi Matabela, Mandla Mkabela, Dikeledi Tshabalala, Zach Modise, Mollet Ngubo and Nontsikelelo Jolingana. Jolingana was the acting head of the Bid Adjudication Committee of the DCS at the time the catering contracts were extended. The commission found that she played a material role in ensuring their extension. In return for this, Jolingana was paid R100,000. Agrizzi, who maintained a 'little black book' of corrupt payments, recorded the payment therein. The commission held that she violated procurement rules and that there was prima facie evidence that she had committed corruption in violation of PRECCA.

The other seven individuals did not dispute or challenge the allegations that were made against them. On this basis, the commission held that they were all jointly involved in facilitating the award of tenders to Bosasa and that there was prima facie evidence that they had all committed PRECCA violations.

## Attempts to capture DCS following Mti's departure

In 2007, Linda Mti was replaced as the National Commissioner of DCS by Vernie Petersen, who held the position until 2008. Petersen passed away in 2011 in allegedly suspicious circumstances; the commission was implored by one witness, Dennis Bloem, to investigate Petersen's death. Petersen was followed by Xoliswa Sibeko.

Petersen and Sibeko were understood to be hostile to Bosasa's role in the DCS. Indeed, Agrizzi testified that he attempted to approach Petersen after his appointment but was rebuffed. Sibeko, when she took over, was reportedly adamant that the Bosasa group should not have anything to do with DCS. Agrizzi recalled that it was not long after her appointment that Bosasa was informed that DCS was not going to renew Sondolo IT's contract for the staffing of control rooms.

Bosasa sought to change both Petersen's and Sibeko's attitudes towards it. After Petersen was appointed, a meeting was held between Gavin Watson, Agrizzi and Khulekani Sithole, the former Commissioner of the DCS. A fourth person, one Sbu, joined, but his identity was not entirely clear in Agrizzi's retelling. It is possible that this Sbu was the general secretary of the Police and Prisons Civil Rights Union (Popcru). The upshot of the meeting, according to Agrizzi, was that Sithole, Sbu and a third person, Mnikelwa Nxele, would receive R1m per month (it is not clear if this was R1m each, or split between them). Nxele was, at the time, the regional Commissioner for the DCS in KwaZulu-Natal. The payment was made specifically so that they could bring their influence to bear to shift Petersen's attitude.

Nxele failed to respond to the evidence led about him to the commission, despite being served with a notice informing him of the evidence and of his rights. Because of this, the evidence against him was unchallenged. The commission thus found that, at least with regards to Nxele, there was good evidence that he was indeed paid to boost Bosasa with Petersen. Nxele was paid R57,500 a month, which the commission found to be a violation of PRECCA.

## Contracts with other state entities

Bosasa was extremely successful in securing tenders with a huge range of government departments. The commission heard evidence about a large number of these contracts, and about allegations of corruption.

In the interests of brevity, I have summarised the contracts awarded to Bosasa by state departments, the key allegations and the commission's findings. However, in certain cases, the commission was not given particularly substantial evidence and thus made no findings. Again, in the interests of saving time and space, I do not include those cases in the accompanying table.

| Detail of contract | Allegation | Commission's finding |
| --- | --- | --- |
| *Department of Justice and Constitutional Development* | | |
| A R601m contract awarded to Sondolo IT in 2013 to provide access control for courts across the country. | 2.5% of the R601m was to be paid to Department of Justice officials. Agrizzi identified two individuals, Mr Thobane and Ms Nyambuse. | The commission was unable to serve Rule 3.3 notices on the two implicated individuals so it could make no finding against them, although it recommended further investigation. |

| Detail of contract | Allegation | Commission's finding |
|---|---|---|
| | Agrizzi alleged that Dr De Wee, the COO of the Department of Justice at the time, was paid cash amounts by Sesinyi Seopela at the time Dr De Wee sat on tender boards assessing the Sondolo contract. | There was no corroboration of the cash payments to Dr De Wee and the evidence was hearsay. Nevertheless, the commission found that Dr De Wee was party to certain decisions that benefited Sondolo IT which were questionable. It recommended further investigations. |
| Sondolo IT was appointed to undertake security upgrades at the South African Legal Union premises rented by the department. | No tender process was followed and no permission was sought from the owners of the buildings. Agrizzi claimed he gave Bosasa's consultant Sesinyi Seopela R1.9m in cash to facilitate the award of the contract. | The evidence against Seopela was undisputed as he did not respond to Rule 3.3 notices. It was likely that departmental officials assisted in the award of the contract. Further investigations recommended. |
| | Desmond Nair, the chief magistrate of the Pretoria magistrate's court, had security systems valued at R252,864.94 installed at his home by Bosasa. Nair denied any wrongdoing and said that it was installed as part of a private relationship he had with a Bosasa employee, Mr Baijoo. | The commission could find no lawful basis for the payment. It recommended further investigation. |

| Detail of contract | Allegation | Commission's finding |
|---|---|---|
| | PRASA | |
| Access control contract with Sondolo IT (unknown value). | Agrizzi claimed that bribes had been paid to secure the contract. It later emerged that the acting chief procurement officer of PRASA, Mbulelo Gingcana, had received free security installations at his house worth R239,468. The installations were made while he served in this role. The installations were noted in Bosasa's records as forming part of something called 'Project PRASA'. | Sondolo IT most likely installed the security system to secure influence with Gingcana. No lawful authority could be found to provide a good reason why the installation was performed. The matter should be referred to law enforcement on the basis that it may uncover a prima facie case of corruption against Gingcana |
| | Department of Health in Mpumalanga Province | |
| A contract to provide services to hospitals in Mpumalanga was successfully negotiated in 2016. | Joe Gumede had negotiated the successful contract and he promised a success fee would be paid to a departmental employee, Mr Netshishivhe. The success fee was made by paying for repairs to Netshishivhe's car to the value of R29,239.79. | Bosasa was awarded the contract and there was corroborating evidence that the repairs were paid for. The commission referred the matter to law enforcement on the basis that this amounted to evidence of the unlawful facilitation of tenders. |

| Detail of contract | Allegation | Commission's finding |
|---|---|---|
| *Department of Social Development in the North West Province* | | |
| Fictitious software purchase equal to R4.5m. | Agrizzi claimed that two officials, Ms Kgasi and Ms Mogale, agreed to create a fictitious contract to raise money for ANC electioneering. Bosasa was paid R4.5m for software services that were never delivered. | Neither Kgasi nor Mogale responded to the allegations. The commission recommended a further investigation by law enforcement, which it believed may prove a prima facie case of criminality. |
| *Airports Company South Africa* | | |
| A five-year contract was awarded in 2001 for guarding multi-storey car parks at OR Tambo Airport (apparently still being run by Bosasa as of 2019). | Agrizzi compiled the tender documents, giving an advantage to Bosasa.<br><br>Gavin Watson knew the head of risk at ACSA, Thele Moema, and head of security, Siza Thanda.<br><br>Agrizzi claimed Moema and Thanda were paid monthly amounts to secure the contract. He also claimed other officials including Reuben Pillay, Joe Serobe, Bongi Mpungose and Mohammed Bashir were also paid cash. Another official, Jason Tshabalala, was also mentioned. Payments were still being made when Agrizzi left Bosasa in 2017. | Moema, Pillay and Serobe did not respond to the allegations.<br><br>The commission failed to send Rule 3.3 notices to Bongi Mpungose, Jason Tshabalala and Mohammed Bashir, so no finding was made regarding them.<br><br>Commission recommended further investigation by law enforcement into Moeme, Pillay and Serobe, as well as Siza Thanda. |

| Detail of contract | Allegation | Commission's finding |
|---|---|---|
| South African Post Office (SAPO) | | |
| Bosasa was awarded contract to provide security services to SAPO (undisclosed value). | The tender was awarded to Bosasa before it was even advertised. <br><br> Agrizzi claimed that regular cash payments were made to the former head of security at SAPO, Siviwe Mapisa, and former CEO, Maanda Manyatshe. They were given additional gifts such as pens and watches. Mapisa was taken on hunting trips at Ronnie Watson's game farm. | Mapisa and Manyatshe failed to respond to Rule 3.3 notices sent to them by the commission. The evidence implicating them was undisputed as a result. <br><br> The commission recommended that the matter by referred to law enforcement for further investigation into charges of corruption against Mapisa and Manyatshe. |

## How Bosasa got away with it

One of the most disturbing aspects of the evidence around Bosasa was how extensively it was able to manipulate and curtail criminal investigations into its conduct. To achieve this, Bosasa secured the illicit help and assistance from officials in the National Prosecuting Authority (NPA), MPs and two of the most politically powerful people in the country, Dudu Myeni and Jacob Zuma.

## *The SIU investigation*

Bosasa's incredible success in securing contracts from the DCS almost immediately started attracting attention. In 2006, the Public Service Commission and the Office of the Auditor General referred specific allegations of wrongdoing to the Special Investigating Unit (SIU). The SIU launched an investigation that delivered a damning report, detailing a litany of wrongdoing, in 2009. The SIU specifically found that the DCS contracts had been awarded to Bosasa after Bosasa staff had written up the specifications, and without any needs analysis or feasibility studies being conducted.

The SIU's investigation into Bosasa was potentially ruinous for the company, and Bosasa did everything it could to thwart it. In 2007, the company brought interdict proceedings against the SIU, trying to stop the investigation. In 2008, the SIU and Bosasa reached an agreement on how the SIU would proceed, and the limitations of its investigation. The SIU, partially based on legal advice it had received, was unable to conduct interviews with senior Bosasa directors. Gavin Watson, for example, was not interviewed at all by the SIU.

The SIU sought access to other evidence and reached an agreement that SIU would be allowed to access data from Bosasa's servers. The transfer was originally due to take place in the first week of December 2008. This was postponed at Bosasa's request. In the second week of December, for eight days, the SIU made forensic copies of Bosasa servers. When SIU reviewed the forensic copies, it was clear that huge amounts of data had been deleted. Agrizzi testified that this was purposely done in the first week of December, during the time in which Bosasa got its postponement. The SIU report confirmed that thousands of documents were deleted and overwritten on 4 and 6 December. Agrizzi claimed that a computer virus had been put on Bosasa's system to clean up documents that might incriminate the company.

Despite these obstacles, the SIU found considerable compelling evidence and made adverse findings against Bosasa. In 2009 it handed over copies of its report to the NPA for action. The SIU made a number of presentations to the NPA to little effect. When SIU's chief investigator on the matter, Clint Oellermann, eventually left in October 2012, the NPA had failed to register any case against Bosasa.

Indeed, a case would only be brought against Bosasa ten years later, when a charge sheet was served in February 2019 against Linda Mti, Patrick Gillingham, Agrizzi, Van Tonder and certain companies within the Bosasa group. The charges emanated substantially from the SIU report. Oellermann, when asked about the delay, claimed it was incomprehensible.

## Capturing the NPA

Sadly, it was all too comprehensible: Bosasa had connections at the very top of the NPA, according to Agrizzi. After the SIU report was completed and handed to the NPA, Agrizzi and Gavin Watson held monthly meetings with Mti to manage the fallout. Mti said Bosasa would need to pay off individuals at the NPA and suggested payments be made to Advocate Nomgcobo Jiba, Advocate Lawrence Mrwebi and Jackie Lepinka. Jiba and Mrwebi were, at the time, in charge of the NPA's investigation into Bosasa. Jiba would later be appointed the Deputy Director of National Prosecutions by Jacob Zuma in December 2010. Lepinka, it emerged at the Commission, was not only involved in the Bosasa case, but had actually served as Mti's secretary between September 2001 and November 2006.

Jiba would eventually be struck from the roll of advocates in 2016 for her handling of politically connected cases, including her decision to drop charges against Richard Mdluli and to pursue charges against the Hawk's Johan Booysen. Booysen would claim that he was targeted by Jiba because he was interested in investigating cases related to Zuma. Mrwebi was removed from the NPA in 2019 following a damning investigation into his and Jiba's conduct chaired by retired Constitutional Court judge Yvonne Mokgoro. In the roll call of Zuma-era nogoodniks, Jiba and Mrwebi loom large.

Following Mti's suggestions, Gavin Watson told Agrizzi to start making monthly payments to Jiba, Mrwebi and Lepinka. Agrizzi testified that Jiba was to receive R100,000 a month, Lepinka R20,000 and Mrwebi R10,000. Mti played a material role in the NPA's wrongdoing: Jiba and Lepinka would meet with Mti on a weekly basis to hand over detailed and confidential information about the NPA's investigation.

In November 2012, Lepinka drafted an email, in which she claimed to speak on behalf of Jiba. The exact recipients of the email are not entirely clear from the commission's telling but appear to have been prosecutors or NPA officials heading various cases. Lepinka complained about the Bosasa case, saying that it needed to be finalised asap. She continued: 'the matter has been investigated for a number of years and from the submitted reports it is clear that there is no evidence and/or prospect of a successful prosecution.' The commission rubbished the claim: there were mountains of evidence. The email, in the commission's mind, thus pointed to 'wrongful attempts to close down the Bosasa investigation and prosecutions'.

The commission would ultimately find that there were reasonable grounds for finding that Agrizzi's version of what happened regarding Jiba and Lepinka had taken place. It did not, however, find that this was true of Mrwebi, who the evidence showed had tried at times to advance the case against Bosasa. While the commission noted that the evidence against Jiba and Lepinka, in particular the evidence of the bribes, amounted to hearsay, it believed there was a 'reasonable prospect' that further investigation would remedy this shortcoming. It also found that further investigation could potentially prove a case of defeating the ends of justice. The commission recommended the NPA conduct a further investigation, focusing on the leaking of specific documents, although it refrained from telling the NPA to focus on any particular individual.

## Neutering Parliament

Bosasa was also potentially vulnerable on another front: Parliament's Portfolio Committee on Correctional Services, which was empowered to request and hear extensive evidence on Bosasa contracts. Agrizzi testified that, as with the NPA, Bosasa used bribery and influence peddling to ensure that Parliament remained toothless in its investigations into the company.

Agrizzi identified a number of parliamentarians who helped Bosasa. The first was Cedric Frolick, the house chairperson of committees. Agrizzi claimed that Gavin Watson had instructed that Frolick be paid R40,000 every month. Frolick, for his part, denied the allegation – he claimed that he had only ever received a single amount of R25,000 from Valence Watson meant as a donation for the ANC, as well as some small gifts from Daniel Watson.

Agrizzi claimed that Frolick was enlisted to help Bosasa with another MP, Vincent Smith. Smith was, at the time of the SIU report being released, the chairperson of the Portfolio Committee on Correctional Services. Bosasa believed that Smith was anti-Bosasa and opposed to outsourcing on principle. Frolick was asked to use his influence with Smith to change his attitude. Frolick, on his own admission, arranged a meeting between Smith, Agrizzi and Gibson Njenje (Njenje was briefly Bosasa's chairperson, albeit without much direct involvement in day-to-day matters). Smith's attitude did, indeed, shift, which Agrizzi attributed, in part, to Frolick's endeavours.

The commission was deeply unimpressed with Frolick's attempts to help Bosasa smooth over its relationship with Smith. This was because he must have known that, at the time, Smith was in charge of the parliamentary body that had significant power to conduct investigations into Bosasa, which would, in turn, have potentially serious and material impacts on the contracts awarded to the company (or the renewal of its contracts).

On this basis, the commission found that, based just on Frolick's own admissions, he was guilty of 'conduct facilitating the unlawful awarding of tenders' in breach of his parliamentary oath and the MPs' Code of Conduct. It also found that there were at least reasonable grounds to believe that he had acted in this way in return for 'payments corruptly made to him' in contravention of PRECCA. The commission referred the matter to the NPA for further investigation.

Frolick's intervention with Smith may have opened the doors for Bosasa, but it was bribery that kept them open. According to Agrizzi, in 2011 Gavin Watson and Agrizzi had a meeting with Smith and two other members of the Portfolio Committee on Correctional Services, Vincent Magagula and Winnie Ngwenya, at a hotel off Rivonia Road in the northern suburbs of Johannesburg. Agrizzi claimed that this meeting was the true turning point in ensuring Smith's positive attitude towards Bosasa.

Agrizzi alleged that the substance of the meeting was that all three MPs would receive payments from Bosasa in return for their adopting a favourable attitude towards Bosasa in portfolio committee meetings. Vincent Smith was alleged to have received R45,000 per month, Magagula R30,000 per month and Ngwenya R20,000 per month. Smith's monthly payment was, according to Agrizzi, boosted to R100,000 per month in 2016, because he had influence over the National Commissioner at the time, Zach Modise.

Smith denied the allegation of cash payments or that he provided any undue benefits or assistance to Bosasa. He did, however, admit that he had a good relationship with Gavin Watson that preceded his election as MP, and that he maintained a friendship thereafter. Smith also conceded that Bosasa had paid his daughter's tuition fees at the University of Aberystwyth in Wales in 2015 and 2016, and that Bosasa had installed a fancy security system at his home. Bosasa contributed R600,000 towards the university fees, which were paid into the account of a company called Euro Blitz, of which Smith was the sole shareholder. Smith's defence was that the university fees were actually a loan, and that he had asked Gavin Watson for an invoice for the security system, which was not forthcoming. He was unable to explain why he failed to declare the 'loan' to Parliament as required.

The commission would ultimately find that there was prima facie evidence of corruption against Smith under PRECCA, based on Smith's admission that he received certain benefits from Bosasa. It also found that Smith acted in breach of the Constitution, the oath he swore to uphold the Constitution, and the MPs' code of conduct. Importantly, the commission found that, on the balance of probabilities, it was likely that Smith had received the cash payments as described by Agrizzi. The commission referred the evidence to law enforcement, although it noted that Smith had already been indicted by the NPA on charges of fraud, corruption and conspiracy to commit corruption.

## Zuma's illicit assistance

As noted previously, Jacob Zuma's appearance before the committee was truncated after he refused, following two and a half days, to answer any further questions. He was sent to jail as a result, which led to an orgy of violence and looting that marred KwaZulu-Natal and parts of Gauteng. The result of this drama, in practical terms, was that Zuma did not provide a denial of the allegations made about him in relation to Bosasa, and the commission could thus treat them as undisputed.

The commission, after explaining this, set out a blunt and brutal summary of the evidence against Zuma. It showed that Zuma was introduced to Gavin Watson in 2009, when Zuma was president of the ANC, but not yet President of the country. The meeting took place at Zuma's Forest Town home in Johannesburg. Zuma was reintroduced to Watson by Dudu Myeni not long afterwards, and this led to a number of further meetings between Zuma and Watson at Zuma's Nkandla compound.

Agrizzi testified that Watson told a large number of people that he had been making payments of R300,000 a month to the benefit of the Jacob G Zuma Foundation, which was run by Myeni. Agrizzi claimed he saw the money being delivered to Myeni on at least three occasions.

During one meeting, it was alleged that Gavin Watson openly asked Zuma to intervene in the criminal case against Bosasa. This meeting was described by Joe Gumede, the executive chair of Bosasa, during an Exco meeting at Bosasa, which was recorded. Agrizzi provided a copy of the transcript of this meeting to the commission.

According to this version, Gavin Watson asked Zuma to call General Anwar Dramat, then in charge of the Hawks, to tell him to shut down the investigation. Agrizzi testified that Gavin Watson told him that he gave Zuma R300,000 in cash at this meeting; Watson also confirmed with Zuma that Myeni was not creaming any money off the top of the R300,000 that Watson was paying to the benefit of Jacob Zuma's foundation.

Agrizzi claimed that, during a meeting at Linda Mti's house, Gavin Watson spoke to Zuma on the phone. Watson handed the phone to Mti, saying, 'Your boss wants to talk to you.' The phone call was concluded by Mti saying to Zuma (or whoever was on the phone), 'I am ready to be deployed,' or a sentence to this effect.

There was testimony that Zuma visited Bosasa facilities on two occasions. On the first, he visited the Bosasa office park in the company of Myeni, where he spent four and a half hours. Another Bosasa employee, Van Tonder, testified that he met Zuma while he was touring a Bosasa-owned prawn-farming facility.

Perhaps most importantly, there was strong evidence that Bosasa had been frequently asked by Myeni to organise high-end functions for Zuma. This included catering for one of Zuma's birthday parties at short notice. Agrizzi claimed that the total cost of these sorts of functions reached about R3.5m a year. Vitally, Myeni admitted that Bosasa was involved in funding the parties, while Agrizzi presented a copy of an email in which Myeni explicitly thanked Bosasa for helping with one of Zuma's birthday parties. Myeni confirmed that Bosasa would pay the service providers used for the parties after they were identified by the Jacob G Zuma Foundation. In one colourful piece of testimony, Agrizzi claimed that he was asked by Gavin Watson to travel to a fancy café, where he would work with one 'Fritz' to design a birthday cake for Zuma's 72nd birthday. Agrizzi provided a picture of the cake, which, while unclear, included Bosasa's logo.

Agrizzi claimed that he was told by Gavin Watson and others of a meeting in about May or June 2016 at Nkandla. This was attended by Zuma, Watson and two representatives of the company Falcon Oil and Gas Group, Phillip O'Quiqley and Liezel Oberholzer. Falcon Oil used the meeting to ask that Zuma help them convince the Minister of Mineral Resources and Energy, Ngoako Ramatlhodi, to amend regulations to their benefit. The regulations were, thankfully, preventing the use of fracking in the Karoo.

Agrizzi claimed that the legal advisors of the department were asked to meet with Oberholzer, although there was no evidence that the regulations were amended. Myeni, while denying any influence in relation to this issue, did admit during her evidence that she helped facilitate a meeting at Nkandla where these issues were addressed. This was confirmed by an email from Myeni to Oberholzer, which the latter provided to the commission, corroborating Myeni's role in setting up the meeting.

Reviewing all this evidence, and the absence of Zuma's own version, the commission would conclude:

> there are reasonable grounds for suspecting that these events took place. Even if the evidence of the R300,000 payments were ignored, there is clear and convincing, non-hearsay evidence, confirmed by Ms Myeni, that Mr Zuma received the benefit of lavish spending by Bosasa on his birthday functions. That on its own required Zuma to come forward and explain publicly and on oath how that spending was justified, how it was dealt with in terms of the Executive Ethics Code and that it was not reciprocated with any form of quid pro quo. His failure to do so warrants an adverse inference.

The commission noted that there was no direct evidence that Zuma was involved in influencing the award of any tender to Bosasa. However, it found, perhaps even more disturbingly, that there were reasonable grounds to believe that he had intervened to help Bosasa with its criminal charges by arranging for Bosasa to be given confidential information. This was based, in large part, on the recording of the Bosasa meeting at which Gumede talked about meeting Zuma. Although what Gumede said was somewhat garbled (which the commission thought was a sign of its authenticity, presumably because it reflected normal speaking patterns), the commission held that the transcripts showed that Zuma, after this meeting, undertook to 'call two people' and that, after this call had taken place, Bosasa was provided with 'confidential information' by a member of the Hawks.

The commission's reading of the transcript was also influenced by the evidence it heard from Myeni (dealt with below) showing that she was directly involved in providing confidential documents to Bosasa.

Zuma's role in helping Bosasa avoid prosecution was not only a criminal offence in its own right: it also facilitated the unlawful awarding of tenders to Bosasa. This was because Zuma's intervention to protect Bosasa inhibited a criminal prosecution of the company for tenders already awarded, which protected them from being set aside. It also enabled Bosasa to continue winning tenders because it had an officially untainted record.

The commission would find that there were 'reasonable grounds to suspect that Mr Zuma's conduct was in breach of his obligations as President under the Constitution, in breach of his obligations under the Executive Ethics Code and in breach of legislation'. Most importantly, the commission found that there was compelling evidence that Zuma had committed PRECCA violations (i.e. he was involved in corruption). It referred the matter to the NPA, commenting that there was a reasonable prospect that a further investigation would 'uncover a prima facie case in terms of Section 3 and/or 4 and/or 11 and/or 12 and/or 13 of PRECCA'.

## *Dudu's dastardly deeds*

As with Zuma, Dudu Myeni's appearance before the commission was marked by evasion rather than disclosure, as we have discussed in the section on SAA. Myeni repeatedly (and wrongly) invoked privilege against self-incrimination to avoid substantive questioning; this meant that in certain respects the commission was also forced to make findings in the absence of her own evidence or recollections.

The commission heard evidence that Myeni received benefits in addition to the funds paid to her as the gatekeeper of the Jacob G Zuma Foundation. Agrizzi testified that he had given Myeni a Luis Vuitton handbag that had been filled with R300,000 in cash. Myeni also received security upgrades at her home worth R486,514.33. Myeni failed to respond to questioning on either claim, and thus failed to explain why these benefits had not been declared in terms of conflict of interest policies at her employers, SAA and the uMhlathuze Water Board.

Agrizzi testified that Myeni was directly involved in helping Bosasa with the Hawks investigation into the company. He testified that he met with Myeni, along with Gavin Watson, at the Sheraton Hotel in Pretoria, where he took R300,000 in cash. They met on the sixth floor of the hotel. Myeni told Watson and Agrizzi that she was trying to arrange to have the investigation terminated. In the interim, she produced a police docket that had allegedly been compiled by the NPA, and handed it to Agrizzi on condition he did not make copies.

Agrizzi failed to live up the agreement. On the pretext that he was taking notes, he took the docket away, laid it on the floor and took photos. The commission was able to forensically verify that the photos had been taken at the Sheraton on 23 September 2015. When a commission investigator, Alan Dutton, visited the Sheraton's sixth floor, he confirmed that it neatly matched Agrizzi's description. Importantly, the carpet installed at the Sheraton was the same carpet appearing in the background of Agrizzi's photos. The hotel also confirmed that Myeni was a guest at the hotel on 22 and 23 September, precisely when the photos were taken. The commission further confirmed with NPA witnesses that the documents appeared to be an internal progress report from August 2015 and that they were being confidentially shared between the NPA and police.

The commission also heard evidence of Myeni's abortive attempts to bring Bosasa into the SAA fold. She facilitated a meeting at OR Tambo Airport between Bosasa officials and Nico Bezuidenhout, then the acting CEO of SAA. During the meeting, a tender for security services was discussed. Myeni indicated that she wanted Bosasa to explore the possibilities of taking over this security contract, as well as a catering contract run by SAA. Bezuidenhout confirmed that the meeting took place. And while nothing appears to have happened in this regard, the commission found that, had contracts been concluded, Bosasa would have benefited; the result being that her conduct amounted to the facilitation of unlawful tenders.

The commission made much the same findings against Myeni as it did with Zuma. It found that there was sufficient evidence to establish a prima facie case of corruption against Myeni in relation to the sharing of confidential information and the attempts to get Bosasa involved at SAA, and that she was also reasonably suspected of other common law offences like defeating the ends of justice. All this was done, the commission found, to benefit Bosasa, herself and Jacob Zuma.

## Bosasa's other networks of influence

Bosasa's tentacles reached far into the South African body politic. In addition to those cases already identified, the commission took aim and made findings about benefits provided by Bosasa to other powerful political players like Nomvula Mokonyane, Gwede Mantashe and Thabang Makwetla – and the ANC itself.

### *Nomvula Mokonyane*

Another individual targeted by Bosasa was Nomvula Mokonyane, who was considered to be particularly influential within the ANC. She served as the Premier of Gauteng between 2009 and 2014, after which she was appointed a cabinet minister under Zuma. She spent four years, between 2014 and 2018, as Minister of Water and Sanitation, during which time she controversially attempted to merge two separate KZN water boards which would be placed under the control of Dudu Myeni. Mokonyane had served on the ANC NEC since 2007, and was elected the first deputy secretary general of the ANC in December 2022.

Agrizzi testified at length about the benefits accruing to Mokonyane. He claimed that she was paid R50,000 per month, which he was involved in delivering at times. Agrizzi buttressed this claim by describing Mokonyane's two houses in considerable and accurate detail. He also claimed that Mokonyane received gifts and groceries from Bosasa, and that Bosasa contributed to the cost of ANC events that fell under her control. Bosasa had also covered the cost of works to Mokonyane's house, according to Agrizzi. Finally, Agrizzi claimed that Bosasa had paid for Mokonyane' surprise 40th birthday party at the Victorian Guest House in Krugersdorp.

Unlike Zuma and Myeni, Mokonyane did respond to the evidence, both on affidavit and in the form of oral testimony. Mokonyane denied Agrizzi's evidence on all its grounds, although, during her testimony, she was forced to concede certain points. For example, even though she declared she had no knowledge of it at the time, she did concede that, on the available evidence, Bosasa had secured the services of a subcontractor to do work on her external fence and had paid for the services.

The commission would ultimately find that Mokonyane's denials were not credible and should be rejected as lies. Fundamental to this finding was the evidence that Mokonyane presented regarding the 40th birthday party. During her first appearance before the commission, she denied, totally, that any party had been held for her benefit at the Victoria Guest House in Krugersdorp. She only conceded that the party had taken place when she was presented with the evidence of the owner of the Victoria Guest House, Mr Coetzee. Coetzee provided evidence to the commission confirming that the party did take place at the venue and that a substantial bill had been incurred for alcohol.

Mokonyane attempted to explain that she had denied the party in error because Agrizzi had wrongly identified it as her 50th birthday party. But the commission was scathing of this attempt, finding that it was extraordinary that she would simply forget her 40th birthday party and its location, not least because it was an important birthday and because of its surprise nature. The commission also found that her own recollection of the party was 'unintelligible'.

The commission would find that Mokonyane's denials all ought to be rejected. It found that there was ample evidence to show that Bosasa had paid for and organised her 40th birthday party, and rejected the idea that she would not have been told this by her husband. It also found that Mokonyane had indeed received the monthly R50,000 payments described by Agrizzi, in addition to other gifts and groceries.

What did Bosasa get for all this? Agrizzi testified that he was originally confused about this too. On one occasion, he claims, he asked Gavin Watson specifically what quid pro quo was achieved. Watson responded that she had 'a lot of clout' and that Bosasa 'needed her support for the protection from the SIU investigation, the Hawks and the NPA'.

Agrizzi also testified that on at least two occasions Mokonyane involved Bosasa in discussions to provide services to institutions under her control. Sometime in 2008–9, when she was Premier of Gauteng, she approached Bosasa to perform an assessment of security at Gauteng hospitals. Agrizzi confirmed that a report was prepared by Bosasa that cost R2m. Agrizzi claimed that the idea was that, if Bosasa produced a good report, the province would issue a tender. No tender was issued. Mokonyane denied this took place, a denial made more credible because the R2m report was never provided to the commission.

Agrizzi claimed that, on a second occasion in 2014, when she was Minister of Water and Sanitation, Bosasa was asked to do an analysis of the security of South Africa's dams, against which a tender might be issued. Mokonyane again denied this and there was no tender ultimately issued. However, on this score, Agrizzi provided a range of ancillary supporting information, including details of the various subcontractors and specialists he spoke to in order to put together the report. This meant that, on this score, his evidence was to be preferred to Mokonyane's bare denial. And if the tender had gone ahead, clearly Bosasa would have been favoured.

The commission held that, even if the tender was not issued, this account would support a charge that Mokonyane's conduct amounted to the unlawful facilitation of a tender; just because a scheme was incomplete does not mean that the scheme was not conceived of and acted on in part.

The commission, reviewing the totality of the evidence, found that Mokonyane did receive benefits, and that this constituted a violation of her oath to the Constitution and the Executive Members' Ethics Act. Most importantly, it found that further investigation would likely confirm a PRECCA offence. The commission thus recommended that her case be referred to law enforcement.

## Gwede Mantashe

Another senior ANC politician who received benefits from Bosasa was Gwede Mantashe, the secretary general of the ANC from December 2007 to December 2017 and national chairperson thereafter. In 2016, Mantashe's home was fitted with sophisticated security systems paid for by Bosasa. Mantashe denied any knowledge that Bosasa had paid for it, or that he was involved in the nitty-gritty of its arrangements. He claimed instead that the installation was facilitated by his head of security and Papa Leshabane, one of Bosasa's men of many talents.

Mantashe admitted that Leshabane was a family friend. He also claimed, at one stage in his testimony, that he was aware that Leshabane was paying for it, but that he believed Leshabane was doing so in his personal capacity. This, Mantashe claimed, was not corrupt or untoward, but instead typical of intra-family help such as one would see in donations to traditional wedding ceremonies. The commission was not impressed.

Mantashe also pointed out that he was not in government at the time, and so would not be able to influence matters to Bosasa's benefit. Mantashe characterised his position as that of the secretary general of an NGO called the ANC, which, because it was an NGO, did not impart on him the duty to declare benefits as it would a minister.

The commission rejected this explanation and, in particular, the idea that the ANC was merely an NGO. Instead, the ANC was, quite clearly, the most powerful political force in the country, and that, as secretary general, Mantashe could wield this power to influence political developments. The commission thus found that there was a reasonable suspicion that Mantashe accepted the free security installations, knowing that Leshabane was seeking to secure influence over him or other office-bearers. The commission could find no lawful reason why the benefit was given to Mantashe. Accordingly, it recommended that the case be referred to law enforcement because there was a reasonable prospect that further investigations could prove a crime of corruption against Mantashe.

## Thabang Makwetla

Thabang Makwetla was another senior politician that the commission found had benefited from Bosasa's security installations. Makwetla testified that, in 2015, he received a call from Gavin Watson asking for a meeting. At the time, Makwetla was the Deputy Minister for Correctional Services. Watson sought an increase in the payments for the DCS's catering contracts because costs had risen. Makwetla promised to take the issue to the accountant general of the department, which he did. During this meeting, Makwetla told Watson that he needed to have his security system checked, and asked if Bosasa could evaluate his residence and give a quote for an upgrade.

Makwetla claimed that, when he returned to his house a few weeks later, he found the installation substantially complete. Makwetla then called Watson and asked him about the cost of the installation. Watson told him not to worry about the costs and that he would explain when they next met. Makwetla claimed he did not do much at the time because the installation was at an advanced stage and because he felt constrained by his respect for Watson.

When they did meet again, Watson was insistent that there would be no charge. Makwetla claimed that he rejected this and told Watson that he couldn't simply accept Bosasa's largesse. Makwetla, who was aware of Watson's reputation from media reports, claimed that he repeatedly asked Watson for an invoice but it was not forthcoming. Disturbed, Makwetla tried to resolve the matter with President Zuma. He had hoped that Zuma would be able to convince Watson that this wasn't allowed and to get Watson to submit an invoice. But he was unable to secure a meeting with Zuma.

Makwetla did eventually meet Ramaphosa in December 2018, by which time Ramaphosa had become President. However, the fact of the installation had become public knowledge and the damage had been done. Makwetla claimed that Watson called to apologise, and thereafter provided an invoice for R90,000, which was presented to the commission. Makwetla could not afford this sum and ended up paying only for those things he had specifically requested, which came to R25,000.

Makwetla, of course, was under an obligation to report the benefit because he was a minister. He claimed that he did not do so because he was attempting to refuse the favour and had hoped that his meeting with Zuma would get Watson to see the light of day. When asked about his knowledge of Bosasa at the time, Makwetla told the commission that he only became aware of the SIU report in 2019. He had been aware of media reports, but, because he was in provincial government, he had not paid them specific attention. The commission found this argument extremely problematic: if he was not aware of his conflict of interest in relation to Bosasa, which was a major issue in the department of which he was Deputy Minister, 'it means he should not be occupying such a senior position in government'.

The commission ultimately found that his attempts to resolve the issues with Zuma and Ramaphosa did not detract from the bald fact that he had received the gratification and that he had not declared it as was required. It thus referred Makwetla to law enforcement to conduct further investigations for potential violations of PRECCA.

## The ANC

The ANC, as an organisation, was also the beneficiary of Bosasa's largesse via the provision of so-called war rooms, or operational centres used to oversee and facilitate electioneering. They were first provided by Bosasa to assist Zuma's campaign during the ANC's Mangaung national conference, and thereafter provided to the ANC for the 2014 national elections and 2016 local elections. Agrizzi testified that they operated from Bosasa facilities and that Bosasa provided equipment valued at millions of rand. The commission reported that the decision to provide the service was made 'at the instance of its directors' at the time, including Gavin Watson, Joe Gumede and Papa Leshabane.

When Ramaphosa testified before the commission, he explained that he was not personally aware that Bosasa had funded the war rooms. However, he said that the ANC's treasurer general and other 'comrades' who ran the election would have known. Ramaphosa conceded under questioning that the ANC had received benefits from Bosasa despite its own rules not to receive benefits from any parties associated with criminality, and that senior ANC officials must have known about the allegations at the time.

The commission was of the view that these services could not be considered a bona fide contribution by Bosasa. Instead, it was of the view that Bosasa was a company that relied for its existence on government tenders, and that it was materially invested in ensuring the success of the ANC so that the ANC would continue to appoint compliant officials to help the company. Bosasa also sought to influence the ANC to ensure that officials employed by the government would favour Bosasa. In addition, the commission held that the ANC 'as a juristic person', and certainly many of its officials, would have been aware that Bosasa was making the facilities available in order to secure influence within the organisation.

On this basis, the commission found that there was a prima facie case of corruption against Gavin Watson, Joe Gumede and Papa Leshabane as directors of Bosasa. It thus recommended that the matter be referred for further investigation to law enforcement, which was additionally advised to identify those ANC officials involved in arranging the war room.

## Andile and Cyril Ramaphosa

Zuma was not the only president of the ANC who received funds from Bosasa: Cyril Ramaphosa did as well. Bosasa (by now renamed African Global Operations) donated R500,000 to Ramaphosa's campaign to become president of the ANC in 2017 (the 'CR17 campaign'). However, because the matter had formed the subject of both a Public Protector investigation and court proceedings, the commission opted to not make any findings in this regard. Ramaphosa, notably, had told the commission that he had distanced himself from the donation-raising and management aspects of his presidential campaign.

The commission also very briefly addressed the relationship between Bosasa and Cyril Ramaphosa's son Andile. Agrizzi testified that an employee of Sondolo IT, Riaan van der Merwe, approached him in 2017 to organise a meeting with the CEO of a company called Dahua and Andile Ramaphosa. Dahua was a Chinese firm that produced surveillance equipment. Agrizzi claimed that he arranged the meeting but did not attend it.

The commission made no adverse finding against Andile

Ramaphosa in this regard. This was because Agrizzi's evidence did not detail any specific wrongdoing against him. Andile Ramaphosa further denied ever being contacted by Agrizzi in this regard.

Andile came up in another piece of testimony. Mr Venter, a tax consultant to Bosasa, testified that Gavin Watson had established a company called Miotto Trading, which was used to make payments so as to disguise the fact that they actually emanated from Bosasa. Venter claimed that he was told to use Miotto Trading to make payments to a number of people and companies, including a trust established by Andile Ramaphosa. Here, too, the commission declined to make a finding because it did not inform him of the allegation, which meant he was not given the opportunity to respond to it.

Considerably more detail about the relationship between Bosasa and Andile Ramaphosa has been put into the public domain, but it did not feature in the proceedings of the commission. In 2019, an investigation by News24 led Andile Ramaphosa to admit that he had been paid R2m by Bosasa via his company Blue Crane Capital. Blue Crane signed a consultancy deal with Bosasa in December 2017 in relation to twenty contracts around Africa. The agreement was terminated in December 2018. News24's investigation claimed that Dahua representatives had introduced Andile Ramaphosa to Bosasa, and that the plan was that Dahua equipment would be used in the African contracts.[7]

---

7    https://www.news24.com/news24/exclusive-andile-ramaphosa-admits-
     bosasa-paid-him-r2m-20190327.

# Recommendations

| Persons/companies | Should be further investigated for potential violations of |
|---|---|
| Angelo Agrizzi, Andries Johannes van Tonder, Carlos Bonifacio, Jacques van Zyl, Riaan Hoeksma, Gregg Lacon-Allin, AA Wholesalers, Riekele Construction, Jumbo Liquor Wholesalers, Lamozest, Equal Trade 4 and Equal Food Traders | Money laundering in terms of section 4 of POCA |
| Angela Aggrizi, Andries Johannes van Tonder, Jacques van Zyl, Johannes Gumede, Papa Leshabane, Thandi Makoko, Leon van Tonder, Richard le Roux, Petrus Venter, William Daniel Mansell, Sesinyi Seopela, Linda Mti, Frans Vorster, Carlos Bonifacio and Riaan Hoeksma | Corruption in terms of section 3 of PRECCA |
| Angela Aggrizi, Andries Johannes van Tonder, Jacques van Zyl, Carlos Bonifacio, Greg Lacon-Allin and Riaan Hoeksma | Fraud |
| Carien Daubert, Rieka Hundermark, Gavin Hundermark, Cedric Frolick, Patrick Littler, Danie van Tonder, Ishmael Dikane, Syvion Dlamini, Trevor Mathenjwa and Ryan Roode | Money laundering and/or corruption and/or fraud |

| Persons/companies | Should be further investigated for potential violations of |
|---|---|
| Angela Aggrizi, Andries Johannes van Tonder, Jacques van Zyl, Carlos Bonifacio, Carien Daubert, Rieka Hundermark, Gavin Hundermark, Johannes Gumede, Papa Leshabane, Thandi Makoko | Failure to report suspicious transactions as required by FICA |
| Gregory Lawrence | Assisting another to benefit from proceeds of unlawful activities in contravention of section 5 of POCA |
| Petrus Venter | Failure to comply with requirement to report illegal transactions under section 34 of PRECCA. Also referred to SA Institute of Tax Practitioners. |
| *Contracts awarded by DCS and protection afforded to Bosasa* | |
| Linda Mti | Corruption under PRECCA and common law offences of fraud, theft and perjury |
| Patrick Gillingham | Corruption under PRECCA and common law offences of fraud, theft and perjury |
| Cedric Frolick | Violation of sections 3 and 7 of PRECCA |
| Nontsikelelo Jolingana, Josiah Maako, Maria Mabena, Shishi Matabella, Mandla Mkabela, Dikeledi Tshabalala, Zach Modise and Mollet Ngubo | Corruption under PRECCA |
| Winnie Ngwenya | Violations of PRECCA |
| Vincent Smith | Unclear, but most likely corruption, fraud and conspiracy to commit fraud |

| Persons/companies | Should be further investigated for potential violations of |
|---|---|
| Mnikelwa Nxele | Violations of PRECCA |
| Contracts with Department of Health in Mpumalanga Province | |
| Ms Kgasi and Ms Mogale | Violations of PRECCA |
| Politicians | |
| Thabang Makwetla | Violations of PRECCA in relation to security upgrades at his home |
| Jacob Zuma | Violations of PRECCA |
| Nomvula Mokonyane | Violations of PRECCA |
| Dudu Myeni | Violations of PRECCA |
| Contracts with ACSA | |
| Thele Moema, Reuben Pillay, Johannes Serobe | Violation of PRECCA in relation to receipt of cash payments |
| Contracts with SAPO | |
| Siviwe Mapisa and Maanda Manyatshe | Corruption under PRECCA |
| Other evidence of wrongdoing | |
| Simon Mofokeng (general secretary of CEPPWAWU) and Sydney Mantata | Corruption under PRECCA in relation to receipt of groceries from Bosasa |
| Angelo Agrizzi, Johannes Andries van Tonder, Leon van Tonder, Matthew Robert Leeson, William Brander and Brian Blake | Destruction of data and evidence to obstruct investigations into Bosasa (defeating the ends of justice) and/ or corruption under PRECCA |

# PART FOUR

# State Capture in the Free State

*The Free State provincial government was a primary site of state capture and, in many ways, acted as a laboratory and talent pool for bigger heists. Indeed, according to the calculations I performed for the commission, it was the third-biggest money-spinner for the Guptas in terms of dodgy contracts. And it was the Estina/ Vrede dairy scandal, delivered on a plate by provincial officials, that served as the Gupta's first taste of serious, big-money state capture.*

*Of course, other players also made hay while the sunshine of political corruption in the Free State bathed its interconnected elites. This led the commission to focus on three additional cases not linked to the Guptas: the Free State housing debacle, the Free State asbestos scandal, and the ludicrous City of Tomorrow.*

# The City of Tomorrow

THE COMMISSION'S INVESTIGATIONS into the Free State were framed by the evidence of Mxolisi Dukoana (also spelt Dukwana), who was the first witness to give evidence on the province at the commission. His evidence indicated that Ace Magashule, the Premier of the province, was extremely close to the Guptas from at least 2008 onwards, and that he received undue benefits as a result. Dukoana claimed to have been threatened by Magashule's lawyers after his first appearance before the commission. He told Magashule, in brief, to 'bring it on'. Magashule failed to submit any affidavits to the commission and made no attempt to cross-examine Dukoana.

Dukoana – who described himself as a 'freedom fighter' and ANC activist during the 1980s – was deployed by the ANC in the Free State provincial legislature, where he served in a number of roles. Between 2008 and 2009, he was the MEC for Safety, Security and Transport. Following the 2009 elections, he was appointed the MEC for Economic Development by Ace Magashule, the Premier. He was fired on 28 February 2012. Perhaps most importantly, Dukoana, in parallel, served as the provincial treasurer for the ANC in the Free State for two terms between 2005 and 2012.

## The first Gupta visit

Dukoana testified that he was taken to the offices of Sahara Computers in 2008 by Ace Magashule, then the Free State MEC for Transport. During the meeting, Magashule handed over his ID book to Tony Gupta, who then briefly left them alone. With Tony now gone, Magashule explained to Dukoana that he was going into business with the Gupta clan. Magashule, however, explained that the business would not be conducted in his name, but rather in the name of his son, Tshepiso. Dukoana recalled that when Tony Gupta returned, he jokingly asked Dukoana where his own ID book was, before seeing them out.

## The City of Tomorrow

Dukoana's second meeting with the Guptas revolved around a project called the City of Tomorrow. This was a plan to build a new city in the Free State, as no new cities had been built there since the end of apartheid. Dukoana claimed that the idea had originally been his, but that it was subsequently in effect stolen by Iqbal Sharma, a key Gupta lieutenant.

On 22 June 2011, local officers in the Free State's developmental clusters were shown a presentation on the City of Tomorrow by the P3I–Nulane Consortium. P3I (P3 International) was an architecture and urban planning firm based in the US while Nulane was a Gupta cut-out, of which Iqbal Sharma was a director. The City of Tomorrow was to be a 'public–private' initiative. Subsequent to this, on 4 July 2011, the acting MEC for Economic Development signed a memorandum recommending that a request for 'in-principle support' be sent to the provincial executive.

Two days later, on 6 July 2011, Dukoana received an email directly from Iqbal Sharma, who attached a 'master agreement' that, if signed, would constitute a contract appointing the P3I–Nulane consortium to develop a 'master plan' for the City of Tomorrow. The agreement stated that the City of Tomorrow would be built in six months, for which the Free State government would pay the consortium R140m.

Iqbal Sharma, when he was asked to give his version, noted that he had initially made contact with Dukoana with the assistance of Ace Magashule's son, Tshepiso. Sharma testified that he and Tshepiso presented Dukoana with the project proposal. To the commission Sharma presented a series of documents that he believed showed that the Free State government had agreed to the project. One document was a signed copy of the master agreement, which purportedly carried the signatures of Dukoana and P3I's John Thomas. He also presented a 'notice to proceed' that was, again, purportedly signed by Dukoana. Sharma claimed that on this basis P3I and Nulane were due payments – which they never received. In fact, according to Sharma, the project did not eventually materialise, despite his threats of legal action to try to force payment on the project.

Dukoana, in response, denied signing the documents or asking Sharma to draft any documents. In fact, Dukoana claimed his signature had been 'brazenly forged'. He pointed out that under the PFMA he would not have had the power to appoint or execute a contract as MEC, as this lay with the head of department as the accounting authority; it would have made no sense to sign a contract to this effect.

The commission ultimately made no definitive finding about whose version was correct. However, it did appoint two forensic handwriting analysts to review the signatures. The two came to the preliminary view that the probabilities suggested that they were in fact Dukoana's signatures. But owing to the pandemic, this evidence wasn't dealt with in oral hearings, so the commission could not take the evidence further. It duly recommended that the police take the matter further.

## Dukoana's second Gupta visit

Dukoana testified to a second visit to the Guptas with Magashule in February 2012, this time to the Gupta compound in Saxonwold. By this stage, Magashule had risen to become Premier of the province and chairperson of the Free State ANC. Dukoana testified that he travelled from Bloemfontein to Johannesburg at Magashule's behest. Magashule explained that he wanted Dukoana, wearing his treasurer general's hat, to meet business people. When he arrived in Johannesburg, he was ferried to the Guptas' compound along with Magashule.

They were, once again, received by Tony Gupta, who reintroduced himself to Dukoana. Tony asked Dukoana to hand over his cell phone; the same was not asked of Magashule. Dukoana claimed in his affidavit to the commission that Magashule's demeanour indicated this was not his first visit. Dukoana was ushered into a room alone. After some time, he was then joined by Magashule,

Tony Gupta and a number of others, including Duduzane Zuma.

Tony then presented Dukoana with a document on a Free State provincial letterhead that purported to come from his office. He asked Dukoana to sign it. The effect of the document was to appoint Nulane to run a project. Somewhat frustratingly, Dukoana simply described this project as 'a whole project I presented in the Cabinet meeting on a turn-key basis'; the precise nature of this project was never disclosed. Dukoana believed that Ace Magashule must have had some role in the creation of the document: Dukoana, at that point, most often went by the spelling Dukwana, and it was only Magashule who knew that his surname was Dukoana. The document presented for signature had his name as Dukoana.

In any event, Dukoana refused to sign the document. He testified that Tony Gupta then informed him that both Magashule and Duduzane Zuma had earned money from a Gupta project involving the Jaggersfontein mine. Neither disputed this claim and simply nodded their heads. Tony then explained that, if Dukoana signed the document, he would be paid R2m immediately and a further R2m a month afterwards. Tony Gupta dispatched somebody who returned with a black pilot bag filled with R200 notes, which he showed to Dukoana.

Dukoana still refused to play ball and instead suggested that the letter of appointment be sent to the Free State provincial legal advisor. He also tried to point out that he had no power as the MEC to sign contracts under the PFMA. Tony Gupta responded by telling Dukoana to fire his head of department (presumably so that a new one could sign the document).

Dukoana further testified that Tony Gupta threatened he would replace Dukoana and had the perfect replacement; after a phone call, Richard Seleke entered the room. Seleke was later appointed head of the Department of Economic Development and then, in a remarkable move, as the director general of Public Enterprises, in which role he would be involved in Gupta-related state capture.

Dukoana left the compound without agreeing to any of the bribe offers.

# The Free State asbestos
# project debacle

THE COMMISSION TURNED its attention next to a truly audacious contract, whose primary function was to funnel vast sums of money into the pockets of politically connected businessmen. On 28 May 2014, the Free State Department of Human Settlements received an unsolicited proposal from a joint venture comprising two companies: Blackhead Consulting and Diamond Hill Trading 71. The proposal was for the assessment and removal of asbestos from houses in the Free State at a total cost of R255 million.

Blackhead Consulting was directed by Edwin Sodi; Diamond Hill was directed by Ignatius 'Igo' Mpambani. Neither Blackhead nor Diamond Hill Trading had any background in asbestos handling, and did not have the skills to undertake the work themselves. Sodi, in his testimony before the commission, explained that Blackhead was to act as a project manager and the intention had been to subcontract the actual work elsewhere. It was 'common cause', the commission found, that Diamond Hill's role was to 'unlock opportunity' through networking with state officials and politicians.

The proposal was received by Nthimotse Timothy 'Tim' Mokhesi, then head of the Department of Human Settlements. The commission commented that Mokhesi's response to the proposal 'affirms the value of and efficacy of the "networking" capabilities of Mr Mpambani'. Despite his claiming otherwise, the commission found that Mokhesi's immediately solicitous response indicated that he had 'foreknowledge of the arrival' of the proposal and that he 'saw no need for any investigation or discussion on the need for or the value of the proposed project'. At the time of the proposal, no allocation had been made for the project in the Free State budget.

Indeed, only three weeks later, on 19 June 2014, Mokhesi wrote back to the joint venture, indicating that he would like to proceed. However, the commission found, there was no desire to put the bid out to tender or to go through any of the normal procurement routes. To regularise the project, therefore, Mokhesi came up with a different route to secure approval of the project. To do this, he would make use of an obscure process developed by Treasury and given the snappy title National Treasury Regulation 16A.6.

Treasury Regulation 16A.6 had the effect of allowing departments to piggyback on contracts that had been awarded to companies by other departments. So, on 15 July 2014, Mokhesi wrote to Anne Diedricks at the Gauteng Department of Human Settlements, which had previously contracted with Blackhead, and asked for permission to extend this contract to the Free State. Diedricks approved the request, but only because Mokhesi had failed to tell her a key fact: the contract for the Free State would be with the joint venture, and not just Blackhead. Diedricks, when asked by the commission, confirmed that she would have refused the request if this detail had been explained.

Mokhesi also wrote to Thabane Zulu, the director general of the Department of Human Settlements in Pretoria, because any changes to the allocation of the provincial budget, and any approval of new projects, had to be approved by the national department. Mokhesi's letter explained the use of the Treasury procedure; Zulu, although it wasn't in his bailiwick to approve its use, nevertheless wrote back saying that he believed that it could be used, and the reallocation of resources was approved.

The commission found that the use of this piggybacking method was flawed in other ways. For example, the scope of services and the costs cited in the Gauteng contract were totally different from those in the Free State contract. In fact, the Gauteng contract was just for the assessment of whether houses damaged in a storm had asbestos roofs that needed attention; the Free State contract was for both assessment and removal.

Consequently, it was 'never permissible', the commission found, for this methodology of approval to be used. More to the point, it found that the use of this method was a 'ruse' rather than a 'legitimate lawful procedure'. Both Mokhesi and Sodi were guilty of this; Sodi, because he had written separately to Diedricks and failed to mention the existence of the joint venture. The commission thus found:

> the only conclusion which can be drawn from the undisputed facts is that Mr Sodi and Mr Mokhesi both knew at all times that Treasury Regulation 16A.6 was not available as a means to legitimise the contract which they both wished to secure without any competitive bidding process. They both took steps to conceal the inconvenient facts ... when they used Treasury Regulation 16A6.6. This was neither incompetence nor negligence, but knowing, deliberate and planned circumvention of lawful processes requiring competitive bidding processes. This process was a sham.

With these formalities out of the way, Mokhesi wrote to the joint venture on 1 October 2014, to say it had been 'exclusively appointed' to conduct the audit of asbestos and its removal. The joint venture was issued an 'instruction to perform' work on 2 December 2014, giving the go-ahead to proceed.

## The outrageous profits and the usefulness of the work

The Blackhead–Diamond Hill joint venture was paid R230m between 22 December 2014 and 4 August 2016. This included a remarkable R55m upfront payment in December 2014. Very little of this money was actually spent on doing the work. To conduct the work on the project, the joint venture appointed a subcontractor, Mastertrade, which was to charge R44m; but Mastertrade's primary function appears to have been to subcontract the services to a company called Ori Group. Ori Group – which did the bulk of the work – was paid about R21m. When Ori Group's director was asked about how he spent his money, it turned out that he made about R11m profit on this amount.

So, when surveying the total spend (there were some expenses incurred by Mastertrade and some payments to additional contractors), the commission estimated that only about R15m of the R230m paid to the joint venture was spent on the work itself.

As one would expect, Blackhead and Diamond Hill both made a killing from the project; a total profit of R186m, according to the commission's calculations. A review of their bank statements showed that of the R230m paid into their account, R70,863,000 was paid to Blackhead's ABSA account and R112,955,500 was paid into 605 Consulting Solutions, which was owned by Igo Mpambani.

To rub additional salt in the wound, the work that was done was basically of no use. The commission asked an independent expert with a long history in asbestos handling and removal – Mr Roets – to review the reports submitted by the joint venture. The work involved workers (who were paid R6.50 per house) approaching houses and taking photos, from which there would be some attempt to establish if there was asbestos in the roof. The work, Roets found, was of no value, as there was no attempt to take any samples or establish whether there was any risk of asbestos contamination. The commission thus found that 'the work conducted by contractors did not constitute a valuable audit and assessment'. So, if the province ever did decide to tackle the problem of asbestos, it would 'need to start from scratch'.

## Just the 'cost of business'

The extraordinary tale of the asbestos 'debacle', as the commission calls it, took on a remarkably different hue when the commission uncovered an explosive spreadsheet called 'Cost of Business'. This set out a detailed accounting for the project. It recorded the names of entities or individuals (sometimes just with initials) with a corresponding figure that they were to be paid: the so-called cost of business. The spreadsheet earmarked R82,608,567.90.

Sodi, when asked about this document, confirmed that he had discussed its creation with Mpambani. After the discussion, Sodi said, Mpambani used Sodi's computer to develop the spreadsheet. Sodi claimed that he understood the spreadsheet was going to be compiled to establish how much 'revenue' would be made from the project. He denied any knowledge of the content of the spreadsheet or that any undue payments were made. He simply said that he 'didn't pay attention' when the spreadsheet was emailed to him at a later stage by Mpambani.

The commission didn't buy his story: 'The Commission concludes that Mr Mpambani, representing one party to the Joint Venture, prepared the schedule setting out the Costs of Business to the Joint Venture and that this schedule was sent to, received by and known and understood by Mr Sodi, representing the other party to the Joint Venture.'

The first beneficiary was listed as TZ, who was due to receive R10m from a number of payments, including one of R5m. The initials TZ showed up elsewhere: on 21 December 2015, Sodi transferred R600,000 from his own account to the ABSA account of SMD Trading Group, with the reference 'TZ'. SMD was the trading name of the Ford dealership in Ballito. The commission confirmed with the dealership that Thabane Zulu – the DG in the national Department of Housing who gave his assent to the project – was a client and that, on 23 March 2016, it invoiced a Range Rover 2013 model to Zulu. The value of the car was R1.3m, of which a cash deposit of R690,000 had been paid towards the purchase.

When Sodi was approached by the commission, he explained that the payment was made in order to settle a debt that Sodi owed to Zulu which had nothing to do with the asbestos project. Sodi claimed that he had spent R600,000 at Zulu's bar called TZ Lounge in Pietermaritzburg. When Zulu asked him about the outstanding bill, Sodi claimed, he told Sodi he was going to buy a car; together they agreed that Sodi would pay back his tab by putting money towards the car. The commission was totally unconvinced: 'the explanation offered by Mr Sodi and Mr Zulu is simply false and dishonest'.

Ballito Ford was graced with further business from Sodi. On 28 May 2015, R1m was transferred from Blackhead's account to SMD/Ballito Ford. The credit description was recorded as 'Thabane Zulu'. The dealership confirmed that R890,000 of the R1m payment was used towards the purchase of a Maserati by Mabheleni Ntuli, although the remaining R110,000 was retained by the dealership, as Ntuli had other debts with them.

When this was put to Thabane Zulu, he initially rejected any knowledge in indignant terms. But, over time, it eventually emerged that Zulu knew Ntuli, and that he had introduced Ntuli to Sodi. The commission was unable to dig any further into the issue but noted that 'one cannot help but strongly suspect that this may well have been another kickback to Mr Zulu's benefit but further investigation is necessary'.

Another beneficiary on the Cost of Business schedule was recorded as 'TM', to whom R5m was allocated.

On 2 April 2015, Blackhead transferred R650,000 into the trust account of Kramer, Weihmann and Joubert Attorneys. The payment related to the sale of a property to Likemo Family Trust, of which Mokhesi was the founder, trustee and beneficiary. Sodi and Mokhesi, who failed to mention any of these issues in their first engagements with the commission, claimed that this was a business venture in which Sodi and Mokhesi were jointly investing in a property. Mokhesi lived in the house, which was never rented out.

Again, the commission was extremely dismissive of the versions put forward by Sodi and Mokhesi: 'the explanation offered by both Mr Mokhesi and Mr Sodi for the payment of this sum of money is so incomprehensible that it must be rejected as false'.

Reviewing the totality of the evidence before it, the commission further found that 'there can only be the inevitable conclusion that Mr Mokhesi [is] the "TM" identified in the "Cost of Business" schedule prepared by Mr Mpambani and to which Mr. Sodi was a Party'. Moreover, the convoluted structure of the purchase of Mokhesi's house 'was made to conceal this transaction because it so clearly constitutes a benefit given by Mr Sodi to Mr Mokhesi'.

Another beneficiary included in the Cost of Business schedule was one 'AM', to whom R10m had been allocated. Sodi refused to speculate as to who AM was and, especially, would not be drawn on whether AM was in fact Ace Magashule. The commission, however, noted the evidence of Dukoana. He claimed that Mpambani was in constant contact with people in Ace Magashule's office and that, shortly after payments were made to the joint venture, requests would be made from Magashule's office to Mpambani.

One such request was to the benefit of Refiloe Mokoena, an advocate who also acted as a High Court judge in the Free State. Mokoena, in July 2015, wrote to Magashule asking for help to pay the school fees of her daughter in the US ($12,149). Magashule's personal assistant then duly wrote to Mpambani and asked him to pay $12,000. Mpambani subsequently sent two emails confirming that payments of R50,000 and R54,000 had been made, the latter of which was made directly to Mokoena's account. Mokoena, for her part, confirmed to the commission that she did, indeed, make the requests to Magashule personally, that she had received the funds, and that, while making the requests, she was serving as an acting judge.

'JT' was the last beneficiary recorded in the Cost of Business schedule considered by the commission; JT was allocated R3m. The commission confirmed that a total amount of R3,858,159.70 was paid to companies controlled by Jimmy Tau from Blackhead's accounts. A further R1.8m was paid to a company controlled by Jimmy Tau by Mpambani's 605 Consulting; a final R1m was paid to a Tau company by NR Projects, which was 50% owned by Sodi.

The commission heard evidence from Sodi about Tau, a former Kaizer Chiefs player, who Sodi claimed was a 'business development consultant' who could help secure business for Blackhead. Tau, however, had no connection to the asbestos project, which made his inclusion on the spreadsheet somewhat odd. The commission, which was also struck by the complex way in which Tau's companies were paid, ultimately found that the evidence 'suggests that both Mr Tau and those entities were no more than conduits for payments to an entity with a real connection to the Asbestos Audit'.

## Blackhead's payments to other politically exposed persons

The commission's investigation into Blackhead found additional business records suggesting that Blackhead had made substantial payments to other politically connected individuals. The recipients of the payments from Blackhead, and their political roles and positions, are set out in the accompanying table.

| Recipient | Total amount | Political roles and positions |
|---|---|---|
| Zizi Kodwa | R174,760 | Deputy Minister for State Security |
| Colin Pitso | R6,504,250 | Former chief of staff to Gauteng MEC for Housing |
| Bongani More | Approx R7,000,000 | Deputy director general of Human Settlements in Gauteng |
| Diane/Anoj Singh | R10,000 | Anoj Singh, CFO of Transnet and Eskom |
| Paul Mashatile (Sodi indicated this was for the benefit of the ANC as Mashatile was provincial treasurer general) | R371,555.87 | MEC of Gauteng Department of Human Settlements and ANC provincial treasurer general |
| Linda Ngcobo | R2,097,627 | Regional manager: Gauteng Housing and chief director of Gauteng Department of Human Settlements (2014–16) |
| Thulas Nxesi | R45,000 | Former Minister of Public Works and Minister of Employment and Labour |
| Pinky Kekana | R170,000 | Deputy Minister of Communications |
| Zweli Mkhize (although Sodi indicated the money was for the ANC as Mkhize was ANC treasurer general) | R6,497,000 | ANC treasurer general |

The commission, which was unable to investigate this fully and, in particular, could not call all implicated parties to give oral evidence, ultimately found:

The result is that the commission is left with the view that Mr Sodi made generous payments through his business accounts to obtain access, secure influence, retain connections with a number of individuals at provincial and national level of government. Whether or not such payments were intended by Mr Sodi to obtain an immediate benefit in return or to create obligations for the future, this would unquestionably indicate an appetite on the part of Mr Sodi for some form of state capture. Such consistent course of action would indicate that a business person made payments to persons who occupied political leadership positions or were employed as government officials with both the intention and the result of obtaining private benefit for himself or his business from persons who were financially obliged to him or those businesses.

The commission further identified payments of R3,523,200 by Blackhead to the ANC between October 2013 and 15 March 2019. The payments were made on an ad hoc basis to cover various ANC costs.

## RECOMMENDATIONS

*Law enforcement should conduct further investigation with a view to prosecution of Timothy Mokhesi for corruption and/or PFMA violations in relation to concluding the agreement that appointed the joint venture.*

*Government should seek legal opinion to recover monies lost due to the asbestos project from Timothy Mokhesi and/or any other implicated government officials.*

*Law enforcement should conduct further investigations for potential PFMA violations with a view to charges being brought against Timothy Mokhesi for his role in the asbestos project.*

*Government should seek a legal opinion as to whether monies paid to the joint venture could be recovered.*

*Law enforcement should conduct further investigation with a view to prosecution of Edwin Sodi and/or Blackhead Consulting and/or Thabane Zulu in relation to Blackhead's R600,000 payment towards a car dealer for the benefit of Thabane Zulu.*

*Law enforcement should conduct further investigation with a view to prosecution of Edwin Sodi and/or Blackhead Consulting and/or Timothy Mokhesi in relation to Blackhead's R600,000 payment towards the purchase of a house owned by a trust controlled by Mokhesi.*

*Law enforcement should give serious consideration to charging Edwin Sodi and/or Blackhead for fraud due to the false representation made by Blackhead that it had the knowledge, qualifications and expertise necessary for the removal of asbestos.*

# The Free State housing debacle

IN A HANDFUL OF MONTHS between the end of 2010 and the beginning of 2011, the Free State Department of Human Settlements paid out over R500m in 'prepayments' towards the building of low-cost housing. Only a tiny number of houses were eventually built – if any at all. The man who oversaw this disaster was Mosebenzi Zwane, whom we have met before in this book.

In February 2010, the Free State Premier announced that the province would start delivering bigger RDP houses than previously. It is not clear that Magashule ever consulted with any of those who would actually deliver on his promises. The result of Magashule's directive was chaos. Contractors had already been selected and contracted to build houses in the 2010/11 financial year; but at an average cost of R50,000 per unit to build smaller houses than Magashule was now promising. Contractors were understandably upset at the prospect of having to build larger houses for the same amount of money.

To fix this situation, the Free State Department of Human Settlements issued a whole new low-cost housing tender to build the larger RDP houses at a rough cost of R70,000 per house. The final closing date for the tenders was supposed to be 16 April 2010. The department received 361 bids, of which 109 were considered to be compliant on first review.

But, for reasons never properly explained, the tender period expired before any contractors were appointed. The 'resolution' of this was that the Bid Adjudication Committee within the Human

Settlements Department resolved that the tender would have to be cancelled, but the department would put the original bidders for the tender onto a database for the provision of future services. It appears that the full list of bidders were entered onto this 'database', despite the fact that 105 of the original 361 bidders did not meet compliance checks and a further 147 were disqualified because they didn't meet basic functionality tests.

The building of low-cost housing in the Free State ground to a halt. By October 2010, the department had only spent 10% of the money that had been allocated to it by the national government; but not a single house had been constructed. This was a disaster for the department. Under regulations of the Division of Revenue Act (the law that basically sets out how Treasury distributes funds to government departments), if the money was unspent, it would be taken away from the Free State government and allocated to other better-performing departments. If this happened, moreover, the government would reduce its future allocations to the Free State as well. So, if the department did not spend the money it had been allocated quickly, it would both lose the money already allocated and receive less money in future years.

This was a real concern; in late October 2010 Tokyo Sexwale, the national Minister of Human Settlements, issued a notice to the Free State department recording its failure to spend its budget, despite the financial year being half over. Sexwale's department requested that its provincial counterpart present a 'recovery plan' that would show how it would accelerate delivery and spending.

The commission was told that officials from the Free State Department of Human Settlements set about developing an 'economic recovery plan' (ERP), hashed out in an office called the war room. Mosebenzi Zwane, the MEC for Human Settlements, attended bi-weekly meetings, while Mpho 'Gift' Mokoena, the head of department, was also involved. Zwane, for his part, later attempted to distance himself from the ERP, saying that he had directed Mokoena to lead the process.

The ERP promised that the department would spend R1bn before the end of the financial year, building 12,800 houses in the four months between November 2010 and March 2011. At least one official testified to the commission that he – and most likely everyone else involved in the ERP – knew that this was simply not feasible. The commission thus believed this plan, and its promises, constituted a fraud committed against the national Department of Human Settlements, being a set of totally unachievable expectations, all designed to prevent money being taken from the Free State department in 2010/11 and thereafter.

How the department then set about implementing the ERP was, frankly, jaw-dropping. Traditionally, the department paid contractors on a milestone basis. So, once a contractor had laid a foundation and this had been verified by inspectors, they would be paid a portion of the total cost, and once they had then put up the walls, they would be paid another milestone payment, again only after an inspection. But the Free State Department of Housing had to spend its allocation in an extremely short space of time: there wasn't time to let people build houses and then be paid.

Instead, the department adopted a whole new model: a system of advance payments. In short, it decided to make payments of hundreds of millions of rand to suppliers and contractors before any work had been done. Practically, this meant jerry-rigging the traditional payment system; officials in the department uploaded documents that improperly 'proved' that contractors had met milestone payments when they did not. One of the officials with knowledge of how this all happened confirmed to the commission that the system was manipulated 'to make it look as though construction work had been executed and that payments were due when in truth this was not the case'.

This was, quite clearly, irregular, and officials from the Free State were told about it. One official was sent to give a briefing about the ERP to a gathering called the Technical Ministerial Member Executive Council (TechMinMech), which acted as a technical discussion forum across provincial and national departments. The Free State official was told by officials from Gauteng that the advance payment plan was unworkable. He additionally testified that the chief of operations at the national Department of Human Settlements had told him that the advance payments were unlawful.

Somewhat unsurprisingly, everyone acknowledged the existence of the advance payment plan, but nobody would claim responsibility for it. Zwane, for his part, claimed that his juniors were responsible for the plan. Mokoena, instead, claimed that it was all Zwane's idea and, further, that Zwane had threatened to fire him if he didn't implement it. In the end, the commission would find that Mokoena and Zwane were equally responsible for its adoption and implementation.

## How much was spent and who got it?

How contractors were selected and paid was the subject of much contested testimony. Some Free State officials testified that Zwane himself used the 'database' that was created from the failed tender to generate a list of 106 contractors, and then told the department to award those suppliers contracts for a specified number of houses. Zwane denied this, and said that he had simply approved a list of suppliers that had been recommended to him by other suppliers. The commission, sifting through this evidence, simply found that it remained 'unclear' exactly who had chosen and appointed the 106 contractors. Nevertheless, what was clear was that none of the suppliers were selected as a result of a competitive bidding process – they were simply awarded contracts without any tender.

Mokoena, in his evidence before the commission, cited an intriguing piece of evidence in favour of the version that Zwane generated the list; Mokoena said that the top six contractors on the 106 contractors list were totally unknown to him and other officials. Moreover, Mokoena claimed that three of those contractors were close to Mosebenzi Zwane, all being from the same region.

Poor record-keeping by the department made it nearly impossible to say for certain how much was paid out through this programme, and what it achieved. A review by the Auditor General found that R481 million was paid out through advanced payments; a review by the Special Investigating Unit found that R831 million was paid in advance payments in both the 2010/11 and 2011/12 financial years. One official then told the commission that R631m in unlawful payments was made; Mokoena indicated it was actually around R500m. And when the department sought to recover monies it had paid out unlawfully, it filed claims equal to R631m.

Whether anything was delivered as a result of this spend was also unclear. Mokoena's testimony was that no houses were built to completion; all that was delivered was a smattering of foundations spread around the province. Zwane, however, claimed that some houses had been built, and that he had opened 50 houses during a ceremony in December 2010. A statement put out by the department in January 2011 said that between 400 and 1,250 houses had been completed, but it was unclear where this figure came from. Ultimately, the commission's take was that 'there was so few houses built compared to those that were supposed to be built that they are not worth mentioning'.

## Findings: Zwane and Mokoena

Zwane and Mokoena – the MEC and head of department respectively – spent much of their time before the commission blaming the other party for any wrongdoing or maladministration. The commission, however, found that they were both at fault, and it did so in stinging terms. Of Zwane, the commission lamented that it was 'surprising and unfortunate' that he had ever been appointed to the position, that he had 'no real intention of understanding his role, learning his duties, becoming informed of the full nature of his responsibilities', and that he was 'unashamed of his ignorance'. Mokoena, for his part, 'failed in every respect' to run the programme properly. Both Mokoena and Zwane were thus 'incompetent and showed themselves to be utterly without concern for relevant legislative and policy provisions as well as fundamental management practices'.

The commission was particularly perturbed by the fact that Zwane suffered no consequences as a result of his mismanagement of the project. Instead, he was shuffled by Ace Magashule into the Department of Agriculture, where he would play a key role in the Estina/Vrede scandal. The commission believed that this was, at its root, a total failure on the part of the ANC to monitor and manage both Magashule and Zwane. The commission concluded its report on the Free State housing debacle by lamenting that 'it is the ANC which gave the people of the Free State Mr Zwane and it is the ANC which gave them the Premier who failed to intervene when Mr Zwane and his Department wasted more than R500m of taxpayers' money which was meant to be used to build low-cost houses for poor people in the Free State'.

# RECOMMENDATIONS

*Law enforcement should investigate with a view to possible prosecution of Mpho Mokoena for violations of the PFMA.*

*Government should take all steps that 'may lawfully be taken' to recover monies spent unlawfully on the project from Mpho Mokoena and Mosebenzi Zwane.*

*Law enforcement should investigate with a view to the possible prosecution of Mpho Mokoena and/or Mosebenzi Zwane and/or other implicated officials for fraud for telling the national Department of Human Settlements that the Free State Department of Human Settlements could build a certain number of houses when they might reasonably have known this not to be possible.*

# The Estina/Vrede dairy scandal

THE FINAL CASE STUDY of state capture in the Free State was the Estina/Vrede dairy scandal, which the commission addressed in a 211-page volume. However, unlike all of the commission's other reports and volumes, this report presented me with something of a challenge. I submitted considerable evidence on the Estina/Vrede dairy scandal which I drew from the GuptaLeaks and other public sources, and spent the better part of a day in testimony before the commission explaining the complex money-laundering systems that were used to steal and launder money paid to Estina by the Free State government. Without being too presumptuous, I think I know quite a lot about this story.

The commission's report is, to put it bluntly, not particularly good. In fact, it is bad. Nothing in the report is actually wrong. But it missed and excluded all sorts of evidence of how the Guptas were involved in the Estina/Vrede project, and it speaks about the evidence of how the funds were stolen and laundered in only the most passing terms. Certain aspects of the evidence heard by the commission were of relevance, but, in other cases, key lines of inquiry were missed, not followed or misunderstood.

This puts me in an invidious position: I want the reader to understand the Estina/Vrede scandal in all of its audacity and outrage. But I also don't want to put words into the commission's mouth about topics on which it did not make any findings. So, what I've done is the following: in the first part of this account, I describe the outline and essence of the Estina/Vrede scandal, as I understand it, which, I hope, will give some grounding to enable readers to understand what follows. And then in the sections that come after, I describe some of the additional evidence the commission heard that is useful to bear in mind, as well as its overall findings and conclusions.

## The Estina/Vrede dairy scandal: My simple summary

On 5 June 2012, the Free State Department of Agriculture entered into a contract with an entity called Estina. The agreement was signed by Peter Thabethe for the Free State government: he was, at the time, the head of department. The agreement, in effect, created a new mega-project: a dairy farm and processing unit. Under the terms of the agreement, a total of R570m was to be invested, of which R228m would come from Estina and the remainder from the Free State government. Estina was shortly thereafter granted a 99-year lease on a local farm (after the farmers who occupied the land had been evicted), for which it paid no rent.

This contract, and the concept notes that preceded it, claimed that the Estina/Vrede dairy farm was to be run for the benefit of the local community. Indeed, it was claimed that local farmers and citizens of Vrede would receive shares in Estina through a special-purpose vehicle that would be created.

Estina was little more than a Gupta cut-out, as revealed by the GuptaLeaks. In my submission to the commission on Estina, I noted the following connections between Estina and the Guptas:

- Estina's sole director from late 2010 onwards was Kamal Vasram, who the GuptaLeaks show was a close associate of the Guptas. Vasram was an IT salesman who had no previous farming experience.
- Estina shared its business address with other Gupta companies in Sandton.
- Ashu Chawla and the Gupta enterprise were directly involved in securing visas for the Indian-born employees of Estina who directed the dairy farm.
- The 'manager' of the farm was Chandrama Prasad, for whom the Guptas secured a work visa. The Guptas knew of Prasad because he was the assistant to a senior police official in India through whom the Guptas were trying to arrange special security

privileges when they travelled back home.
- Estina's day-to-day financial record-keeping was done on a piece of software called Fincon, which was housed on Sahara's servers.
- Certain day-to-day payments were routed through and approved by Sahara Computers employees.

But, most importantly, the vast majority of the money that was paid into Estina was stolen and laundered into the accounts of Gupta companies. In the calculations I performed for the commission (which it cites in this report but does not explore in any depth), I showed that the Free State government paid R280.2m to Estina between 2012 and 2016. This included payments to Estina of R106m between May 2015 and May 2016, *after* Estina had been booted from the project.

Of the R280.2m paid to Estina:
- R59.5m was paid to Vargafield (Pty) Ltd, another Gupta cut-out whose sole director, Sanjay Grover, oversaw the Gupta's money-laundering vehicles in Dubai.
- R205.7m was paid to Gateway Ltd in Dubai. Gateway was controlled by the Guptas. Of this amount, $3.3m was then transferred into the accounts of Linkway, another Gupta company, and a further $3.1m was paid to Oakbay Investments, the Gupta flagship company.

A key part of my evidence before the commission was about how the Guptas used various money-laundering techniques to move and disguise the money. The most important of these were round-tripping and loan-backing, whereby money paid to Estina by the Free State was moved between a series of fixed deposit accounts and loans, and then redeposited back into Estina. I told the commission that this was likely done to make it look as if Estina had invested its own money in the project when, in fact, the vast majority of the money flowing via Estina's accounts actually emanated from payments made to it by the Free State government, which it had laundered through round-tripping and loan-backs.

Two officials were implicated in the award of the contract to Estina, both of whom had close connections to the Guptas. The first was Mosebenzi Zwane, who, at the time of the Estina scandal, was the MEC for Agriculture. The GuptaLeaks revealed that Zwane had met with the Guptas frequently at their compound. As we have seen in the chapter on Eskom, Zwane was later deployed as the Minister of Mineral Resources, in which role he was implicated in the Guptas' capture of Eskom.

The second was Peter Thabethe, the head of department during the conceptualisation and initiation of the Estina project. Thabethe entered into the various contractual agreements that gave life to the project. The GuptaLeaks show that Thabethe was scheduled to visit the Gupta compound on two occasions with Zwane. Moreover, Thabethe had, as part of his 'conceptualisation' of the Estina project, travelled to India, ostensibly as part of a 'research trip' to visit Indian dairy farmers who might partner on the project. The GuptaLeaks show that Thabethe's visa was arranged and supported by Sahara Computers. He was accompanied on the 'research trip' by Ashok Narayan, who had only recently been appointed by Ace Magashule as an advisor. More importantly, Narayan was a key Gupta lieutenant – he was, for example, the person who came forward to claim control over Homix, which received kickbacks from Neotel in relation to Transnet contracts.

## The work done by Estina
The commission heard useful evidence from a number of witnesses about what went on at the farm: this provided a graphic description of just how much of a fatuous ruse the project really was.

Albert Radebe, a local councillor and farmer, testified that he had heard that cows from the Estina project were dying, and that their carcasses had been dumped next to a stream that provided the local water supply. When he confirmed that the cows had been dumped, he alerted local authorities and the press.

Another witness before the commission, Willie Basson, gave insight into why so many cows died on the project. Basson ran a local engineering and agricultural supply firm called Vrede Trekkers, which was hired on occasion by Estina. In 2013, Basson was asked to help excavate a ditch to bury 100 cattle that had died on the farm. Basson said it was obvious that the cattle were malnourished, and that he would end up burying more cows as the year progressed. Basson testified that Prasad, the Indian policeman-turned-farmer, had no idea why the cows were dying. Prasad believed that the cows could survive simply by eating the grass on the farm; Basson had to explain that they also needed to be given cattle feed, and ended up supplying R1m worth.

Basson also described how, in 2013, he was approached by Chandrama Prasad, the farm manager, for help in installing the dairy processing unit that Estina had bought from India. Basson testified that the unit – which was supposed to turn raw milk into other products – was in extremely poor condition. It was so badly rusted, Basson noted, that large peels of rust were falling off like fish scales.

Another witness who gave evidence to the commission, in the form of a statement, was David Andreas Maree, an agricultural economist employed by FNB. In late 2013, Maree had provided an assessment of the project to assist a National Treasury investigation into the farm and its funding. Maree confirmed that the business proposal used to justify the farm project was unrealistic and academic. He advised that, based on the proposal, the project should not have proceeded.

## Zwane's choir trip to India

The commission also heard important evidence about a potential benefit that accrued to Mosebenzi Zwane. The GuptaLeaks included email correspondence between Ashok Narayan and the email address zwanemail@gmail.com. The correspondence showed that, in October 2012, Narayan was helping to arrange a detailed itinerary for a visit to India by a choir called Umsingizane. Zwane was some sort of patron of the choir. The choir did indeed travel to India, where they were hosted at a lunch with Tony Gupta. The itinerary in the GuptaLeaks confirmed that Zwane, Narayan and another Free State official, Ms Motau, would attend the lunch.

When Zwane was originally asked about the matter, he responded that he was aware that they had taken a trip, but he had no idea who had sponsored them. He also explained that he refused to answer any answers related to the GuptaLeaks, from where details of the choir trip had emerged, because this was 'information extorted from the leaks' that he did not want to 'fall prey to legitimising'.

In the most remarkable coincidence, Zwane travelled to India at precisely the same time as the choir. Indeed, during his second appearance before the commission, he admitted that he was on the same plane. He also admitted that zwanemail@gmail.com was his email, but he wasn't aware of the content of the emails: he claimed that he sometimes let members of the choir, who did not have great knowledge of IT matters, use his email for their purposes.

Zwane still had to explain what he was doing in India at precisely the same time that his choir was being given a tour of the country at the behest of the Guptas. Zwane's version was that he travelled to India to meet the representatives of Paras Dairy. This needs some explaining. In the earliest stages of the fraud, Estina submitted proposals to the effect that the dairy project would be pursued in partnership with a large Indian dairy firm, Paras. When Peter Thabethe travelled to India in February 2012 with Ashok Narayan, they did so, in part, to meet with Paras Dairy representatives. Even this had the fingerprints of the Guptas: the GuptaLeaks show that, in addition to organising Thabethe's visa to travel to India, the Gupta enterprise also organised the visas of Paras employees who visited South Africa in early 2012. Strangely, the commission totally overlooked this fact.

Ultimately, the inclusion of Paras was a ruse. Paras was never involved in the dairy project. The only party that signed an agreement with the Free State government was Estina, and that agreement made no mention at all of any undertakings or obligations on the part of Paras.

Zwane's story was probed by the commission. He claimed that he travelled to Paras in order to check on the work of Thabethe: to confirm for himself that Paras could do the work on the project. Even on the face of it, this was absurd: the contract with Estina had already been signed, so it would be somewhat strange to check if one of its ostensible partners could do the job months after the contract had been awarded.

Under further pressure, his version became increasingly insane. When it was put to him that Paras had no role in the project, and that the only contracting party was Estina, Zwane testified that he only became aware of Estina's involvement in 2014, after he had left the department. Zwane could act in such staggering ignorance, he claimed, because he never reviewed the contract with Estina that created the project. The commission was blunt: 'Mr Zwane was obviously being untruthful when he said he did not know Estina's involvement in this project. He was simply lying.'

Frustratingly, the commission made no actual finding of fact on the choir trip beyond describing these exchanges. It did, however, recommend, in general terms, that law enforcement investigate Zwane's role in the project.

## The beneficiary experience: Murder, death threats and fear

As we have seen, the Estina/Vrede dairy project had been touted in government circles on the basis that local citizens of Vrede would become participants and beneficiaries. It will surprise no one that this never happened, but how it played out was shocking.

The commission heard evidence from two local Vrede residents who had submitted their names to the project: Ephraim Dlamini and Meshack Mpaleni Ncongwane. Dlamini testified about multiple meetings he attended with Free State officials in connection with the project. The first took place in June 2012 and was convened by Zwane, with Thabethe and other officials in attendance. Zwane used the meeting to give details of the project and asked for people to indicate their willingness to participate. A representative of Zwane took down the list of names.

A second meeting was held shortly thereafter. Again, the meeting was convened by Zwane with Thabethe, the local mayor and other Free State officials in attendance. Further details were provided about the Vrede dairy project. Most disturbingly, Dlamini testified that local farmers who attended the meeting and were keen to join the project were told to sell their existing cattle, especially if they were meat cattle, as the government would shortly give them each ten cows towards the project. It appears that some farmers did indeed sell their cows on this suggestion, leading to serious hardship.

Dlamini recalled three further meetings through 2013 and 2014. Besides a request for the ID numbers of participants at one meeting, nothing ever materialised, and beneficiaries were left without any further information. In 2017, the leader of the opposition Democratic Alliance, Mmusi Maimane, visited the project as part of a fact-finding mission, and met with Dlamini and toured the farm. This was the only time, Dlamini testified, that any of the alleged beneficiaries were ever allowed into its gates.

Dlamini testified that he received frequent and persistent death threats because he refused to keep quiet about the project. At one stage, he was sent a video that showed somebody threatening him because of his public attitude towards the project. Dlamini forwarded the video to the Hawks and also gave it to the local SAPS station commander in Vrede. No docket was ever opened and the allegations were never investigated by the police.

Dlamini further claimed that other beneficiaries, who were publicly critical of the project, were murdered. Dlamini named Philemon Ngwenya as one public critic of the project who was found killed; Dlamini recalled that Ngwenya had been threatened in public by a henchman of Zwane's. Two people were killed in the nearby town of Warden, shot from an unidentified black vehicle. Another individual, Moses Chauke, was allegedly kidnapped, tortured and murdered. Chauke was rumoured to be investigating the project.

Another key witness was Albert Radebe, who, as I noted, alerted local authorities and the media to the dumping of Estina's dead cows. Radebe testified that he had been physically assaulted, beaten up and sprayed with pepper spray. Radebe identified his assailants as employees of the Free State Department of Agriculture linked to Zwane.

When Radebe attempted to open a case at the local SAPS office, he was bizarrely told that no docket could be opened because it was a criminal matter, and that he would have to wait for a visiting officer from the nearby town of Bethlehem to process his complaint. He was never contacted by this supposed official. Radebe also claimed that, as part of the retribution meted out against him, he was denied access to the local state veterinarian. As a result, Radebe lost 45 cows that could otherwise have been treated.

The commission was clearly extremely disturbed by this evidence; both because of the threats themselves and because of the failure of law enforcement to do anything to protect individuals who reported the threats against them. The commission recommended further probes into why the SAPS had so badly dropped the ball.

## Conclusion: Where the fault lay

The commission concluded its assessment of the Estina project by identifying the individuals most at fault, and it did so in a bracingly blunt paragraph:

The whole Vrede Dairy Project happened because Mr Thabethe dismally failed to do his job and failed to protect the interests and assets of the DARD [Department of Agriculture and Rural Development] and to protect taxpayers' money. It also happened because Mr Mosebenzi Zwane as MEC was pursuing the agenda of the Guptas and did not do his job to perform oversight over Mr Thabethe. It also happened because the Premier of the Province, Mr Ace Magashule, would have also been pursuing the agenda of the Guptas.

## RECOMMENDATIONS

*Law enforcement should investigate Mosebenzi Zwane and Ace Magashule to establish if any laws were broken in relation to the Vrede dairy project.*

*Consideration should be given to getting legal advice to institute recovery proceedings against Mosebenzi Zwane and Ace Magashule where their conduct involved losses to the state.*

*Law enforcement should investigate further whether any members of the Gupta family, including Tony Gupta, and their associates, including Ashok Narayan and directors of Estina, are guilty of any offence with a view to bringing criminal charges.*

# PART FIVE

# Flashpoints

*In two brief reports, the commission set out the result of its investigations into two notable scandals: the Waterkloof landing, which effectively announced the Guptas to the public, and the decision by various banks to shut down Gupta-related bank accounts in early 2016. These two flashpoints generated a media storm, and raised serious concerns about whether the state was, under President Zuma, being repurposed into a vehicle to be used for the benefit of the Guptas.*

# The Waterkloof landing

ON 30 APRIL 2013, a plane carrying 200 guests landed at the Waterkloof Air Force Base in Gauteng. Waterkloof is, as the name suggests, a military installation and national key point, whose use is strictly governed by national security concerns. The plane disgorged its passengers onto a red carpet. Some guests walked, while others were ferried, to a reception area, where they were treated to snacks and the dubious entertainment of 'traditional dancers'. A presiding officer, Colonel Visser, was confused as to who among the 200 attendees was a dignitary or VIP, and so greeted every person who they met.

Following the sort of rapid passport processing one can only dream of when landing at OR Tambo, the guests were whisked away to Sun City in a police convoy consisting of 31 cars and 62 officers of the Gauteng police service; at the border with North West Province, NW police took over to see them to their final destination. Approximately seventy security vehicles attended to the safety of these hallowed guests. It later emerged that some of the security staff were, in fact, personnel of Tshwane Police who were illegally moonlighting, casually violating the law by carrying their official firearms.

Besides a lack of taste, there were two major problems with this whole affair, which shortly afterwards came into the media spotlight. The first was that Waterkloof, as a security installation, was supposed to be reserved for the use of diplomatic VIPs – ministers and presidents, who had specific security requirements.

The second was that not a single one of the 200 passengers met these requirements. They were, instead, an assorted collection of Indian wedding guests, who were being flown in to celebrate the wedding of Vega Gupta and Aakash Jahajgarhia; Vega was the daughter of Achla Gupta, sister of Tony, Atul and Ajay.

The commission's investigation sought to understand how this had happened and, in particular, whether this lavish and unlawful treatment was meted out at the behest, or at least with the knowledge, of Jacob Zuma. The commission, in turn, relied extensively on witness testimony it heard, as well as the results of an investigation led by Nonkululeko Sindane, the director general of the Department of Justice. Sindane performed the investigation at the behest of the government, which ordered a probe in the immediate aftermath of the story breaking in the media.

Sindane's investigation revealed that the Guptas had been trying to get favourable treatment for their guests for some time. In February 2013, Tony Gupta approached officials at ACSA about a plane arriving with heads of state and ministers from India, asking whether it could land at OR Tambo. Shortly thereafter, he met Bruce Koloane, then the acting CEO of ACSA, and Ben Martins, Minister of Transport. Tony Gupta again asked about landing at OR Tambo, but this was rejected as it would disrupt the airport's passport counters; they suggested a smaller airport nearer to Sun City.

Undeterred, in March 2013, Atul Gupta approached the Minister of Defence and Military Veterans, while Ashu Chawla addressed his inquiries to the minister's advisor. They asked about the possibilities of landing elsewhere. The ministers and their advisor asked the chief of the SAAF, Lieutenant FZ Msimang, whether it was possible for the landing to take place at Waterkloof. They were told that it would be impossible. It is not clear from the commission's report whether the idea of landing at Waterkloof came, specifically, from a suggestion made by the Guptas or whether it was the brainwave of the minister.

Koloane, who the commission confirmed was a key player in the debacle, took it upon himself to pressure others. In his role as chief of state protocol, he contacted the minister's advisor and told him that he was under pressure from 'No. 1' to resolve the landing situation; all concerned thought No. 1 referred to Zuma. The Presidency denied that any pressure was applied to Koloane, although the commission would, as we'll see later, come to a different conclusion.

The matter moved forward when Koloane contacted Major Ntshisi at the base and asked him about the progress in resolving the landing; Ntshisi replied the base would only receive heads of state and their deputies. Koloane then responded that there would be several Indian ministers on the flight, and that the Minister of Transport and the Guptas had reached out for assistance. However – and this was key – Koloane explained that the request could not be put in writing. Ntshisi was adamant that approval could only be granted with something on paper.

Ntshisi was also approached by another SAAF member working at the base, Colonel Anderson. Anderson claimed Koloane told her that the President had been inquiring about the landing. When Ntshisi approached Anderson about the matter, she reportedly told him that the matter was 'political' and that 'Number 1' knew about it. Ntshisi then approached the person who had the power to approve the request – Lieutenant SJ van Zyl. Van Zyl issued the clearance based on the conversations he had with Ntshisi and others, and based documents presented to him.

Cutting through the extended denials and retractions, the commission laid the blame for the affair primarily at the feet of two people. The first was Koloane. This was hardly surprising. When the landing was first investigated, Koloane was charged with three separate disciplinary offences, among them that he had 'abused diplomatic channels' to facilitate the landing, and that he had misrepresented facts to make this happen. Koloane admitted guilt in all three cases. His punishment was a two-month suspension. Not long after, however, Koloane was appointed to a new, cushy position as Ambassador to the Netherlands, despite the fact that he had only recently been found guilty of abusing the diplomatic process.

The second person to receive blame was Jacob Zuma, who, when he appeared before the commission, denied any involvement. The commission found that this was simply not credible. In making this finding, it pointed to all the evidence it had heard of how Zuma had defended the Guptas and sought to promote their interests. The commission also quoted the evidence of Rajesh Sundaram, whose account of his travails with the Guptas was discussed earlier. Sundaram's book included a recollection of a meeting at which Atul

Gupta spoke at length about the Waterkloof landing. Atul predicted that Zuma would 'help us [Guptas] through this as well', and pointed out how many ministers had attended the wedding, which was seen as an endorsement. Atul also predicted that 'the personnel against whom action is taken will be reinstated very soon'. And, indeed, Koloane was, as we have seen, promoted shortly afterwards to ambassador.

The commission thus found:

> the probabilities are overwhelming that President Zuma knew about the plans for a Gupta private aircraft to land at the Waterkloof Military Air Base and had no objections to the plans being implemented. In fact all indications are that he would have taken steps to have the landing at the airport facilitated. If that is what the Guptas wanted from him, how could he not do it for them when the evidence has shown that he could even fire his own comrades if that is what the Guptas wanted.

The commission, however, stopped short of finding that Koloane or any other official had acted as they did because any particular 'officer or institution' had been captured. This was not explained in any depth, and the commission's reasoning was not laid out; I have to admit that I find this conclusion somewhat confusing in the light of what preceded it. In any event, the commission concluded that, when seen in its broader context, 'the positive purpose' of the entire Waterkloof saga was that it served to 'starkly demonstrate to the media and wider public the scandalous influence that the Guptas exercised in the highest office in the Republic and how shamelessly they flaunted it. It is hoped that an incident like the Waterkloof saga will never happen again in this country.'

# The closure of Gupta bank accounts

ITEM 1.7 OF THE commission's terms of reference required it to investigate whether 'any member of the National Executive had unlawfully, corruptly or improperly intervened in the matter of the closing of banking facilities'. The accounts that were closed belonged to the Guptas and were linked to their flagship company, Oakbay Investments. ABSA was the first bank to move on the Guptas. In November 2014, ABSA's Politically Exposed Committee reviewed the Guptas' accounts and advised ABSA to withdraw banking facilities from the Guptas. For reasons left unexplained, ABSA waited until December 2015 to issue a notice to the Guptas that they intended to close their bank accounts. Two months later, in February 2016, ABSA closed the Gupta accounts. In addition to the reputational risk of being associated with potential criminality, ABSA was also concerned that they only provided one small part of the Gupta's banking facilities. This meant that they lacked insight into the totality of the Gupta's transactional activities and, as a result, could not have the confidence that they fully understood and reviewed the money coming into the Guptas' ABSA accounts.

The other members of the so-called Big Four followed suit shortly thereafter. First National Bank (FNB) wrote to the Guptas on 1 April 2016 to say that it intended to close Gupta accounts by 31 May 2016. On 6 April 2016, Standard Bank gave notice to the Guptas that they intended to shut down 27 accounts related to the Guptas, including those of Oakbay, Sahara Computers and Optimum coal mine. The accounts were closed on 6 June 2016. On 7 April 2016, Nedbank also issued its decision to terminate the accounts.

The decision of the banks led to a media furore. Senior ANC members angrily said that the banks had colluded and were doing so in league with 'white monopoly capital' in order to undermine black empowerment.

On 8 April 2016, the day after FNB's decision, Nazeem Howa, the Guptas' de facto spokesperson, published a letter saying that Oakbay's attorneys had written to Jacob Zuma and three ministers: Mosebenzi Zwane, Mildred Oliphant and Pravin Gordhan. The letter from Oakbay requested that the government intervene, which it did. On 13 April 2016, Cabinet resolved to appoint an Inter-Ministerial Committee (IMC) to investigate the matter. The IMC was supposed to be composed of Zwane, Oliphant and Gordhan; Gordhan, however, was not at the 13 April 2016 Cabinet meeting and ultimately appears not to have participated.

The IMC wrote to the four banks and asked to meet to discuss the issues although, after extended correspondence, neither FNB nor ABSA met with the IMC. The first bank to meet with the IMC was Standard Bank, on 5 May 2016. The government delegation included Zwane, Oliphant and Jimmy Manyi. The commission noted that Manyi's inclusion was somewhat strange as he had no government role at the time.

Standard Bank's Ian Sinton, who attended the meeting with the CEO of Standard Bank, testified before the commission about the meeting. He said that Standard Bank attempted to impress on the IMC that it could not talk about individual cases. Nevertheless, according to Sinton, the IMC put forward an argument in favour of the Gupta companies, claiming they employed 7,500 people. The IMC also suggested that Standard had colluded with other banks and with 'white monopoly capital'. Members of the IMC – although precisely who was not disclosed – also pointed out that banks operated with the permission of government through the issuance of licences; the inference, of course, was that the government could make life tough for the banks if it so chose.

Unsurprisingly, Sinton's view was that the meeting was not called to investigate the complexities of legal compliance for banks, but to advance the interests of Oakbay and the Guptas. This was also the view of Michael Thomas Brown, who gave evidence on behalf of Nedbank. He attended an IMC meeting that was attended by Zwane and a representative of Oliphant. Again, despite Nedbank stating that it would not discuss individual cases, Zwane tried to ask what had triggered the closure decision. He also suggested that Nedbank could step in to become the Guptas' new transactional bank and help save Gupta-related jobs. Brown would not be drawn on the suggestion and the meeting soon closed, but not before Zwane expressed his confusion out loud as to why other banks didn't meet with the IMC, considering that government controlled the issuance of banking licences. Brown testified that he viewed this as a veiled threat.

At the same time that the IMC was meeting with the banks, the ANC also decided to investigate. It met with Oakbay, to hear its side of the story. And it called representatives of all four banks to Luthuli House to meet with, among others, Gwede Mantashe and Jessie Duarte. The meetings with the banks followed much the same lines as those with the IMC; the banks tried to say they could not comment on individual accounts but were then forced to answer questions about whether they were colluding, or were tools of white monopoly capital, or otherwise nefariously motivated.

On 23 May 2016, the ANC team that led the investigations reported its findings to the National Working Committee (NWC); the NWC then made its own observations. It stated that the closure of the bank accounts 'smacks of collusion', and that the powers wielded by banks to shut accounts could be abused. The NWC also fretted about the adoption of the idea of Politically Exposed Persons (PEPs), which it believed could be used to imply that PEPs were 'morally corrupt until proven otherwise'. The ANC NEC noted and adopted the NWC report at the end of May 2016, although little was said about concrete steps forward.

Nothing much then happened on the matter until 1 September 2016, when Zwane, out of the blue, issued a media statement. He claimed that Cabinet had resolved to appoint a commission of inquiry to look into the mandates of the Banking Tribunal and Banking Ombudsman in the light of the Oakbay decisions. President Zuma, the following day, was forced to put out a statement denying that any commission of inquiry had been appointed.

The following month, Pravin Gordhan took a further, highly unusual step: he applied to the High Court for a declaratory order. Gordhan asked the High Court to confirm that, as the Minister of Finance, he had no power to intervene in the relationship between banks and their clients. Gordhan, in his application, attached an explosive report that had been compiled by the Financial Intelligence Centre (FIC), which discussed 73 suspicious transactions by Gupta companies that had been reported to the FIC by South African banks.

Gordhan's application was eventually rejected on 18 August 2017. The High Court found that there was no need for it to make any declaratory order as the law was quite clear on the powers and responsibilities of government ministers. It also balked at what it saw as an attempt to get the judiciary to stray into matters that should, under a proper separation of powers, be reserved for the executive.

The last public act in this sordid affair played out the following month. In November 2016, President Zuma spoke in public for the first time about the closure of the accounts. Answering a question in Parliament about whether the banks' actions were part of an attempt by 'imperialists' to control the financial sector, Zuma revealed his own belief: that the banks had done something untoward and had rebuffed the 'polite' overtures made by the government. Zuma stated:

> This is precisely the reason why government cannot ignore such an action. The action looks suspicious and as government responsible to govern this country, we certainly have to investigate this. We started very politely by sending a team to meet the banks to investigate what is happening. The banks did not say, these are the faults that this company has done or what led to our actions. So, up to now, we do not know. We have laws in this country. If, let us say, any company violates the laws, there are enforcement institutions that you will report to. Just to stand willy-nilly and close simultaneously a number of banks as well as other financial institutions, it does not look innocent.

## Conclusion
The commission's findings on this issue were both straightforward and robustly expressed. Three particular findings stand out. First,

the commission found that there was absolutely zero evidence that the banks had colluded as part of a campaign on behalf of 'white monopoly capital'. The banks, instead, were complying with their legal duty. Indeed, questions could be reasonably asked about why the banks took so long to act:

> The accusation that the termination decisions to close bank accounts were taken to advance the agenda of white monopoly capital was entirely unjustified on the facts of this case. There is absolutely no evidence to support that accusation. The decisions of the banks were taken in the light of their legal obligations when a client appears to be involved in suspicious transactions that could cause a bank reputational damage.

Second, the commission found that there was clear evidence that the investigation on the part of the IMC was not, as stated, to broadly investigate the vagaries of banking law in South Africa. Instead, it was obviously attempting to help the Guptas:

> It is quite clear with regard to the meetings that representatives of various banks had with the Inter-Ministerial Task Team chaired by Mr Zwane that that Task Team's focus, as they seem to have understood it themselves, was to get the banks to reverse their decisions to close the bank accounts of the Gupta-owned companies. Therefore, that Task Team improperly intervened in the matter of the closing of the bank facilities of the Gupta-owned companies to advance the cause of the Guptas.

Finally, the commission found that Zuma himself sought to advance the interests of the Guptas. In so doing, Zuma violated section 2 of the Executive Members' Ethics Act, which, among other things, banned MPs and Cabinet ministers from using their official position to improperly advance the interests of third parties. The commission found that Zuma's statements in Parliament, when seen against the conduct and approach of the IMC, showed that he 'sought to improperly interfere in the matter of the closing of the banking facilities of the Gupta-owned companies in order to assist his friends'.

## The private power of banks

Interestingly, the commission took the opportunity to explore an issue that perturbed many people: the 'enormous power' of banks to unilaterally deny services to clients. This power, the commission commented, 'would become very clear if all the banks were to refuse that you hold an account with them'.

What particularly irked the commission was that the evidence of the banks had shown that, in some cases, they had merely informed the Guptas of their decision, without seeking any input from them. While the commission was hardly sympathetic towards the Guptas, it was of the opinion that it 'is unacceptable that an institution as powerful as a bank should have no option to hear – whether in discussion or in writing – what a client has to say before the Bank may close that client's account'. The commission believed that this potentially arbitrary exercise of power was against the spirit of the Constitution, and recommended that Parliament seek to introduce a notion of fairness into this process.

### RECOMMENDATION

*Parliament should amend existing legislation, or promulgate new legislation, that would introduce the requirement of fairness into the process by which banks close the accounts of their clients.*

# PART SIX

# Bits and Pieces and Findings on Specific Individuals

*The commission used its final volume to address a small handful of disparate topics, tying up certain loose ends and making findings about particular individuals. In some cases, the commission weighed in on matters that don't appear particularly germane to its terms of reference. So, in the interests of highlighting the important stuff, I have not included them here, instead focusing on the four topics that had the most heft and political consequence. I've also included, in this section, a summary of a matter that fits somewhat oddly within the commission's other work, and that appeared in its fourth volume: the contracts between EOH and the City of Johannesburg.*

# The testimony of Vytjie Mentor

In 2016, Vytjie Mentor claimed that she had been approached by Atul Gupta, with the knowledge of Jacob Zuma, to accept the position of Minister of Public Enterprises. In addition to posting about it on Facebook, Mentor laid criminal charges flowing from the experience, and deposed her version of events with the Public Protector for Thuli Madonsela's *State of Capture* report. Madonsela's report recommended that Mentor's version be assessed by the judicial commission of inquiry which her report also recommended be established. As a result, the commission's terms of reference specifically required the commission to assess the veracity of Mentor's version.

Following a youth of activism, Mentor served in Parliament as an ANC MP between 2002 and 2014. Between 2009 and 2010, she chaired the Parliamentary Portfolio Committee on Public Enterprises.

In August 2010, Mentor travelled to China to meet with officials to discuss solutions to Eskom's power supply issues; she did so in her capacity as chairperson of the Public Enterprises Portfolio Committee. She travelled at the same time that Jacob Zuma was making a formal state visit. Mentor alleged that, during her flight, she was introduced by Duduzane Zuma to his companion, Tony Gupta, as his business partner. Tony apparently indicated that his brother was part of Zuma's 'advance team'. Zuma also introduced Mentor to Fana Hlongwane. She initially claimed that Zuma called Hlongwane his 'chairperson', although she later withdrew this allegation.

On landing, she noticed three Indian men who were arranging logistics for the visit. She later realised that they were the three Gupta brothers. Following a formal reception, Mentor claimed she travelled to her hotel and there received a phone call from one of the Gupta brothers who said Zuma had invited Mentor to his guesthouse. The Gupta brother offered to take her there. Mentor refused, saying it would be insane to travel with a stranger in a foreign country.

In October 2010, Mentor claimed she received a call from Ms Kaunda, an assistant to Jacob Zuma, who said Zuma wanted to meet her and that Atul Gupta would contact her to make the arrangements. Following a conversation with Atul, Mentor flew to Johannesburg where she was met by Atul and Tony Gupta. At first she was taken to the offices of Sahara Computers and, after a conversation, to the Gupta compound.

According to Mentor, she was showed into a waiting room on her arrival; after an extended period of time, she was joined by Ajay Gupta. Ajay started by asking Mentor about uranium supplies in the Northern Province, where she came from; he said that, in anticipation of a nuclear deal, the Guptas were moving to become the primary uranium suppliers in the country. Most notably, he opined that the SAA turn-around strategy was failing, and that he believed the SAA route to India was not profitable. He suggested that, if SAA stopped this route, the Guptas were partnered with an airline that could take it over.

According to Mentor, Ajay then very casually offered her the position of Minister of Public Enterprises, which he could ensure if she agreed to oversee the closure of the SAA India route. Mentor refused and started raising her voice. Soon thereafter, Jacob Zuma joined them and tried to calm her down. Mentor explained to Zuma what Ajay had just said: Zuma did nothing more than invite her to calm down.

Mentor claimed that she told a number of people about the event, including the chairperson of the Joint Standing Committee on Intelligence, Siyabonga Cwele, and two other members of the committee. She also testified that she had told Gwede Mantashe and Jessie Duarte, as well as a good friend, Ms Mashile-Nkosi.

## The commission's evaluation

The commission concluded that there were too many 'unsatisfactory features' of Mentor's evidence for it to make a finding that the meeting had happened. Or, more simply, the commission did not find that the meeting had happened, or that Ajay Gupta had offered her the ministerial position.

The commission identified several problems in her evidence:

- It was unable to corroborate Mentor's version that she had travelled to Johannesburg to visit the Guptas and back to Cape Town on the same day. There were no flight records to attest to her version despite the commission's extensive efforts to locate them.

- Mentor described the physical features of the Gupta compound and the rooms she entered in some detail. When the commission and Department of Public Works did a tour of the compound, her descriptions did not match the actual layout or decor that was found.

- Mentor's friends, including Mashile-Nkosi, did not corroborate her version. Mentor claimed that she had a conversation with Mashile-Nkosi in which she relayed some of the content of the meeting. The commission found it striking that Mentor's friends would not back her up.

On this basis, the commission concluded that 'on the probabilities and on the evidence before the commission, the incident did not happen and Ms Mentor was not offered a position as Minister of Public Enterprises by a member of the Gupta family at the Gupta residence'.

# The Guptas' knowledge of Fikile Mbalula's appointment to Cabinet

THE COMMISSION'S TERMS of reference required it to investigate 'whether the appointment of any member of the National Executive, functionary and/or office bearer was disclosed to the Gupta family or any other unauthorised person before such appointments were formally made and/or announced, and if so, whether the President or any member of the National Executive is responsible for such conduct'. The commission was thus compelled to look into one of the earliest allegations of Gupta-related state capture: the appointment of Fikile Mbalula as the Minister of Sport.

The allegation was straightforward: in August 2011, at a meeting of the ANC NEC, the assembled comrades were discussing the influence of the Guptas on the country. Fikile Mbalula was alleged to have tearfully and emotionally told the NEC members that, in October 2010, he had had a conversation with one of the Gupta brothers. During the conversation, the Gupta brother told him that Zuma was going to appoint him Minister of Sport in an upcoming Cabinet reshuffle, and congratulated him on the appointment. This was prior to Zuma informing Mbalula.

Mbalula was a long-time confidant and supporter of Zuma – a position of loyalty he maintained throughout JZ's period in power. As a result, Mbalula was initially at pains to refute the allegation. He denied the incident took place at all when he was interviewed by the Public Protector. The commission found that Mbalula most likely lied in his interview as he was 'protecting his political position in the ANC and the government by shielding the then still powerful President Zuma from the Public Protector's investigation into his relationship with the Guptas'.

Mbalula was initially also reluctant to give any evidence to the commission. He only deposed a statement after both Trevor Manuel and General Siphiwe Nyanda were called to give evidence before the commission. Although Manuel's and Nyanda's evidence disagreed on certain particulars, they both testified to the same basic story: Mbalula had told the NEC that a Gupta brother told him of his appointment before Zuma notified him.

Once Manuel and Nyanda gave evidence, Mbalula reluctantly came forward to give his own. He deposed an affidavit in which he confirmed that he had indeed told the NEC about his conversation with Ajay Gupta. He confirmed that he felt 'angered and perturbed' that his appointment had been leaked to Ajay, and that he was 'extremely troubled' and 'emotionally distraught' because his appointment had been 'tainted by circumstances beyond my control'.

Ajay Gupta, for his part, denied the essence of the allegation, namely, that he had heard about Mbalula's appointment prior to the decision being made. Instead, he claimed that media reporting at the time had hinted at a Cabinet reshuffle and Mbalula's promotion from a deputy minister to a full minister position. He admitted that he did talk to Mbalula, but that he merely joked broadly about the promotion predicted by the media. The commission found this version implausible.

Thus, the commission found:

despite Mr Mbalula having given a different version to the Public Protector in 2016, it should be accepted on the balance of probabilities that his evidence to the Commission regarding what he said at the NEC meeting in August 2011 is true. One may say this with confidence because two witnesses whose evidence should be accepted in this regard – Mr Manuel and Gen Nyanda – were present at that meeting and heard him speak. On this basis it is clear that he lied to the Public Protector and told the truth to the commission in this particular respect.

The commission then took this line further in order to ask who had told the Guptas about Mbalula's appointment. Its answer was straightforward: considering the nature of the relationship between the Guptas and Zuma, 'there can be no doubt that the Guptas got the information from President Zuma'. In addition, Zuma must have been aware by August 2011, when Mbalula told his version to the NEC meeting, that the Guptas were 'privy to and used important confidential information' for their own ends. Despite knowing this, Zuma made no attempt to investigate the matter at all, despite its being raised with him by Gibson Njenje, then the head of the domestic branch of the State Security Agency.

On this basis, the commission found that, unless Zuma could provide a satisfactory answer otherwise, 'a finding that he was in dereliction of his constitutional duty in terms of [section] 195 of the Constitution in regard to the Mbalula matter would seem to be justified'. Section 195, in broad terms, requires that government is conducted in fulfilment of democratic values and with a high degree of professional ethics.

# The role of Duduzane Zuma in state capture

DUDUZANE ZUMA LURKS throughout the pages of the commission's reports; sitting in various meetings, mute, while one or other Gupta brother does his dirty work. In these fleeting moments he feels a bit like a ghost, incorporeal and not particularly influential. This feeling, however, dissipates when the fullness of the evidence involving Duduzane is set out in a single conspectus.

The commission began by looking at the publicly available evidence. It showed that Duduzane worked for several years at Sahara Computers, eventually becoming a director. He was appointed to the board of Mabengela Investments, a Gupta company, in August 2008. He was 26 at the time. He became a director of a further 11 Gupta companies over the next year and a half. Duduzane owned a 25% share in Mabangela, which was gifted to him in July 2008. He was given a further 20% share in 2009. Mabangela was the vehicle through which Duduzane purchased a R4m home in Saxonwold 600 metres from the Guptas' Saxonwold compound.

Importantly, Duduzane was a director or shareholder (both direct and indirect) in a number of companies that I identified as receiving state capture benefits in my own evidence before the commission, which the commission now cited. Duduzane had direct or indirect stakes in Westdawn Investments, Shiva Uranium, Tegeta Exploration and Resources, and VR Laser. He further sat on the boards of other Gupta companies that received state capture cash, including Sahara,

Westdawn, Shiva Uranium and Islandsite Investments.

Both Jacob Zuma and Duduzane testified to the long and close relationship between Duduzane and the Guptas. Duduzane claimed that Tony Gupta, in particular, was 'a very dear and close friend' and, 'more than particularly close, that is my guy'. They spent loads of time together, often on a daily basis. Jacob Zuma confirmed that the Guptas had helped Duduzane during JZ's period in the political wilderness. JZ claimed that nobody would employ Duduzane in the period before JZ was elected president of the ANC.

The commission then ran through all the evidence implicating Duduzane in key moments of state capture, which I've summarised in the accompanying table.

| Site of capture | Duduzane's involvement |
|---|---|
| National Treasury | Mcebisi Jonas testified that he was offered a bribe and the position of Minister of Finance in a meeting with Tony Gupta at Saxonwold. Jonas was brought to the meeting by Duduzane, who also sat in on the meeting. |
| | Nhlanhla Nene testified that he was removed as Minister of Finance because he opposed various deals, including the nuclear deal. Duduzane would have benefited from the nuclear deal as a shareholder in Shiva Uranium. Shiva Uranium was bought by Oakbay using a loan granted to it by the Industrial Development Corporation (IDC). The commission quoted my calculations showing that the IDC loan was repaid, in part, through money linked to state capture. |
| | Duduzane's bank accounts were closed alongside the Gupta accounts in 2015/16; the efforts that Cabinet went to, particularly those of Mosebenzi Zwane, to 'improperly intervene' on the closures would have helped Duduzane. |

| Site of capture | Duduzane's involvement |
|---|---|
| Free State | Mxolisi Dukoana testified that Tony Gupta offered him a bribe at a meeting in Saxonwold. Duduzane was present. |
| Department of Mineral Resources | Susan Shabangu, the Minister for Minerals and Energy, deposed a statement to the commission. She claimed that Duduzane arranged a meeting with her, which he attended with Tony Gupta. At a subsequent meeting with the two, Tony Gupta asked Shabangu to pressure a mining company, Lonmin, to make the Guptas their BEE partner. Shabangu reported the matter to Essop Pahad.<br><br>Ngoako Ramatlhodi testified that, after his appointment as minister, Duduzane repeatedly tried to get him to meet the Guptas. Ramatlhodi was asked to assist with a 'stop order' that the department had placed that stopped work on a Gupta mine. Ramatlhodi refused; Duduzane denied this evidence.<br><br>On 31 July 2015, Mosebenzi Zwane and Tony Gupta were in contact. On the same day, businessman France Oupa Mokoena emailed a copy of Zwane's CV to Tony Gupta, who forwarded it to Duduzane on 1 August 2015. Zwane was appointed as Minister of Mineral Resources the following month. The commission found Zwane was appointed at the behest of the Guptas. |

| Site of capture | Duduzane's involvement |
|---|---|
| SAA | Vuyisile Kona, CEO of SAA at the time, testified that he was brought to a meeting in Saxonwold in 2012 by Siyabonga Mahlangu, the advisor to Malusi Gigaba. Kona testified that Tony Gupta offered him a bribe to get a turn-around contract for SAA. Duduzane and Tshepiso Magashule (the son of Ace Magashule) were present, according to Kona. |
| Transnet | Mafika Mkwanazi, chair of Transnet, testified he was invited to meet at Saxonwold in 2011. The Guptas started by emphasising their relationship with Jacob Zuma. They then asked Transnet to divert 30%–50% of their advertising to *The New Age*. Duduzane was present at the meeting. Mkwanazi testified that Duduzane confirmed the relationship between JZ and the Gupas, but was otherwise quiet. |
| Denel | Riaz Saloojee, then CEO of Denel, testified that he was invited to a series of meetings in Saxonwold by Salim Essa in 2012. He met with Tony Gupta. Duduzane and one of Ace Magashule's sons were present in one meeting where Tony Gupta suggested that the Guptas could help Denel break into the Asian defence market.<br><br>Duduzane was an indirect shareholder in VR Laser with Tony Gupta via Westdawn Investments. VR Laser was partly owned by a Salim Essa company. The commission found that Denel designed sole supplier contracts for the benefit of VR Laser.<br><br>Travel Excellence, the travel agent used by the Guptas, invoiced Westdawn for flights to Dubai in 2015 for Duduzane Zuma, his wife and Daniel Mantsha, then the Chair of Denel. |

| Site of capture | Duduzane's involvement |
| --- | --- |
| Eskom | Duduzane was an indirect shareholder in Tegeta via his shares in Westdawn. Funds from the capture of Eskom were used to assist Tegeta buy Optimum coal mine.<br><br>Collin Matjila was appointed acting GCEO in April 2014. This happened days after his CV had been sent by Essa to Tony Gupta and then to Duduzane. The commission found that Matjila facilitated capture at Eskom, and so Duduzane 'can therefore be linked to Mr Matjila's appointment, and the capture of Eskom'. |
| Department of Public Enterprises | Malusi Gigaba made regular visits to Saxonwold. Gigaba's special advisor, Siyabonga Mahlangu, travelled to a Gupta wedding in India with Duduzane. The trip was paid for by Sahara. Tony Gupta and Duduzane met with Mahlangu on a number of occasions.<br><br>Richard Seleke was appointed director general at the DPE after he had sent his CV to Essa's infoportal email address, which was then forwarded to Duduzane. |
| Communications and SABC | General Siphiwe Nyanda testified that Duduzane tried to arrange meetings with the Guptas, but Nyanda refused.<br><br>Lulama Mokhobo testified that after she was appointed GCEO of SABC, Hlaudi Motsoeneng took her to Saxonwold. The Guptas expressed their desire to start a news channel on SABC's network. Duduzane was present at the meeting.<br><br>Former Minister of Communications Faith Muthambi shared confidential information via email with Duduzane, Tony Gupta and Ashu Chawla in 2014. |

| Site of capture | Duduzane's involvement |
|---|---|
| PRASA | Lucky Montana, the CEO of PRASA, testified that he met with Minister Ben Martins. Tony Gupta and Duduzane joined the meeting. Tony Gupta tried to influence the award of the rolling stock renewal programme. |
| Law Enforcement | General Johan Booysen testified that Duduzane took him to Saxonwold to meet the Guptas ahead of Booysen's interview to become head of the Hawks. Booysen testified that he believed the purpose of the meeting was to show that, if he was chosen, the Guptas had a hand in his appointment. Duduzane denied this version. |
| ANN7 | Rajesh Sundaram, who wrote a tell-all book about the creation of ANN7, claimed that Duduzane owned about a third of ANN7. |

The commission also addressed one of the disturbing parts of the state capture experience: the role of the UK PR firm Bell Pottinger. The commission noted that it was Duduzane who had originally approached Bell Pottinger to help with the Guptas' PR. The result of this was the creation of Pottinger's lamentable astro-turfing campaign that claimed that allegations of corruption against the Guptas were part of counter-revolutionary agenda pursued by white monopoly capital. Duduzane also helped Mosebenzi Zwane answer media questions, alongside Nazeem Howa and others.

Finally, the commission reviewed what was revealed by the GuptaLeaks. The GuptaLeaks indicated that the Guptas planned and paid for Duduzane's wedding, as well as for other trips and holidays. They also showed that, in 2014, Duduzane travelled to India with Salim Essa and Malcolm Mabaso, the special advisor to Mosebenzi Zwane and one of Des van Rooyen's 'unofficial' advisors during his weekend stint as Minister of Finance. Finally, in late 2015 and early 2016, Duduzane travelled to Dubai alongside a number of other guests, all of whom stayed at the Oberoi Hotel. Among those present were Salim Essa, Fana Hlongwane, Gift and Tshepiso Magashule,

Ayanda Dlodlo, Anoj Singh, Des van Rooyen, Tom Moyane, Daniel Mantsha, Siyabonga Gama and Matshela Koko.

The commission, after reviewing this evidence, thus concluded that Duduzane Zuma

> was a shareholder in several Gupta-related companies and thereby stood to gain financially from contracts awarded to those companies. In some instances, Mr D Zuma appears to have taken part in the decision-making that would lead to the award of those contracts by SOEs to the Gupta-linked companies.
>
> Mr D Zuma also seems to have been involved in the appointment of key individuals in SOEs, who in turn facilitated the capture of those SOEs. He also seems to have acted as a conduit between the Guptas and government, particularly his father, Mr JG Zuma. In several cases, Mr D Zuma was present when bribes were offered to individuals at the Guptas' Saxonwold residence.

## RECOMMENDATION

*Law enforcement agencies should conduct investigations to establish if Duduzane Zuma may have facilitated bribes or failing to report corruption that happened in his presence when Tony Gupta offered bribes to Mcebisi Jonas, Mxolisi Dukoana and Vusi Kona.*

# The case against Gigaba

WHEN THE COMMISSION FIRST published its final volume of factual findings, it appears to have lopped off one of the most interesting sections: the evidence against Malusi Gigaba testified to by his ex-wife, Nomachule Mngoma. This was only rectified in October 2022, when a new and updated version of part 6, volume 3 was published, which has slipped somewhat under the radar: more's the pity, considering how combustible the evidence was.

Ms Nomachule Mngoma first met Malusi Gigaba in 2009. At the time, Gigaba was the Deputy Minister of Home Affairs. They moved in together in the same year, and married in August 2014. Mngoma claimed that, during this period, Gigaba provided her with a credit card, but instructed her to spend no more than R100,000 per month.

Mngoma's evidence painted a lurid picture of her ex-husband's relationship with the Guptas. She claimed that Gigaba regularly visited the Guptas after he was appointed Minister of Public Enterprises. Gigaba referred to them as his 'advisors'. She met the Guptas in person in 2011, during which meeting Ajay gave a gold necklace to her son. She continued to visit the compound with Gigaba throughout 2012. They also attended the Sun City wedding, although they ended up leaving at midnight due to the extremely negative publicity. Thamsanqa Msomi and Siyabonga Mahlangu (Gigaba's chief of staff and special advisor respectively) were often at the compound when they visited, as was Duduzane. In total, she estimated that she visited the Gupta compound with Gigaba at least 20 times between 2011 and 2014.

She testified that, from 2014 onwards, Gigaba's relationship with the Guptas cooled, as did his relationship with Dudu Myeni. Gigaba allegedly told her that this was the reason why he was effectively demoted from the position of Minister of Finance to Minister of Home Affairs.

Mngoma claimed Gigaba was also loose-lipped when it came to SOE appointments. He informed her ahead of time of Molefe's move from Transnet to Eskom, and that the move was prompted because the Guptas wanted to replace the erstwhile CEO, Brian Dames, who was not playing ball with the Guptas. He also allegedly told her about Siyabonga Gama's imminent return to Transnet Freight Rail, which he supported.

Perhaps not coincidentally, Mngoma claimed that Gigaba had told her that he intended to approach Gama to get his sister Gugu Gigaba employed at Transnet. She was subsequently employed at Transnet and remained employed there at the time of the commission's final report. Mngoma claimed that, in addition to this interaction, Gigaba had helped his sister Nozipho during a period when she was in financial straits. Mngoma testified that Nozipho lived with them for a time in Pretoria, at which point she was employed by Sahara. Gigaba denied that he had any role in securing this employment, which the commission rejected as implausible.

Mngoma also testified that Gigaba had received benefits from the Guptas. This included a white BMW that was given to Gigaba by Ajay Gupta at the Sahara offices; the car was then given for her use. The commission was, however, unable to verify the existence of the car. She also claimed that, while the Guptas did not attend the Gigabas' 2014 wedding, they made a cash donation towards the cost of the wedding and their honeymoon in Dubai. Other 'donations' identified by Mngoma included a payment of R425,000 to help pay off the debts of Gigaba's sister, cash given to Gigaba by the Guptas used to pay school fees, and cash given to Gigaba to pay for renovations to his father's home in KZN.

Gigaba, she further alleged, had carried a leather bag into and out of the private meetings at the Saxonwold compound, which would be put into his boot by private protection staff. She claimed to have seen Gigaba removing cash from this bag to transfer it into a smaller shoulder bag during a shopping trip to Sandton City. She also claimed to have interrupted Gigaba while unpacking bundles of cash from the bag into a safe in his study.

Gigaba denied everything, putting up a totally different version. He also pointed out that Mngoma was testifying in the context of their separation and divorce. He claimed that she had used her potential appearance at the commission as leverage during divorce settlement proceedings.

The commission was wary of aspects of Mngoma's evidence. On certain occasions, she had testified to matters that could not be corroborated, and had deposed to certain issues on oath 'without paying proper attention to the contents'. As a result, the commission decided to foreground and focus on the 'one area of commonality' in their two versions: both Gigaba and Mngoma testified and confirmed that Gigaba had a long-standing association with the Guptas and was particularly friendly with Ajay Gupta.

Gigaba's own admissions had to be seen in the light of an important piece of context. In 2019, the legal and audit firm Fundudzi investigated wrongdoing at Transnet. In his interview with Fundudzi investigators, Gigaba claimed that he had no relationship with the Guptas. 'The fact that he chose to cover this up in 2019 is telling,' the commission commented. Gigaba had also denied that he travelled to the Saxonwold compound for anything other than cultural and social events; Mngoma's evidence suggested otherwise and, most importantly, was corroborated by Riaz Saloojee, the Denel CEO, who testified to Gigaba's presence at a meeting in Saxonwold.

Mmgoma's evidence also received a degree of support – although not total corroboration – from Witness 3. As I discussed in the chapter on Transnet, Witness 3 was Gigaba's close protection officer who testified to handling cash on behalf of Gigaba; on this basis the commission believed there were reasonable grounds to suspect that Gigaba had received cash payments at the Saxonwold compound. That another witness alleged this fact was 'sufficiently corroborative to at least give rise to a reasonable suspicion that Gigaba received cash' from the Guptas on two occasions.

So, in two instances at least, the commission found it was likely that Gigaba *had* received benefits from the Guptas: the first was their employment of Gigaba's sister at Sahara Computers, which it found was done as a favour to Gigaba, and the cash payments that were made to him in person.

Mngoma's evidence of Gigaba's relationship with the Guptas was, in essence, that Gigaba had been captured by the Guptas. On this, the commission could not agree more. The commission recounted ten different situations or incidents in which Gigaba was involved, as Minister of Public Enterprises, in decisions that benefited the Gupta enterprise. These examples included the appointment of Collin Matjila to the board of Eskom, of Gupta nominee Dr Rajesh Naithani to the board of SAA, of Salim Essa to Broadband Infraco, and of Iqbal Sharma as a board member of Transnet (and his ill-fated attempt to get Sharma appointed chairperson).

## RECOMMENDATIONS

*Law enforcement should investigate Gigaba's receipt of cash from the Gupta residence under PRECCA and POCA, based on the evidence of Witness 3 and Mngoma.*

*Law enforcement should investigate Gigaba for corruption under PRECCA and/or racketeering under POCA related to the employment of his sister Nozipho Gigaba by Sahara Computers in 2013.*

*Law enforcement should investigate Gigaba for corruption under PRECCA and/or racketeering under POCA to determine whether:*

- *the Guptas contributed cash to the costs of the Gigaba wedding in 2014;*
- *the Guptas paid for the honeymoon trip of Malusi Gigaba and Mngoma to Dubai in 2014/2015;*
- *the Guptas gave cash to Gigaba to assist pay for renovations to Gigaba's father's home in KZN;*
- *the Guptas gave R425,000 or more to settle the debts of Malusi Gigaba's sister Nozipho;*
- *Ajay Gupta gave Gigaba two watches during trips to Dubai;*
- *the cash Gigaba received from the Guptas was used to settle his children's school fees.*

# EOH and the City of Johannesburg

THE COMMISSION'S HEARINGS on EOH were unique. EOH, an information and communications technology company, proactively approached the commission to set out how its previous management had secured contracts through seeming corruption. The evidence was largely presented by Stephen van Coller, the CEO of EOH since 2018. He spearheaded a process by which EOH appointed forensic investigators, ENS Forensics, to probe its previous state contracts, so as to make this information available to law enforcement agencies and the commission.

## EOH, Jehan Mackay and Geoff Makhubo

In 2011, EOH acquired a company called Tactical Software Solutions Managed Services (TSS Managed Services). Prior to the acquisition, the company was owned by Jehan Mackay and his father, Danny Mackay. Jehan served as the managing director of TSS Managed Services and continued in a senior role after TSS Managed Services was acquired by EOH. In this capacity he worked closely with Patrick Makhubedu, who was also employed by TSS prior to 2011 as the business development director. Makhebedu moved from TSS to EOH as an employee in 2014.

Makhubedu shared a close personal relationship with Geoff Makhubo, who acted as the regional treasurer for the ANC in Greater Johannesburg until his appointment as regional leader in

2018. From 2011, and while acting as treasurer general, Makhubo served as the member of the mayoralty committee (MMC) for finance at the Johannesburg municipality under the mayoral leadership of Parks Tau. He became mayor of Johannesburg in 2018. Makhubo passed away from complications related to Covid-19 in 2021.

In 2009, and thus prior to its acquisition by EOH, TSS Managed Services entered into a 'teaming arrangement' with the company Molelwane Consulting CC, which was owned by Geoff Makhubo and his mother. At the time, Makhubo was not a City of Johannesburg employee. According to the commission's report, the 'teaming arrangement' envisaged that Molelwane would provide a set of vague and undefined services such as business advisory and development services. The 'teaming arrangement' remained in place after EOH's acquisition of TSS Managed Services.

During the period of the 'teaming arrangement', EOH was awarded two contracts by the City of Johannesburg. The first, valued at R26m, was awarded to the EOH subsidiary EOH Mthombo in December 2010 and was supposed to run until November 2012, during which period Makhubo became MMC for finance. However, the contract was irregularly extended on a number of occasions.

The second was awarded to EOH Mthombo for the provision of SAP support services for a four-year period between 2012 and February 2016; this contract was also extended on a number of occasions. According to the commission, evidence was presented showing that Makhubo had played a key role in ensuring that the contract was not re-advertised once it expired.

EOH made a number of payments to third parties, which performed no discernible services, in relation to this contract. Most importantly, EOH paid Molelwane, Makhubo's company, R1.25m in 2012.

## The two big contracts

The commission delved deeply into two further contracts awarded to EOH. The first was a 2014 contract with TSS Managed Services to supply network and security infrastructure upgrades. This contract emanated from an unsolicited proposal sent by EOH to the City of Johannesburg on 16 April 2014. EOH quoted a cost estimate of R106,185,39.36 (including VAT).

On the very same day that EOH made the unsolicited proposal,

EOH donated R3m to the Greater Johannesburg Region of the ANC. Makhubo, as treasurer, wrote to his friend Patrick Makhubedu, now employed at EOH, to acknowledge the donation. Four months later, in August 2014, Makhubo emailed Makhubedu, asking for a donation towards accommodation costs for a regional ANC Youth League event. TSS Managed Services made the donation the day after the request, transferring R582,100 into the account of the ANC's Greater Johannesburg Region.

The day after this generous donation, Makhubo wrote to Jehan Mackay asking for even more money, this time to cover various expenses equalling R6,180,000. Just less than two weeks later, Makhubedu transferred R20,527.30 to the Sandton Convention Centre to pay an ANC bill. The payment was made by a company called Prime Molecular, of which Makhubedu was the director. Two days later, another company called Mfundi Mobile, transferred R70,000 to the ANC. Mfundi Mobile was controlled by Reno Barry, a former employee of TSS, who worked with Makhubedu. The latter sent proof of payment to Makhubo.

Mfundi Mobile made two notable payments to Molelwane, Makhubo's company, during this period. First, it paid R80,000 to Molelwane on the same day it had made its R70,000 donation to the ANC. Later in the same month, Mfundi paid a further R1.2m to Molelwane. This payment corresponded exactly with a 'special invoice' that Mfundi had issued to EOH in June 2014, suggesting that Molelwane was in effect paid by EOH.

At the end of August 2014, after this flurry of payments, Makhubedu sent the unsolicited proposal which it had first submitted in April 2014, directly to Makhubo. Makhubo had no role in procurement in his position at the City of Johannesburg. When he was asked why he received the proposal when officially he had nothing to do with procurement, Makhobo was unable to explain himself.

Two days later, on 29 August 2014, Makhubedu emailed Makhubo an invoice on a TSS Managed Services letterhead. This was for R106,185,395.83, the amount included in EOH's original unsolicited proposal. Makhubo was again unable to explain why he was sent the invoice. Two days later, on 1 September 2014, at the instruction of Makhubedu, a further R100,000 was transferred by

Reno Barry to Molelwane. Eight days later, on 9 September 2014, Makhubedu emailed Makhubo to remind him of the donations made by EOH to the ANC. These donations included R151,000 paid on 11 November 2013; R2m paid on 13 December 2013; and R3m paid in April 2014 (discussed above), which was made on the same day as the unsolicited proposal. Three days later, on 12 September 2014, the City of Johannesburg issued an order for the immediate payment of R109,737,278.52 to TSS Managed Services (approximately R3m more than the original unsolicited proposal). Three days later, Prime Molecular, of which Makhubedu was a director, paid R70,000 to Molelwane.

Remarkably, on the same day Molecular paid Molelwane, Makhubedu sent a draft letter of award to Makhubo, which informed TSS that it was successful in its bid. So Makhubedu and TSS literally wrote the letter through which it was awarded the contract, and this was distributed after the City of Johannesburg had already issued its payment order.

Further correspondence, payments and donations took place throughout September. On 18 September, when Makhubedu was scheduled to meet Geoff Makhubo, he forwarded a request for a R300,000 donation for the Tshwane branch of the ANC. On 20 September, a further R570,000 was paid to Molelwane. And on 2 October 2014, following a request made by Makhubo to Makhubedu in September 2014, TSS Managed Services paid R1.5m into the account of the ANC's Greater Johannesburg Region.

Based on this evidence, the commission found that 'Mr Makubhedu, Mr Barry and Mr Makhubo conspired to procure the improper acceptance by the City of the 16 April 2014 unsolicited proposal from TSS Managed Services ... to the value of R100m'. The commission recommended that law enforcement investigate the award of the contract.

The second contract related to an upgrade of SAP services, which was awarded to EOH Mthombo on 2 June 2016. The award letter stipulated the aggregate contract price of R404m. As with the first contract, the award was preceded and then followed by a flurry of correspondence, donations and payments. The correspondence included repeated reference to meetings held by senior EOH staff and Geoff Makhubo. It also included a coded euphemism, included in an email written by a senior employee, Ebrahim Laher, of the need to make a payment to the ANC for 'goodwill :)'.

During the period between the advertisement of the tender and its award, EOH made a number of payments to Makhubo's Molelwane, despite there being no evidence of any work done. The payments included:

a.  R200,000 paid on 1 February 2016 by Mfundi to Molelwane;
b.  R50,000 on 25 April 2016 from Mfundi to Molelwane;
c.  R570,000 paid to Molelwane pursuant to a R500,000 (excluding VAT) invoice sent by Molelwane to TSS Managed Services. Of this amount, R200,000 was transferred into Makhubo's personal account.

In the weeks after the contract was awarded to EOH, two notable payments or donations were made to the ANC. The first was an order of R204,095 worth of computer equipment which was placed by EOH for its own divisions, though it was delivered to the ANC Greater Johannesburg Region for the attention of 'Geoff'. The delivery instruction included Makhubo's phone number. The second donation was made via Mfundi, which invoiced EOH for R16m in July 2016. After this amount was paid to Mfundi by EOH, Mfundi transferred R15,439,068 to pay for the election expenses incurred by the ANC Greater Johannesburg Region.

In addition to this, EOH also issued a purchase order worth R512,000 to Serendipity Tours. The payment was made in respect of a project run by the wife of the mayor of Johannesburg at the time, Parks Tau, which involved sending learners to New York.

The commission, unsurprisingly, found that there was good evidence that Makhubedu, Makhubo, Barry, Jehan Mackay, Ebrahim Laher and Nyiko Mutileni (another EOH employee) had conspired to procure the award of the contract to EOH Mthombo. It recommended further investigations by law enforcement.

## Payments to Zizi Kodwa

EOH's evidence included details of how ANC spokesman Zizi Kodwa was paid R1.68m by EOH-related entities and Jehan Mackay. This included a payment of R1m to assist Kodwa to buy a Jeep, and payments for luxury accommodation. Kodwa, at the time, was not a government employee but an employee of the ANC. Jehan Mackay and his PA also sent multiple emails to Kodwa inviting him to ask for donations from EOH or otherwise asking for his advice on various ANC donations.

The commission found that Mackay was 'attempting to buy influence' by making 'loans' to Kodwa and providing him with luxury accommodation. Mackay's emails show that he repeatedly reached out to Kodwa about tenders that EOH was interested in. The commission was, however, ultimately unable to investigate what Kodwa may or may not have done. So while it acknowledged that it was eminently plausible that a senior ANC official could induce his colleagues in government to swing contracts certain ways, it could not make a definitive finding in this regard.

Nevertheless, the commission noted that Kodwa was in an 'impossible position'. In 2021, he was appointed the Deputy Minister of State Security, a position he still held at the time of the commission's report and at the time of my writing this book. The commission noted that, if the payments to Kodwa by Mackay were indeed loans, he was now beholden to an individual who the commission had recommended face multiple criminal investigations. On this basis, the commission urged President Ramaphosa to revisit Kodwa's appointment.

## RECOMMENDATIONS

*Law enforcement should investigate the network and security infrastructure contract awarded to TSS Managed Services and the SAP upgrade contract awarded to EOH Mthombo. The investigations should be conducted with a view to the prosecution of Patrick Makhubedu, Reno Barry, Jehan Mackay, Ebrahim Laher and/or any other implicated EOH employee, for violations of PRECCA.*

*Law enforcement should investigate Jehan Mackay in relation to his payments to Zizi Kodwa and his attempts to procure Kodwa's assistance in tenders.*

*President Cyril Ramaphosa should consider Kodwa's position as Deputy Minister of State Security in the light of the revelation of payments made to him by Jehan Mackay.*

# PART SEVEN

# President, Party, Parliament

*State capture was a process rather than a single event. Indeed, as the commission would find in reviewing the totality of the evidence, state capture was a 'political project' that set out to control the levers of state power both to enrich its participants and to consolidate political power in furtherance of this scheme. In this context, the commission sought to investigate how state capture was allowed to happen and, in particular, what Cyril Ramaphosa, the ANC and Parliament did to halt the extraordinary corruption of the Zuma era. Its findings are set out in three reports, dealt with in this section. The first focused on Ramaphosa, both in his role as Deputy President and President of the country and in his role within the ANC. The second addressed the role and contribution of the ANC to state capture. The third and final report considered the role of Parliament.*

# Ramaphosa as Deputy President and President of South Africa

As MOST READERS OF this book will know, Cyril Ramaphosa was appointed Deputy President of the country on 25 May 2014 following the elections that year. He served in this position until Jacob Zuma's resignation as President in February 2018, whereafter Ramaphosa was elected unopposed to become President on 15 February 2018. He has held that position ever since.

Ramaphosa thus held the second most powerful position in the country – at least on paper – during the egregious final term of Jacob Zuma's Presidency – precisely when state capture was both flourishing and, importantly, coming to the attention of the South African public. What, then, did Ramaphosa, who has spoken repeatedly about the need to fight corruption, do about it?

The commission deposed Ramaphosa over multiple days to get answers to these questions. Somewhat artificially, the commission split its discussion of Ramaphosa's experiences and responses in two: first, in his position as Deputy President (and then President) of the country and, second, in his position as deputy president (and then president) of the ANC.

The commission's report on Ramaphosa's role in the ANC covered much the same ground traversed in a further report discussing the role of the ANC in state capture in general terms. To prevent duplication, I have decided to combine and interweave the commission's two discussions of Ramaphosa's role as ANC president and the role of the ANC at large.

## When and how Ramaphosa became aware of state capture

Ramaphosa's evidence was clear: state capture definitely occurred during the Presidency of Jacob Zuma. State capture, on his version, was defined by a number of key features; it was organised, facilitated by the protection of wrongdoers, and enabled by the appointment of 'certain people' to key positions where they colluded with those inside and outside the state to 'syphon' as much money from the state as possible.

Despite this clear acceptance of the existence of state capture, Ramaphosa claimed to know only as much as the general public. He testified that he found out about state capture through investigative reporting, the results of investigations by Chapter 9 institutions (such as the Public Protector), numerous court cases, the versions put forward by whistleblowers, and, of course, the GuptaLeaks.

Ramaphosa noted three 'signposts' along the way that should have served as a warning that state capture was occurring, in particular the removal of Nhlanhla Nene and then Pravin Gordhan, and the manner in which Cabinet went to bat for the Guptas over the closure of their bank accounts. Nevertheless, he maintained that the overall pattern was not clear and that those involved in state capture 'hid their machinations', which meant that he and others failed to 'join the dots'.

The commission, in evaluating Ramaphosa's evidence, was distinctly unimpressed by this view. It noted that since at least 2010, media reports had started to reveal the motives and means of the Gupta enterprise. Ramaphosa, in his evidence, failed to properly explain when he began to believe that the media articles pointed to valid concerns and what the tipping point was.

The commission, however, was not going to let Ramaphosa get away with claiming ignorance as a defence. Instead, it questioned whether Ramaphosa *ought* to have known about it: 'The wealth of evidence before this Commission suggests that the answer is yes. There was surely enough credible information in the public domain, long before December 2015, to at least prompt him to inquire and perhaps act on a number of serious allegations. As the Deputy President, he surely had the responsibility to do so.'

## Ramaphosa's strategy to resist state capture

Ramaphosa testified that, confronted with the corruption of the Zuma era, he had five options: resign, speak out, acquiesce and abet, remain and keep silent, and remain and resist. He was morally opposed to acquiescing and remaining silent. If he resigned, Ramaphosa claimed, he would be unable to stop state capture from the inside. And yet, if he was confrontational, he believed he would have been removed. As a result, he took the option of remaining and resisting where possible behind closed doors.

The commission was struck by the fact that Ramaphosa would not be drawn on precisely who would fire him, although it noted that, realistically, it was only Jacob Zuma who would have had the power to do so. It also drew the inference that Ramaphosa must have believed that, if he was fired, the ANC would not protect him.

Ramaphosa also noted that the extent of his resistance was curtailed by the political realities of the time; that the 'balances of forces' in the government and ANC were a constraining factor. His decision, therefore, to remain so that he could run for president of the ANC (and then the country) was part of a process whereby he could shift these 'balance of forces'.

Ramaphosa cited three moments when he resisted state capture, which he also cited as examples of how his strategy bore fruit. The first related to the firing of Nhlanhla Nene and the appointment of Des van Rooyen. According to Ramaphosa's version, he was not consulted by Jacob Zuma about the decision to fire Nene and appoint Van Rooyen, nor were the 'Top 6' of the ANC. Ramaphosa speculated that it was Nene's resistance to the nuclear deal that led to his removal. He further claimed that Nene's removal signalled to him that 'the process of state capture had now succeeded to an extent that the most strategic organ of the state, Treasury, had now been captured'.

Shortly after Van Rooyen's appointment, Ramaphosa was contacted by Lungisa Fuzile, the long-serving director general of the National Treasury, who asked to meet him urgently. Fuzile was extremely concerned about Van Rooyen's arrival and the two advisors he had appointed – both of whom, as it turned out, had strong Gupta links. Fuzile's warnings, combined with the extremely negative response of the capital markets, prompted Ramaphosa to act.

Ramaphosa met with Jessie Duarte, the deputy secretary general of the ANC. Ramaphosa said that he would resign unless something was done; Duarte apparently conveyed this to Zuma. Following a 'flurry of consultations', Ramaphosa, according to his own version, went with Duarte and Gwede Mantashe, the secretary general of the ANC, to meet with Zuma. There was some confusion as to whether Mantashe attended this meeting – Ramaphosa testified that he was there, but this was not mentioned in Mantashe's evidence. In any event, Ramaphosa and Duarte, at the very least, told Zuma that he needed to appoint Pravin Gordhan in order to calm the markets.

The second act of resistance took place when Pravin Gordhan and Nhlanhle Nene were removed as Minister and Deputy Minister of Finance in March 2017. Ramaphosa testified that, prior to their removal, the President met with ANC officials including Ramaphosa. Zuma indicated that his relationship with Gordhan had deteriorated and he wanted to remove him. Zuma also presented a three-page 'intelligence' report – 'Operation Checkmate' – that claimed that Gordhan and Nene were conspiring against the South African government. Ramaphosa recalled that the document was a 'photographed piece of paper', written in large font and 'very badly drafted'.

Ramaphosa claims that he told Zuma that he disagreed with him on his reasoning to remove Gordhan and Nene, and would make this known publicly. Ramaphosa did, indeed, make his objection known publicly, in an interview he gave on 31 March 2017. Asked about the decision to remove Gordhan, Ramaphosa responded: 'I think it is totally unacceptable that he fired someone like Gordhan, who has served the country excellently, for his own gain and survival.' In another interview, Ramaphosa said he would not resign as Deputy President, but that he had made his views known, along with other ANC members.

But the key act of resistance, according to Ramaphosa, was when Zuma suggested appointing Brian Molefe as the new Minister of Finance. Ramaphosa and other ANC officials, he recalled, resisted the suggestion, saying that Molefe did not have the right 'profile' and pointing to how he had recently left Eskom in ignominious circumstances. Zuma, instead, appointed Malusi Gigaba.

The third and final act of resistance cited by Ramaphosa centred on Cabinet's response to the closure of the Guptas' bank accounts in April 2016. Ramaphosa provided a detailed account of the way in which Cabinet handled the issue. On 2 June 2016, Cabinet held a meeting, chaired by Ramaphosa, in which the issue was discussed. During the meeting, Mosebenzi Zwane submitted a memorandum that suggested a commission of inquiry be established to investigate the banks. Ramaphosa claims that he rejected this, saying that 'it would be wholly inappropriate for a commission of inquiry to be established for the purpose of addressing unique challenges faced by one private company in the banking sector'.

Ramaphosa's evidence did not identify other interventions on this issue although, in his oral evidence before the commission, he testified that he and others pushed back to prevent the appointment of a commission of inquiry into the banks:

> The view was [to] set up a commission of inquiry because there was collusion in the way [the banks] acted, without actually really proving it, and it was supposed to be a judicial commission of inquiry, and some of us said that will be the wrong thing to do, because immediately one of the strongest institutions we have in this country, in our economy, is one of the best banking systems in the world … So it looked like a sledgehammer was going to be used to kill a mosquito. So there was a very strong push, a strong thrust to help this commission, and we resisted that.

While largely accepting this version, the commission was nevertheless critical of Ramaphosa's further statement on the issue, in which he said he believed that Cabinet should merely have inquired as to the reasons for the account closure, rather than push for a commission of inquiry. The commission noted that this was problematic, as there was no seemingly good reason for Cabinet to get involved in this matter to assist the Guptas at all.

But was this resistance enough? The commission was of the view that it was not and, indeed, that Ramaphosa's reasoning for his strategic choices was flawed. The commission noted, with subtle acidity, that Ramaphosa's claim that he stayed in place in order to resist 'suffers from his inability to provide any further examples of his resistance', beyond these three moments. In addition, Ramaphosa's argument that he would be dismissed if he was too confrontational was not fully explained: '[Ramaphosa] did not provide any evidence as to why he believed this was the case. How did he arrive at this fifth option [to remain and resist]? Had he tried to act in some way against corruption and state capture and been rebuked? Had he seen others suffer the consequences from the former President?'

Moreover, Ramaphosa's evidence that he successfully resisted key moments of state capture actually undermined the argument in defence of his 'remain and resist' strategy. Following these interventions, the commission notes, '[Ramaphosa] was not dismissed and did not face any consequences for his action. It is difficult, then, to understand why other allegations in the public domain – in some cases made by loyal ANC members themselves – continued to go unaddressed so long.' The result was that the commission was unconvinced that Ramaphosa's strategy was successful or prudent: 'considering the dire straits we find ourselves in, the effectiveness of President Ramaphosa's decision to remain within the party and state is not a given'.

## Ramaphosa as President: Concerns about intelligence

Ramaphosa's evidence also covered his period as President. In his testimony Ramaphosa sought to burnish his credentials as an anti-corruption President. But the commission noted serious concerns about decisions that had been made under Ramaphosa's watch when it came to South Africa's out-of-control intelligence services.

Ramaphosa testified about the appointment of the High Level Review Panel into the State Security Agency. He noted that the panel's findings had been received by Cabinet and the response had included the appointment in 2020 of a Ministerial Task Team whose job was to 'unpack' the recommendations and turn them into concrete action, while investigations were ongoing to unravel the full extent of wrongdoing. Ramaphosa, on this basis, claimed that the implementation of the panel's recommendations was at an 'advanced stage'.

The commission, however, was perturbed by the derailing of Project Veza, which had been investigating the SSA, and the allegation that qualified investigators had been removed from the probe. It was extremely concerned that the investigation had been unduly curtailed and that evidence had been placed under 'lock and key' behind closed doors.

The commission put it to Ramaphosa that, in fact, the implementation of the High Level Review Panel's recommendations was not anywhere near an 'advanced stage', not least because the investigations premised on its recommendations had been halted. Ramaphosa's response – that the investigations would have to start again but they would build on previous work – clearly did not pass muster with the commission: 'Ultimately, far from being at an "advanced stage of completion", this evidence shows that the HLRP recommendations regarding internal investigations have come to a halt. The reason seems to be interference from the highest powers in the SSA and the Ministry. There appear to have been no consequences for this interference.'

The commission was also scathing of Ramaphosa's decision-making with regard to Arthur Fraser and David Mahlobo. The HLRP had made serious findings against Mahlobo, who oversaw the SSA at a time when it showed 'an almost complete disregard for the Constitution, policy, legislation and other prescripts'. The HLRP had also found it had 'more than enough information' to show that Mahlobo had 'involved himself directly in operations'. Serious findings were also made about Arthur Fraser and his management of the so-called PAN programme while he served as director general.

In both cases, however, Ramaphosa saw fit to appoint them to senior positions. Fraser was appointed as the director general of Correctional Services in April 2018 while Mahlobo was appointed as the Deputy Minister for Water, Sanitation and Housing in May 2019.

When both appointments were put to Ramaphosa, his answer was simply that he was awaiting the report of the commission before he acted. Judge Zondo pushed back on this during Ramaphosa's evidence. He explained that it was possible that the commission's findings might be taken on review, which could take years to resolve. This could then be used as an excuse or reason not to act on the commission's findings until they had been upheld by other courts. Ramaphosa remained steadfast, simply repeating that he would soon have the commission's reports in his hands, and would act accordingly.

The commission felt that this was a 'concerning statement':

Even if Mr Mahlobo and Mr Fraser have not been found guilty

of criminal offences, the state of the SSA under their leadership – which President Ramaphosa freely acknowledges is both dire and dangerous – is surely a reflection on their competence and integrity. It is therefore difficult to understand how they could reasonably be considered suitable for appointment to senior positions in the state.

# The role of the ANC in state capture

As I NOTED ABOVE, the commission dedicated an entire section of its report on Ramaphosa to discussing his behaviour within the ANC. This was followed in turn by a separate report on the role of the ANC in state capture more generally. But, because the second report on the role of the ANC drew heavily on Ramaphosa's own evidence, the two reports are remarkably repetitive. So I have opted to interweave the findings of the two reports here.

**What did the party do internally to fight state capture?**
Both Ramaphosa, wearing his hat as ANC deputy president and then president, and Gwede Mantashe, as ANC secretary general, maintained that there was no direct evidence of state capture until quite a late stage. The commission's rebuttal, which it also repeated during Ramaphosa's evidence as the country's President, was that media articles had been published since 2010 exposing the rot.

However, even when it became clear that things were going wrong, the ANC did not do nearly enough, according to the commission. This was illustrated in March 2016, when Mcebisi Jonas told the public about the Guptas' attempt to bribe him; this was followed by others, such as Barbara Hogan, Vytjie Mentor and Themba Maseko, coming forward to give their own version of events.

The response of the ANC's National Executive Committee (NEC), the highest decision-making body in the party, was to announce its intention to investigate the statements. It called on people with evidence to come forward to tell their story. In the end, only a single person was willing to put his or her version on paper. Mantashe, in his evidence, noted that some individuals feared that, if they did come forward with proper testimony, the only result would be a severe curtailing of their political career. The result was that, two months later, the ANC NEC tamely suggested that people with concerns should approach law enforcement or Chapter 9 institutions.

The commission was particularly critical of the way in which the ANC NEC announced this lacklustre investigation, which it found must have played a role in the way it failed. In the very same statement in which the investigation was announced, the ANC NEC stated that, while it condemned corruption, it had 'full confidence' in Jacob Zuma. The result was that 'this was not a neutral or independent space'.

The commission also highlighted the fact that Ramaphosa, at the time of the announcement of the investigation, stated that the ANC would conduct a 'methodical' investigation. This, of course, never happened. 'There is no evidence provided by either President Ramaphosa or Mr Mantashe that the ANC ever proactively sought to make even basic enquiries,' the commission found. 'The ANC collected complaints from members and did not do anything with them. That was the entirety of this process.'

Another key moment when the ANC opted to do nothing in the face of overwhelming evidence was the publication of Thuli Madonsela's *State of Capture* report in November 2016, which painted an utterly damning picture of Zuma's conduct. Despite this, the ANC NEC refused to call for Zuma to step down. Instead, the NEC stated that 'it was more urgent to direct the energies of the ANC in entirety towards working towards the unity of the movement'. The commission was damning in its assessment of this response: 'the implication of this statement is that the NEC decided to prioritise the survival and success of the party over acting on allegations of state capture'.

## What did the ANC do in Parliament?

The commission, in assessing the behaviour of the ANC's

parliamentary caucus (which was overseen by Ramaphosa during Zuma's Presidency), focused on two developments. The first was the party's response to the March 2016 revelations of Mcebisi Jonas and others. At the time, a motion was put forward by the Opposition calling for a full parliamentary investigation into the allegations. The ANC, however, resisted this call and, indeed, submitted a competing motion, which was carried with the ANC's majority. The ANC's motion rejected the call for a parliamentary inquiry and instead suggested that evidence of wrongdoing be handed over to law enforcement and Chapter 9 institutions.

The second issue the commission focused on was the multiple motions of no confidence in President Zuma, all of which were defeated (even after the Constitutional Court, in a landmark judgment, permitted MPs to cast their votes in secret). Ramaphosa was extensively probed about the failure of these votes and, in particular, the freedom MPs had to exercise their vote in line with their consciences. Ramaphosa testified that, because MPs served at the discretion of the party, they did not have a free vote: MPs had to submit to discipline and act in accordance with collective decisions.

The commission was unimpressed. It noted that MPs, upon being sworn in, were bound by an oath to act in the best interests of the country. Surely, the commission argued, MPs should be bound to this oath rather than the directions of a political party that might be compromised by its own corruption and inaction. Ramaphosa remained unmoved by this argument.

Mantashe was similarly doctrinaire on this issue. Indeed, when he was asked about the motions of no confidence, he rejected them as the 'ploys' of the Opposition. Attempts by the Opposition to remove a sitting President were 'mischief that we should resist all the time'. Mantashe also noted that the need to protect party unity was paramount at these moments; were any of the motions of no confidence successful, Mantashe argued, it would have split the party into warring factions.

The commission drew two implications from the evidence of Ramaphosa and Mantashe. The first was that, because MPs were not given free rein to exercise their conscience when it came to motions of no confidence, this important mechanism of accountability was rendered null and void. 'This means in effect that a President of a country can only be removed by Parliament through a motion of no confidence if the majority party has lost confidence in them already,' the commission commented. 'In that case, however, the Party can use its own processes to recall them.'

The second implication was that the ANC, as a party, did not properly respect the duties of MPs to put their country first. Thus, when Ramaphosa and Mantashe argued that the ANC might have split in the event of a successful motion of no confidence, the commission commented that 'the natural conclusion of this argument is that the ANC prioritises its own survival and strength over the Constitutional obligations of its members'.

As I'll discuss later, Parliament did, eventually, get its act together and start investigating state capture, but this was only done in 2017, long into Zuma's term, and most likely because of the imminent ANC elective conference in December 2017, which would see the downfall of the Zuma faction.

## The loyalty test: The ANC's Deployment Committee

By far the most in-depth and arguably most important section of the commission's report focused on the role of the ANC's Deployment Committee. The committee, briefly, is a body in the ANC that oversees appointments to senior positions in government. It is chaired by the deputy president of the ANC, and thus by Ramaphosa between 2012 and 2017.

In a jaw-dropping admission, the ANC claimed that it could find no minutes at all of the Deployment Committee while Ramaphosa served as its chair. Ramaphosa, when questioned about it, was not particularly helpful – he wasn't even sure if meetings were minuted. The commission was, however, provided with minutes of the committee subsequent to Ramaphosa's chairmanship.

Ramaphosa, in evidence, sought to downplay the importance and power of the Deployment Committee. His evidence was to the effect that the committee limited itself to appointments at the deputy director general and director general level and above. He also testified that the committee had no role in judicial appointments. But Ramaphosa was then confronted with minutes of the Deployment Committee showing that it had made two recommendations for appointment to the Constitutional Court and one to the Supreme Court. The commission, of course, was concerned that these recommendations would put undue pressure on the Judicial Services Commission, which is responsible for approving appointments to the bench.

Ramaphosa's response was a clumsy pivot: he argued that this was just a function of the ANC trying to transform the judiciary. But, if this argument was true, it implied that the ANC was involved in judicial appointments.

Both Ramaphosa and Mantashe argued that the Deployment Committee made recommendations only, and did not directly dictate appointments. In fact, Ramaphosa argued, it was not uncommon for ministers to approach the Deployment Committee to argue on behalf of specific individuals. Ramaphosa testified that this showed how the committee could work like a quality-assurance filter, ensuring the best candidate. The commission took a somewhat different view: ministers would hardly bother lobbying the Deployment Committee if its powers were only advisory. Clearly the committee's decisions were, in reality, central to the appointment of the most senior figures in government.

The commission's review of the minutes of the Deployment Committee – where they were available – clearly undercut the argument that the committee was only advisory. The minutes, on occasion, reflected how ministers approached the committee with recommendations which were then sent back for 'refinement'. In one case, the committee members complained that their recommendations were not being followed: an act of 'ill-discipline' that could not be countenanced.

The commission, on reviewing Mantashe's and Ramaphosa's evidence, as well as the minutes of Deployment Committee meetings, concluded that the real power for appointments lay within the party. Moreover, the Deployment Committee's findings were, in fact, binding on Cabinet. 'Its "recommendations" are in reality instructions,' the commission found.

The commission was perturbed by the Deployment Committee for two reasons. The first was that state capture was facilitated, at least in part, by the appointment of corrupt and unsuitable people to places of influence and, in particular, to the highest level of SOEs. If the Deployment Committee was involved in these appointments, it must therefore have been implicated in state capture, either through ignorance or design. In reviewing Ramaphosa's admission that unfit persons were appointed with the support of the committee, the commission was stinging in its criticism: 'His own admission, that the Committee had previously deployed unfit or corrupt individuals to positions of power, undermines his evidence in regard to the general integrity of the Deployment Committee and its acts. That the Committee did not prevent these appointments is an indictment of either its integrity or its ability, or both.'

The second reason was that the commission believed that the operation of the Deployment Committee was likely to be unlawful and unconstitutional. The Constitution is forthright and explicit about the need to create an unbiased and professional civil service. This is particularly true of section 197(3), which forbids any favouritism in the appointment of people to the civil service.

In addition, the Public Service Act (PSA) prescribes how appointments are to be made to the civil service. To understand the importance of this, one needs to understand the meaning of prescription. In non-legalese, if something is prescribed by law, it means that the law says that only those things being prescribed must be considered. So, if a law is passed about whose turn it is to make tea in a household, that law may prescribe that the only considerations are (a) who made the last cup and (b) who is closest to the kettle. The decision-makers in this instance would not be allowed to consider whose feet were the most sore, or who made the best or worst cup of tea.

The PSA states that any appointment that is not prescribed by the PSA is unlawful. So, simply put, all state appointments must abide by the PSA. Moreover, the PSA prescribes that appointments must have regard to constitutional principles. When the PSA and Constitution are read together, the commission argued, government appointments have to be made in such a way that there is equality in the treatment of candidates, as well as transparency, accountability, and fairness. The PSA further prescribes the specific criteria that should be used in determining appointments. Section 11(2)(b) thus prescribes that appointment decisions be 'based on training, skills, competence, knowledge and the need to redress the imbalances of the past to achieve a public service broadly representative of the South African people, including representation according to race, gender and disability'.

The Deployment Committee, the commission argued, fell foul of these principles. For example, it only reviewed the candidacy of ANC members; it also required that these ANC members be loyal to the party. Party loyalty, of course, is not prescribed by the Public Service Act, and should not play any role in appointments. In addition, the committee only considers a small handful of candidates. It does not review the quality of candidates who are not ANC members, nor does it conduct interviews with other candidates with whom the ANC candidate may be competing. The Deployment Committee's recommendations can't be relied upon as they are based on partial and limited information.

In a conclusion that could have profound implications for the governance of South Africa long into the future (if it is ever taken into account), the commission found:

> What is said above makes it clear that within the current constitutional and statutory framework it is unlawful and unconstitutional for a President of this country and any Minister, Deputy Minister or Director-General or other government official, including those in parastatals, to take into account recommendations of the ANC Deployment Committee or any deployment committee or any similar committee of any other political party in deciding who should be appointed to a position in the public service or in organs of state or parastals.

## The ANC's lack of internal discipline

The ANC's failure to tackle state capture at its highest levels, in Parliament, and in the Deployment Committee was mirrored in its total disregard for internal disciplinary proceedings.

The commission was provided with minutes of the ANC's National Disciplinary Committee and National Disciplinary Committee of Appeal from 2014 to 2021. They made for grim and unimpressive reading. All the cases that were referred to these committees related to organisational ill-discipline. In the entire period between 2014 and 2021, only two new cases were heard by the committees; most of the work of the committees consisted of appeals from provincial disciplinary committees about matters before 2014. The most serious sanction that was levelled was a temporary sanction. Not a single person was expelled from the party in this entire period. And not a single case brought before these committees had anything to do with corruption. This is quite extraordinary.

When this questionable record was put to Ramaphosa, he noted that where matters involved criminality, corruption or fraud, 'the institution of disciplinary proceedings is dependent on a conviction in a court of law'. As a result of this principle, no action could be taken by the party until court processes had run their course.

The commission had no time for this argument; it was simply not true that the ANC could not act in cases where allegations or actual charges of corruption were being contemplated. There were simply no legal barriers in place to prevent the ANC from doing so. Ramaphosa, while conceding this point, nevertheless argued that it would be embarrassing for the ANC if it disciplined somebody only for them to be found innocent in court. This was the reason why the ANC had developed the so-called step-aside rule, according to which people would step down from their pubic positions while due process ran its course, but the ANC would take no further action.

The commission was unconvinced by this argument. First, the ANC disciplinary bodies have their own standards of proof and an appeals process. They are empowered by organisational regulations to deal with many types of misconduct; they also do not have the 'bureaucratic trappings' of criminal proceedings, which can take years to be finalised. The ANC disciplinary mechanisms could, as a result, move rapidly to implement discipline.

Second, while the disciplinary committees may be ill-equipped to deal with complex cases of corruption, it is not credible that they would be unable to navigate *all* cases of corruption. There was no reason the committees could not consider matters on a case-by-case basis. Any argument to the contrary would be unsatisfactory: 'for the ANC to decide not to consider *any* corruption cases is not acceptable,' the commission found. 'One would also expect that the ANC would hold its members, and especially its leaders, to a higher standard than "has not been convicted in a court of law".'

The commission was clearly disturbed by the failure of the ANC to properly grapple with corruption through its internal disciplinary proceedings, and was not mollified by the introduction of the step-aside rule. Surveying the evidence, the commission sounded a pessimistic note:

> It is clearly against the Party's best interest to allow its leadership positions to be occupied by those credibly accused of corruption and other crimes. Not only does this practice bring the ANC into disrepute, but there is a high risk that corrupt persons in powerful positions will continue to abuse their offices. This is a risk that the Party, by failing to discipline those accused of corruption, has deemed [corruption] acceptable. This certainly does not augur well for the prevention of corruption in future. Nor does it give positive reassurance that state capture will not recur. I am afraid that the step aside rule will not address this problem.

## Conclusion

The commission's conclusions on both Ramaphosa's evidence and that of the ANC were sobering and bruising. Ramaphosa's adoption of his 'remain and resist' strategy was particularly strongly criticised in the context of ANC rather than national politics. The commission was of the opinion that, in fact, Ramaphosa may have had considerably more scope to resist state capture vocally and publicly.

Moreover, if he had been removed by Jacob Zuma from his formal position in the state, Ramaphosa would still have remained deputy president of the ANC – a position of considerable strength, as Jacob Zuma showed when he successfully used it to lobby for his presidency after being fired by Thabo Mbeki. Ramaphosa's removal might have acted as a lightning rod for resistance to state capture; he could have become a centre of gravity around which anti-corruption forces could coalesce.

Finally, the commission, worried about the precedent that Ramaphosa's approach might set if it was considered to be without flaw. 'It would be untenable to send a message that if the same scenario were to happen again sometime in the future, the right thing is not to speak out,' the commission concluded.

In assessing the evidence of the ANC, the commission made four comments. First, it strongly criticised the ANC's unwillingness to discipline members who have been accused of corruption until they have been dealt with by a court of law. This attitude in effect means that the ANC will only take action against people when they are found guilty according to the extremely exacting standard of 'guilt beyond reasonable doubt' when, in fact, there is enough evidence to make a compelling case under a civil law standard. Without making changes to this approach, the commission believed, 'it is difficult to see how the ANC will succeed in getting people to think it is serious about fighting corruption'.

Second, the commission noted that the ANC failed to countenance or support any parliamentary investigations while, at the same time, failing to conduct any meaningful investigations of its own. The commission found that, if this attitude had not been adopted, there was a chance that the Guptas could have been stopped in their tracks.

Third, the commission criticised the work of the Deployment Committee, which it found played an important role in elevating unsuitable people to senior positions. In so doing, the committee was complicit in the weakening of key state institutions.

Finally, the commission criticised the ANC's total unwillingness to countenance any motions of no confidence in Jacob Zuma, despite the scale of state capture being apparent to most observers. The result of this approach was that 'the ANC protected Zuma and ensured that he remained in office as President which also means that the Guptas got more time to pursue state capture and continued to loot taxpayers' money'. The commission concluded that the ANC should have considered Zuma's removal in the wake of the Waterkloof scandal but, instead, allowed him to remain in power for five more years. If the ANC had not protected Zuma, 'the Guptas would probably have fled as they did in 2018 and therefore not looted in the way that they did'.

# The failure of parliamentary oversight

THE COMMISSION'S FINDINGS on the ANC prefigured much of what it would find in relation to the role that Parliament played in tackling state capture or, more accurately, failing to do so. Indeed, the commission found repeatedly in its assessment of the ANC's approach to state capture that it consistently prevented meaningful action being taken in Parliament. Unsurprisingly, therefore, the commission found that Parliament had failed to make any substantial steps to tackle state capture until the eleventh hour – and then only because the political stars began to realign.

## What should Parliament do – and who should do it?

The commission begins its analysis of the role of Parliament by analysing its position within South Africa's constitutional democracy. After considering the country's constitutional architecture, the commission was at pains to point out that Parliament has a role beyond just making legislation: Parliament has a constitutional duty to actively and diligently exercise oversight over the executive.

Section 42(3) of the Constitution emphasises that Parliament's role is 'represent the people and to ensure government by the people under the Constitution'. This requires, among other things, that it is actively involved in 'scrutinizing and overseeing executive action'. Moreover, as the commission clarifies, scrutiny 'implies a careful and thorough examination or a penetrating or searching reflection'.

The important point, here, is that Parliament is not just enabled to exercise oversight: it is duty-bound to scrutinise the executive. Or, more simply, it is not enough that Parliament *can* exercise oversight – it *must* exercise oversight. This is particularly true where there is credible evidence of wrongdoing. Parliament has a 'duty to investigate or enquire (or take other reasonable and appropriate measures) where there is reasonable cause to suspect unconstitutional, unlawful or improper conduct on the part of senior representatives of the executive,' the commission confirmed.

Parliament is run under a set of agreed rules (currently in its ninth edition). One of the most important parts is that they empower the Speaker of Parliament to create Parliamentary Portfolio Committees (PPCs), specialist committees that are formed to exercise oversight over a particular portfolio, or a department of government under a minister. So, for example, the running of SOEs, which falls under the control and authority of the Department of Public Enterprises, should be scrutinised by the Department of Public Enterprises Parliament Portfolio Committee.

PPCs are important because they are the bodies through which oversight is properly achieved. So while the executive can be held to account during parliamentary question time, or subject to votes of no confidence, the true nitty-gritty of examining executive conduct is performed by PPCs. And so they are given wide powers to do precisely this, including the power to summon people to testify under oath. Moreover, because Parliament is duty-bound to investigate and inquire, so too are PPCs 'obliged' to hold departments to account.

## Parliament and state capture – too little, too late

The commission was damning about the failure of Parliament to exercise its constitutional duties of oversight. In a lengthy and depressing timeline, the commission set out how, since at least 2010, serious allegations and credible evidence of state capture began emerging. This accelerated after the Waterkloof incident, and culminated in both the *State of Capture* report and the revelations of the GuptaLeaks. There was simply no reasonable person, the commission implied, that could have denied that there was, at the very least, a problem with how the state was being run.

The commission interweaved this timeline of public allegations of state capture with notes on how Parliament reacted. In summary, it did nothing, largely because the ANC component in Parliament resisted any attempts to get Parliament involved. In September 2016, for example, the Democratic Alliance (DA) proposed a motion for Parliament to establish an ad hoc committee to investigate state capture. The motion was defeated by 160 to 103. Every ANC MP in attendance voted down the motion. The ANC's argument in response to the motion was that all evidence of wrongdoing should be sent to law enforcement or Chapter 9 institutions. The commission was highly critical of this reasoning, as it meant that Parliament was effectively abdicating its responsibility to law enforcement, which was 'not consistent … with Parliament's constitutional responsibilities'.

It was only in mid-2017 that Parliament started getting its act together – and, even then, its performance was markedly patchy. In May 2017, the Portfolio Committee on Public Enterprises received a request from the DA's Natasha Mazzone, requesting that the committee call the minister and the Eskom board to give evidence. Mazzone had previously attempted to get the committee to act in 2016 but had been breezily dismissed. This time, however, Mazzone's request landed on the desk of Zukiswa Rantho, who had recently taken over chairmanship of the committee. Rantho was a rare thing: an ANC MP who saw the necessity of exercising oversight. She approved the request.

Minister Lynne Brown duly appeared, as did the Eskom board. The answers they gave to probing questions were considered unsatisfactory by the portfolio committee members; the result was that the committee agreed to the appointment of a full inquiry. For the first time in nearly the entire life of Parliament under Zuma, the dysfunction of the SOEs would be subject to scrutiny.

The GuptaLeaks revelations began coming thick and fast from the end of May 2017. This provided the background to a remarkable about-turn on the part of the ANC. On 15 June 2017, Cedric Frolick, the house chairman of committees, wrote to the chairs of four portfolio committees (Public Enterprises, Transport, Home Affairs and Mineral Resources), requesting that these committees convene investigations into the allegations of state capture pertinent to each of their portfolios.

This change in attitude was remarkable – a full 180-degree change in the ANC's previous position. The commission tried to understand exactly why the ANC had such a dramatic change of heart, which must have had, at the very least, the imprimatur of the ANC's Political Committee overseeing Parliament. After considering various arguments, the commission came to a much more prosaic and pessimistic conclusion: 'it was known that at the end of 2017 the ANC was going to hold its elective conference in which a new President of the organisation would be elected and Mr Ramaphosa, being Deputy President of the ANC, would be a candidate. That was enough for many within the ANC to seek to position themselves favourably on Mr Ramaphosa's side.'

The result of the Frolick letters was markedly mixed. The PPC on Transport conducted no investigation. According to the DA Shadow Minister of Transport, the chair of the PPC, PD Magadzi, failed to even share Frolick's letter with the committee. The PPC on Minerals and Energy tried a bit harder than Transport, but even there the commission found that it 'ultimately failed to inquire effectively into allegations of state capture referred to it'. The committee did, once, get Mosebenzi Zwane to appear to answer questions; but he thereafter evaded the committee, thereby limiting its effectiveness. Battles over budgetary allocations also bogged it down in bureaucratic mire.

The PPC on Home Affairs was more effective, but even its efforts produced limited results. The committee was tasked with investigating the role of Malusi Gigaba and the department in approving the citizenship applications of Gupta family members. The first meeting on this matter took place on 20 June 2017; it was only in March 2019 that the committee finalised its report. This recommended that Ajay Gupta and his family members be referred to law enforcement for submitting false information in their naturalisation claims.

The only PPC that dug into the topic of state capture with any rigour was the PPC on Public Enterprises. The committee ended up conducting a detailed and incisive investigation into the mismanagement of Eskom. The commission commented that the PPC's investigation was useful for its own inquiries, and that it relied on some of the results of this investigation.

## Other failures of parliamentary oversight

The commission noted that Parliament did not just fail when it came to dealing with Gupta-related state capture; evidence led before the commission showed that Parliament was utterly ineffective in conducting oversight over the award of contracts to Bosasa by the Department of Correctional Services.

As shown previously, the problems with Bosasa were well known from an early stage. In 2009, for example, the Special Investigating Unit investigated Bosasa, found serious issues and recommended prosecutions. This was relayed to the PPC on Correctional Services on 19 November 2009. But nothing much happened. At the time, the chairperson of the committee was Dennis Bloem, an ANC MP. He testified that he tried to investigate Bosasa but was put under pressure by the minister and the ANC chief whip. James Selfe, the DA Shadow Minister, confirmed that Bloem would frequently call him to discuss Bosasa. During these conversations, Bloem gave Selfe information and suggestions about questions he could pose, but told him that he was unable to do so himself due to political pressure.

According to Bosasa's bagman, Angelo Agrizzi, Bosasa also bribed MPs to prevent the PPC from investigating the company. Agrizzi testified that Bosasa paid bribes to PPC members, including Vincent Smith (the committee chair from mid-2009), Winnie Ngwenya and VV Magagula. (He also claimed to have paid bribes to Cedric Frolick.) Agrizzi said that he initially paid monthly bribes of R45,000 to Smith, R30,000 to Magagula and R20,000 to Ngwenya. When the latter two were removed from the committee, Smith's bribe was increased to R100,000 a month, according to Agrizzi. All of those implicated denied wrongdoing.

The commission noted that Vincent Smith was facing criminal charges, and thus refrained from making any particular finding about his guilt. Nevertheless, it recommended that the National Director of Public Prosecutions consider bringing charges against Smith, Frolick, Magagula and Ngwenya.

## Why did Parliament fail – and what can be done?

The commission's damning assessment of Parliament led it to inquire into the reasons why Parliament had failed so spectacularly over this period. At the heart of the commission's analysis was the reality that during this period ANC MPs voted according to the party line, because failure to do so could lead to serious repercussions for their career and even their safety.

The commission heard from evidence led by the political analyst Richard Calland, who gave the example of what happened to my good friend and colleague Andrew Feinstein when he tried to investigate the Arms Deal, at a time when this was being resisted fiercely by the executive. Andrew was harassed by the party and eventually resigned the day before he was about to be removed from Parliament. Calland also testified that, from 2009 onwards, an atmosphere of fear pervaded Parliament. Calland, who met with MPs frequently, was struck by how often they would refuse to talk on their cell phones or removed their phone batteries when they met in person.

But running through all this analysis was the simple fact that MPs are, under a proportional representation system, appointed by their party and serve at its pleasure. They can also be dismissed as MPs through the same process. MPs are thus totally dependent on their political parties to hold on to their jobs. This constrains the freedom that MPs can exercise, and may bring MPs into conflict with their oath to act in the national interest.

The commission thus solicited and heard evidence about the possibilities for electoral reform, which was provided by, among others, the Council for the Advancement of the South African Constitution (CASAC). CASAC argued for the implementation of a constituency-based system, in which voters elect their MPs directly in their own constituencies. MPs would not be able to be removed from their positions by the party, as is currently the case. The commission was receptive to this argument, but also not convinced that it was a panacea: 'it will not be a proverbial silver bullet, but it is likely to help'. It thus recommended that Parliament consider legislation that would introduce a constituency-based system that was still proportionally representative, as required by the Constitution.

The commission also contemplated possible limits to the exercise of power over MPs by the party that appoints them to Parliament, especially when it comes to disciplinary action. In particular, the commission was of the view that there have to be some limits to the power of a political party to discipline an MP, where the MP takes the good faith view that the duty of Parliament to oversee the executive and to hold it to account compels him or her to act in a manner not favoured by the Party leadership or a decision by a Party structure. Can the Party direct its MPs to collude in or cover up illegal or unconstitutional conduct? Can it issue instructions based on the personal interests of one or more of its leaders, where those interests manifestly conflict with the interests of the citizens of the Republic? Surely not.

The commission, on this basis, recommended that Parliament consider promulgating legislation that would provide some legal protection to MPs when they acted reasonably and in good faith in trying to exercise their power of oversight.

In addition to a number of rather technical and administrative issues, the commission also considered two further meaty issues: how to hold the Presidency to account; and the limits of parliamentary power to force the executive to change its ways. On the former, the commission noted that the Parliamentary Portfolio Committee systems did not currently provide for a committee that would exercise oversight over the Presidency directly. This was because the Presidency was not considered a portfolio on its own, and because the President ultimately delegates his or her functions to other Cabinet members. The commission, unsurprisingly, found this situation undesirable, and recommended that Parliament consider introducing a PPC focused on the Presidency.

Finally, the commission considered the limits of parliamentary power. Under the current legislative framework, Parliament is empowered to call members of the government to answer questions and provide information. But Parliament does not have the power to compel the executive to do anything; the executive can effectively ignore Parliament, while Parliament is ultimately limited in its powers to levying criticism and making recommendations. The only real power that it has is to put forward motions of no confidence in the Cabinet or President – an extreme intervention that is clearly not suitable in every instance.

The commission was particularly impressed with the idea of 'amendatory accountability', which was outlined by Hugh Corder, who had conducted a review of parliamentary structures in 1999. Under this system, Parliament would have the power to insist that the executive correct its behaviour when it fell foul of parliamentary scrutiny: the executive would have to make amends, through correcting its behaviour. Corder recommended the introduction of an Accountability Standards Act that would give Parliament power under law to ensure this remedial action was taken. The commission, in turn, recommended that Parliament consider the concept of amendatory accountability and, if it was in favour, introduce legislation that would put it into effect.

## RECOMMENDATIONS

*Parliament should consider the desirability of:*
- *creating a committee that provides oversight over the President and Presidency;*
- *introducing a constituency-based system that is still proportionally representative;*
- *enacting legislation that would protect MPs from being dismissed for merely exercising their duties of oversight in good faith;*
- *amendatory accountability;*
- *appointing opposition MPs more frequently as chairs of committees;*
- *amending its rules regarding its role in appointments along the lines suggested by Corruption Watch, thereby introducing greater transparency;*
- *amending the Intelligence Services Act to ensure that the Joint Standing Committee on Intelligence report to Parliament as much as possible preceding an election.*

*If Parliament decides these recommendations are desirable, it should either promulgate legislation or make changes to its rules to give effect to them.*

*Parliament should:*
- *enhance the resources made available to portfolio committees to enable them to conduct research and investigations;*

- *make clear to ministers that their non-attendance at PPC meetings will not be tolerated and action will be taken; and consider the possibility of legislation being passed to this effect;*
- *introduce a 'track and monitor' system for committee reports;*
- *establish an Oversight and Advisory Section to provide advice and technical assistance to PPCs;*
- *create a system whereby a PPC can put a minister 'on terms' regarding remedial action and follow this up through the Speaker or other appropriate offices.*

# PART EIGHT

# The Money

*For an extremely intense six months, I worked alongside a remarkable team of advocates and investigators at the commission who formed part of what was called the 'Flow of Funds' team. Their job was to track and trace the money that was spent on state capture contracts, estimate how much the Gupta enterprise got, unravel the Guptas' money-laundering schemes and, finally, discover how the Guptas' loot was routed back into the country to buy assets like Optimum coal mine. The result of this investigation was a report I authored running to just under 500 pages, which formed part of a 7,023-page evidence bundle. Thousands of pages of supporting material, including banking documentation and bank statements, were attached to prove the veracity of the work.*

*The commission dealt with this report in a dedicated volume, one of the last to be published. Broadly, the commission accepted my findings and conclusions, and then made a series of recommendations on that basis. The commission's volume was, as a result, something of a straight summary of my report.*

*In the light of this, I've taken some liberties in how I present the findings here. There are also aspects of my report which the commission addressed in part, but which I feel may be understated* or may have excluded certain things that I think are worthy of attention.

In the next sections, I set out my findings in my lengthy report to the commission, in which I also include graphics to make some of the funds flows easier to understand. Once I've covered this, I will then describe the commission's overall findings and recommendations.

# The total cost of Gupta-related state capture

R57,064,461,144.82 IS THE total amount of money that the South African government paid on contracts tainted by state capture involving the Gupta enterprise. I calculated this figure simply. I worked with the commission to identify the contracts awarded by the South African government where they were tainted by state capture and how much was paid against them. This was quite a wide definition, but the essence is that the contracts involved and benefited the Gupta enterprise in some way, most notably where the Gupta enterprise eventually took a cut. In some cases – in fact, the vast majority of cases – the involvement of the Gupta enterprise was an obvious and clear predictor of some sort of irregularity in the awarding of contracts by the state.

In a small number of cases, however, the involvement of the Gupta enterprise didn't necessarily mean that the original contract was corrupt or irregular. Instead, I found that in certain cases money flowing from state capture was used to fulfil those contracts. One example of this is the R250m loan given by the Industrial Development Corporation (IDC) to enable the Guptas and their partners to buy Shiva Uranium. There is no evidence that the IDC made the loan irregularly. However, in paying back a portion of the loan to the IDC, the Guptas made use of money sourced from other state capture money flows.

Two further things should be emphasised before I move on. First,

413

these are state capture contracts linked only to the Gupta enterprise. They do not include, for example, the horrific looting of PRASA and many other cases of grand corruption. Second, when I say the cost of Gupta-linked state capture, I mean only the amount of money paid by the state in contracts. I do not calculate the opportunity cost or the real, long-term and profound social cost of state capture, which includes denuding the state of the wherewithal to realise its citizens' socio-economic rights. But I am very confident that this amount would be orders of magnitude more than the R57bn figure I quote above.

## The five biggest earners

State capture earned a number of companies, both multinational conglomerates and South African entities, serious money. The contractors that received the most amount of money in state capture related to the Guptas were China South Rail, China North Rail, and the company they formed when they merged, CRRC. These three companies were awarded contracts to deliver locomotives (and associated services) by Transnet: 95 20E electric locomotives, 232 45D diesel locomotives, 100 21E electric locomotives and 359 22E locomotives. As we've already seen, these contracts involved an absolute orgy of corruption. In total, these companies were paid R26.32bn by Transnet – 46% of the total value of all the contracts I identified that were tainted by Gupta state capture.

The second biggest recipient of Gupta-related state capture contracts was T-Systems, the enormous multinational conglomerate with headquarters in Frankfurt, Germany. It is a subsidiary of German giant Deutsche Telekom, which is part-owned by the German government. Deutsche Telekom reported total revenue of €101 billion in 2020.

T-Systems was awarded two huge contracts (referred to as master services agreements or MSAs) to supply IT services and equipment rental to Transnet and Eskom; their connection to the Guptas is discussed below. In total, T-Systems was paid R12.3bn. That's 21% of the total amount paid by the state in state capture contracts linked to the Guptas.

| Description | Recipient company | Total amount (ZAR) |
|---|---|---|
| 95 20E locomotives (all-in cost) | CSR | R3,432,869,565.21 |
| 232 45D locomotives (all-in cost, inc. Durban relocation) | CNR | R2,823,869,773.71 |
| 100 21E locomotives (all-in cost) | CSR | R5,159,831,654.92 |
| 359 22E locomotives (all-in cost) | CSR | R14,910,751,921.66 |
| Subtotal: Locomotive contracts | CSR/CNR | R26,327,322,915.50 |

| SOE | Amount paid to T-Systems |
|---|---|
| Eskom | R7,805,558,985.49 |
| Transnet | R4,529,377,797.46 |
| Total | R12,334,936,782.95 |

The third highest earner was Neotel, which was paid R5.581bn by Transnet in relation to three contracts. That's 9.78% of the total Gupta-linked state capture tally.

The fourth highest earner was Tegeta Exploration and Resources (TER), the Gupta enterprise vehicle that held the Guptas' mining assets. In total, Eskom paid TER R4,124,550,047.21. Of this, R2.4bn was paid by Eskom directly to TER and the remaining R1.6bn was paid to Optimum Coal after this asset was bought by the Guptas (using over R1bn from Eskom to do so).

| Gupta company paid by Eskom | Amount [ZAR] |
|---|---|
| Tegeta Exploration and Resources | R2,442,523,980.95 |
| Optimum Coal | R1,682,026,066.26 |
| Total | R4,124,550,047.21 |

Coming in at fifth place is McKinsey. It earned R1,898,659,064.26 in total from contracts it shared with Regiments and Trillian: R784,287,306 from Transnet and R1,108,164,558.26 from Eskom. McKinsey's income was 3.3% of all state capture payments connected to the Gupta enterprise.

| Company | Total income from Gupta-linked state capture | Percentage of Gupta-linked state capture expenditure |
|---|---|---|
| CSR/CNR/CSSR | R26,327,322,915.50 | 46% |
| T-Systems | R12,334,936,782.95 | 21% |
| Neotel | R5,581,955,471.63 | 9.78% |
| Tegeta Exploration and Resources (including Optimum Coal) | R4,124,550,047.21 | 7.2% |
| McKinsey | R1,898,659,064.26 | 3.3% |

## The primary sites of state capture

The three primary sites of state capture, when measured against total state spend, were Transnet, Eskom and the Free State provincial government.

| Organ of state or government department | Total amount disbursed related to Gupta-linked state capture (ZAR) | Percentage of total state payments related to Gupta-linked state capture |
|---|---|---|
| Transnet including the Transnet Second Defined Benefit Pension Fund | R41,203,679,801.43 | 72.21% |
| Eskom | R14,765,761,250.07 | 25.88% |

| Organ of state or government department | Total amount disbursed related to Gupta-linked state capture (ZAR) | Percentage of total state payments related to Gupta-linked state capture |
|---|---|---|
| FS provincial government including the Office of the Premier | R441,042,621.08 | 0.77% |
| Total | R56,410,483,672.58 | 98.85% |

## Europe's biggest state capture collaborator, T-Systems

When I first presented my report to the commission, I pointed out I had seen that T-Systems had been making regular payments to Zestilor starting in 2012, and suggested that the commission identify the reason. As I've discussed elsewhere, Zestilor was owned by Zeenat Osmany, Salim Essa's wife.

T-Systems had paid R3,051,639.21 to Zestilor between August 2012 and mid-July 2015, 73.9% of Zestilor's total income in that period. Essa was paid R501,010.10 by Zestilor between June 2012 and July 2015.

The discovery of the Zestilor payments led to another discovery: T-Systems had earned R7.8bn through a nearly decade-long contract with Eskom that was closely linked to the Gupta enterprise. T-Systems had first won the contract to supply IT services to Eskom in December 2009. This contract was supposed to run for five years, starting on 1 January 2010 and ending on 31 December 2015. But the contract never ended. Instead, it was extended, without competition, through a series of 'modifications' – the most recent in June 2018 – that transformed a five-year contract to nearly double that length. The repeated renewal of the contract was particularly strange as Eskom had attempted to cancel T-Systems' contract and put it up for competitive tender. Letters from Eskom were sent to T-Systems on 26 August 2013 and 29 September 2014 making it clear that Eskom would not extend the contract and would put it out to tender. This never happened.

On 24 June 2015, T-Systems' global compliance monitor

completed an internal compliance review, which had been tasked with investigating T-Systems South Africa's 'non-IT consultancy agreements'. This review revealed that T-Systems opted to 'informally' engage with Salim Essa (referred to as S.E.) because T-Systems recognised that he 'has a strong network to Eskom officials and stakeholders'.

T-Systems chose an 'informal' route, rather than make Essa a formal consultant or agent, after it had started a compliance check. This included getting legal opinion on the 'use of S.E. as a sales consultant – specifically the Prevention and Combating of Corruption Act'. The inference is that T-Systems quickly came to realise how problematic it would be to have Essa on board formally, yet it continued to engage with him and his allies 'informally'. Despite this, the compliance review concluded that 'the decision to engage S.E. in an informal way and without any contractual basis led to a vast number of legal and compliance risks'.

The compliance report acknowledged that Essa's 'reward' for helping T-Systems with his 'informal network' was that he introduced 'several local and start-up companies to TSSA [T-Systems South Africa] decision makers and he requested TSSA to provide these companies with the opportunity to be included in the value chain where possible'. No surprises for guessing who owned the 'local and start-up companies' that T-Systems eventually included in its 'value chain'. T-Systems made Sechaba Computer Systems its 'supplier development partner' for the Transnet and Eskom contracts; the GuptaLeaks show that by 2015 Sechaba was controlled by the Guptas. Sechaba would ultimately earn R323m as T-Systems' supplier development partner.

The other 'start-up' that made a fortune was Zestilor, the company controlled by Essa's wife. Zestilor earned R238m from these T-Systems contracts. The bulk of this was earned when T-Systems agreed to cede the equipment rental portion of its contract with Transnet to Zestilor. Later, Zestilor would also be paid R75m from Trillian.

Zestilor's bank statements show it was largely a front for Sahara. Of R319m paid to Zestilor in relation to the T-Systems and other contracts, 95% was paid onwards to Sahara Computers. Sahara was thus paid R302m by Zestilor between May 2015 and September 2017.

The real kicker is how the Trillian Group compliance audit ended. Despite the obvious quid pro quo between T-Systems, Essa and Gupta companies, the report concluded that relationship between T-Systems, Sechaba and Zestilor was a 'normal contractual relationship in place without any irregularities. There is no indication for corruption or any other illegal behaviour.' And so, despite everything that would become known about Essa, Zestilor and Sechaba, T-Systems' group compliance department gave T-Systems the green light to keep doing what it was doing.

# How much the Guptas earned from state capture

THE TOTAL AMOUNT earned by the Gupta enterprise was R15,543,960,171.22. There is a caveat with this figure, however. The commission used my calculations on this and came to a slightly different figure; I had originally calculated a figure of R16,217,793,047.18. This difference was based on one or two different assumptions (and the commission picked up an error in my final calculation table, for which I'd like to thank Microsoft). In the interests of consistency, and in deference to the commission's calculations, I've gone with its calculation rather than mine.

As with the cost of state capture, this figure was calculated simply. I worked with the commission to identify every contract or payment made to the Gupta enterprise where there was an obvious irregularity, wrongdoing or conflict of interest. Taking this approach meant that I excluded those amounts paid to the Gupta enterprise by the state where there was no obvious irregularity. For example, the commission identified that Sahara was paid R102m by the state. But because of a lack of evidence, this could not be definitively deemed irregular, and was thus excluded.

The payments to the Gupta enterprise were made in four broad categories:
a. payments directly by the state to the Gupta enterprise;
b. payments made to the Gupta enterprise by contractors to the state whose contracts were tainted by Gupta state capture;

c.   payments made to what I call 'first-level laundry vehicles';
d.   the known kickbacks paid to the Gupta enterprise, all related to locomotive and crane contracts awarded by Transnet.

## Payments made directly to the Gupta enterprise by the state

The second biggest contribution to the Gupta's illicit earnings was payments made directly to Gupta enterprise companies by the state. In total, the Gupta enterprise was paid R6.403bn directly by the state in irregular contracts. Two companies received 64% of these payments: Tegeta Exploration and Resources and Optimum Coal. Together, these two companies were paid R4.1bn.

| SOE making payment | Gupta enterprise recipient | Amount (ZAR) | Percentage of direct payments to the Gupta enterprise (rounded down) |
|---|---|---|---|
| Eskom | Tegeta Exploration and Resources | R2,442,523,980.95 | 38% |
| Eskom | Optimum Coal (after its April 2016 purchase by Tegeta) | R1,682,026,066.26 | 26% |
| Total | | R4,124,550,047.21 | 64% |

Other notable recipients included
a.   Estina, which was directly under the control of the Gupta enterprise. Estina was paid over R280m to deliver the Vrede dairy project;
b.   VR Laser, which earned over R242m from Denel contracts after it was taken over by the Guptas;
c.   TNA Media, which was paid R248m by Eskom, Transnet, the

Free State Treasury, and Offices of the Premiers of Mpumalanga, Free State and North West Province, often without any contracts.

## Payments made to the Gupta enterprise by state contractors

The Gupta enterprise earned R877m through payments made to Gupta enterprise companies by contractors to the state. By far the biggest winner here was Sechaba Computer Systems. As we have seen, Sechaba earned R323m as T-Systems' supplier development partner. The funds started flowing to Sechaba after it came under the effective control of the Guptas.

Another notable recipient was CAD House, which earned R99m from the multinational software firm Systems Application Products (SAP).

## Payments to first-level laundry vehicles

As I will explore below, the Gupta enterprise made use of extensive and complex local and international laundries to move funds from state capture. The first stop in the laundering process was the first-level laundry vehicles. These companies received payments flowing from state capture (often simultaneously from multiple state capture cases). From the first-level laundry vehicles, the money was sent to the local laundry.

In calculating the total earned by the Gupta enterprise, I used the total payments flowing from state capture paid into these vehicles and arrived at the figure of over R1.2bn.

The top-five first-level laundry vehicles were:

| First-level laundry vehicle | Amount (ZAR) | Percentage of total payments to first-level laundry vehicles (rounded down) |
|---|---|---|
| Homix | R395,418,856.44 | 32% |
| Albatime | R311,556,446.04 | 26% |
| Chivita Trading | R144,093,427.25 | 11% |

| First-level laundry vehicle | Amount (ZAR) | Percentage of total payments to first-level laundry vehicles (rounded down) |
|---|---|---|
| Fortime Consultants | R105,543,369.69 | 8% |
| Medjoul | R95,148,371.74 | 7% |

## Known kickbacks paid to the Gupta enterprise

The largest contribution to the Gupta enterprise's illicit income was kickbacks paid in relation to contracts placed by Transnet. In total, I estimate that the Gupta enterprise earned R7.3bn through this route.

Of this, we can confirm that the Gupta enterprise was paid R3.4bn by CNR, CSR and CRRC in relation to the infamous loco procurements, based on hard documentary evidence. The Gupta enterprise was also due to earn a further R3.7bn in kickbacks from these contracts, and though the paper trail goes cold, I believe it did.

Although they were much smaller than the loco procurements, the Gupta enterprise also scored from crane contracts issued by Transnet. As I discussed in the section on Transnet, Gupta enterprise companies in Dubai were paid R33m in relation to crane contracts given to ZPMCC (a Chinese firm). The Guptas' Dubai companies were paid a further R26.5m by Liebherr Cranes, the Swiss mega-multinational, which was also related to crane contracts with Transnet.

## The land-speed record

One contract that we came across during our deep dig into the Guptas was particularly remarkable: not for its size, but as a reflection of how easily the Guptas could fleece the state. Under this contract, R71m was paid to Cutting Edge by Eskom. This contract sets a land-speed record for dodgy contracting. On 29 April 2016, Cutting Edge submitted an unsolicited proposal to Eskom for data management. On 9 May 2016, Eskom gave it the contract. On 16 May, Eskom paid the full amount to Cutting Edge. It took only 17 days to go from unsolicited proposal to full payment.

# The local and international laundries

THE GUPTAS USED A large number of different laundering mechanisms to move their money into and out of South Africa. These were, at points, extremely complicated, and describing them in any depth will get quickly stuck in the weeds. What follows, as a result, is a high-level overview rather than a blow-by-blow account.

## The Dubai fronts

In the earliest stages of state capture the focus was initially on provincial government (and the Free State in particular). In this stage, the Gupta enterprise was remarkably unsubtle in the way it laundered money. The modus operandi of the Guptas was to create a front company (or use one that they or their colleagues had lying around) to get a contract from the government. After spending a small fraction of the amount paid to them to deliver a 'service', most of the money was sent directly abroad to Dubai.

In particular, the Gupta enterprise ran and controlled four Dubai entities that received and disbursed state capture money: Accurate Investments, Fidelity Enterprises, Gateway Limited and Global Corporation LLC. A good example of this is Estina: as I've already discussed, Estina was little more than a corporate shell controlled by Kamal Vasram, who took his directions from the Gupta enterprise head honchos. Estina was paid over R280m by the Free State government. Of this amount, over R169m was paid directly to Gateway Limited in Dubai.

Quite often, the Gupta enterprise decided to move this money back into their other businesses in South Africa, most frequently invoiced against bogus contracts. Again, Estina is instructive. Of the R169m transferred to Gateway Limited, over $3.2m (about R33m at the time) was paid into the accounts of the Gupta flagship, Oakbay Investments, while Linkway Trading, another Gupta company, was paid over $3.3m (about R34m at the time). Infamously, the Linkway Trading payment was justified by Linkway issuing an invoice for the costs incurred at the Sun City wedding of Vega Gupta and Aakash Jahajgarhia.

The Dubai fronts became increasingly important once the Guptas started earning serious money from their locomotive kickbacks (over R7bn). When the Guptas first started being paid this money, it was laundered on their behalf by two companies, JJ Trading (JJT) and Century General Trading (CGT), which were controlled by the Worlds Window Group, a scrap metal and general trading company in India. As I described in the Transnet chapter, JJT and CGT, after receiving the money from the locomotive manufacturers, transferred 85% of the kickback amounts into the Dubai front companies for the Guptas. JJT retained 15% as a fee. During the period in which it used JJT (until about mid-2014), the Gupta enterprise was paid over $98m by JJT and CGT from the loco kickbacks.

The amount that was eventually repatriated into South Africa via the Dubai fronts (and almost all derived from criminal sources) was astonishing: over R630m to Gupta companies.

| | Fidelity (ZAR) | Accurate (ZAR) | Global Corporation LLC (ZAR) | Total |
|---|---|---|---|---|
| Oakbay Investments | R312,300,859.94 | R189,399,975.21 | | R501,700,835.15 |
| Sahara Computers | R16,226,959 | | R37,658,741.16 | R53,885,700 |
| Goldridge Trading | R46,174,511.41 | | | R46,174,511.41 |
| Double Excellence | R293,494 | | | R293,494 |
| Linkway Trading | | R29,430,913.15 | | R29,430,913.15 |
| Marvis Jewellers | | | R1,760,000 | R1,760,000 |
| Browns the Diamond Store | | | R600,000 | R600,000 |
| Total | R374,995,824.35 | R218,830,888.36 | R40,018,741.16 | R633,845,453.71 |

# The first-level laundry vehicles and the local laundries

As noted above, the Gupta enterprise often received payments from companies like Regiments through 'first-level laundry vehicles'. These vehicles were the first stop on the laundering route. The Gupta enterprise made use of 15 laundries (the top five were listed in table on page 418), which were used roughly chronologically in four different laundry systems (see table on page 419).

| First-level laundry entity | Period used | Amount paid (ZAR) |
|---|---|---|
| *First laundry* | | |
| Chivita | May 2013 to May 2014 | R144,093,427.25 |
| *Second laundry* | | |
| Homix | April 2014 to May 2015 | R395,418,856.44 |
| *Third laundry* | | |
| Forsure Consultants | May to July 2015 | R19,809,329.70 |
| Hastauf | May to July 2015 | R12,360,769.62 |
| Subtotal | | R32,170,099.32 |
| *Fourth laundry – the spider's web* | | |
| Fortime Consultants | July 2015 to August 2016 | R105,543,369.69 |
| Medjoul | August 2015 to August 2016 | R95,148,371.74 |
| Birsaa Projects | January 2016 to September 2016 | R49,230,737.23 |
| Maher Strategy | November 2015 to January 2017 | R28,928,450 |
| Pactrade | October 2016 | R4,291,766 |
| Matson | October 2016 | R1,970,000 |
| Jacsha | October 2016 | R2,150,000 |
| Shacob Commerce | October 2016 to July 2017 | R24,589,767.40 |

| First-level laundry entity | Period used | Amount paid (ZAR) |
|---|---|---|
| Birtusa | April 2017 | R3,097,200 |
| Subtotal | | R314,949,662.06 |

The Guptas would make use of a first-level laundry vehicle until some event made them dump the vehicle and move on to something new. For example, Homix was used for approximately a year to receive over R395m. In May 2015, Homix made payments directly to a Hong Kong company called Morningstar, which had been flagged by the South African Reserve Bank (SARB) as suspicious. Again, Homix was the vehicle through which the Guptas were paid kickbacks by Neotel. The SARB subsequently froze the assets in Homix's account, and Homix was promptly dumped.

From the first-level laundry, the funds were then paid onwards into an intermediary company. This company would take all the funds from state capture and other criminal sources (more on this below), and either pay them into another layer of local laundry or pay them into what I call an onshore-offshore bridge. Onshore-offshore bridges were companies that received and bulked funds from multiple sources (including state capture funds) and then transferred them offshore. In the majority of cases, the onshore-offshore bridges would pay money into what I call the Hong Kong–China laundry, but it would also make payments to companies in Dubai.

In total, I was able to trace over R388m paid from state capture moving abroad via onshore-offshore bridges, following specific routes out of the country, mostly into the Hong Kong–China laundry. Generally speaking, the different laundries use different onshore-offshore bridges.

To make this a bit simpler, let's look at the graphic on page 422, which shows how money moved from Combined Private Investigations into Medjoul and eventually abroad. Combined Private Investigations, while not forming a part of the main body of the commission's findings, was addressed in the report on financial flows. It provided security services to various parastatals and paid large sums of money directly to the Guptas' first-level laundry vehicles.

| Onshore-offshore bridge | Route of funds | Amount (ZAR) |
|---|---|---|
| FGC Commodities | Homix to FGC Commodities | R186,700,560.81 |
| IPocket | Hastauf to IPocket | R14,201,614.53 |
| IPocket | Forsure to IPocket | R11,356,000 |
| One Last Trading | Fortime to One Last Trading | R34,919,987.01 |
| ENY/Studio De Pablo | Ismer and Saamed Bullion directly to ENY | R33,851,201.30 |
| ENY/Studio De Pablo | Saamed Bullion to Graincor to ENY | R6,287,522.61 |
| ENY/Studio De Pablo | Saamed to Dial Square to ENY | R3,584,078.16 |
| Pine Peak Wholesalers | Saamed to Pine Peak Wholesalers and Saamed to Graincor to Pine Peak | R43,536,506.83 |
| Eng 38 Pty Ltd | Saamed to Eng 38 Pty Ltd | R2,833,200 |
| Damla Trading | Saamed to Dial Square and Charly Wholesalers to Damla Trading | R19,175,000 |
| Seattle Clothing Manufacturers/ Lionhead | Saamed to Shazari to Seattle/Lionhead | R23,509,527.16 |
| Varlozone | Saamed to Zokubyte to Varlozone | R7,675,000 |
| CCE Holdings | Saamed to CMC Distributors to CCE Holdings | R1,000,000 |
| Total | | R387,630,198.41 |

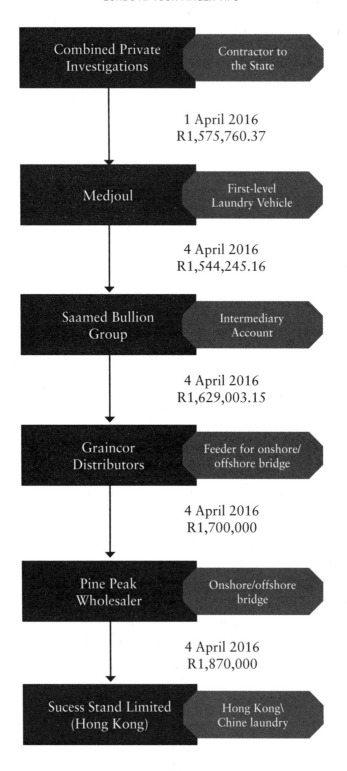

## Tracing money to known recipients: Some examples

Given the use of these complex laundries, it is extremely difficult to trace them to their final destination. But there are a number of cases where we can trace the laundry payments to some important recipients.

The first example relates to Integrated Capital Management (ICM). The accompanying graphic on page 424 shows how money was paid by China North Rail to Business Expansion Structured Products (BEX) in the outrageously corrupt contract related to the CNR relocation issue, and then onwards to ICM. At the time ICM received the money, one of its directors was Stanley Shane, a Transnet board member and chair of the Board Acquisition and Disposal Committee (BADC) which oversaw the locomotive contracts.

The second example also relates to payments to BEX from CNR. In the accompanying graphic on page 425, the funds flow from CNR to BEX and eventually into the accounts of a company controlled by the Guptas, Confident Concepts, which received R33,730,000.

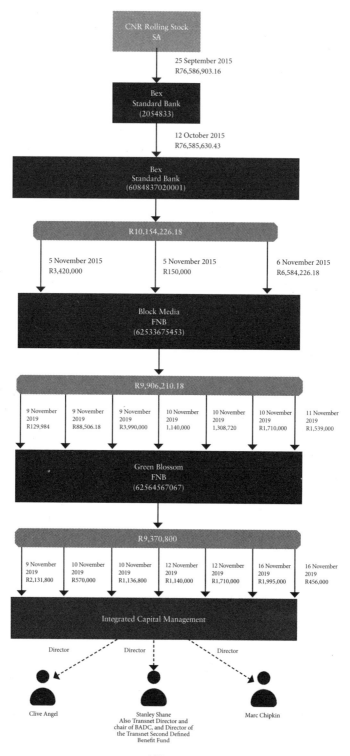

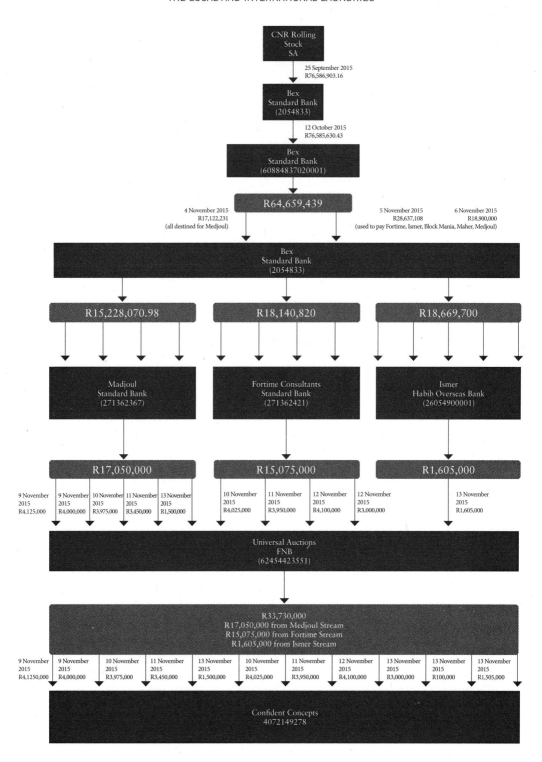

# The Guptas' criminal bedfellows

ONE OF THE MOST disturbing discoveries made when following the flow of Gupta-related state capture money was the scale of money laundering taking place in South Africa, and, in particular, the amounts of money flowing out of the country into offshore laundry networks. In total, I was able to track over R387m of Gupta enterprise state capture money moving through 12 different onshore-offshore bridges. But the Gupta funds flows through these accounts were only a small fraction of the total moved abroad through these laundering vehicles: R8.835bn in 4,019 transactions between 2013 and 2020. This is the amount moved just by those companies discovered by tracing the Gupta enterprise money, and doesn't include every onshore-offshore bridge. I have no doubt that we only have a small and partial picture of the real extent of the problem.

| Onshore-offshore bridge | Total number of offshore payments | Total value of offshore payments[8] |
|---|---|---|
| Ukuzuza | 1,586 | R3,839,193,805.63 |
| Syngen Distribution | 409 | R1,325,007,774.56 |
| FGC Commodities | 360 | R1,030,605,584.68 |
| Lionhead | 613 | R940,048,019.02 |

---

8   $333,842,939.62 @ USD:ZAR 11.5.

| Onshore-offshore bridge | Total number of offshore payments | Total value of offshore payments[8] |
|---|---|---|
| CCE Motor Holdings | 360 | R767,601,728.73 |
| Studio De Pablo | 185 | R328,326,130.97 |
| Seattle Clothing Manufacturers | 215 | R256,842,214.20 |
| Truhaven | 143 | R146,208,484.42 |
| Pine Peak Wholesalers | 53 | R116,676,411.57 |
| Damla Trading | 20 | R40,419,762 |
| Varlozone | 37 | R26,788,550.71 |
| Eng 38 Pty Ltd | 38 | R17,860,180.84 |
| Total | 4,019 | R8,835,578,647.33 |

## The pre-existing networks used by the Guptas

Throughout the process of laundering money out of South Africa via the first-level vehicles, the Guptas piggy-backed on existing criminal networks. Indeed, all the onshore-offshore bridges used by the Guptas operated independently of the Gupta enterprise, moving money for all and sundry.

One example of this is Chivita Trading. The Gupta enterprise paid over R144m of state capture money to Chivita in 2013 and 2014. Prior to this, Chivita was receiving a vast number of electronic and – most importantly – cash deposits. Between July 2010 and May 2013 (when the Guptas started paying Chivita), it received thousands of cash and electronic deposits equal to over R354m, almost all of which was immediately transferred to other recipients.

Chivita distributed these funds in two rough flows, paying them onwards to either a company called Ballatore Brands or another onshore-offshore bridge called Syngen Distribution, which, as I show above, transferred R1.3bn into offshore laundries. Ballatore was even more active as a local laundering front, operating two FNB accounts. In the first, Ballatore received 4,106 electronic and cash deposits equal to R660m between April 2012 and August 2013; in the second, Ballatore received 17,501 deposits equal to a truly astonishing R2.158bn in six months between January 2014 and June 2014.

## The organised crime connections: Ukuzuza, Tian Wang and the Mafia

Some of the laundering networks used by the Gupta enterprise were grisly.

In May 2015, Homix was dropped when SARB flagged payments it made directly to companies in Hong Kong. It was replaced by two stopgap first-level laundry vehicles: Forsure Consultants and Hastauf. Together, they were paid over R61m from state capture contracts, either from Regiments or Albatime.

| | Direct from Regiments Capital (ZAR) | Via Albatime (ZAR) | Total (ZAR) |
|---|---|---|---|
| Forsure Consultants | R16,890,928.70 | R14,820,000 | R31,710,928.70 |
| Hastauf | R12,360,369.62 | R17,670,000 | R30,030,369.62 |
| Total | | | R61,741,298.32 |

Both Hastauf and Forsure Consultants transferred a portion of these funds into the accounts of IPocket Global: R14m by Hastauf and R11.3m by Forsure Consultants.

In 2015, SARB initiated an investigation into a company called Ukuzuza after payments it made had been flagged as suspicious. SARB discovered that Ukuzuza had been fraudulently registered against the name of an unemployed resident of Germiston.

SARB's investigation showed that IPocket Global acted as a proxy account for Ukuzuza Trading. The owners of IPocket claimed that they had agreed to receive deposits and make payments at the instructions of the controlling mind of Ukuzuza, Miss Tian Wang. The funds paid by Hastauf and Forsure to IPocket were thus destined for Ukuzuza, which, in turn, made the payments abroad through the currency trader Gro Capital. Ukuzuza was by far the largest onshore-offshore bridge identified in my investigation; as noted above, it transferred over R3bn offshore, almost all into companies into the Hong Kong–China laundry.

In November 2015, Tian Wang was caught in a failed bribery attempt. When she found out her company was being investigated, she offered an upright SARB official, André Malherbe, a R5m bribe to get him to assist in releasing funds frozen by SARB. Malherbe duly reported the offer to his superiors and to the Hawks. The Hawks then created a sting: Wang was told to deposit R4m in a specific account and to bring a further R1.2m to a restaurant, where she was immediately arrested. Wang was subsequently prosecuted for corruption and sent to jail for eight years.

In bringing the charges, the National Director of Public Prosecutions, Shaun Abrahams, told the court that the money handled by Wang, which the state had seized, was the proceeds of 'unlawful activities including serious offences such as murder, rape, extortion, fraud and sexual offences, among others'. The Guptas were thus using the same money-laundering network as serious violent organised crime involved in the most heinous offences.

There is another astonishing part to this story. During its investigations, SARB was told that the owners of IPocket had been physically threatened by Tian Wang and Yusuf Omarjee so that IPocket would not terminate their relationship with Wang. Omarjee was convicted of fraud in 2013. At the time, he was additionally fingered for being the person who organised the fake passport of Samantha Lewthwaite, the so-called White Widow. She is one of the world's most wanted terrorists, who is alleged to have connections to the terrorist group al-Shabaab. She travelled on a fake South African passport in 2012 to Kenya, where it is alleged she was involved in terrorist attacks responsible for the deaths of 400 people.

## The Cape gangs connection

In August 2016, six individuals each transferred R1m into the accounts of three Hong Kong–China laundry entities: Morningstar International (which had been paid by Homix), PAI International and Vedia Trading. These six payments were funded by state capture money: the R235m paid by Eskom to Trillian Management Consulting in August 2016, as the accompanying graphic on page 430 shows. As it emerged, none of the six individuals had any idea that the payments had been made and that accounts had been opened in their name. Their identities had all been stolen.

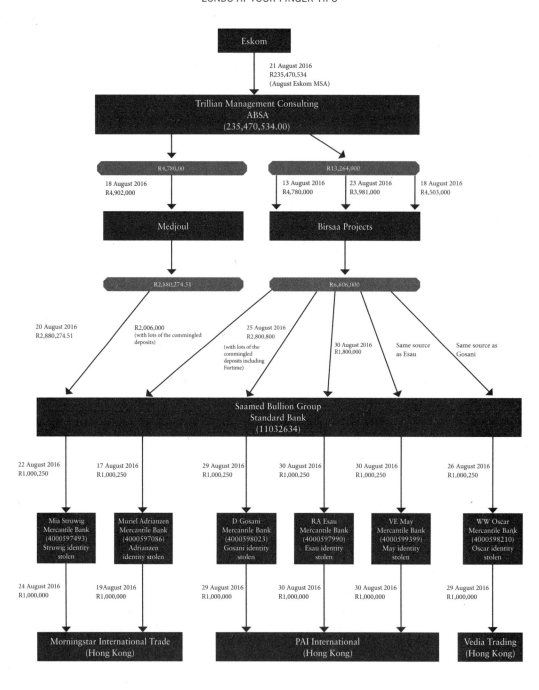

The true mind behind the payments was revealed when the documents seeking approval of the transfers was examined. They all bore a contact email address that was a variation of sheldonbreet@gmail.com.

As Morningstar had been flagged, SARB launched an investigation into the payments made. This confirmed that the payments were orchestrated by Sheldon Breet (including one payment in his own name), who had to forfeit funds as a result.

In 2018, Sheldon Breet's brother, Matthew, pleaded guilty to the murder of Brian Wainstein, the 'steroid king' responsible for smuggling steroids into South Africa. Matthew was Wainstein's bodyguard. Sheldon was charged and remains accused of being party to the conspiracy to murder Wainstein. Sheldon's co-conspirators included Cheslin Adams and Fabian Cupido, the former allegedly a member of the '27s' gang and the latter allegedly associated with the Spoilt Bratz street gang. The Guptas kept some interesting company.

## The Hong Kong–China laundry

So far I have been referring to the Hong Kong–China network. Let me explain what I'm referring to. As we have seen in the section about Transnet, Chinese rail companies paid hundreds of millions of dollars in kickbacks into the HSBC accounts of Regiments Asia and Tequesta Group, both registered in Hong Kong and both controlled by Salim Essa. As soon as Regiments Asia and Tequesta Group received these payments, they paid them out in thousands of transactions to a range of Chinese and Hong Kong companies. (These companies were also paid by Morningstar International.) A few names really stood out; Success Stand Limited, Celertus, Honourway Garment, and Freedom Trading. My investigations showed that they were little more than shelf companies in Hong Kong with no notable trading or online presence.

When the commission asked SARB to run these names through its database of inflows and outflows, it turned out that they had been paid by many companies in South Africa, including a range of onshore-offshore bridges. When those bridges were reviewed, it emerged that they were all also making payments into a network of Hong Kong companies like Sanny Trading, Vic Charm Limited, Pavantex HK, and Samantha Trading. The implication was obvious: these Hong Kong companies were part of a much larger international laundry.

This was borne out by an internal investigation conducted by HSBC in April 2017, following media reports about Regiments Asia and Tequesta, in an attempt to establish the extent of HSBC's exposure to the Gupta enterprise's corruption. The investigation not only supported the conclusion that the Gupta enterprise (as well as all the onshore-offshore networks) was using a sophisticated laundry; it also showed that this laundry was truly vast. One investigation tracked payments into 60 accounts that had received payments from Regiments Asia and Tequesta Group. It identified over 50,339 deposits. HSBC, as is well known, has been investigated and prosecuted in relation to a large number of other money-laundering scandals, such as for failing to prevent the laundering of huge sums of money belonging to ultra-violent Mexican drug cartels through HSBC accounts.

## The Altaf Khanani network: Drugs, al-Qaeda and … quilts?

In tracing payments made to the Hong Kong–China laundries, the trail eventually led me and the commission to two companies: Truhaven and Donsantel 133 CC. Both of these companies had made payments into Hong Kong–China laundry vehicles like Samantha Trading, Pavantex and Derik Fashion. At the same time, they were also making payments to a number of notable companies in Dubai. Donsantel 133 CC paid over R43m to Aydah Trading and Seven Seas Golden Trading. Truhaven paid over R52m to four Dubai companies between July and September 2015: Aydah Trading, Jetlink General Trading, Seven Seas Golden Trading and Wadi Al Afrah Trading LLC.

In November 2015, the US Treasury's Office of Foreign Asset Control (OFAC) designated the Altaf Khanani Money Laundering Organisation (Khanani MLO) a transnational money-laundering organisation. Altaf Khanani was once described as the world's most wanted money launderer. The Khanani MLO laundered billions of dollars 'for organised crime groups, drug trafficking organizations, and designated terrorist groups throughout the world', including the Taliban and al-Qaeda.

OFAC identified five key companies that the Khanani MLO used to receive and launder these criminal funds. Four of them were paid by Truhaven; two were paid by Donsantel 133 CC. Thus, there were at least two companies making payments to both the Hong Kong–China laundry and the Khanani MLO at the same time.

But, you may be asking, what has this to do with the Guptas? Further digging revealed that Truhaven and Donsantel 133 were also making use of the same local laundries used by the Guptas. Key to this was the company Smart Fabrics, which received payments from Truhaven and also made outward payments to Donsantel 133 CC. Crucially, Smart Fabrics also received one payment from the Gupta enterprise first-level laundry company Fortime Consultants. It also received deposits from other companies used by the Guptas to launder state capture funds, like Rich Rewards Trading; and it made 13 outgoing payments to Anchor Import and Export. This was controlled by the same man who controlled laundry vehicles used to move Gupta state capture funds abroad: Pine Peak Wholesalers, Graincor Distributors and Damla Trading.

Both Truhaven and Donsantel 133 CC were investigated by SARB and subject to forfeiture orders. Truhaven's director, Thair Gasee, is also currently facing corruption charges for trying to bribe a bank official to release funds seized by SARB.

SARB's investigation into Donsantel 133 CC revealed that the man controlling it – Ahmed Mulla – had a long history of international money laundering. Between April 2007 and May 2011, he used a company called Maverick Trading 239CC to pay over R437m offshore to companies in Hong Kong and China. When Maverick Trading was rumbled, he created Donsantel, through which he paid R592m abroad between May 2013 and November 2015. When Donsantel was stopped, he opened up StyleUp Fashions, which also paid money out to the Hong Kong–China laundry.

Importantly, StyleUp Fashions made a payment of R1.6m into the account of CMC Distributors, a feeder account for an onshore-offshore bridge called CCE Motor Holdings (also subject to a SARB forfeiture order). My tracing shows that the Guptas' money-laundering network paid over R1m to CMC Distributors in April 2016.

So, while the Guptas weren't making payments via the Khanani network directly, they were using the same local and international networks as companies that did so. Only time will tell if there are any further links between the Hong Kong–China laundry, the Khanani MLO, South Africa's sprawling local network of criminal launderers, and the Guptas.

# How the Guptas used their loot

You may be asking what the Guptas did with all their stolen loot and, in particular, the loot that had been so aggressively laundered. The answer is twofold: first, they paid for a shed-load of weddings. To steal a joke from my estimable evidence leader Advocate Matthew Chaskalson: they really should have just been wedding planners. Second, they used their state capture gains to buy more assets in South Africa so that they could benefit from even further state capture.

## Tegeta purchases Optimum Holdings

On 14 April 2016, Tegeta Exploration and Resources transferred R2.084bn from its Bank of Baroda current account into the trust account of the law firm Werksmans. The transfer secured and finalised Tegeta's purchase of Optimum Holdings from Glencore. Considerable evidence has emerged showing that Glencore only undertook the sale after pressure from Gupta-linked officials and Eskom. To finance this, the Gupta enterprise mobilised R1.82bn in capital that was derived from criminal or questionable sources. In the accompanying table on page 435, I provide a summary of these flows, and then delve deeper into two particularly notable streams: the Centaur and Albatime flows.

Note, however, my very specific phrasing: I say that the Gupta enterprise mobilised R1.73bn in questionable *capital* to purchase Optimum, not that that Gupta enterprise *paid* this amount. This is because the Gupta enterprise's financial manoeuvring involved a good portion of this capital flowing back to its source, while over R1bn of the real costs actually derived from Eskom.

| Paying entity | Criminal or questionable links | Amount paid (ZAR) |
|---|---|---|
| Eskom | A dodgy 'prepayment' for future coal deliveries that plugged a gap in the Gupta funding stream | R659,558,079.38 |
| Eskom | A payment for coal supplies by Tegeta to Eskom, which had awarded contracts to Tegeta on extremely favourable terms | R68,653,781.78 |
| Subtotal: Eskom | | R728,211,861 |
| Albatime | These funds derived from money stolen from the Transnet Second Defined Benefit Fund and from fees paid to Regiments by Transnet in relation to the 'Club Loan' | R104,500,000.00 |
| Trillian Management Consulting | These funds derived from money stolen from the Transnet Second Defined Benefit Fund | R152,000,000.00 |
| Centaur Mining | These funds ultimately derived from money recycled back into South Africa by Griffin Line, a Gupta enterprise front company in Dubai | R842,231,000.00 |
| Total | | R1,826,942,861.16 |

## Stream 1: Griffin Line and Centaur

In late 2015, the Guptas opened a new company based in Dubai called Griffin Line Trading. In one email from the GuptaLeaks, the Guptas' chief lieutenant, Ronica Ragavan, appears to explain to Tony Gupta that Griffin Line would be controlled or represented by Kamal Singhala, Ajay Gupta's son. Beginning in 2013, the Gupta enterprise also started discussing potential investments with Daniel McGowan and Simon Hoyle, directors of Centaur Asset Management, who also directed a company called Centaur Holdings.

### CENTAUR VENTURES LTD STRUCTURE CHART

Centaur Ventures LTD.
(Bermuda) *CVL

50% Centaur Holdings, 50% Aakash Garg

Centaur Mining (Mauritius)
(Mauritius) *CMM

100% CVL

Centaur Mining
South Africa (Pty) Ltd
(South Africa) *CMSA

100% CM

Tokicap (Pty) Ltd
(South Africa) *TOKI

74% CMSA, 26% Aerohaven

By 2015, the Gupta enterprise and Centaur had established a joint venture called Centaur Ventures. Centaur Ventures' shareholding was split 50-50 between Centaur Holdings and Aakash Garg (Aakash Jahajgarhia), the man who married Vega Gupta at the infamous Sun City wedding. Centaur Ventures held a 100% shareholding in Centaur Mining in Mauritius, which in turn held a 100% share of Centaur Mining in South Africa. In effect, Centaur Mining in South Africa was 50% owned by Aakash Jahajgarhia – in reality, the Gupta enterprise. These relationships were visualised in an application filed by Centaur Mining with Standard Bank in South Africa.

In January 2016, Centaur Mining and Centaur Ventures entered into a loan agreement whereby the latter would loan R1.5bn to the former. But this money was actually sourced from Griffin Line, which had given a $100m loan to Centaur Ventures. These back-to-back loans allowed Griffin Line – a Gupta enterprise company – to move the money it hoarded from questionable sources abroad, back into South Africa, without anybody being the wiser as to the source. Indeed, we only know of these back-to-back loans because Centaur and the Guptas fell out and became involved in acrimonious court battles in Bermuda, where Centaur Ventures is based.

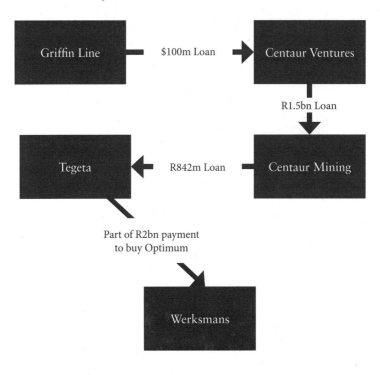

This back-to-back loan – in reality, Gupta enterprise money – was moved from Centaur Ventures to Centaur Mining, from Centaur Mining to Tegeta Exploration and Resources, and from Tegeta to Werksmans. This was achieved as follows. First, between 26 February and 1 April 2016, Centaur Mining drew down R885m into its Standard Bank account. Between 9 March 2016 and 4 April 2016, Centaur Mining transferred this amount into its Bank of Baroda current account, where it was then transferred into a fixed deposit account on 12 April 2016. On the same day, the Bank of Baroda issued a loan to Tegeta Exploration and Resources worth R842m. This amount was then paid to Werksmans.

But this does not mean that Griffin Line–Centaur actually paid R842m towards the purchase of Optimum; it only means that they provided R842m in capital towards the purchase. In fact, about 40% of this was returned to Centaur Ventures and the shortfall was covered by Eskom and Glencore. It worked like this: First, on 5 April 2017, Eskom paid R249m to Optimum and Koornfontein mine (the latter an asset the Gupta enterprise acquired when it bought Optimum). Of this, R242m was paid into Tegeta's loan which it had taken out against the Centaur Mining fixed deposit. Second, on the following day, Centaur Mining closed its fixed deposit with the Bank of Baroda and eventually paid the capital and accumulated interest (R905m) back to Centaur Ventures, thereby settling part of the R1.5bn loan facility.

The fact that Centaur Mining was able to close its fixed deposit with Baroda at this point reflects particularly poorly on the bank. By this point, Tegeta had only paid back R242m of the R842m loan that was secured against the Centaur Mining fixed deposit. By letting Centaur Mining close this fixed deposit, which secured Tegeta's loan, the Bank of Baroda exposed itself to R600m in loans that might not be repaid. Either Baroda knew what was really going on or it was astonishingly cavalier about its own potential losses.

Third, between 11 April 2017 and 20 April 2017, Centaur Ventures recycled R651m of the R905m it had just been repaid, back into South Africa. This money was deposited into Optimum Coal's Baroda account. Of this, R470m was paid to Tegeta, which immediately used it to pay down its mega-loan, while the remainder was paid out to various other Gupta enterprise companies. Finally,

Glencore paid R135m to Optimum on 26 April 2017, of which R130m was used to pay off the Tegeta loan.

The net effect of all this was that, while Centaur had provided R842 in capital, it actually only paid R470m towards the purchase of Optimum. The remainder was made up of R135m paid by Glencore and, most importantly, R249m paid by Eskom.

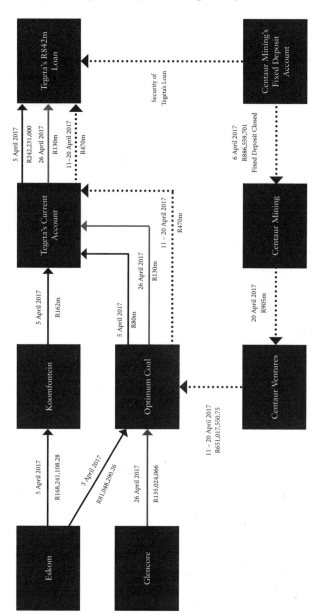

Key
Eskom = Solid black lines
Glencore = Dark grey lines
Centaur Mining/Centaur Ventures
ultimately funded by Griffin = Dotted lines

447

## *Stream 2: Albatime*

The second stream of interest flowed via Albatime.

As noted ealier, Albatime sourced its funding for this tranche from both Transnet directly (R93.4m) and Transnet's Second Defined Benefit Pension Fund (R56.1m). These amounts transited either via Regiments or Trillian to Albatime. Albatime repeated the Centaur trick, paying R110m of this into a fixed deposit, against which Tegeta took out a loan of R104.5m, which it used to contribute to the purchase of Optimum.

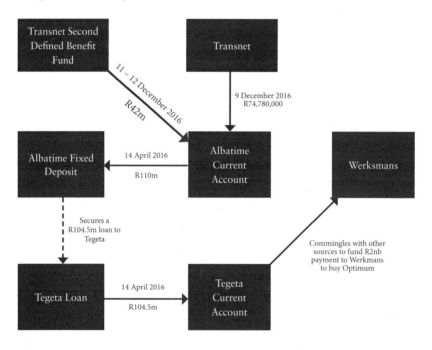

But the interesting thing about the Albatime portion is what happened next. On 20 April 2016, less than a week after the Optimum purchase happened, Albatime closed its fixed deposit account and paid R110m back into its Baroda current account. Of this R110m, Albatime transferred a total of R26,710,400 into three first-level laundry entities: Medjoul, Fortime Consultants and Birsaa Projects.

Following this money, I've been able to track that $450,416 of the R26.7m paid to the first-level laundry entities was paid via a local laundry into two separate onshore-offshore bridges and, ultimately, to Griffin Line Trading. So we have money from state capture first being used to help the Guptas finance the purchase of Optimum, and once that objective had been achieved, a portion of the same money was then paid out to a Gupta enterprise front company in Dubai.

## Eskom's real contribution

As a result of the Gupta enterprise's financial manoeuvring, over half of the actual contribution towards the purchase of Optimum was paid by the taxpayer via Eskom.

Thus, the Gupta enterprise relied on state capture to force the sale of Optimum to Tegeta, then relied on state capture to get Eskom to pay hundreds of millions to help that sale, and then used the asset they had bought to secure more illicit state capture funding. On my calculations, Eskom ultimately contributed R1.046bn to the purchase of Optimum Holdings – all for the benefit of the Gupta enterprise.

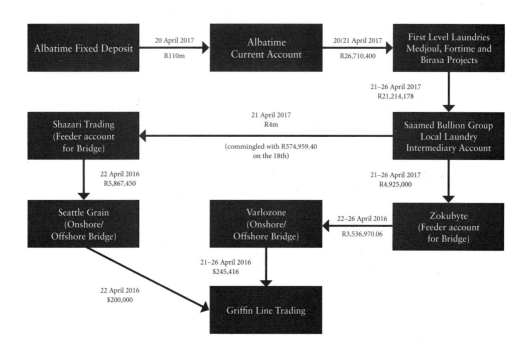

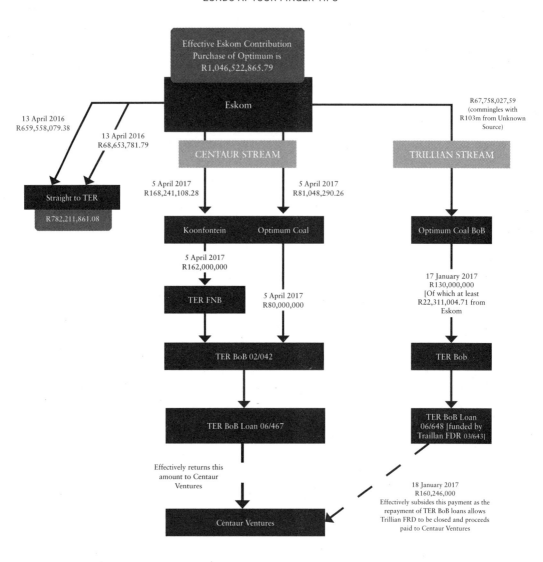

# The commission's findings and recommendations

The commission made a number of findings and recommendations based on my report. I include the recommendations below but highlight two of the features of my work about which the commission made some useful and interesting comments. First, the commission was clearly perturbed by the size and scale of the money-laundering networks that were uncovered, and commented that there was 'ample evidence' for the National Prosecuting Authority to consider prosecutions of a very wide range of individuals and for a very wide range of offences. But the commission worried that, even if those prosecutions did happen, taking on historical offences would likely not be enough. The money-laundering networks were, if anything, flexible and persistent. It would be imperative, going forward, for a proper strategy to be employed to disrupt these criminal networks.

The commission's suggestions were based on a number of observations about money laundering:

- Because money laundering is used by multiple criminal actors in different spheres of the illicit economy, a 'holistic' approach needs to be taken in tackling it. Coordination is required from all law enforcement agencies, including, at the very least, the Asset Forfeiture Unit, Hawks, Financial Intelligence Centre, the NPA's Investigating Directorate, SARS, SARB and the SIU.
- It is important to use the existing anti-money-laundering powers of the banks in a more proactive way than is currently

the case. The commission noted that the FIC had created a SA Anti-Money Laundering Task Force (SAMLIT) so that banks can share information and trends with one another. But current statutory provisions make it hard to share this information.

- There is a need to review the current system of suspicious transaction reporting to the FIC. The commission thus recommended an urgent review of the FIC's activities, which I set out in the recommendation box below.

The second comment and finding of the commission related to the purchase of Optimum coal mine. The commission noted my calculations of the sources of funds used to buy the mine and, on that basis, made its own calculation that R1,758,942,861.61 was derived from criminally sourced funds. The eagle-eyed reader might have noticed that this is a little bit less than my calculation of R1.82bn; this is because the commission, generously, removed the R68m prepayment by Eskom to Tegeta from its own calculations. The commission then used this figure and plotted it against the ownership of Tegeta to show how much each individual shareholder would have benefited from the acquisition of the mine.

| Shareholder | Percentage shares in Tegeta (held directly or indirectly) | Amount of benefit derived from criminally sourced funds (ZAR) |
| --- | --- | --- |
| Gupta family members/ companies | 65.15% | R1,145,527,852.53 |
| Duduzane Zuma | 19.49% | R342,750,991.89 |
| Salim Essa | 6.73% | R118,330,242.57 |
| Ronica Ragavan | 6.49% | R114,250,330.63 |
| Ashu Chawla and other Gupta enterprise employees | 2.16% | R38,083,443.54 |

On this basis, the commission recommended that all of those listed in the accompanying table be investigated by law enforcement for violations of POCA.

## RECOMMENDATIONS

*The NPA should consider the 'three reports of Mr Holden' with a view to instituting criminal prosecutions against a 'wide range of individuals' under POCA in relation to the laundering of state capture proceeds.*

*The FIC should conduct an urgent review to establish:*

- *whether banks were compliant in their reporting under FICA as far as the laundering of state capture money was concerned, to establish whether the FIC was alerted to the transactions and, if so, to what extent;*
- *what action the FIC took in relation to any suspicious activity reports involving state capture money;*
- *what recommendations were made by the FIC to other law enforcement agencies;*
- *what steps, if any, were taken by law enforcement based on those referrals.*

*The NPA should investigate Duduzane Zuma, Salim Essa, Ronica Ragavan, Ashu Chawla and members of the Gupta family for potential POCA violations in relation to the acquisition of Optimum coal mine by using criminal or suspicious sources.*

# PART NINE

# Reflections and Big Picture Recommendations

*Why did state capture happen, and what can be done about it? This is, of course, the million dollar question, which the commission took some time to answer. It did so in a punchy and debate-worthy volume that rapidly surveyed the detritus of state capture to identify some key themes, and then made some intriguing recommendations. I must admit that I am unconvinced by some of the recommendations, which I will address below. Nevertheless, the commission's suggestions are a useful jumping-off point to begin a national conversation about how to protect South Africa from further state capture.*

# The problems

THE FIRST PART OF THE commission's report on the underlying causes and types of state capture spent considerable time identifying a series of interlocking and mutually reinforcing problems that allowed state capture to happen, and that might, if unchecked, allow it to flourish again.

## Problems in procurement

The first part of the commission's overview of the types of dysfunction focused on the country's procurement framework. It quoted from numerous academic studies to point out that South Africa's procurement system had been creaking under the weight of numerous problems – inefficiency, lack of skills, confusing legislation – for a long period prior to the Zuma presidency. However, when it was faced with the systematic attack on good governance that state capture presented, the procurement system's failings made for easy pickings.

The commission then provided a detailed typology of the 'patterns of abuse at each stage of the procurement cycle': a rather depressing litany of the tricks that were used to skew procurement.

In the pre-tendering phase (before the process of buying even started), the commission noted these types of abuse:

- *The procurement of goods and services that weren't actually needed, or weren't even intended to be supplied, or were duplications of work already done*

One example of this was Transnet's award of contracts to Regiments and Trillian to give financial advice when Transnet Treasury was either already doing the job or could have done the job.

- *The abuse of the policy of deviation*
  Deviations from the normal procurement approach, which is an open-tender competition, were frequently used for instance to stipulate that contracts would not go out on open tender. In the worst cases, contracts would be awarded to single bidders on grounds of 'emergency' or where there was no obvious second bidder. One of the most notorious examples of this was the Vrede/Estina dairy scandal, in which the Free State decided not to go out to open tender at all but simply gave the contract to Estina to develop the project.

- *The misuse of confinements*
  A confinement occurs when a department chooses to confine the number of bidders for a tender; in the worst-case scenarios, the tender is confined to a single bidder. This is supposed to happen only in real emergencies or where the services are extremely specialised. One example of the abuse of confinement was Transnet's award of the 100 loco contracts to China South Rail (CSR), without any competitive bidding, thus eliminating the much more suitable locos provided by Mitsui.

The patterns of abuse in the tendering phase (when bidders were invited to make bids) included:

- *Parcelling*
  This happens when a large contract is split into multiple parts to produce a series of smaller contracts with lower values. This is particularly problematic when it is done to reduce the smaller contracts below the so-called delegation of authority (DOA) limit – the ceiling amount of the costs at which a CFO or CEO of an SOE can confine a contract; for any sum below that cost, a CFO or CEO can decide to issue a contract on confinement. One example of this process occurred when, over four days, McKinsey was given four contracts on confinement. The total cost of the four contracts was R619m, but each was split into amounts ranging from R100m to R239m. This kept the contracts

below the R250m DOA limit at which the contracts would have had to go to the adjudication committee for approval.

- *Abuse of preferential procurement and 'supplier development policies'*

  Preferential procurement seeks to award contracts, or portions of contracts, to black-owned businesses as part of empowerment. With supplier development, a primary contractor agrees to give the work from a contract to an up-and-coming firm in the interests of transformation and empowerment. While the commission was at pains to point out how important – and legitimate – transformation truly is, it also noted that it was used to create opportunities for corruption. The commission cites, as one example, how Regiments 'got its foot in the door' by partnering with McKinsey in their dealings with Transnet. Strangely, the commission did not cite what I think is the most obvious example: T-Systems, which received questionable contracts from Eskom after giving huge supplier development contracts to Zestilor and Sechaba, both Gupta-related companies.

- *Communication with bidders*

  This is pretty self-explanatory. One of the examples cited by the commission was the award of contracts to Bain by SARS. It noted that Bain had had lengthy communication with Jacob Zuma and Tom Moyane prior to getting contracts at SARS. When Bain eventually obtained its SARS contract, it emerged that the firm had actually drafted the tender documents.

- *Retroactive changes to bidding criteria*

  This happens when, while bids being considered, the bid specifications were altered, sometimes to benefit specific bidders. One example of this was the change in the evaluation criteria to benefit CSR in its Transnet contracts. Here, if you recall, CSR faced problems because it did not have a local subsidiary and therefore received no BBBEE score, which should have knocked it out of contention in the first round. It was then decided to consider the BBBEE scores only at the end of the whole bidding process, which gave CSR the time and chance to open a local subsidiary.

The following problems were noted after contracts were awarded and were being delivered by contractors:

* *Contract variations*

  On occasion, a contract, which has already been awarded, was amended to extend its length or scope of services. Bain, for example, was initially awarded a contract worth R2.6m for six weeks of work but, through variations, was ultimately paid R164m on a contract that was repeatedly extended to run to 27 months

## The collapse in governance at SOEs

Of course, the various procurement problems identified in the previous section only took place because there were people, largely in SOEs, who found ways to use them for corrupt advantage. This testified to the near-total collapse in good governance at multiple SOEs during the Zuma presidency.

The commission's focus here was primarily on the highest level of SOE governance. The two most important bodies or individuals responsible for SOE governance were the 'shareholder minister' and the board of the SOE. The 'shareholder minister' is the minister who represents the government as the SOE's sole shareholder. This role is played by the Minister of Public Enterprises. The shareholder minister is responsible for appointing the board of directors, which is responsible for overseeing the affairs of an SOE. Directors are bound by 'onerous' fiduciary and regulatory responsibilities that can be summed up as: spend money wisely and legally. The senior management of SOEs – the CFOs and CEOS – run the organisations on a day-to-day basis. But they ultimately report to the board. Boards are thus critical in ensuring that the managers of SOEs do their jobs well and in good faith.

Reviewing the catastrophes at every SOE it considered, the commission concluded that 'the evidence received by the commission demonstrates that in many cases and in fundamental respects, the boards of the SOEs have shirked their responsibilities, or worse, used their powers to corrupt the SOEs which they have been appointed to protect'. This was particularly problematic because boards during this period implemented or introduced centralised procurement processes so that they – or their subcommittees – were directly involved in procurement decisions. This happened at Transnet, where the Board Acquisition and Disposal Committee (BADC) became the locus of corruption in the award of a whole range of huge government contracts.

The commission identified two particularly concerning features of the management of SOEs during the period it investigated:

- *Strategic appointments and dismissals*

  The commission noted that the capture of SOEs involved the appointment of compromised individuals to key positions within SOEs, such as CEOs, CFOs or senior positions in procurement. Two of the most obvious examples of this were the appointment of Brian Molefe as CEO of Transnet and then Eskom, and Dudu Myeni as the CEO of SAA.

- *Blurring the lines of management and oversight*

  The commission noted that, in addition to political involvement and interference in the appointment of the boards of SOEs, boards put themselves in a conflicted position – on the one hand, they were supposed to perform neutral oversight of the running of the SOEs, while, on the other, they were increasingly involved in the operational running of SOEs. One of the most obvious examples of this was the LSG Skychefs contract. This contract was awarded to LSG Skychefs following an open tendering process by SAA's management and procurement. But the award was then overturned by the board, which then took it upon itself to award the contract to Air Chefs instead.

## The legislative framework and structure of public procurement

After this gloomy dissection, the commission then moved on to discuss other problems that put South Africa's procurement system under serious strain. The first notable problem was the extremely complicated and diffuse nature of the legislative framework guiding procurement. Basically, procurement in South Africa is guided by multiple pieces of overlapping legislation like the Public Finance Management Act, Preferential Procurement Policy Framework Act, the Municipal Finance Management Act and the End of the Month Salticrax Act. I'm just kidding with this last one, of course, but I bet your eyes were already glazing over when you got to it. Now

461

can you imagine the poor procurement officer in rural North West Province who is simply trying to buy toilet paper and needs to make sense of this?

The irony is that, despite this web of legislation – which is also imbricated with other pieces of legislation and jurisprudence – there is no actual template for how good procurement should be done. This is because each of the bodies in South Africa that procure services (ranging from SOEs to municipalities) adopts what is called a supply chain management policy (SCM), which sets out how procurement should be carried out, including very specific rules and guidance about what to do in different situations. But SCMs are not uniform and are not coordinated. Each body adopts its own SCM, which might be different from that of all sorts of other bodies. This gives procuring bodies a good deal of flexibility, but it means a huge amount of discontinuity across government.

The commission also makes a compelling constitutional point: South Africa's Constitution requires procurement to achieve two sometimes conflicting things. On the one hand, it requires the implementation of a system that is cost-effective and efficient – that, in simple terms, requires that goods and services are bought in the most cost-effective manner. On the other, the Constitution also envisages that procurement will be used for the purposes of transformation, which is an equally valid undertaking.

While it may be possible to achieve both things in most cases of procurement, this is not to be taken for granted. In some cases, the choice will have to be made between the best-value bidder or the bidder that offers the best possibilities for transformation. The result, the commission finds, is that 'there is an inevitable tension when a single process is simultaneously [used] to achieve different aspirational objectives'.

In the commission's view, there is an urgent need for clarity on how to balance these potentially competing imperatives. In the commission's view, this should be done by focusing on best-value procurement: 'the primary national interest is best served when government derives the maximum value-for-money in the procurement process and procurement officials should be so advised'.

The second problem, related to the first, is the extent to which procurement has become decentralised. South Africa's legislative framework grants a vast number of public sector bodies the power to undertake their own procurement, such as national government departments, major public entities, municipalities and constitutional bodies. In local government alone, 44 district municipalities and 226 local municipalities all undertake their own procurement using their own SCM policies and systems. This decentralisation comes up against the very uneven distribution of skills across the country and across government, which the commission highlights as being of particular concern. Procurement is a highly specialised function, the commission notes, which, to be done properly, requires high levels of training and institutional support – which are all currently lacking.

While the commission does not suggest a fully centralised system, it nevertheless is of the view that some things could be rationalised. For example, it may make sense for sectoral procurement to take place on a centralised basis. Another suggestion was to create specific requirements for high-value tenders, such as the inclusion of the National Treasury in a watchdog function.

## And here's some more problems

The commission next moved its attention away from issues with procurement and governance, and identified a number of other issues that needed to be addressed in order to guard against future state capture. The first was the impact of political funding. The commission, throughout its life, heard evidence that donors had given money to the ANC, in particular, in order to gain corrupt advantage in procurements. Some examples of this include the donations to the ANC by EOH and by Bosasa.

The commission noted the passing of the Party Political Funding Act (PPFA) during its life. This, in short, requires parties and donors to report donations they received or made above a certain threshold. But the commission believed that, while important, the PPFA 'does not go as far as it should' because it failed to make any provision to 'prohibit donations linked to the grant of tenders'. The commission, in short, believed that the PPFA should be amended so that it would criminalise the attempt to gain favour in procurements through political donations, although, as will be seen a bit later, it gave very little by way of concrete advice about how to formulate this.

The commission was also concerned about the lack of protection given to whistleblowers in South Africa. Two pieces of legislation give basic protection to whistleblowers at present: the Protected Disclosures Act and the Protection from Harassment Act. The former basically allows people to share otherwise classified material if it reveals criminal conduct and is disclosed to the appropriate people; the latter applies to all forms of harassment and makes provision for protection or restraining orders.

The commission found that these two pieces of legislation were not sufficient to provide guidance to whistleblowers and to protect those that came forward. For example, the law makes no provision for providing physical protection, nor does it incentivise whistleblowing. It also fails to create a single mechanism whereby people can report wrongdoing. The commission thus suggested the creation of a new body that could receive whistleblowing reports, as well as the development of physical protection resources. It also recommended the adoption of a US-style system, whereby whistleblowers are paid a portion of whatever fine is levied, or assets seized, if their information is material to a prosecution or asset seizure.

The third issue was the thorny matter of who gets to appoint the boards of SOEs, and how the most senior management positions within SOEs are filled. If one thing was proved by the commission's work, it was that the country's Public Enterprise ministers had repeatedly appointed people who were totally unfit for the roles. This had to stop, the commission duly warned, if state capture was to be halted in future; the recommendations to achieve this are set out below.

The fourth issue was, quite simply, corrupt intent on the part of bidders and their accomplices in the state. The commission was of the view that this is best dealt with by four interventions, some of which are codified in the recommendations that follow. These interventions would include blocking corrupt firms from bidding for contracts, the introduction of deferred prosecution agreements, a presidentially appointed review of the National Prosecuting Authority to identify why it has performed so poorly, and, finally, civil recovery cases to reclaim money lost by the state.

The fifth issue was the general failure of oversight that the commission found was essential to the enabling of state capture.

This included the failure of Parliament to exercise any meaningful oversight, the inability of National Treasury to deal with corruption, especially when political forces protected wrongdoers and limited Treasury's reach, and the total lack of any meaningful consequences when state bodies were given qualified audits by the Auditor General.

The sixth issue identified by the commission was the failure on the part of government to engage constructively with actors outside government. Here, it noted the robust and useful contributions of private sector representatives, civil society organisations and academics. The commission believed that some mechanisms should be introduced to bring these actors into the fold to provide their own insights and expertise.

The final issue was that of transparency, which, admittedly, the commission pays only the briefest attention to. In essence, it believed that mechanisms should be put in place to make tender documents, government deliberations and the results of procurement processes more readily available to the public.

# The solutions

IN ITS INITIAL VOLUME about structural issues, and the recommendations to deal with them, the commission presented a very pleasing list of ten suggested actions, which I deal with below. But, as it emerged, the commission made additional recommendations throughout its various volumes that have the same sort of effect (of changing the political architecture of the country), including a headline-grabbing final recommendation that it added as its last breath. In the interests of completeness, I deal with all these recommendations together.

## A National Charter against Corruption

The first recommendation was to introduce a National Charter against Corruption that would include a Code of Conduct. The Charter – a commitment to anti-corruption – would be signed by people at all levels of society, from the President through to SOEs, private companies and civil society organisations. Procurement officers, in particular, would be expected to sign a commitment to uphold the charter, while any person or entity tendering for government services would have to do the same. The charter would be 'given legal status and effect by an Act of Parliament'.

## An Independent Anti-Corruption Agency

The second recommendation was to introduce legislation that would establish an independent Public Procurement Anti-Corruption

Agency (PPACA). PPACA would be independent and financed by the government and through fees paid to the agency by every person or tenderer trying to get government business. The agency's essential function would be to monitor, oversee, report and prevent corruption. It would provide a vertically integrated system that would include policy advisory services, investigative units to put together cases and make proposals for interventions, and tribunals and courts to make judgments and determinations on cases presented to it.

This would be achieved by five bodies that would be incorporated within PPACA:

a. A council: this would provide guidelines and recommendations and initiate measures on procurement at a high level to ensure it was functional and transparent.

b. An inspectorate: this would monitor procurement to detect and expose corruption, and would have the power to intervene in specific procurements to issue mandatory compliance notices that would force government bodies to immediately correct any problems detected in any procurement, and also act as a national centre to receive reports from whistleblowers.

c. A litigation unit: this would be the effective investigative unit that would put together cases for referral to the tribunal or court of the PPACA. The unit would undertake investigations and bring applications to the tribunal for remedial action such as debarring individuals from procurement or putting together applications for recouping money lost from corruption.

d. A tribunal: this would act as the body that receives applications from the litigation unit on which it would act, by granting the litigation unit search warrants or agreeing with and enforcing applications to debar people from taking part in procurements.

e. A court: this would determine and judge the cases brought by the litigation unit where they concerned civil actions for recouping funds, and act as a court of appeal on decisions made by the tribunal.

## Protection for whistleblowers

The commission recommended that legislation be amended or new legislation be developed, to:

• ensure that whistleblowers are given protections as envisaged in the UN Convention Against Corruption, in particular protection from physical threats through relocation or other interventions;

- codify the PPACA inspectorate as the place where whistleblower reports can be lodged and managed;
- allow whistleblowers to receive a portion of the proceeds flowing from any case where their testimony was material; this would be agreed with the litigation unit of PPACA;
- allow the granting of immunity to whistleblowers when they have made an honest disclosure of information.

## Deferred prosecution agreements

The commission recommended that the government introduce legislation that would introduce deferred prosecution agreements (DPAs) into South Africa's criminal enforcement framework. DPAs are an American invention that has been adopted in other countries such as England. In short, they are settlements that companies can enter into to settle corruption claims against them. In return for certain undertakings – such as paying large fines, introducing corporate monitors, and agreeing to the publication of facts about the case – the companies avoid prosecution for a certain period. When that period expires, the prosecution lapses and can no longer take place.

The upside for the company is that it avoids a criminal charge; the prosecution is deferred and, if the company meets certain requirements, is eventually set aside permanently. The advantage for the state is that it allows prosecutors to conclude and finalise cases that might otherwise take much longer to prosecute through the courts. Because DPAs also require that companies come clean, they can also make accessing information and evidence easier.

This is the one recommendation that I am totally opposed to; in fact, my organisation, Shadow World Investigations, and our colleagues in Open Secrets made a joint submission to the commission in which we argued against DPAs. There are a number of reasons for this.

First, I don't think it is morally appropriate for companies to be allowed to negotiate settlements that wouldn't be open to individuals; there is no reason why companies and corporations should be given this privilege. Second, experience in the US and the

UK has shown that DPAs can turn anti-corruption enforcement into a simple 'cost of doing business'. If a business knows it can enter into a DPA and pay a fine to make criminal charges go away, the risk–reward calculation changes: the company can risk being corrupt, and potentially earn loads of money, in the knowledge that it can pay a fine to settle the issue.

Third, despite rhetoric to the contrary, there are almost never prosecutions of the business people guilty of corruption. In the US and the UK, there have been a vanishingly small number of company directors or employees who have been prosecuted for wrongdoing. This is a genuinely huge problem: I don't think you can tackle corporate corruption if people who work for companies can get off scot-free just because their companies are willing to pay a settlement.

Fourth, to my mind the most powerful disincentive for corrupt behaviour is if companies, when they are found corrupt, are debarred from government procurement. But in most countries around the world, and especially in the EU and OECD countries, debarment rules only come into force once a company is actually convicted. Because DPAs don't lead to a criminal conviction, companies can admit corruption and still avoid debarment.

Fifth, the longer that DPAs are in place, the more the prosecution services lose the skills they need to undertake corruption investigations outside the slightly artificial confines of a 'play nice' negotiation. If the authorities rely on companies to self-disclose and self-report, less and less time is put into developing the tools that allow corruption investigators to undertake their own investigations. And companies will be much less scared of being investigated for corruption if they don't have to face bad-ass investigators who are experienced in raiding offices, digging through materials and building a case. This becomes a self-fulfilling cycle, in which anti-corruption bodies are only really capacitated to achieve DPAs.

Finally, the rate of recidivism in DPAs is, frankly, absurd. In the US, which concludes the most DPAs of any enforcement agency in the world, it is not uncommon for companies to enter into multiple DPAs over time. This makes a total mockery of the idea that using DPAs can deter economic crime. One of the most notorious examples of this was the US pharmaceutical manufacturer Pfizer, which entered four successive DPAs between 2002 and 2009.

DPAs are seductive: they offer a short-cut to investigations and criminal proceedings, which can be expensive, long-winded and uncertain of outcome. But I believe there is no short-cut that can be taken to navigate us out of the simple reality that corruption is often complicated, law enforcement is difficult, and trials can be arduous. Instead, it is far better to work diligently to create the resilience and capacity in the state to deal with these issues than introduce a model that treats corporations like special citizens that can buy their way out of the rule of law.

## Coming soon: The professional procurement officer

The commission was very clear that procurement officers are not simply civil servants who perform a function every now and again. Instead, they perform highly specialised tasks that require knowledge of a complex legal framework and constant training to keep abreast of new regulations and Treasury instructions. They are also in uniquely powerful positions and are vested with great responsibility by the state to oversee the effective use of scarce resources.

In light of this, the commission recommended that the government introduce legislation that would have the effect of professionalising the position and make procurement officers akin to lawyers and chartered accountants. This could be achieved by creating a professional body that – like the Bar Council – sets the rules for the type of qualifications that are needed for people to become procurement officers, and that can monitor, review and potentially discipline officers if they violate their professional code of conduct.

## Enhanced transparency

The commission, in an extremely brief recommendation, suggested that National Treasury develop a set of regulations and rules that would require every procurement system to include true transparency. Although this is not fleshed out in great detail, I assume that the commission has a system in mind similar to that used in the EU. Here every tender has to be advertised, along with all sorts of important information like details of the scoring system that will be used, the total price and how this is calculated, and contact details for the procurement officers responsible. Once tenders are awarded, additional information has to be uploaded, such as the tender award deliberations and justifications for why bidders were selected.

## Protection for accounting officers and authorities acting in good faith

The commission, in its review of the South African procurement landscape, was concerned that responsible and non-corrupt accounting officers and authorities (these are the people who are considered legally responsible for procurement in a government body, in terms of the PFMA) were terrified of falling foul of South Africa's complicated legal framework. This led to them taking little or no action, even though they were often required under law to monitor and prevent violations of good procurement practice.

Practically, you could have a situation where accounting officers know that their seniors or some other decision-making body is possibly doing something wrong. But, because they are so scared of violating procurement law, they don't do anything beyond the bounds of routine. The result is that many accounting officers, who are supposed to act as enforcers of the PFMA, are too worried to take the action they need.

The commission thus recommended that a new paragraph be introduced into the current legislation. This would prevent accounting officers from being prosecuted if they violated procurement rules but did so either inadvertently or in good faith.

## Amendments to PRECCA

The commission was concerned that the Prevention and Combating of Corruption Act (PRECCA) currently does not include what is commonly known in international anti-corruption circles as a 'failure to prevent' provision. As a result, the commission recommended amendments to section 34A of PRECCA by introducing two new paragraphs.

I won't quote them here because they are somewhat technical in their wording, but, in essence, they would make it an offence for individuals and companies to fail to prevent bribery. Practically, as we've seen internationally, this means that companies are duty-bound to put in place compliance systems and rules that make it clear to employees that they are not allowed to act corruptly, and that they can be disciplined or fired as a result.

However, and this is an important point, a company will not be held liable for the action of an employee or agent (or, in technical terms, any individual that is associated with the company by performing services for it) if it can show that the company had systems in place to prevent corruption. This is included to protect companies from rogue employees who might go around bribing everyone in sight, without the knowledge the company, but whose corruption might lead to the company itself being prosecuted.

I have to admit that I've always been slightly iffy on this issue. Practically, the 'failure to prevent' model has turned out to be a bit of a get-out-of-jail-free card for companies where corruption is found. It is relatively easy for a big company to pay a bit of money to create a compliance department, do some tick-box exercises and deliver a half-hearted 30-minute presentation every year about why bribery is bad. This can then be used to show that the company itself should not be found guilty when its employees go off and do bad things.

I don't buy the 'rogue employee' narrative, especially when it comes to grand corruption and properly big contracts. In those cases, the contracts are swung by the payment of huge bribes to powerful and influential people. It just isn't believable that there might be employees who somehow find ways to obtain $50m to pay a bribe without the company knowing about it, not least because the bribe is usually paid from company rather than employee resources.

It is also common for there to be two cultures at play in corporations: a formal culture that pays lip service to anti-corruption and a 'hardball' culture that disdains anti-corruption as being unrealistic or unfeasible. The number of senior managers and CEOs who have told me, while a little bit sozzled, that you can't do business with 'that' sort of person or in 'this' sort of country without paying bribes is, frankly, absurd. This is the culture of the pub or the golf course, where nods and winks rule the day, and executives can do their dirty work knowing that they can prove they have 'prevented corruption' because they can wheel out Mr Smith in Compliance and his 40-page PowerPoint presentation.

And that is saying nothing about the bastardisation of the compliance process itself. It is astonishing how well-trained lawyers hired to do anti-corruption compliance can make themselves totally blind to obvious wrongdoing. We have a really good example of this in state capture: the case of T-Systems. As I've shown elsewhere, T-Systems' international compliance department barely batted an eyelid about the fact that Salim Essa was telling it whom to subcontract with, and to give hundreds of millions in contracts to one company owned by his wife and another owned by the Guptas.

That is not to say that there can't be the rare situation in which a rogue employee does get an otherwise innocent company in trouble. But these are issues that require a far more subtle set of regulations to deal with, and that might be better dealt with on a case-by-case basis during criminal trials themselves, rather than the somewhat bald and undeveloped paragraphs put forward by the commission.

## Party funding

The commission also recommended amendments to the Political Party Funding Act in order to remedy those issues I've identified earlier. It proposed that the Act be amended in order to 'criminalise the making of donations to political parties in the expectation or with a view to the grant of procurement tenders or contracts as a reward for or in recognition of such grants having been made'. The commission, sadly, does not develop this recommendation further and, I think, suffers as a result. While the underlying motive is good – to stop political funding from corrupting procurement – this is a very difficult area to navigate. As it stands, I find it hard to conceive of a law or a system that can accurately determine whether a political donation is inherently or overwhelmingly tied to a specific procurement, rather than being made for other motivations. It may be that this is obvious on a case-by-case basis (the EOH case, for example, was pretty cut and dried), but I would personally have liked a bit more meat on the bones of this recommendation.

## Appointments to SOEs

As you are already no doubt very aware, the commission's work paid considerable attention to the SOEs falling under the Department of Public Enterprises. Based on all the evidence it considered, the commission found that 'the SEOs which were captured by the

Guptas were captured because some members of these boards of those SOEs, particularly their Chairpersons, as well as the Group Chief Executive Officers and Chief Financial Officers were people who had no integrity and knowledge and experience required for their position or were people who had the right knowledge, skills or experience but simply lacked the integrity'.

The commission, after providing a potted summary of the role dodgy appointments played in the capture of SOEs, made a number of recommendations that would fundamentally alter the way in which boards of SOEs are appointed. The first was that legislation be promulgated to create a Standing Appointment and Oversight Committee. The committee would receive applications and interview candidates, and make recommendations to the minister. It would also publish a Code of Conduct, and receive and investigate complaints of wrongdoing.

The commission further prescribed what a minister must do upon receipt of the recommendation and, in particular, what would happen if the minister disagreed. In that case, the minister would have 30 days to reject the candidate but would have to supply written reasons to the committee. The committee would then select an additional list of candidates ranked in terms of preference. If the minister ultimately refused to appoint any of the candidates, the person ranked first by the committee in either the first or alternative lists would have to be appointed by the minister – he or she could no longer refuse to accept the recommendation.

The committee was to include:
- a retired judge nominated by the Chief Justice, to act as chairperson;
- the Minister of Finance or his or her delegate;
- a legal practitioner appointed by the Legal Practice Council;
- a representative appointed by National Economic Development and Labour Council;
- a trade union rep selected by the National Economic Development and Labour Council;
- an auditor selected by the chairperson of the Independent Regulatory Board for Auditors;
- an industry expert selected by the SOE concerned; and
- a senior representative of an anti-corruption non-profit

operating in the private sector, with the chairperson choosing the appropriate non-profit.

## Centralising procurement

The final recommendation related to some generalised proposals for improving procurement in broad terms. Three of these proposals were pretty anodyne and uncontroversial, and included considering legislation that would allow for:

- centralising certain types of procurement;
- finding ways to properly harmonise and simplify procurement regulations and laws; and
- giving greater guidance and training to procurement officials.

The fourth proposal, while not elaborated in any detail, was actually quite profound: the commission recommended that legislation be considered that would discontinue 'any deviation based on the concept of a sole source provider'. This, if implemented, is actually a huge intervention: it would have the effect of ensuring that all bids, and especially those done under deviation, be subject to at least some limited competition. It would no longer be possible to let only a single bidder tender for a project and for that tender to be awarded on this basis.

## The constitutional and political architecture and a directly elected President

As I've discussed earlier, the commission dedicates a report to unpacking the manner in which Parliament failed to conduct meaningful oversight during state capture, and why this happened. The result of this discussion was that the commission made a number of recommendations with potentially broad-ranging implications for how South Africa's democracy might look in the long term. Because I've already addressed them, I don't go into them in great detail here but note that the commission recommended that Parliament consider the desirability of (and pass legislation to enact, where desirous):

- the introduction of a constituency-based system that would still be proportionally representative;
- the introduction of mechanisms to prevent MPs being fired by

their parties when they exercise their duties in good faith;

- the introduction of a specific committee that would exercise direct oversight over the Presidency;
- the introduction of amendatory accountability that would make it a legal violation for the executive to ignore the remedial recommendations of Parliament.

The commission saved the most dramatic recommendation for last; indeed, it was included as the very last recommendation in the last volume published: a 200-page compendium of all its recommendations. The commission, in brief, recommended that the country consider introducing a new model of voting in which voters directly elect the President. This would change the current system, in which the majority party elects the President in Parliament.

The commission makes the argument that this would ensure that Presidents are elected on the basis of their *own* popularity with the people rather than their party. This would give voters greater choice and discretion as to how they cast their vote. The example provided by the commission is that of Jacob Zuma: there were plenty of ANC supporters that wanted and supported an ANC government but did not necessarily support Zuma for President. Under the current arrangement, this imaginary voter was caught in a bind: do they vote for the party they wanted in government because of its policy platforms (or for whatever reason) but do so regretfully because it elevated Zuma to the presidency? Or do they withhold their vote for the ANC because of Zuma, but then vote for a different political party that may not align with their philosophical or political principles? By introducing a directly elected President, this sort of difficult and intractable choice could be avoided.

Of course, the commission was also sanguine: it was possible that, even with a direct election, terrible people could be elected. Donald Trump, the commission noted, was directly elected. It may not guarantee that a future Jacob Zuma, or even somebody worse, would not be elected – if chosen by the people. But, the commission noted, 'if that were to happen ... the consolation will be that the people elected their own queer character or person who has no integrity, and if he or she ever facilitated a capture of the State by private individuals or entities as Mr Zuma did, the people can blame themselves for electing such a person to the highest office in the land.'

# PART TEN

# Zondo in Review

*The Zondo Commission's work was, in many ways, extraordinary. It heard a huge amount of oral testimony and conducted extensive and detailed investigations, most of which were of undoubted quality. It probed a wide range of complex crimes and left very few stones unturned, especially when it came to the bigger and most consequential cases of wrongdoing.*

*My own experience was, I believe, instructive. I was struck by the diligence and commitment of the team of investigators and advocates I worked with. They were all very conscious of the weight of expectation on them and on the commission as a whole, as a unique opportunity to both understand and make history.*

*But the commission was not without flaws and omissions. That is, indeed, to be expected from such a mammoth endeavour. Nevertheless, without sounding churlish, I think the problems with the commission are important to acknowledge: not to undermine its work, but to draw attention to issues that must be borne in mind as South Africa moves forward.*

# The good

BEFORE MOVING ON TO my criticisms, I think it is worthwhile taking stock. South Africans – myself included – can lapse into cynicism and criticism very easily. It is, perhaps, a defence mechanism, a way of moderating hope because the dashing of hopes is so painful. There has been a tendency to dismiss the work of the commission, or to downplay its significance, in part because it has taken so long to come to its lengthy conclusions. The very scale of the commission's work, and the staggered publication of its findings, probably works against it, as it is beyond the abilities of most citizens, no matter how engaged, to make sense of 5,000 pages of dense forensic and legal discussion.

So this is why I think the commission should be accorded considerable respect. First, as I've already noted, the commission really dug deep into its subject matter. It deployed resources to find the truth in a way that most likely cannot be matched in the entire post-apartheid period, coming close even to the Truth and Reconciliation Commission in scope and scale.

Second, the commission has created a political reality that cannot be obscured or denied. It wasn't so long ago that South Africans were gaslit by a parade of captured officials and public representatives adamantly claiming that what was clearly a swimming pool for summery dips was, in fact, a fire pool. Having something like the truth confirmed by the commission – even if there are aspects to be contested – must be recognised for the powerful thing it is.

Third, the commission is, truly, globally unique. There are only a handful of examples of any state or quasi-judicial inquiry being given the task and resources to delve so deeply into the corruption of the ruling party. Having lived and engaged in politics in both the UK and South Africa, I can tell you that something like the scale, importance and independence of the Zondo Commission could *never* happen in the UK.

Fourth, the commission acted as a really powerful centralised node to draw in the various investigative capacities of the state. It was able to subpoena and summon evidence from various statutory bodies and law enforcement agencies. This was so incredibly important because a big part of state capture was to ensure that these bodies did not work together, coordinate or share information.

In my own investigations with the commission, it was a total revelation to find out that the South African Reserve Bank (SARB) had been conducting investigations into the very same onshore-offshore bridges that we were encountering by following the money from the other end of the pipeline. The material from SARB was fundamental to unpicking these complex laundries. And it was when we combined that information with all the other data that had been collected by the commission that we could start to see the outlines of something quite profound.

Fifth, the commission was unapologetic about locating state capture within South Africa's political dynamics. It spent a whole volume explaining how the ANC as an organisation was responsible for state capture. It took a long look at the most fundamental parts of our constitutional architecture and found them wanting. The commission didn't satisfy itself with some technical recommendations and platitudes. Its recommendations could seriously transform the form and content of South African politics. At the very least, they would inject a level of accountability that has been distinctly lacking from the country's parliamentary democracy for so long.

Sixth, we are seeing concrete results based on the commission's work. Law enforcement – the Special Investigating Unit (SIU) and Asset Forfeiture Unit (AFU) in particular – has been moving on the cases investigated by the commission. The AFU successfully froze the assets of Optimum coal mine, just as they were about to be handed over to a one-time Gupta associate. The SIU has won multiple cases against multinationals to recoup funds. In some of those cases, the work of the commission led directly to those actions; in two cases so far, for example, I have been asked to provide supporting affidavits so that the money-laundering analysis I undertook can be used in evidence.

The Independent Directorate (ID) has also moved swiftly and arrested a large number of the core officials behind state capture. Although there has been some concern about the scale of those cases and the strategic challenges they present, if they are pursued with vigour and ingenuity, we could start seeing jail time for a whole coterie of wrongdoers. This was simply inconceivable just five years ago.

Seventh, the commission was an act of unparalleled and quite radical transparency. Not since the Truth and Reconciliation process have South Africans witnessed high-level officials being forced to explain themselves in public. The commission levelled the playing field, dragging once-protected officials and technocrats into the public gaze. In so doing, it powerfully illustrated how a culture of openness and transparency can act as a powerful antidote to a culture of impunity.

Finally, the commission's approach to civil society was a breath of fresh air. For years, civil society organisations were seen as the enemy of the state. It was not uncommon for senior ANC leaders to claim that civil society organisations and NGOs were stalking horses for hostile foreign powers. The commission took a very different approach. It was open to the evidence and expertise of organisations that had been fighting bravely for years to expose corruption. In some of its recommendations, too, it envisaged an important and permanent role for civil society in key decision-making. We can only hope that the commission's attitude rubs off on other parts of the country's decision-making apparatus, and that citizens are again allowed to play an active and empowering role in their own governance.

# The bad

I HAVE SEVEN primary criticisms of the commission.

First, the commission's final reports vary quite widely in terms of quality and readability. Clearly it was under extreme pressure to produce its findings in time, and this shows. In some cases, I found it hard to follow the narrative, and it took a lot of concentration and rereading to make sense of what was being described. This was rare, and not typical of all the commission's reports: the reports on Transnet, SAA and Eskom, by comparison, are particularly shocking precisely because of the forensic precision with which they were written.

On some occasions – again, thankfully, a rare occurrence – I was unimpressed by the actual analysis of the commission. One example of this is the commission's report on Estina. There is nothing actually *wrong* in the commission's report on Estina: I agree with almost everything it said. But the analysis really missed the mark in understanding how profoundly the Guptas were involved in the project, from its very origin until its conclusion. When I worked with the Flow of Funds team, we found out a Gupta company called Nulane had been paid millions to develop the Free State's rural agricultural strategy, which led directly to the Vrede dairy project. The Guptas were, quite literally, conceiving of a project, ensuring its implementation, and then stealing the money that resulted. This is absolutely vital context and it is sad that it was left out.

Second, the commission arguably missed a key opportunity to delve into the real human costs and consequences of state capture –

how lives of people who stood up were ruined, and how communities struggled as a result of being deprived of the services they needed. One of the most powerful moments of the commision was when the intended 'beneficiaries' of the Vrede dairy project appeared and described the death threats and intimidation they faced in holding their local politicians to account. Their appearance highlighted that state capture could have life-and-death consequences, and grounded the commission's sometimes rarified proceedings in the lived experience of ordinary South Africans.

Third, the commission was soft on the very many multinational corporations that were involved in state capture. It is particularly striking that the commission's recommendations simply do not mention these companies. Instead, they focused almost exclusively on the individual officials involved in wrongdoing. The commission did not recommend any action be taken against companies like T-Systems, Liebherr and SAP. This is strange considering that all these companies had South African subsidiaries with South African directors, none of whom were called to face the music by the commission. As a consequence, the commission also failed to place state capture and South Africa in an international context, where corporate malfeasance preys on captured societies and replicates those conditions of capture.

The commission also limited its recommendations to South Africa. In only one case – a recommendation about HSBC – does the commission contemplate law enforcement engaging with authorities in a foreign jurisdiction. I had hoped that the commission would have recommended to law enforcement in South Africa to report the wrongdoing of multinationals to their counterparts abroad. If South African authorities approached international law enforcement to report this corruption, it would carry extraordinary weight. There will only ever be limited accountability if the likes of T-Systems, SAP and Liebherr are not investigated and prosecuted in their home countries.

It is this approach to corporations and their role in state capture that most likely informs the commission's recommendations to introduce deferred prosecution agreements in South Africa. I've already explained why this is such a bad idea previously, so I won't go into it here, except to note that this would introduce a legal mechanism that would, in effect, treat corporations differently from ordinary citizens. It may also have perverse incentives in that corporations can now take a calculated risk to pay bribes in the knowledge that some hand-wringing and a fine will solve any problems down the line.

Fourth, the commission did not pay enough attention to the role of enablers in state capture. That is not to say that the commission was not aware of this; at times, especially in its broader conclusions, it does acknowledge the role of enabling service providers in state capture. Yet the role of auditors in allowing state capture was only really explored in any depth in the commission's report on SAA.

Fifth, and partly as a consequence of this, the commission was way too lenient on South African banks. In my investigation, it was astonishing how many bank accounts we came across where the money laundering taking place was gob-smackingly obvious. In certain cases, these accounts moved huge sums of money over lengthy periods of time. The commission, to its credit, did recommend an investigation into whether the banks filed suspicious activity reports, and what the Financial Intelligence Centre did with these reports. But this is simply not enough. If banks were submitting suspicious activity reports and then doing nothing thereafter, this was still a dereliction of duty. Indeed, the closure of the Guptas' bank accounts shows that the banks could act swiftly, decisively, and in fact without obstruction, to close down accounts for suspected wrongdoing. Why didn't they do this with all those many accounts whose involvement in money laundering was blindingly obvious?

Sixth, the commission was way too soft on Ramaphosa and the ANC on one particular thing, which, when I read it, truly shocked me. In the chapter on the ANC and Ramaphosa, the commission stated that the ANC was unable to provide a single minute from any of the ANC Deployment Committee meetings between 2014 to 2019, when Ramaphosa was its chair. This is an extraordinary admission. And, frankly, I just don't believe it. I don't believe that no minutes were taken, or that the minutes were simply lost. I do believe that their contents would have been very embarrassing for the ANC both past and present, and they were withheld from the commission as a result. The commission, I think, should either have demanded much more disclosure (I find it hard to believe that emails discussing the content of the meetings don't exist somewhere) or made a much more damning finding on this point.

Finally, the commission could sometimes take an ahistorical approach to the problems it encountered. The result was that it failed to understand how much of what happened in the Zuma period flowed from the groundwork laid in the Mbeki era. One example of this was the commission's report on Denel. It argued that Denel had been well governed prior to Zuma and then collapsed into corruption and dysfunction only under Zuma's watch. But this ignores Denel's profound role in the Arms Deal, in which it was implicated in all sorts of irregularities before those deals were inked. It also ignored how Denel was the cash cow of the politically connected during the Mbeki era. So, while the contracts awarded to the Guptas' VR Laser were clearly an outrage, how different was this from the Mbeki era when political allies (and even family members) could benefit from the Arms Deal?

Most profoundly, the commission didn't place the failure of intelligence during the Zuma era within its proper context, namely, the all-out and vicious intelligence-led warfare of the period between Zuma's firing as Deputy President and his election as President of South Africa. By the time Zuma won the presidency, the intelligence services had already been politicised and abused by both the Mbeki and Zuma factions. What followed under Zuma was nothing substantively new, even if it was bigger in scale and intensity than what preceded it.

Of course, all these roads run directly to the Arms Deal. Now, I don't expect the commission to have reported on that, too, and there are clearly limits to how far one goes back in time to explain a contemporary dysfunction. Nevertheless, it is equally clear that the Arms Deal truly began the process through which the state was eroded: it was because of the Arms Deal that the ANC dropped the idea of bipartisan Parliamentary Portfolio Committees, and why so much of South Africa's law enforcement was denuded of talent and political will by the time Zuma took over. The corruption of the Zuma era, despite popular myths otherwise, was the result of both Mbeki's and Zuma's involvement in the Arms Deal.

One of my own personal bugbears is Fana Hlongwane, who lurks in the background of the commission's work. Hlongwane was one of the biggest beneficiaries of 'commission' payments made by BAE Systems in the Arms Deal. He was there when Mcebisi Jonas was offered a bribe at the Gupta compound; he was the man who introduced the Guptas to Bell Pottinger because the daughter of one of Hlongwane's BAE colleagues worked there; Vytjie Mentor claimed that he was accompanying Duduzane Zuma when she met him on her way to China.

And then there is Simphiwe Nyanda, Hlongwane's business colleague, who was also implicated in Arms Deal decisions. He, too, makes frequent cameo appearances in the commission's reports; on one occasion, as someone testifying to statements made by Fikile Mbalula about the Guptas, and, on another, as the proprietor of General Nyanda Security, which benefited from deals with Transnet in ways that the commission was extremely critical of.

There is something quite profound, and quite disturbing, about how state capture under Zuma featured actors who had made their fortune during the Arms Deal and, most importantly, were able to thrive through the political protection afforded them by Mbeki. And I think the commission should have tried to grapple with how the unresolved corruption in the Arms Deal may have interacted with and empowered the corruption of the Zuma years.

I am concerned that people will look at the Zondo report and be tempted to respond: well, why don't we just bring back all those professionals who ran things during the Mbeki era? That would be a deep and serious failure – as much, arguably, as failing to rid the state of the most serious enablers of state capture under Zuma. Bluntly, South Africa does not need to go back in time to some imagined past of good governance under Mbeki; it needs to make a radical break from the various forms of corruption and political influence trading that have characterised South African democracy since at least 1999. A slightly less brazen form perpetuated by more refined operators will get us nowhere.

# The ugly

AND NOW WE MUST RETURN, after our brief sojourn in the somewhat rarefied world of the commission's genteel proceedings and legal rituals, to the rough and tumble of the day-to-day political contestation that unfolds around us.

I, for one, hope that there will never be anything like a Zondo Commission in South Africa again, for two reasons. First, I hope, although I sadly don't totally expect, that after surviving the corrupt onslaught of the Zuma years, the state can be slowly rebuilt and our democracy emerge more resilient and less corrupt.

Second, it will be a great day indeed when South African politics are conducted without reference to the courts. The criminalisation of our political elite has led to a decade in which the activities (or lack thereof) of law enforcement and the judgments of our courts have dominated our political cycles. There is only so much political pressure those institutions can take.

The ultimate privilege will be when the cut-and-thrust of politics is not about whether someone is guilty of corruption; but, instead, about policy, about the right choices to help every citizen live their best life, about the ways to navigate our way out of centuries of repression, dispossession and domination that still scar the political fabric, so that we can jointly create a truly post-colonial society.

I sincerely hope we all get to experience that privilege sooner rather than later.

# References

| Part 1: Capture of State Ministries or Institutions | |
|---|---|
| The attempted capture of the National Treasury | |
| The attempted capture of the National Treasury | Part 6, vol. 1, paras. 1–10 |
| The context: Evidence of Lungisa Fuzile | Ibid., para. 11 |
| Jonas meets the Guptas | Ibid., paras. 13–81 |
| Nene's resistance to state capture and his eventual dismissal | Ibid., paras. 82–165 |
| The Weekend Special and the hand of the Gupta enterprise | Ibid., paras. 166–204 |
| The reappointment of Gordhan – and the race to his dismissal | Ibid., paras. 204–239 |
| The exception to the rule: State capture resisted | Ibid., para. 237 |
| Recommendation | Ibid., para. 241 |
| The capture of SARS | |
| The Nugent Commission | Part 1, vol. 3, paras. 9–20 |
| Zuma, Bain and Ambrobrite | Ibid., paras. 42–71 |
| Bain, Moyane and plans for SARS | Ibid., paras. 66–67 and 73–89 |

| | |
|---|---|
| Moyane gets the job – and Bain gets its contracts | Ibid., paras. 112–138 and 141–146 |
| Moyane's reign of terror and that 'rogue unit' | Ibid., paras. 149–160 and 197–212 |
| Dismantling SARS | Ibid., paras. 162–189 |
| Moyane, Gordhan and the Vlok Symington hostage debacle | Ibid., paras. 220–257 |
| Moyane vs Gordhan at the Zondo-dome | Ibid., paras. 263–318 |
| Conclusion: A clear example of state capture | Ibid., paras. 319–325 |
| Recommendations | Ibid., para. 326 |
| The State Security Agency | |
| The commission's findings | Part 5, vol. 1, paras. 3–133 |
| Recommendations | Ibid., paras. 844–940 |
| **Part 2: The Capture of State-Owned Enterprises** | |
| Transnet | |
| The processes that enabled the capture of Transnet | Part 2, vol. 1, paras. 39–53 |
| Zuma, Hogan and the battle to appoint Transnet's group CEO | Ibid., paras. 57–109 |
| In comes Molefe | Ibid., para. 110–114 |
| The resurrection of Siyabonga Gama | Ibid., paras. 115–158 |
| The Gupta dream team | Ibid., paras. 167–197 |
| The cash bribes | Ibid., paras. 198–249 |
| The GNS/Abalozi contract | Ibid., paras. 250–284 |
| The 95 locomotive contract | Ibid., paras. 285–326 |
| The 100 locos contract | Ibid., paras. 328–380 |
| The 1,064 locos deal | Ibid., paras. 386–537 |
| The Gupta kickbacks | Ibid., paras. 21–25, 321–322, 381; Part 6, vol. 3, paras. 10–12 |

| | |
|---|---|
| The CNR/BEX relocation contract | Part 2, vol. 1, paras. 538–587 |
| The financial advisors: McKinsey, Regiments and the Gupta enterprise | Ibid., paras. 589–608 |
| The financing of the 1,064 contracts | Ibid., paras. 660–741 |
| The Manganese Expansion Project | Ibid., paras. 797–874 |
| Neotel and Homix | Ibid., paras. 878–962 |
| The dodgy T-Systems IT contract | Ibid., paras. 963–1004 |
| The other dodgy deals: ZPMC and Liebherr Cranes | Ibid., paras. 33–38 |
| Recommendations | Ibid., paras. 1088–1125 |
| Eskom | |
| Eskom's 2014 board | Part 4, vol. 3, paras. 1255–1338 |
| The dismissal of the four executives | Ibid., paras. 1364–1505 |
| Completing the takeover: Removing Tsotsi and Baloyi, welcoming Molefe and Singh | Ibid., paras. 1505–1579 |
| The acquisition of Optimum coal mine | Ibid., paras. 1588–1665 |
| The R1.68bn guarantee | Ibid., paras. 1666–1717 |
| The outrageous R659m prepayment | Ibid., paras. 1721–1794 |
| Screwing South Africa just a little bit more | Ibid., paras. 1795–1804 |
| The Brakfontein debacle: The Guptas score big | Part 4, vol. 4, paras. 1936–2080 |
| The testing farce | Ibid., paras. 2015–2069 |
| The cost of Brakfontein | Ibid., paras. 2070–2074 |
| Friends reunited: Singh, Molefe, McKinsey, Regiments and Trillian | Ibid., paras. 2144–2370 |
| Crisis averted: The Huarong financing deal | Ibid., paras. 2066–2143 |
| Koko's international travel | Ibid., paras. 2374–2412 |
| Recommendations | Ibid., paras. 2485–2586 |

| SAA | |
|---|---|
| The move from governance to dysfunction | Part 1, vol. 1, paras. 24–63 |
| Kona, SAA and the Guptas | Ibid., paras. 65–78 |
| Myeni's strategy at the commission and her revelation of Witness X | Ibid., paras. 97–120 |
| Pembroke Capital | Ibid., paras. 82–96 |
| The collapse of the board | Ibid., paras. 123–143 |
| The Airbus swap and Emirates deals | Ibid., paras. 145–154 |
| LSG Skychefs and Air Chefs | Ibid., paras. 155–197 |
| The fake whistleblowers | Ibid., paras. 198–202 |
| The '30% set-aside' and the disturbing downfall of Dr Dahwa | Ibid., paras. 211–306 |
| The extraordinary tale of BNP Capital | Ibid., paras. 312–493 |
| Swissport and JM Aviation | Ibid., paras. 500–553 |
| The sale of the GPUs | Ibid., paras. 533–553 |
| AAR and JM Aviation | Ibid., paras. 555–615 |
| The kickbacks to Kwinana and Memela | Ibid., paras. 679–744 |
| SAA, Regiments and Ramosebudi | Ibid., paras. 747–763 |
| Why was Myeni not stopped? | Ibid., paras. 833–845 |
| Fast money at SA Express | Ibid., paras. 978–1081 |
| Recommendations | Ibid., paras. 1082–1121 |
| Denel | |
| The rarest jewel: A successful SOE | Part 2, vol. 2, paras. 20–29 |
| The Guptas' circle | Ibid., paras. 34–44 |
| The acquisition of VR Laser | Ibid., paras. 45–57 |
| The Guptas' first score: The 'hulls' contract | Ibid., paras. 58–92 |

| The Guptas and their cronies take control | Ibid., paras. 107–123 and 144–234 |
| Making the Guptas indispensable | Ibid., paras. 235–337 |
| The Denel Vehicle Services (DVS) and VR Laser single-source contract | Ibid., paras. 339–378 |
| Denel Asia | Ibid., paras. 379–390 |
| Findings | Ibid., paras. 414–432 |
| Recommendations | Ibid. |
| SABC | |
| Jacob Zuma, ANN7 and the testimony of Rajesh Sundaram | Part 5, vol. 2, paras. 1394–1396 and 1489–1535 |
| Zuma and the Ethics Code | Ibid., paras. 1576–1599 |
| The capture of the SABC: The business breakfasts | Ibid., paras. 1348–1362 |
| The theft of SABC's archival footage | Ibid., paras. 1363–1388 |
| Digital migration and Faith Muthambi | Ibid., paras. 1552–1575 |
| Recommendations | Ibid., paras. 1598–1611 |
| *The New Age* | |
| The dismissal of Themba Maseko and the capture of GCIS | Part 1, vol. 2, paras. 23–147 |
| What did the Guptas get from Manyi's GCIS? | Ibid., paras. 148–156 |
| TNA and Eskom | Ibid., paras. 161–207 |
| The ratification: Regularising the irregular | Ibid., paras. 207–296 |
| Eskom and TNA subscriptions | Ibid., paras. 300–304 |
| TNA and Transnet sitting in a tree: L.O.O.T.I.N.G. | Ibid., paras. 314–404 |
| SAA: Paying first-class prices for economy-class products | Ibid., paras. 406–429 |
| Recommendations | Ibid., paras. 434–451 |

| Alexkor | |
|---|---|
| Gupta associates all the way down | Part 4, vol. 1, paras. 299–325 |
| The irregular appointment of Scarlet Sky Investments | Ibid., paras. 326–358 |
| Was Alexkor ripped off? | Ibid., paras. 359–378 |
| Alexkor as an example of state capture | Ibid., paras. 397–398 |
| Recommendations | Ibid., para. 398 |

| PRASA | |
|---|---|
| Swifambo | Part 5, vol. 2, paras. 1818–1861 |
| The 'bombshell affidavit' and the money flows investigations | Ibid., paras. 1849–1892 |
| The Siyangena contracts | Ibid., paras. 1914–1933 |
| Montana's property empire | Ibid., paras. 1933–1968 |
| Resistance to the clean-up of PRASA | Ibid., paras. 1735–1817 |
| Continued instability at PRASA | Ibid., paras. 2065–2118, 2134–2154 and 2194 |
| Recommendations | Ibid., paras. 2190–2193 |

| Part 3: Bosasa | |
|---|---|
| The big fish: Bosasa | Part 3, vol. 1, paras. 1–5 |
| The Bosasa group and its key players | Part 3, vol. 1, paras. 151–164, 174; Part 3, vol. 3, paras. 1470–1489; Part 3, vol. 4, paras. 2201–2202 and 2173–2174 |
| Bosasa's cash bribery system | Part 3, vol. 1, paras. 261–295 and 300–305; Part 3, vol. 4, para. 1734 |
| The catering contracts | Part 3, vol. 1, paras. 449–486; Part 3, vol. 4, paras. 1909–1936 |
| The access control contract | Part 3, vol. 1, paras. 487–491; Part 3, vol. 4, paras. 1916–1920 |
| The fencing contracts | Part 3, vol. 1, paras. 493–583; Part 3, vol. 4, para. 1926 |

| | |
|---|---|
| The 'television contract' | Part 3, vol. 1, paras. 506–509; Part 3, vol. 4, paras. 1927–1930 |
| The DCS officials captured by Bosasa | Part 3, vol. 1, paras. 445–571; Part 3, vol. 4, paras. 1940–1960 and 1973–1983 |
| Attempts to capture DCS following Mti's departure | Part 3, vol. 1, paras. 636–644 |
| Contracts with other state entities | Part 3, vol. 4, paras. 1861–1878, 2028–2058, 2185–2186 and 2188–2194 |
| The SIU investigation | Part 3, vol. 2, paras. 863–932 |
| Capturing the NPA | Part 3, vol. 2, paras. 916–1002; Part 3, vol. 4, paras. 1855–1860 |
| Neutering Parliament | Part 3, vol. 1, paras. 588–634; Part 3, vol. 3, paras. 1270–1312; Part 3, vol. 4, paras. 1962–2020 |
| Zuma's illicit assistance | Part 3, vol. 4, paras. 2079–2121 |
| Dudu's dastardly deeds | Part 3, vol. 3, paras. 1202–1258; Part 3, vol. 4, paras. 2144–2168 |
| Nomvula Mokonyane | Part 3, vol. 3, paras. 1063–1197; Part 3, vol. 4, paras. 2143–2174 |
| Gwede Mantashe | Part 3, vol. 4, paras. 1782–1801 |
| Thabang Makwetla | Part 3, vol. 4, paras. 2059–2073 |
| The ANC | Part 3, vol. 4, paras. 1802–1815 |
| Andile and Cyril Ramaphosa | Part 3, vol. 4, para. 1815 and 2046–2051 |
| Recommendations | Part 6, vol. 4, paras. 129–238 |
| **Part 4: State Capture in the Free State** | |
| City of Tomorrow | |
| The first Gupta visit | Part 4, vol. 2, paras. 408–411 |
| The City of Tomorrow | Ibid., paras. 414–440 |
| Dukoana's second Gupta visit | Ibid., 412–413 |
| The Free State asbestos debacle | |

| | |
|---|---|
| The Free State asbestos debacle | Ibid., paras. 485–613 |
| The outrageous profits and the usefulness of the work | Ibid., paras. 670–764 |
| Just the 'cost of business' | Ibid., paras. 771–844 |
| Blackhead's payments: other politically exposed persons | Ibid., paras. 850–904 |
| Recommendations | Ibid., paras. 906–922 |
| The Free State housing debacle | |
| The Free State housing debacle | Part 4, vol. 2, paras. 923–1069 |
| How much was spent and who got it? | Ibid., paras. 1070–1111 and 1159–1192 |
| Findings: Zwane and Mokoena | Ibid., paras. 1194–1217 |
| Recommendations | Ibid., paras. 1218–1222 |
| The Estina/Vrede dairy scandal | |
| The work done by Estina | Part 6, vol. 1, paras. 114 and 136–185 |
| Zwane's choir trip to India | Ibid., para. 98 |
| The beneficiary experience: Murder, death threats and fear | Ibid., paras. 186–286 |
| Conclusion: Where the fault lay | Ibid., para. 620 |
| Recommendations | Ibid., paras. 600–625 |
| **Part 5: Flashpoints** | |
| The Waterkloof landing | Part 5, vol. 2, paras. 1612–1708 |
| The closure of Gupta bank accounts | |
| The closure of Gupta bank accounts | Part 6, vol. 1, paras. 699–791 |
| Conclusions | Ibid., paras. 779–793 |
| The private power of banks | Ibid., paras. 794–798 |
| Recommendation | Ibid. |

# Index